Python Automation Cookbook

Second Edition

CW00547930

75 Python automation ideas for web scraping, data wrangling, and processing Excel, reports, emails, and more

Jaime Buelta

BIRMINGHAM - MUMBAI

Python Automation Cookbook
Second Edition

Producer: Ben Renow-Clarke
Acquisition Editor – Peer Reviews: Suresh Jain
Content Development Editors: Alex Patterson, Bhavesh Amin
Technical Editor: Karan Sonawane
Project Editor: Janice Gonsalves
Copy Editor: Safis Editing
Proofreader: Safis Editing
Indexer: Priyanka Dhadke
Presentation Designer: Sandip Tadge

First published: September 2018
Second published: May 2020

Production reference: 1270520

Published by Packt Publishing Ltd.
Livery Place
35 Livery Street
Birmingham B3 2PB, UK.

ISBN   978-1-80020-708-0

www.packt.com

Contributors

About the author

Jaime Buelta has been a professional programmer for 20 years and a full-time Python developer for over 10. During that time, he has been exposed to many different technologies. He has developed software for different industries, including aerospace, networking, industrial systems, video game online services, and finance services. In these industries, he has worked in various areas, such as marketing, management, sales, and game design, helping companies achieve their goals. He is a strong proponent of automating everything and making computers do most of the heavy lifting so users can focus on the important stuff. He is currently living in Dublin, Ireland, and is a regular speaker at PyCon Ireland.

This book could not have happened without the support and encouragement of my amazing wife, Dana. For this second edition I've worked closely with more people in the Packt team, and their help has been invaluable. Also, great thanks to the reviewers – their comments have improved this book. Finally, I'd like to thank the whole Python community. I can't overstate what a joy it is to be a developer in the Python world.

About the reviewer

Michal Jaworski has more than 10 years of professional experience in writing software using various programming languages. Michał has spent most of his career writing high-performance and highly distributed backend services for web applications. His beloved language of choice was always Python.

He has had various roles at different companies, from an ordinary full-stack developer, through software architect, to VP of engineering in a fast-paced start-up. He is currently a full-time senior software engineer at Showpad. Whenever he finds any free time, he provides Python consulting for local start-ups. Michał is also an active contributor to many open source Python projects and authored the last two editions of *Python Expert Programming*.

Table of Contents

Preface

We are all probably spending time doing small manual tasks that don't add much value. It may be scanning through information sources in search of the small bits of relevant information, working with spreadsheets to generate the same graph over and over, or searching files one by one until we find the data we're looking for. Some—probably most—of those tasks are, in fact, automatable. There's an investment upfront, but for the tasks that get repeated over and over, we can use computers to do these kinds of menial tasks and focus our own efforts instead on what humans are good for—high-level analysis and decision making based on the result. This book will explain how to use the Python language to automate common business tasks that can be greatly sped up if a computer is doing them.

Given the expressiveness and ease of use of Python, it's surprisingly simple to start making small programs to perform these actions and combine them into more integrated systems. Throughout the book, we will show small, easy-to-follow recipes that can be adapted to your specific needs, and we will combine them to perform more complex actions. We will perform common actions, such as detecting opportunities by scraping the web, analyzing information to generate automatic spreadsheet reports with graphs, communicating with automatically generated emails, getting notifications via text messages, and learning how to run tasks while your mind is focused on other more important stuff.

Though some Python knowledge is required, the book is written with non-programmers in mind, giving clear and instructive recipes that will further the reader's proficiency while being oriented to specific day-to-day goals.

Who this book is for

This book is for Python beginners, not necessarily developers, that want to use and expand their knowledge to automate tasks. Most of the examples in the book are aimed at marketing, sales, and other non-tech areas. The reader needs to know a little of the Python language, including its basic concepts.

What this book covers

Chapter 1, Let's Begin Our Automation Journey, presents some basic content that will be used all through the book. It describes how to install and manage third-party tools through virtual environments, how to do effective string manipulation, how to use command-line arguments, and introduces you to regular expressions and other methods of text processing.

Chapter 2, Automating Tasks Made Easy, shows how to prepare and automatically run tasks. It covers how to program tasks to be executed when they should, instead of running them manually; how to be notified of the result of a task that's run automatically; and how to be notified if there has been an error in an automated process.

Chapter 3, Building Your First Web Scraping Application, explores sending web requests to communicate with external websites in different formats, such as raw HTML content; structured feeds; RESTful APIs; and even automating a browser to execute steps without manual intervention. It also covers how to process results to extract relevant information.

Chapter 4, Searching and Reading Local Files, explains how to search through local files and directories and analyze the information stored there. You will learn how to filter through relevant files in different encodings and read files in several common formats, such as CSVs, PDFs, Word documents, and even images.

Chapter 5, Generating Fantastic Reports, looks at how to display information given in text format in multiple formats. This includes creating templates to produce text files, as well as creating richly formatted and properly styled Word and PDF documents.

Chapter 6, Fun with Spreadsheets, explores how to read and write spreadsheets in the CSV format; in rich Microsoft Excel, including with formatting and charts; and in LibreOffice, a free alternative to Microsoft Excel.

Chapter 7, Cleaning and Processing Data, presents techniques to deal with multiple sources of information and cleanup of data before processing it. You will learn how to batch process to speed up working with big amounts of data, including using specific data analysis libraries like Pandas.

Chapter 8, Developing Stunning Graphs, explains how to produce beautiful charts, including common examples such as pie, line, and bar charts, as well as other advanced cases, such as stacked bars and even maps. It also explains how multiple graphs can be combined and styled to generate rich graphics and show relevant information in an understandable format.

Chapter 9, Dealing with Communication Channels, explains how to send messages in multiple channels, using external tools to do the most of the heavy lifting. This chapter goes into sending and receiving emails individually as well as *en masse*, communicating through SMS messages, and creating a bot in Telegram.

Chapter 10, Why Not Automate Your Marketing Campaign?, combines the different recipes included in the book to generate a full marketing campaign, including steps such as detection of opportunity, generation of promotion, communication to potential customers, and analyzing and reporting sales produced by promotion. This chapter shows how to combine different elements to create powerful systems.

Chapter 11, Machine Learning for Automation, explains how to use the Machine Learning APIs from Google for text analysis, detecting a location of an image landmark, and extracting text from images. The chapter includes the creation and training of a model for detecting, based on text, which department an email should be assigned.

Chapter 12, Automatic Testing Routines, explores the write and execute tests to verify that code is behaving as expected. To do so, the test framework `pytest` is presented with common situations to effectively work with tests.

Chapter 13, Debugging Techniques, features different methods and tips to help in the debugging process and ensure the quality of your software. It leverages the great introspection capabilities of Python and its out-of-the-box debugging tools for fixing problems and producing solid automated software.

To get the most out of this book

- Before reading this book, readers need to know the basics of the Python language. We do not assume that the reader is an expert in the language.

- The reader needs to know how to input commands in the command line (Terminal, Bash, or equivalent).

- To understand the code in this book, you need a text editor, which will enable you to read and edit the code. You can use an IDE that supports the Python language, such as PyCharm and PyDev—which you choose is up to you. Check out this link for ideas about IDEs: `https://realpython.com/python-ides-code-editors-guide/`.

Download the example code files

You can download the example code files for this book from your account at `http://www.packtpub.com`. If you purchased this book elsewhere, you can visit `http://www.packtpub.com/support` and register to have the files emailed directly to you.

You can download the code files by following these steps:

1. Log in or register at `http://www.packtpub.com`.
2. Select the **SUPPORT** tab.
3. Click on **Code Downloads & Errata**.
4. Enter the name of the book in the **Search** box and follow the on-screen instructions.

Once the file is downloaded, please make sure that you unzip or extract the folder using the latest version of:

- WinRAR / 7-Zip for Windows
- Zipeg / iZip / UnRarX for Mac
- 7-Zip / PeaZip for Linux

The code bundle for the book is also hosted on GitHub at `https://github.com/PacktPublishing/Python-Automation-Cookbook-Second-Edition`. We also have other code bundles from our rich catalog of books and videos available at `https://github.com/PacktPublishing/`. Check them out!

Download the color images

We also provide a PDF file that has color images of the screenshots/diagrams used in this book. You can download it here: `https://static.packt-cdn.com/downloads/9781800207080_ColorImages.pdf`.

Conventions used

There are a number of text conventions used throughout this book.

`CodeInText`: Indicates code words in text, object names, module names, folder names, filenames, file extensions, pathnames, dummy URLs and user input. Here is an example: "For this recipe, we need to import the `requests` module."

A block of code is set as follows:

```
# IMPORTS
from sale_log import SaleLog
def get_logs_from_file(shop, log_filename):
def main(log_dir, output_filename):
...

    if __name__ == '__main__':
        # PARSE COMMAND LINE ARGUMENTS AND CALL main()
```

Note that code may be edited for concision and clarity. Refer to the full code when necessary, which is available at GitHub.

Any command-line input or output is written as follows (notice the $ symbol):

```
$ python execute_script.py parameters
```

Any input in the Python interpreter is written as follows (notice the >>> symbol):

```
>>> import delorean
>>> timestamp = delorean.utcnow().datetime.isoformat()
```

To enter inside the Python interpreter, call the python3 command with no parameters:

```
$ python3
Python 3.8.2 (default, Mar 11 2020, 00:28:52)
[Clang 11.0.0 (clang-1100.0.33.17)] on darwin
Type "help", "copyright", "credits" or "license" for more information.
>>>
```

Verify that the Python interpreter is Python 3.8 or higher. It may be necessary to call python or python3.8, depending on your operating system and installation options. See *Chapter 1*, *Let's Begin Our Automation Journey*, specifically the *Activating a virtual environment* recipe—for further details about the use of different Python interpreters.

Bold: Indicates a new term, an important word, or words that you see on the screen, for example, in menus or dialog boxes. For example: "Select **System info** from the **Administration** panel."

Warnings or important notes appear like this.

Tips and tricks appear like this.

Get in touch

Feedback from our readers is always welcome.

General feedback: Email `feedback@packtpub.com`, and mention the book's title in the subject of your message. If you have questions about any aspect of this book, please email us at `questions@packtpub.com`.

Errata: Although we have taken every care to ensure the accuracy of our content, mistakes do happen. If you have found a mistake in this book we would be grateful if you would report this to us. Please visit, `http://www.packtpub.com/submit-errata`, selecting your book, clicking on the Errata Submission Form link, and entering the details.

Piracy: If you come across any illegal copies of our works in any form on the Internet, we would be grateful if you would provide us with the location address or website name. Please contact us at `copyright@packtpub.com` with a link to the material.

If you are interested in becoming an author: If there is a topic that you have expertise in and you are interested in either writing or contributing to a book, please visit `http://authors.packtpub.com`.

Reviews

Please leave a review. Once you have read and used this book, why not leave a review on the site that you purchased it from? Potential readers can then see and use your unbiased opinion to make purchase decisions, we at Packt can understand what you think about our products, and our authors can see your feedback on their book. Thank you!

For more information about Packt, please visit `packtpub.com`.

1

Let's Begin Our Automation Journey

The objective of this chapter is to lay down some of the basic techniques that will be useful throughout the whole book. The main idea is to create a good Python environment to run the automation tasks that follow and be able to parse text inputs into structured data.

Python has a good number of tools installed by default, but it also makes it easy to install third-party tools that can simplify many common operations. We'll see how to import modules from external sources and use them to leverage the full potential of Python.

We will install and use tools to help process texts. The ability to structure input data is critical in any automation task. Most of the data that we will process in this book will come from unformatted sources such as web pages or text files. As the old computer adage says, *garbage in, garbage out*, making the sanitizing of inputs a very important task.

In this chapter, we'll cover the following recipes:

- Activating a virtual environment
- Installing third-party packages
- Creating strings with formatted values
- Manipulating strings
- Extracting data from structured strings

- Using a third-party tool—parse
- Introducing regular expressions
- Going deeper into regular expressions
- Adding command-line arguments

We will start by creating our own self-contained environment to work in.

Activating a virtual environment

As a first step when working with Python, it is a good practice to explicitly define the working environment.

This helps you to detach from the operating system interpreter and environment and properly define the dependencies that will be used. Not doing so tends to generate chaotic scenarios. Remember, *explicit is better than implicit!*

 Explicit is better than implicit is one of the most quoted parts of the Zen of Python. The Zen of Python is a list of general guidelines for Python, to provide clarity on what is considered Pythonic. The full Zen of Python can be invoked from the Python interpreter by calling `import this`.

This is especially important in two scenarios:

- When dealing with multiple projects on the same computer, as they can have different dependencies that clash at some point. For example, two versions of the same module cannot be installed in the same environment.
- When working on a project that will be used on a different computer, for example, developing some code on a personal laptop that will ultimately run in a remote server.

A common joke among developers is responding to a bug with "it runs on my machine," meaning that it appears to work on their laptop, but not on the production servers. Although a huge number of factors can produce this error, a good practice is to produce an automatically replicable environment, reducing uncertainty over what dependencies are really being used.

This is easy to achieve using the `venv` module, which sets up a local virtual environment. None of the installed dependencies will be shared with the Python interpreter installed on the machine, creating an isolated environment.

In Python 3, the `venv` tool is installed as part of the standard library. This was not the case in the previous version where you had to install the external `virtualenv` package.

Getting ready

To create a new virtual environment, do the following:

1. Go to the main directory that contains the project:

    ```
    $ cd my-directory
    ```

2. Type the following command:

    ```
    $ python3 -m venv .venv
    ```

    This creates a subdirectory called .venv that contains the virtual environment.

    The directory containing the virtual environment can be located anywhere. Keeping it on the same root keeps it handy, and adding a dot in front of it avoids it being displayed when running `ls` or other commands.

3. Before activating the virtual environment, check the version installed in `pip`. This is different depending on your operating system and installed packages. It may be upgraded later. Also, check the referenced Python interpreter, which will be the main operating system one:

    ```
    $ pip --version
    pip 10.0.1 from /usr/local/lib/python3.7/site-packages/pip (python 3.7)
    $ which python3
    /usr/local/bin/python3
    ```

 Note that `which` may not be available in your shell. In Windows, for example, `where` can be used.

Now your virtual environment is ready to go.

How to do it...

1. Activate the virtual environment if you use Linux or macOS by running:

    ```
    $ source .venv/bin/activate
    ```

Depending on your operating system (for example, Windows) and shell (for example, fish), you may need a different command. View the documentation of venv in the Python documentation here: https://docs.python.org/3/library/venv.html.

You'll notice that the shell prompt will display (.venv), showing that the virtual environment is active.

2. Notice that the Python interpreter used is the one inside the virtual environment, and not the general operating system one from *step 3* of the *Getting ready* section. Check the location within a virtual environment:

```
(.venv) $ which python
/root_dir/.venv/bin/python
(.venv) $ which pip
/root_dir/.venv/bin/pip
```

3. Upgrade the version of pip and then check the version:

```
(.venv) $ pip install --upgrade pip
...
Successfully installed pip-20.0.2
(.venv) $ pip --version
pip 20.0.2 from /root_dir/.venv/lib/python3.8/site-packages/pip
(python 3.8)
```

 An alternative is to run python -m ensurepip -U, which will ensure that pip is installed.

4. Get out of the environment and run pip to check the version, which will return the previous environment. Check the pip version and the Python interpreter to show the existing directories before activating the virtual environment directories, as shown in *step 3* of the *Getting ready* section. Note that they are different pip versions:

```
(.venv) $ deactivate
$ which python3
/usr/local/bin/python3
$ pip --version
pip 10.0.1 from /usr/local/lib/python3.8/site-packages/pip (python 3.8)
```

How it works...

Notice that inside the virtual environment you can use `python` instead of `python3`, although `python3` is available as well. This will use the Python interpreter defined in the environment.

In some systems, like Linux, it's possible that you'll need to use `python3.8` instead of `python3`. Verify that the Python interpreter you're using is 3.8 or higher.

Inside the virtual environment, *step 3* of the *How to do it* section installs the most recent version of `pip`, without affecting the external installation.

The virtual environment contains all the Python data in the `.venv` directory, and the `activate` script points all the environment variables there. The best thing about it is that it can be deleted and recreated very easily, removing the fear of experimenting in a self-contained sandbox.

Remember that the directory name is displayed in the prompt. If you need to differentiate the environment, use a descriptive directory name, such as `.my_automate_recipe`, or use the `-prompt` option.

There's more...

To remove a virtual environment, deactivate it and remove the directory:

```
(.venv) $ deactivate
$ rm -rf .venv
```

The `venv` module has more options, which can be shown with the `-h` flag:

```
$ python3 -m venv -h
usage: venv [-h] [--system-site-packages]
            [--symlinks | --copies] [--clear]
            [--upgrade] [--without-pip]
            [--prompt PROMPT]
            ENV_DIR [ENV_DIR ...]


Creates virtual Python environments in one or more target directories.


positional arguments:
  ENV_DIR               A directory to create the
                        environment in.
```

```
optional arguments:
  -h, --help                show this help message and
                            exit
  --system-site-packages
                            Give the virtual
                            environment access to the
                            system site-packages dir.
  --symlinks                Try to use symlinks rather
                            than copies, when symlinks
                            are not the default for the
                            platform.
  --copies                  Try to use copies rather
                            than symlinks, even when
                            symlinks are the default
                            for the platform.
  --clear                   Delete the contents of the
                            environment directory if it
                            already exists, before
                            environment creation.
  --upgrade                 Upgrade the environment
                            directory to use this
                            version of Python, assuming
                            Python has been upgraded
                            in-place.
  --without-pip             Skips installing or
                            upgrading pip in the
                            virtual environment (pip is
                            bootstrapped by default)
  --prompt PROMPT           Provides an alternative
                            prompt prefix for this
                            environment.
```

Once an environment has been created, you may wish
to activate it, e.g. by sourcing an activate script
in its bin directory.

A convenient way of dealing with virtual environments, especially if you often have to swap between them, is to use the `virtualenvwrapper` module:

1. To install it, run this:

   ```
   $ pip install virtualenvwrapper
   ```

2. Then, add the following variables to your shell startup script, these are normally `.bashrc` or `.bash_profile`. The virtual environments will be installed under the WORKON_HOME directory instead of the same directory as the project, as shown previously:

   ```
   export WORKON_HOME=~/.virtualenvs
   source /usr/local/bin/virtualenvwrapper.sh
   ```

Sourcing the startup script or opening a new terminal will allow you to create new virtual environments:

```
$ mkvirtualenv automation_cookbook
...
Installing setuptools, pip, wheel...done.
(automation_cookbook) $ deactivate
$ workon automation_cookbook
(automation_cookbook) $
```

For more information, view the documentation of `virtualenvwrapper` at `https://virtualenvwrapper.readthedocs.io/en/latest/index.html`.

 An alternative tool for defining environments is Poetry (`https://python-poetry.org/`). This tool is designed for creating consistent environments with clear dependencies, and provides commands for upgrades and managing dependency packages. Check it out to see whether it's useful in your use case.

Hitting the *Tab* key after `workon` autocompletes the command with the available environments.

See also

- The *Installing third-party packages* recipe, covered later in the chapter.
- The *Using a third-party tool – parse* recipe, covered later in the chapter.

Installing third-party packages

One of the strongest capabilities of Python is the ability to use an impressive catalog of third-party packages that cover an amazing amount of ground in different areas, from modules specialized in performing numerical operations, machine learning, and network communications, to command-line convenience tools, database access, image processing, and much more!

Most of them are available on the official Python Package Index (`https://pypi.org/`), which has more than 200,000 packages ready to use. In this book, we'll install some of them. In general, it's worth spending a little time researching external tools when trying to solve a problem. It's very likely that someone else has already created a tool that solves all, or at least part, of the problem.

More important than finding and installing a package is keeping track of which packages are being used. This greatly helps with **replicability**, meaning the ability to start the whole environment from scratch in any situation.

Getting ready

The starting point is to find a package that will be of use in our project.

A great one is `requests`, a module that deals with HTTP requests and is known for its easy and intuitive interface, as well as its great documentation. Take a look at the documentation, which can be found here: `https://requests.readthedocs.io/en/master/`.

We'll use `requests` throughout this book when dealing with HTTP connections.

The next step will be to choose the version to use. In this case, the latest (2.22.0, at the time of writing) will be perfect. If the version of the module is not specified, by default it will install the latest version, which can lead to inconsistencies in different environments as newer versions are released.

We'll also use the great `delorean` module for time handling (version 1.0.0: `http://delorean.readthedocs.io/en/latest/`).

How to do it...

1. Create a `requirements.txt` file in our `main` directory, which will specify all the requirements for our project. Let's start with `delorean` and `requests`:

```
delorean==1.0.0
requests==2.22.0
```

2. Install all the requirements with the `pip` command:

```
$ pip install -r requirements.txt

...

Successfully installed babel-2.8.0 certifi-2019.11.28
chardet-3.0.4 delorean-1.0.0 humanize-0.5.1 idna-2.8 python-
dateutil-2.8.1 pytz-2019.3 requests-2.22.0 six-1.14.0
tzlocal-2.0.0 urllib3-1.25.7
```

Show the available modules installed using `pip list`:

```
$ pip list
Package          Version
---------------  ----------
Babel            2.8.0
certifi          2019.11.28
chardet          3.0.4
Delorean         1.0.0
humanize         2.0.0
idna             2.8
pip              19.2.3
python-dateutil  2.8.1
pytz             2019.3
requests         2.22.0
setuptools       41.2.0
six              1.14.0
tzlocal          2.0.0
urllib3          1.25.8
```

3. You can now use both modules when using the virtual environment:

```
$ python
Python 3.8.1 (default, Dec 27 2019, 18:05:45)
[Clang 11.0.0 (clang-1100.0.33.16)] on darwin
Type "help", "copyright", "credits" or "license" for more
information.
>>> import delorean
>>> import requests
```

How it works...

The `requirements.txt` file specifies the module and version, and pip performs a search on `pypi.org`.

Note that creating a new virtual environment from scratch and running the following will completely recreate your environment, which makes replicability very straightforward:

```
$ pip install -r requirements.txt
```

Note that *step 2* of the *How to do it* section automatically installs other modules that are dependencies, such as `urllib3`.

There's more...

If any of the modules need to be changed to a different version because a new version is available, change them using `requirements` and run the `install` command again:

```
$ pip install -r requirements.txt
```

This is also applicable when a new module needs to be included.

At any point, the `freeze` command can be used to display all of the installed modules. `freeze` returns the modules in a format compatible with `requirements.txt`, making it possible to generate a file with our current environment:

```
$ pip freeze > requirements.txt
```

This will include dependencies, so expect a lot more modules in the file.

Finding great third-party modules is sometimes not easy. Searching for specific functionality can work well, but, sometimes, there are great modules that are a surprise because they do things you never thought of. A great curated list is Awesome Python (`https://awesome-python.com/`), which covers a lot of great tools for common Python use cases, such as cryptography, database access, date and time handling, and more.

In some cases, installing packages may require additional tools, such as compilers or a specific library that supports some functionality (for example, a particular database driver). If that's the case, the documentation will explain the dependencies.

See also

- The *Activating a virtual environment* recipe, covered earlier in this chapter.
- The *Using a third-party tool – parse* recipe, covered later in this chapter, to learn how to use one installed third-party module.

Creating strings with formatted values

One of the basic abilities when dealing with creating text and documents is to be able to properly format values into structured strings. Python is smart at presenting good defaults, such as properly rendering a number, but there are a lot of options and possibilities.

We'll discuss some of the common options when creating formatted text using the example of a table.

Getting ready

The main tool to format strings in Python is the `format` method. It works with a defined mini-language to render variables this way:

```
result = template.format(*parameters)
```

The `template` is a string that is interpreted based on the mini-language. At its simplest, templating replaces the values between the curly brackets with the parameters. Here are a couple of examples:

```
>>> 'Put the value of the string here: {}'.format('STRING')
"Put the value of the string here: STRING"
>>> 'It can be any type ({}) and more than one ({})'.format(1.23,
'STRING')
"It can be any type (1.23) and more than one (STRING)"
>> 'Specify the order: {1}, {0}'.format('first', 'second')
'Specify the order: second, first'
>>> 'Or name parameters: {first}, {second}'.format(second='SECOND',
first='FIRST')
'Or name parameters: FIRST, SECOND'
```

In 95% of cases, this formatting will be all that's required; keeping things simple is great! But for complicated times, such as when aligning strings automatically and creating good looking text tables, the mini-language `format` has more options.

How to do it...

1. Write the following script, `recipe_format_strings_step1.py`, to print an aligned table:

```python
# INPUT DATA
data = [
    (1000, 10),
    (2000, 17),
    (2500, 170),
    (2500, -170),
]

# Print the header for reference
print('REVENUE | PROFIT | PERCENT')

# This template aligns and displays the data in the proper
format
TEMPLATE = '{revenue:>7,} | {profit:>+6} | {percent:>7.2%}'

# Print the data rows
for revenue, profit in data:
    row = TEMPLATE.format(revenue=revenue, profit=profit,
percent=profit / revenue)
    print(row)
```

2. Run it to display the following aligned table. Note that PERCENT is correctly displayed as a percentage:

```
REVENUE | PROFIT | PERCENT
  1,000 |    +10 |   1.00%
  2,000 |    +17 |   0.85%
  2,500 |   +170 |   6.80%
  2,500 |   -170 |  -6.80%
```

How it works...

The TEMPLATE constant defines three columns, each one defined by a parameter named revenue, profit, and percent. This makes it explicit and straightforward to apply the template to the format call.

After the name of the parameter, there's a colon that separates the format definition. Note that everything is inside the curly brackets. In all columns, the format specification sets the width to seven characters, to make sure all the columns have the same width, and aligns the values to the right with the > symbol:

- revenue adds a thousands separator with the , symbol — [{revenue:>7,}].

- profit adds a + sign for positive values. A - sign for negatives is added automatically — [{profit:>+7}].

- percent displays a percent value with a precision of two decimal places — [{percent:>7.2%}]. This is done through .2 (precision) and adding a % symbol for the percentage.

There's more...

You may have also seen the available Python formatting with the % operator. While it works for simple formatting, it is less flexible than the formatted mini-language, and it is not recommended for use.

A great new feature since Python 3.6 is to use f-strings, which perform a format action using defined variables:

```
>>> param1 = 'first'
>>> param2 = 'second'
>>> f'Parameters {param1}:{param2}'
'Parameters first:second'
```

This simplifies a lot of the code and allows us to create very descriptive and readable code.

Be careful when using f-strings to ensure that the string is replaced at the proper time. A common problem is that the variable defined to be rendered is not yet defined. For example, TEMPLATE, defined previously, won't be defined as an f-string, as revenue and the rest of the parameters are not available at that point. All variables defined at the scope of the string definition will be available, both local and global.

If you need to write a curly bracket, you'll need to repeat it twice. Note that each duplication will be displayed as a single curly bracket, plus a curly bracket for the value replacement, making a total of three brackets:

```
>> value = 'VALUE'
>>> f'This is the value, in curly brackets {{{value}}}'
'This is the value, in curly brackets {VALUE}'
```

This allows us to create meta templates — templates that produce templates. In some cases, this will be useful, but they get complicated very quickly. Use with care, as it's easy to produce code that will be difficult to read.

 Representing characters that have a special meaning usually requires some sort of special way to define them, for example, by duplicating the curly bracket like we see here. This is called "escaping" and it's a common process in any code representation.

The Python Format Specification mini-language has more options than the ones shown here.

As the language tries to be quite concise, sometimes it can be difficult to determine the position of the symbols. You may sometimes ask yourself questions, like "*is the + symbol before or after the width parameters?*" Read the documentation with care and remember to always include a colon before the format specification.

Please refer to the full documentation and examples on the Python then it would look like website: `https://docs.python.org/3/library/string.html#formatspec` or at this fantastic web page — `https://pyformat.info` — that shows lots of examples.

See also

- The *Template Reports* recipe in *Chapter 5, Generating Fantastic Reports*, to learn more advanced template techniques.

- The *Manipulating strings* recipe, covered later in this chapter, to learn more about working with text.

Manipulating strings

When dealing with text, it's often necessary to manipulate and process it; that is, to be able to join it, split it into regular chunks, or change it to be uppercase or lowercase. We'll discuss more advanced methods for parsing text and separating it later; however, in lots of cases, it is useful to divide a paragraph into lines, sentences, or even words. Other times, words will require some characters to be removed or a word will need to be replaced with a canonical version to be able to compare it with a predetermined value.

Getting ready

We'll define a basic piece of text and transform it into its main components; then, we'll reconstruct it. As an example, a report needs to be transformed into a new format to be sent via email.

The input format we'll use in this example will be this:

```
AFTER THE CLOSE OF THE SECOND QUARTER, OUR COMPANY, CASTAÑACORP
HAS ACHIEVED A GROWTH IN THE REVENUE OF 7.47%. THIS IS IN LINE
WITH THE OBJECTIVES FOR THE YEAR. THE MAIN DRIVER OF THE SALES HAS
BEEN
THE NEW PACKAGE DESIGNED UNDER THE SUPERVISION OF OUR MARKETING
DEPARTMENT.
OUR EXPENSES HAS BEEN CONTAINED, INCREASING ONLY BY 0.7%, THOUGH THE
BOARD
CONSIDERS IT NEEDS TO BE FURTHER REDUCED. THE EVALUATION IS
SATISFACTORY
AND THE FORECAST FOR THE NEXT QUARTER IS OPTIMISTIC. THE BOARD
EXPECTS
AN INCREASE IN PROFIT OF AT LEAST 2 MILLION DOLLARS.
```

We need to redact the text to eliminate any references to numbers. It needs to be properly formatted by adding a new line after each period, justified with 80 characters, and transformed into ASCII for compatibility reasons.

The text will be stored in the `INPUT_TEXT` variable in the interpreter.

How to do it...

1. After entering the text, split it into individual words:

```
>>> INPUT_TEXT = '''
...        AFTER THE CLOSE OF THE SECOND QUARTER, OUR COMPANY,
CASTAÑACORP
...        HAS ACHIEVED A GROWTH IN THE REVENUE OF 7.47%. THIS IS IN
LINE
...
'''
>>> words = INPUT_TEXT.split()
```

2. Replace any numerical digits with an `'X'` character:

```
>>> redacted = [''.join('X' if w.isdigit() else w for w in word)
for word in words]
```

3. Transform the text into pure ASCII (note that the name of the company contains the letter ñ, which is not ASCII):

```
>>> ascii_text = [word.encode('ascii', errors='replace').
decode('ascii')
...                     for word in redacted]
```

4. Group the words into 80-character lines:

```
>>> newlines = [word + '\n' if word.endswith('.') else word for
word in ascii_text]
>>> LINE_SIZE = 80
>>> lines = []
>>> line = ''
>>> for word in newlines:
...         if line.endswith('\n') or len(line) + len(word) + 1 >
LINE_SIZE:
...             lines.append(line)
...             line = ''
...         line = line + ' ' + word
```

5. Format all of the lines as titles and join them as a single piece of text:

```
>>> lines = [line.title() for line in lines]
>>> result = '\n'.join(lines)
```

6. Print the result:

```
>>> print(result)
 After The Close Of The Second Quarter, Our Company, Casta?Acorp
Has Achieved A Growth In The Revenue Of X.Xx%. This Is In Line
With The Objectives For The Year. The Main Driver Of The Sales
Has Been The New Package Designed Under The Supervision Of Our
Marketing Department. Our Expenses Has Been Contained, Increasing
Only By X.X%, Though The Board Considers It Needs To Be Further
Reduced. The Evaluation Is Satisfactory And The Forecast For The
Next Quarter Is Optimistic.
```

How it works...

Each step performs a specific transformation of the text:

- The first step splits the text into the default separators, whitespaces, and new lines. This splits it into individual words with no lines or multiple spaces for separation.

- To replace the digits, we go through every character of each word. For each one, if it's a digit, an `'X'` is returned instead. This is done with two list comprehensions, one to run on the list, and another on each word, replacing them only if there's a digit – `['X' if w.isdigit() else w for w in word]`. Note that the words are joined together again.

- Each of the words is encoded into an ASCII byte sequence and decoded back again into the Python string type. Note the use of the `errors` parameter to force the replacement of unknown characters such as ñ.

> The difference between strings and bytes is not very intuitive at first, especially if you never have to worry about multiple languages or encoding transformations. In Python 3, there's a strong separation between strings (internal Python representation) and bytes. So most of the tools applicable to strings won't be available in byte objects. Unless you have a good idea of why you need a byte object, always work with Python strings. If you need to perform transformations like the one in this task, encode and decode in the same line so that you keep your objects within the comfortable realm of Python strings. If you are interested in learning more about encodings, you can refer to this brief article: `https://eli.thegreenplace.net/2012/01/30/the-bytesstr-dichotomy-in-python-3` and this other, longer and more detailed one: `http://www.diveintopython3.net/strings.html`.

- The next step adds an extra newline character (the \n character) for all words ending with a period. This marks the different paragraphs. After that, it creates a line and adds the words one by one. If an extra word will make it go over 80 characters, it finishes the line and starts a new one. If the line already ends with a new line, it finishes it and starts another one as well. Note that there's an extra space added to separate the words.

- Finally, each of the lines is capitalized as a Title (the first letter of each word is uppercased) and all the lines are joined through new lines.

There's more...

Some other useful operations that can be performed on strings are as follows:

- Strings can be sliced like any other list. This means that `"word"[0:2]` will return `"wo"`.

- Use `.splitlines()` to separate lines with a newline character.

- There are `.upper()` and `.lower()` methods, which return a copy with all of the characters set to uppercase or lowercase. Their use is very similar to `.title()`:

```
>>> 'UPPERCASE'.lower()
'uppercase'
```

- For easy replacements (for example, changing all *As to Bs or changing mine \ to ours*), use `.replace()`. This method is useful for very simple cases, but replacements can get tricky easily. Be careful with the order of replacements to avoid collisions and case sensitivity issues. Note the wrong replacement in the following example:

```
>>> 'One ring to rule them all, one ring to find them, One ring
to bring them all and in the darkness bind them.'.replace('ring',
'necklace')
'One necklace to rule them all, one necklace to find them, One
necklace to bnecklace them all and in the darkness bind them.'
```

This is similar to the issues we'll encounter with regular expressions matching unexpected parts of your code. There are more examples to follow later. Refer to the regular expressions recipes for more information.

> To wrap text lines, you can use the `textwrap` module included in the standard library, instead of manually counting characters. View the documentation here: `https://docs.python.org/3/library/textwrap.html`.

If you work with multiple languages, or with any kind of non-English input, it is very useful to learn the basics of Unicode and encodings. In a nutshell, given the vast amount of characters in all the different languages in the world, including alphabets not related to the Latin one, such as Chinese or Arabic, there's a standard to try and cover all of them so that computers can properly understand them. Python 3 greatly improved this situation, making the internal objects of the strings can deal with all of those characters. The default encoding that Python uses, and the most common and compatible one, is currently UTF-8.

A good article to learn about the basics of UTF-8 is this blog post: `https://www.joelonsoftware.com/2003/10/08/the-absolute-minimum-every-software-developer-absolutely-positively-must-know-about-unicode-and-character-sets-no-excuses/`.

Dealing with encodings is still relevant when reading from external files that can be encoded in different encodings (for example, CP-1252 or windows-1252, which is a common encoding produced by legacy Microsoft systems, or ISO 8859-15, which is the industry standard).

See also

- The *Creating strings with formatted values* recipe, covered earlier in the chapter, to learn the basics of string creation.

- The *Introducing regular expressions* recipe, covered later in the chapter, to learn how to detect and extract patterns in text.

- The *Going deeper into regular expressions* recipe, covered later in the chapter, to further your knowledge of regular expressions.

- The *Dealing with encodings* recipe in *Chapter 4*, *Searching and Reading Local Files*, to learn about different kinds of encodings.

Extracting data from structured strings

In a lot of automated tasks, we'll need to treat input text structured in a known format and extract the relevant information. For example, a spreadsheet may define a percentage in a piece of text (such as 37.4%) and we want to retrieve it in a numerical format to apply it later (0.374, as a float).

In this recipe, we'll learn how to process sale logs that contain inline information about a product, such as whether it has been sold, its price, profit made, and other information.

Getting ready

Imagine that we need to parse information stored in sales logs. We'll use a sales log with the following structure:

```
[<Timestamp in iso format>] - SALE - PRODUCT: <product id> - PRICE:
$<price of the sale>
```

For example, a specific log may look like this:

```
[2018-05-05T10:58:41.504054] - SALE - PRODUCT: 1345 - PRICE: $09.99
```

Note that the price has a leading zero. All prices will have two digits for the dollars and two for the cents.

 The standard ISO 8601 defines standard ways of representing the time and date. It is widely used in the computing world and can be parsed and generated by virtually any computer language.

We need to activate our virtual environment before we start:

```
$ source .venv/bin/activate
```

How to do it...

1. In the Python interpreter, make the following imports. Remember to activate your `virtualenv`, as described in the *Creating a virtual environment recipe*:

   ```
   >>> import delorean
   >>> from decimal import Decimal
   ```

2. Enter the log to parse:

   ```
   >>> log = '[2018-05-05T11:07:12.267897] - SALE - PRODUCT: 1345 - PRICE: $09.99'
   ```

3. Split the log into its parts, which are divided by - (note the space before and after the dash). We ignore the SALE part as it doesn't add any relevant information:

   ```
   >>> divide_it = log.split(' - ')
   >>> timestamp_string, _, product_string, price_string = divide_it
   ```

4. Parse the `timestamp` into a datetime object:

   ```
   >>> timestamp = delorean.parse(timestamp_string.strip('[]'))
   ```

5. Parse the `product_id` into an integer:

   ```
   >>> product_id = int(product_string.split(':')[-1])
   ```

6. Parse the price into a `Decimal` type:

   ```
   >>> price = Decimal(price_string.split('$')[-1])
   ```

7. Now you have all of the values in native Python format:

```
>> timestamp, product_id, price
(Delorean(datetime=datetime.datetime(2018, 5, 5, 11, 7, 12,
267897), timezone='UTC'), 1345, Decimal('9.99'))
```

How it works...

The basic working of this is to isolate each of the elements and then parse them into the proper type. The first step is to split the full log into smaller parts. The – string is a good divider, as it splits it into four parts—a timestamp one, one with just the word SALE, the product, and the price.

In the case of the timestamp, we need to isolate the ISO format, which is in brackets in the log. That's why the timestamp has the brackets stripped from it. We use the delorean module (introduced earlier) to parse it into a datetime object.

The word SALE is ignored. There's no relevant information there.

To isolate the product ID, we split the product part at the colon. Then, we parse the last element as an integer:

```
>>> product_string.split(':')
['PRODUCT', ' 1345']
>>> int(' 1345')
1345
```

To divide the price, we use the dollar sign as a separator, and parse it as a Decimal character:

```
>>> price_string.split('$')
['PRICE: ', '09.99']
>>> Decimal('09.99')
Decimal('9.99')
```

As described in the next section, do not parse this value into a float type, as it will change the precision.

There's more…

These log elements can be combined together into a single object, helping to parse and aggregate them. For example, we could define a class in Python code in the following way:

```python
class PriceLog(object):
  def __init__(self, timestamp, product_id, price):
    self.timestamp = timestamp
    self.product_id = product_id
    self.price = price
  def __repr__(self):
    return '<PriceLog ({}, {}, {})>'.format(self.timestamp,
                                            self.product_id,
                                            self.price)


  @classmethod
  def parse(cls, text_log):
    '''
    Parse from a text log with the format
    [<Timestamp>] - SALE - PRODUCT: <product id> - PRICE: $<price>
    to a PriceLog object
    '''
    divide_it = text_log.split(' - ')
    tmp_string, _, product_string, price_string = divide_it
    timestamp = delorean.parse(tmp_string.strip('[]'))
    product_id = int(product_string.split(':')[-1])
    price = Decimal(price_string.split('$')[-1])
    return cls(timestamp=timestamp, product_id=product_id,
  price=price)
```

So, the parsing can be done as follows:

```
>>> log = '[2018-05-05T12:58:59.998903] - SALE - PRODUCT: 897 - PRICE:
$17.99'
```

```
>>> PriceLog.parse(log)
```

```
<PriceLog (Delorean(datetime=datetime.datetime(2018, 5, 5, 12, 58, 59,
998903), timezone='UTC'), 897, 17.99)>
```

Avoid using float types for prices. Floats numbers have precision problems that may produce strange errors when aggregating multiple prices, for example:

```
>>> 0.1 + 0.1 + 0.1
```

```
0.30000000000000004
```

Try these two options to avoid any problems:

- **Use integer cents as the base unit**: This means multiplying currency inputs by 100 and transforming them into `Integers` (or whatever fractional unit is correct for the currency used). You may still want to change the base when displaying them.

- **Parse into the decimal type**: The `Decimal` type keeps the fixed precision and works as you'd expect. You can find further information about the `Decimal` type in the Python documentation at `https://docs.python.org/3.8/library/decimal.html`.

If you use the `Decimal` type, parse the results directly into `Decimal` from the string. If transforming it first into a float, you can carry the precision errors to the new type.

See also

- The *Creating a virtual environment* recipe, covered earlier in the chapter, to learn how to start a virtual environment with installed modules.

- The *Using a third-party tool – parse* recipe, covered later in the chapter, to further your knowledge of how to use third-party tools to deal with text.

- The *Introducing regular expressions* recipe, covered later in the chapter, to learn how to detect and extract patterns from text.

- The *Going deeper into regular expressions* recipe, covered later in the chapter, to further your knowledge of regular expressions.

Using a third-party tool—parse

While manually parsing data, as seen in the previous recipe, works very well for small strings, it can be very laborious to tweak the `exact` formula to work with a variety of inputs. What if the input has an extra dash sometimes? Or it has a variable length header depending on the size of one of the fields?

A more advanced option is to use regular expressions, as we'll see in the next recipe. But there's a great module in Python called `parse` (`https://github.com/r1chardj0n3s/parse`), which allows us to reverse format strings. It is a fantastic tool that's powerful, easy to use, and greatly improves the readability of code.

Getting ready

Add the `parse` module to the `requirements.txt` file in our virtual environment and reinstall the dependencies, as shown in the *Creating a virtual environment* recipe.

The `requirements.txt` file should look like this:

```
delorean==1.0.0
requests==2.22.0
parse==1.14.0
```

Then, reinstall the modules in the virtual environment:

```
$ pip install -r requirements.txt
...
Collecting parse==1.14.0
  Downloading https://files.pythonhosted.org/packages/4a/ea/9a16ff9167522
41aa80f1a5ec56dc6c6defc5d0e70af2d16904a9573367f/parse-1.14.0.tar.gz
...
Installing collected packages: parse
  Running setup.py install for parse ... done
Successfully installed parse-1.14.0
```

How to do it...

1. Import the `parse` function:

   ```
   >>> from parse import parse
   ```

2. Define the log to parse, in the same format as in the *Extracting data from structured strings* recipe:

   ```
   >>> LOG = '[2018-05-06T12:58:00.714611] - SALE - PRODUCT: 1345 -
   PRICE: $09.99'
   ```

3. Analyze it and describe it as you would do when trying to print it, like this:

   ```
   >>> FORMAT = '[{date}] - SALE - PRODUCT: {product} - PRICE:
   ${price}'
   ```

4. Run `parse` and check the results:

   ```
   >>> result = parse(FORMAT, LOG)
   >>> result
   <Result () {'date': '2018-05-06T12:58:00.714611', 'product':
   '1345', 'price': '09.99'}>
   >>> result['date']
   '2018-05-06T12:58:00.714611'
   ```

```
>>> result['product']
'1345'
>>> result['price']
'09.99'
```

5. Note the results are all strings. Define the types to be parsed:

```
>>> FORMAT = '[{date:ti}] - SALE - PRODUCT: {product:d} - PRICE:
${price:05.2f}'
```

6. Parse once again:

```
>>> result = parse(FORMAT, LOG)
>>> result
<Result () {'date': datetime.datetime(2018, 5, 6, 12, 58, 0,
714611), 'product': 1345, 'price': 9.99}>
>>> result['date']
datetime.datetime(2018, 5, 6, 12, 58, 0, 714611)
>>> result['product']
1345
>>> result['price']
9.99
```

7. Define a custom type for the price to avoid issues with the float type:

```
>>> from decimal import Decimal
>>> def price(string):
...     return Decimal(string)
...
>>> FORMAT = '[{date:ti}] - SALE - PRODUCT: {product:d} - PRICE:
${price:price}'
>>> parse(FORMAT, LOG, {'price': price})
<Result () {'date': datetime.datetime(2018, 5, 6, 12, 58, 0,
714611), 'product': 1345, 'price': Decimal('9.99')}>
```

How it works...

The `parse` module allows us to define a format, as a string, that reverses the `format` method when parsing values. A lot of the concepts that we discussed when creating strings apply here—put values in brackets, define the type after a colon, and so on.

By default, as seen in *step 4*, the values are parsed as strings. This is a good starting point when analyzing text. The values can be parsed into more useful native types, as shown in *steps 5* and *6* in the *How to do it* section. Please note that while most of the parsing types are the same as the ones in the Python Format Specification mini-language, there are some others available, such as `ti` for timestamps in ISO format.

> Though we are using timestamp in this book in a more liberal way as a replacement for "Date and time," in the strictest sense, it should only be used for numeric formats, such as *Unix timestamp* or *epoch*, defined as the number of seconds since a particular time.
>
> The usage of a timestamp that includes other formats is common anyway as it's a clear and understandable concept, but be sure to agree to formats when sharing information with others.

If native types are not enough, our own parsing can be defined, as demonstrated in *step 7* of the *How to do it* section. Note that the definition of the `price` function gets a string and returns the proper format, in this case, a `Decimal` type.

All the issues about floats and price information described in the *There's more* section of the *Extracting data from structured strings* recipe apply here as well.

There's more...

The timestamp can also be translated into a `delorean` object for consistency. Also, `delorean` objects carry over time zone information. Adding the same structure as in the previous recipe gives the following object, which is capable of parsing logs:

```python
import parse
from decimal import Decimal
import delorean


class PriceLog(object):
    def __init__(self, timestamp, product_id, price):
        self.timestamp = timestamp
        self.product_id = product_id
        self.price = price

    def __repr__(self):
        return '<PriceLog ({}, {}, {})>'.format(self.timestamp,
                                                self.product_id,
                                                self.price)
```

```
    @classmethod
    def parse(cls, text_log):
        '''
        Parse from a text log with the format
        [<Timestamp>] - SALE - PRODUCT: <product id> - PRICE: $<price>
    to a PriceLog object
        '''
        def price(string):
            return Decimal(string)
        def isodate(string):
            return delorean.parse(string)
        FORMAT = ('[{timestamp:isodate}] - SALE - PRODUCT: {product:d}

             'PRICE: ${price:price}')
        formats = {'price': price, 'isodate': isodate}
        result = parse.parse(FORMAT, text_log, formats)
        return cls(timestamp=result['timestamp'],
                   product_id=result['product'],
                   price=result['price'])
```

So, parsing it returns similar results:

```
>>> log = '[2018-05-06T14:58:59.051545] - SALE - PRODUCT: 827 - PRICE:
$22.25'

>>> PriceLog.parse(log)

<PriceLog (Delorean(datetime=datetime.datetime(2018, 6, 5, 14, 58, 59,
51545), timezone='UTC'), 827, 22.25)>
```

This code is contained in the GitHub file, `https://github.com/PacktPublishing/Python-Automation-Cookbook-Second-Edition/blob/master/Chapter01/price_log.py`

All supported parse types can be found in the documentation at `https://github.com/r1chardj0n3s/parse#format-specification`.

See also

- The *Extracting data from structured strings* recipe, covered earlier in this chapter, to learn how to use simple processes to get information from text.

- The *Introducing regular expressions* recipe, covered later in this chapter, to learn how to detect and extract patterns from text.

- The *Going deeper into regular expressions* recipe, covered later in this chapter, to further your knowledge of regular expressions.

Introducing regular expressions

A **regular expression**, or **regex**, is a pattern to *match* text. In other words, it allows us to define an **abstract string** (typically, the definition of a structured kind of text) to check with other strings to see if they match or not.

It is better to describe them with an example. Think of defining a pattern of text as *a word that starts with an uppercase A and contains only lowercase "n"s and "a"s after that.* Let's show some possible comparisons and results:

Text to compare	Result
Anna	Match
Bob	No match (No initial A)
Alice	No match (l is not n or a after initial A)
James	No match (No initial A)
Aaan	Match
Ana	Match
Annnn	Match
Aaaan	Match
ANNA	No match (N is not n or a)

Table 1.1: A pattern matching example

If this sounds complicated, that's because it is. Regexes can be notoriously complicated because they may be incredibly intricate and difficult to follow. But they are also very useful because they allow us to perform incredibly powerful pattern matching.

Some common uses of regexes are:

- **Validating input data**: For example, a phone number that is only numbers, dashes, and brackets.
- **String parsing**: Retrieve data from structured strings, such as logs or URLs. This is similar to what's described in the previous recipe.
- **Scrapping**: Find the occurrences of something in a long piece of text. For example, find all of the emails in a web page.
- **Replacement**: Find and replace a word or words with others. For example, replace *the owner* with *John Smith*.

Getting ready

The python module to deal with regexes is called `re`. The main function we'll cover is `re.search()`, which returns a `match` object with information about what matched the pattern.

 As regex patterns are also defined as strings, we'll differentiate them by prefixing them with an `r`, such as `r'pattern'`. This is the Python way of labeling a text as raw string literals, meaning that the string within is taken literally, without any escaping. This means that a "\" is used as a backslash instead of an escaping sequence. For example, without the `r` prefix, \n means a newline character.

Some characters are special and refer to concepts such as *the end of the string, any digit, any character, any whitespace character*, and so on.

The simplest form is just a literal string. For example, the regex pattern `r'LOG'` matches the string `'LOGS'`, but not the string `'NOT A MATCH'`. If there's no match, `re.search` returns `None`. If there is, it returns a special `Match` object:

```
>>> import re
>>> re.search(r'LOG', 'LOGS')
<_sre.SRE_Match object; span=(0, 3), match='LOG'>
>>> re.search(r'LOG', 'NOT A MATCH')
>>>
```

How to do it...

1. Import the `re` module:

   ```
   >>> import re
   ```

2. Then, match a pattern that is not at the start of the string:

   ```
   >>> re.search(r'LOG', 'SOME LOGS')
   <_sre.SRE_Match object; span=(5, 8), match='LOG'>
   ```

3. Match a pattern that is only at the start of the string. Note the ^ character:

   ```
   >>> re.search(r'^LOG', 'LOGS')
   <_sre.SRE_Match object; span=(0, 3), match='LOG'>
   >>> re.search(r'^LOG', 'SOME LOGS')
   >>>
   ```

4. Match a pattern only at the end of the string. Note the $ character:

```
>>> re.search(r'LOG$', 'SOME LOG')
<_sre.SRE_Match object; span=(5, 8), match='LOG'>
>>> re.search(r'LOG$', 'SOME LOGS')
>>>
```

5. Match the word 'thing' (not excluding things), but not something or anything. Note the \b at the start of the second pattern:

```
>>> STRING = 'something in the things she shows me'
>>> match = re.search(r'thing', STRING)
>>> STRING[:match.start()], STRING[match.start():match.end()],
STRING[match.end():]
('some', 'thing', ' in the things she shows me')
>>> match = re.search(r'\bthing', STRING)
>>> STRING[:match.start()], STRING[match.start():match.end()],
STRING[match.end():]
('something in the ', 'thing', 's she shows me')
```

6. Match a pattern that's only numbers and dashes (for example, a phone number). Retrieve the matched string:

```
>>> re.search(r'[0123456789-]+', 'the phone number is 1234-567-
890') <_sre.SRE_Match object; span=(20, 32), match='1234-567-890'>
>>> re.search(r'[0123456789-]+', 'the phone number is 1234-567-
890').group()
'1234-567-890'
```

7. Match an email address naively:

```
>>> re.search(r'\S+@\S+', 'my email is email.123@test.com').
group() 'email.123@test.com'
```

How it works...

The re.search function matches a pattern, no matter its position in the string. As explained previously, this will return None if the pattern is not found, or a Match object.

The following special characters are used:

- ^: Marks the start of the string
- $: Marks the end of the string

- \b: Marks the start or end of a word
- \S: Marks any character that's not a whitespace, including characters like *
  or $

More special characters are shown in the next recipe, *Going deeper into regular expressions*.

In *step 6* of the *How to do it* section, the r'[0123456789-]+' pattern is composed of two parts. The first one is between square brackets, and matches any single character between 0 and 9 (any number) and the dash (-) character. The + sign after that means that this character can be present one or more times. This is called a **quantifier** in regexes. This makes a match on any combination of numbers and dashes, no matter how long it is.

Step 7 again uses the + sign to match as many characters as necessary before the @ and again after it. In this case, the character match is \S, which matches any non-whitespace character.

Please note that the naive pattern for emails described here is *very* naive, as it will match invalid emails such as john@smith@test.com. A better regex for most uses is r"(^[a-zA-Z0-9_.+-]+@[a-zA-Z0-9-]+\.[a-zA-Z0-9-.]+$)". You can go to http://emailregex.com/ to find it, along with links to more information.

Note that parsing a valid email including corner cases is actually a difficult and challenging problem. The previous regex should be fine for most uses covered in this book, but in a general framework project such as Django, email validation is a very long and hard-to-read regex.

The resulting matching object returns the position where the matched pattern starts and ends (using the start and end methods), as shown in *step 5*, which splits the string into matched parts, showing the distinction between the two matching patterns.

The difference displayed in *step 5* is a very common one. Trying to capture GP (as in General Practitioner, for a medical doctor) can end up capturing eggplant and bagpipe! Similarly, things\b won't capture things. Be sure to test and make the proper adjustments, such as capturing \bGP\b for just the word GP.

The specific matched pattern can be retrieved by calling `group()`, as shown in *step 6*. Note that the result will always be a string. It can be further processed using any of the methods that we've previously seen, such as by splitting the phone number into groups by dashes, for example:

```
>>> match = re.search(r'[0123456789-]+', 'the phone number is 1234-567-890')
>>> [int(n) for n in match.group().split('-')]
[1234, 567, 890]
```

There's more...

Dealing with regexes can be difficult and complex. Please allow time to test your matches and be sure that they work as you expect in order to avoid nasty surprises.

> *"Some people, when confronted with a problem, think "I know,*
> *I'll use regular expressions." Now they have two problems."*

– Jamie Zawinski

Regular expressions are at their best when they are kept very simple. In general, if there is a specific tool to do it, prefer it over regexes. A very clear example of this is with HTML parsing; refer to *Chapter 3, Building Your First Web Scraping Application,* for better tools to achieve this.

 Some text editors allow us to search using regexes as well. While most are editors aimed at writing code, such as Vim, BBEdit, or Notepad++, they're also present in more general tools, such as MS Office, Open Office, or Google Documents. But be careful, as the particular syntax may be slightly different.

You can check your regexes interactively with some tools. A good one that's freely available online is `https://regex101.com/`, which displays each of the elements and explains the regex. Double-check that you're using the Python flavor:

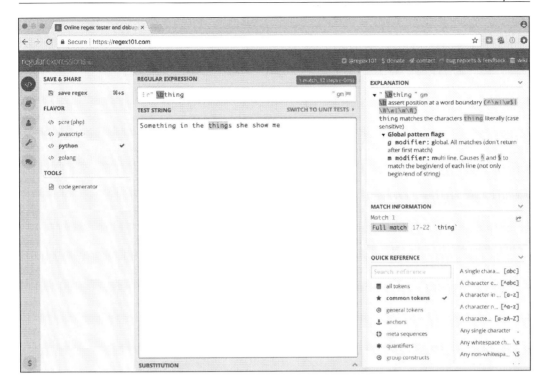

Figure 1.1: An example using RegEx101

Note that the **EXPLANATION** box in the preceding image describes that \b matches a word boundary (the start or end of a word), and that *thing* matches literally these characters.

Regexes, in some cases, can be very slow, or even susceptible to what's called a **regex denial-of-service attack**, a string created to confuse a particular regex so that it takes an enormous amount of time. In the worst-case scenario, it can even block the computer. While automating tasks probably won't get you into those problems, keep an eye out in case a regex takes too long to process.

See also

- The *Extracting data from structured strings* recipe, covered earlier in the chapter, to learn simple techniques to extract information from text.

- The *Using a third-party tool – parse* recipe, covered earlier in the chapter, to use a third-party tool to extract information from text.

- The *Going deeper into regular expressions* recipe, covered later in the chapter, to further your knowledge of regular expressions.

Going deeper into regular expressions

In this recipe, we'll learn more about how to deal with regular expressions. After introducing the basics, we will dig a little deeper into pattern elements, introduce groups as a better way to retrieve and parse strings, learn how to search for multiple occurrences of the same string, and deal with longer texts.

How to do it...

1. Import `re`:

```
>>> import re
```

2. Match a phone pattern as part of a group (in brackets). Note the use of \d as a special character for any digit:

```
>>> match = re.search(r'the phone number is ([\d-]+)', '37: the
phone number is 1234-567-890')
>>> match.group()
'the phone number is 1234-567-890'
>>> match.group(1)
'1234-567-890'
```

3. Compile a pattern and capture a case-insensitive pattern with a yes|no option:

```
>>> pattern = re.compile(r'The answer to question (\w+) is
(yes|no)', re.IGNORECASE)
>>> pattern.search('Naturally, the answer to question 3b is YES')
<_sre.SRE_Match object; span=(10, 42), match='the answer to
question 3b is YES' >
>>> pattern.search('Naturally, the answer to question 3b is YES').
groups()
('3b', 'YES')
```

4. Match all the occurrences of cities and state abbreviations in the text. Note that they are separated by a single character, and the name of the city always starts with an uppercase letter. Only four states are matched for simplicity:

```
>>> PATTERN = re.compile(r'([A-Z][\w\s]+?).(TX|OR|OH|MI)')
```

```
>>> TEXT ='the jackalopes are the team of Odessa,TX while the
knights are native of Corvallis OR and the mud hens come from
Toledo.OH; the whitecaps have their base in Grand Rapids,MI'
```

```
>>> list(PATTERN.finditer(TEXT))
```

```
[<_sre.SRE_Match object; span=(31, 40), match='Odessa,TX'>, <_sre.
SRE_Match object; span=(73, 85), match='Corvallis OR'>, <_sre.SRE_
Match object; span=(113, 122), match='Toledo.OH'>, <_sre.SRE_Match
object; span=(157, 172), match='Grand Rapids,MI'>]
```

```
>>> _[0].groups() ('Odessa', 'TX')
```

How it works...

The new special characters that were introduced are as follows:

- \d: Marks any digit (0 to 9).

- \s: Marks any character that's a whitespace, including tabs and other whitespace special characters. Note that this is the reverse of \S, which was introduced in the previous recipe.

- \w: Marks any letter (this includes digits, but excludes characters such as periods).

- . : (dot): Marks any character.

 Note that the same letter in uppercase or lowercase means the opposite match, for example, \d matches a digit, while \D matches a non-digit.

To define groups, put the defined groups in parentheses. Groups can be retrieved individually. This makes them perfect for matching a bigger pattern that contains a variable part to be processed in the next step, as demonstrated in *step 2*. Note the difference with the *step 6* pattern in the previous recipe. In this case, the pattern is not only the number, but it includes the prefix text, even if we then extract only the number:

```
>>> re.search(r'the phone number is ([\d-]+)', '37: the phone number is
1234-567-890')
```

```
<_sre.SRE_Match object; span=(4, 36), match='the phone number is 1234-
```

```
567-890'>
>>> _.group(1)
'1234-567-890'
>>> re.search(r'[0123456789-]+', '37: the phone number is 1234-567-890')
<_sre.SRE_Match object; span=(0, 2), match='37'>
>>> _.group()
'37'
```

Remember that group 0 (.group() or .group(0)) is always the whole match. The rest of the groups are ordered as they appear.

Patterns can be compiled as well. This saves some time if the pattern needs to be matched over and over. To use it that way, compile the pattern and then use that object to perform searches, as shown in *steps 3* and *4*. Some extra flags can be added, such as making the pattern case insensitive.

Step 4's pattern requires a little bit of information. It's composed of two groups, separated by a single character. The special character "." (dot) means it matches everything. In our example, it matches a period, a whitespace, and a comma. The second group is a straightforward selection of defined options, in this case, US state abbreviations.

The first group starts with an uppercase letter ([A-Z]) and accepts any combination of letters or spaces ([\w\s]+?), but not punctuation marks such as periods or commas. This matches the cities, including those that are composed of more than one word.

The final +? makes the match of letters *non-greedy*, matching as few characters as possible. This avoids some problems such as when there are no punctuation symbols between the cities. Take a look at the result where we don't include the *non-greedy* qualifier for the second match and how it includes two elements:

```
>>> PATTERN = re.compile(r'([A-Z][\w\s]+).(TX|OR|OH|MI)')
>>> TEXT ='the jackalopes are the team of Odessa,TX while the knights
are native of Corvallis OR and the mud hens come from Toledo.OH; the
whitecaps have their base in Grand Rapids,MI'
>>> list(PATTERN.finditer(TEXT))[1]
<re.Match object; span=(73, 122), match='Corvallis OR and the mud hens
come from Toledo.OH>
```

Note that this pattern starts on any uppercase letter and keeps matching until it finds a state, unless separated by a punctuation mark, which may not be what's expected, for example:

```
>>> re.search(r'([A-Z][\w\s]+?).(TX|OR|OH|MI)', 'This is a test, Escanaba
MI')
<_sre.SRE_Match object; span=(16, 27), match='Escanaba MI'>
>>> re.search(r'([A-Z][\w\s]+?).(TX|OR|OH|MI)', 'This is a test with
Escanaba MI')
<_sre.SRE_Match object; span=(0, 31), match='This is a test with Escanaba
MI'>
```

Step 4 also shows you how to find more than one occurrence in a long text. While the .findall() method exists, it doesn't return the full match object, while .findalliter() does. As is common now in Python 3, .findalliter() returns an iterator that can be used in a for loop or list comprehension. Note that .search() returns only the first occurrence of the pattern, even if more matches appear:

```
>>> PATTERN.search(TEXT)
<_sre.SRE_Match object; span=(31, 40), match='Odessa,TX'>
>>> PATTERN.findall(TEXT)
[('Odessa', 'TX'), ('Corvallis', 'OR'), ('Toledo', 'OH')]
```

There's more...

The special characters can be reversed if they are case swapped. For example, the reverse of the ones we used are as follows:

- **\D**: Marks any non-digit.
- **\W**: Marks any non-letter.
- **\B**: Marks a position that's **not** at the start or end of a word. For example, r'thing\B' will match *things* but not *thing*.

> The most commonly used special characters are typically \d (digits) and \w (letters and digits), as they mark common patterns to search for.

Groups can be assigned names as well. This makes them more explicit at the expense of making the group more verbose in the following shape— (?P<groupname>PATTERN). Groups can be referred to by name with .group(groupname) or by calling .groupdict() while maintaining its numeric position.

For example, the *step 4* pattern can be described as follows:

```
>>> PATTERN = re.compile(r'(?P<city>[A-Z][\w\s]+?).
(?P<state>TX|OR|OH|MN)')
>>> match = PATTERN.search(TEXT)
>>> match.groupdict() {'city': 'Odessa', 'state': 'TX'}
>>> match.group('city') 'Odessa'
>>> match.group('state') 'TX'
>>> match.group(1), match.group(2) ('Odessa', 'TX')
```

Regular expressions are a very extensive topic. There are whole technical books devoted to them and they can be notoriously deep. The Python documentation is a good reference to use (https://docs.python.org/3/library/re.html) and to learn more.

If you feel a little intimidated at the start, it's a perfectly natural feeling. Analyze each of the patterns with care, dividing them into smaller parts, and they will start to make sense. Don't be afraid to run a regex interactive analyzer!

Regexes can be really powerful and generic, but they may not be the proper tool for what you are trying to achieve. We've seen some caveats and patterns that have subtleties. As a rule of thumb, if a pattern starts to feel complicated, it's time to search for a different tool. Remember the previous recipes as well and the options they presented, such as `parse`.

See also

- The *Introducing regular expressions* recipe, covered earlier in the chapter, to learn the basics of using regular expressions.
- The *Using a third-party tool – parse* recipe, covered earlier in the chapter, to learn a different technique to extract information from text.

Adding command-line arguments

A lot of tasks can be best structured as a command-line interface that accepts different parameters to change the way it works, for example, scraping a web page from a provided URL or other URL. Python includes a powerful `argparse` module in the standard library to create rich command-line argument parsing with minimal effort.

Getting ready

The basic use of `argparse` in a script can be shown in three steps:

1. Define the arguments that your script is going to accept, generating a new parser.
2. Call the defined parser, returning an object with all of the resulting arguments.
3. Use the arguments to call the entry point of your script, which will apply the defined behavior.

Try to use the following general structure for your scripts:

```
IMPORTS
def main(main parameters):
    DO THINGS


if __name__ == '__main__':
    DEFINE ARGUMENT PARSER
    PARSE ARGS
    VALIDATE OR MANIPULATE ARGS, IF NEEDED
    main(arguments)
```

The `main` function makes it easy to know what the entry point for the code is. The section under the `if` statement is only executed if the file is called directly, but not if it's imported. We'll follow this for all the steps.

How to do it...

1. Create a script that will accept a single integer as a positional argument, and will print a hash symbol that amount of times. The `recipe_cli_step1.py` script is as follows, but note that we are following the structure presented previously, and the `main` function is just printing the argument:

```
import argparse


def main(number):
    print('#' * number)


if __name__ == '__main__':
    parser = argparse.ArgumentParser()
    parser.add_argument('number', type=int, help='A number')
```

```
        args = parser.parse_args()

        main(args.number)
```

2. Call the script and check how the parameter is presented. Calling the script with no arguments displays the automatic help. Use the automatic argument -h to display the extended help:

```
$ python3 recipe_cli_step1.py

usage: recipe_cli_step1.py [-h] number

recipe_cli_step1.py: error: the following arguments are required:
number

$ python3 recipe_cli_step1.py -h

usage: recipe_cli_step1.py [-h] number


positional arguments:

  number      A number

optional arguments:

 -h, --help show this help message and exit
```

3. Calling the script with the extra parameters works as expected:

```
$ python3 recipe_cli_step1.py 4

####

$ python3 recipe_cli_step1.py not_a_number

usage: recipe_cli_step1.py [-h] number

recipe_cli_step1.py: error: argument number: invalid int value:
'not_a_number'
```

4. Change the script to accept an optional argument for the character to print. The default will be "#". The recipe_cli_step2.py script will look like this:

```
import argparse


def main(character, number):
    print(character * number)


if __name__ == '__main__':
    parser = argparse.ArgumentParser()
    parser.add_argument('number', type=int, help='A number')
    parser.add_argument('-c', type=str, help='Character to
print',
```

```
                          default='#')

        args = parser.parse_args()
        main(args.c, args.number)
```

5. The help is updated, and using the -c flag allows us to print different characters:

```
$ python3 recipe_cli_step2.py -h
usage: recipe_cli_step2.py [-h] [-c C] number
positional arguments:
  number      A number
optional arguments:
 -h, --help show this help message and exit
 -c C Character to print
$ python3 recipe_cli_step2.py 4
####
$ python3 recipe_cli_step2.py 5 -c m
mmmmm
```

6. Add a flag that changes the behavior when present. The recipe_cli_step3. py script is as follows:

```
import argparse


def main(character, number):
    print(character * number)



if __name__ == '__main__':
    parser = argparse.ArgumentParser()
    parser.add_argument('number', type=int, help='A number')
    parser.add_argument('-c', type=str, help='Character to print',
                        default='#')
    parser.add_argument('-U', action='store_true', default=False,
                        dest='uppercase',
                        help='Uppercase the character')
    args = parser.parse_args()
```

```
         if args.uppercase:
              args.c = args.c.upper()
         main(args.c, args.number)
```

7. Calling it uppercases the character if the -U flag is added:

```
$ python3 recipe_cli_step3.py 4 -c f
ffff
$ python3 recipe_cli_step3.py 4 -c f -U
FFFF
```

How it works...

As described in *step 1* of the *How to do it* section, the arguments are added to the parser through .add_arguments. Once all of the arguments are defined, calling parse_args() returns an object that contains the results (or exits if there's an error).

Each argument should add a help description, but their behavior can change greatly:

- If an argument starts with a -, it is considered an optional parameter, like the -c argument in *step 4*. If not, it's a positional argument, like the number argument in *step 1*.

- For clarity, always define a default value for optional parameters. It will be None if you don't, but this may be confusing.

- Remember to always add a help parameter with a description of the parameter; help is automatically generated, as shown in *step 2*.

- If a type is present, it will be validated, for example, number in *step 3*. By default, the type will be a string.

- The actions store_true and store_false can be used to generate flags, arguments that don't require any extra parameters. Set the corresponding default value as the opposite Boolean. This is demonstrated in the U argument in *steps 6* and *7*.

- The name of the property in the args object will be, by default, the name of the argument (without the dash, if it's present). You can change it with dest. For example, in *step 6*, the command-line argument -U is described as uppercase.

Changing the name of an argument for internal usage is very useful when using short arguments, such as single letters. A good command-line interface will use -c, but, internally, it's probably a good idea to use a more verbose label, such as configuration_file. Remember, explicit is better than implicit!

- Some arguments can work in coordination with others, as shown in *step 3*. Perform all of the required operations to pass the `main` function as clear and concise parameters. For example, in *step 3*, only two parameters are passed, but one may have been modified.

There's more...

You can create long arguments as well with double dashes, for example:

```
parser.add_argument('-v', '--verbose', action='store_true',
default=False,

                            help='Enable verbose output')
```

This will accept both `-v` and `--verbose`, and it will store the name `verbose`.

Adding long names is a good way of making the interface more intuitive and easy to remember. It's easy to remember after a couple of times that there's a verbose option, and it starts with a `v`.

The main inconvenience when dealing with command-line arguments may be that you end up with too many of them. This creates confusion. Try to make your arguments as independent as possible and don't make too many dependencies between them; otherwise, handling the combinations can be tricky.

In particular, try to not create more than a couple of positional arguments, as they won't have mnemonics. Positional arguments also accept default values, but most of the time, that won't be the expected behavior.

For advanced details, refer to the Python documentation of `argparse` (`https://docs.python.org/3/library/argparse.html`).

See also

- The *Creating a virtual environment* recipe, covered earlier in this chapter, to learn how to create an environment installing third-party modules.
- The *Installing third-party packages* recipe, covered earlier in this chapter, to learn how to install and use external modules in the virtual environment.

2
Automating Tasks Made Easy

To properly automate tasks, we need a way to make them execute automatically at the proper times. A task that needs to be started manually is not really fully automated.

However, in order to be able to leave them running in the background while worrying about more pressing issues, the task will need to be adequate to run in *fire-and-forget* mode. We should be able to monitor that it executes correctly, be sure that we capture relevant information (such as receiving notifications if something interesting arises), and know whether there have been any errors while running it.

Ensuring that a piece of software runs consistently with high reliability is actually a very big deal. It is one area that, in order to be done properly, requires specialized knowledge and staff, who typically go by the names of sysadmin, operations, or **SRE (Site Reliability Engineering)**. Big operations, such as Amazon and Google, require huge investment in ensuring that everything works 24/7.

The objective for this book is way more modest than that, as most software doesn't require this kind of high availability. Designing systems with downtimes of less than a few seconds per year is challenging, but executing a task with reasonable reliability is a much easier thing to do. However, be aware that there's maintenance to be done, and plan accordingly.

In this chapter, we'll cover the following recipes:

- Preparing a task
- Setting up a cron job
- Capturing errors and problems
- Sending email notifications

We'll begin by going over how we ought to prepare a task before we automate it.

Preparing a task

It all starts with defining precisely the work that needs to be executed, and designing it in a way that doesn't require human intervention to run.

Some ideal characteristic points are as follows:

1. **Single, clear entry point**: No confusion on how to start the task.
2. **Clear parameters**: If there are any parameters, they should be as explicit as possible.
3. **No interactivity**: Stopping the execution to request information from the user is not possible.
4. **The result should be stored**: In order to be checked at a different time than when it runs.
5. **Clear result**: When we oversee the execution of a program ourselves, we can accept more verbose results, such as unlabeled data or extra debugging information. However, for an automated task, the final result should be as concise and to the point as possible.
6. **Errors should be logged**: To analyze what went wrong.

A command-line program has a lot of those characteristics already. It always has a clear entry point, with defined parameters, and the result can be stored, even if just in text format. And it can be improved ensuring a config file that clarifies the parameters, and an output file.

Note that point 6 is the objective of the *Capturing errors and problems* recipe, and will be covered there.

To avoid interactivity, do not use any function that waits for user input, such as `input`. Remember to delete debugger breakpoints!

Getting ready

We'll start by following a structure in which a main function will serve as the entry point, and all parameters are supplied to it.

This is the same basic structure that was presented in the *Adding command-line arguments* recipe in *Chapter 1, Let's Begin Our Automation Journey*.

The definition of a main function with all of the explicit arguments covers points 1 (single, clear entry point) and 2 (clear parameters). Point 3 (no interactivity) is not difficult to achieve.

To improve points 2 (clear parameters) and 5 (clear result), we'll look at retrieving the configuration from a file and storing the result in another. Another option is to send a notification, such as an email, which will be covered later in this chapter.

How to do it...

1. Prepare the following command-line program by multiplying two numbers, and save it as prepare_task_step1.py:

```python
import argparse


def main(number, other_number):
    result = number * other_number
    print(f'The result is {result}')


if __name__ == '__main__':
    parser = argparse.ArgumentParser()
    parser.add_argument('-n1', type=int, help='A number',
default=1)
    parser.add_argument('-n2', type=int, help='Another
number', default=1)

    args = parser.parse_args()

    main(args.n1, args.n2)
```

Run prepare_task_step1.py by multiplying two numbers:

```
$ python3 prepare_task_step1.py -n1 3 -n2 7
The result is 21
```

2. Update the file to define a config file that contains both arguments, and save it as prepare_task_step3.py. Note that defining a config file overwrites any command-line parameters:

```python
import argparse
import configparser
```

```
def main(number, other_number):
    result = number * other_number
    print(f'The result is {result}')


if __name__ == '__main__':
    parser = argparse.ArgumentParser()
    parser.add_argument('-n1', type=int, help='A number',
default=1)
    parser.add_argument('-n2', type=int, help='Another
number', default=1)

    parser.add_argument('--config', '-c', type=argparse.
FileType('r'),
                        help='config file')

    args = parser.parse_args()
    if args.config:
        config = configparser.ConfigParser()
        config.read_file(args.config)
        # Transforming values into integers
        args.n1 = int(config['ARGUMENTS']['n1'])
        args.n2 = int(config['ARGUMENTS']['n2'])

    main(args.n1, args.n2)
```

3. Create the config file, `config.ini`. See the ARGUMENTS section and the n1 and n2 values:

```
[ARGUMENTS]
n1=5
n2=7
```

4. Run the command with the config file. Note that the config file overwrites the command-line parameters, as described in *step 2*:

```
$ python3 prepare_task_step3.py -c config.ini
The result is 35
$ python3 prepare_task_step3.py -c config.ini -n1 2 -n2 3
The result is 35
```

5. Add a parameter to store the result in a file, and save it as `prepare_task_step6.py`:

```python
import argparse
import sys
import configparser


def main(number, other_number, output):
    result = number * other_number
    print(f'The result is {result}', file=output)


if __name__ == '__main__':
    parser = argparse.ArgumentParser()
    parser.add_argument('-n1', type=int, help='A number',
default=1)
    parser.add_argument('-n2', type=int, help='Another
number', default=1)

    parser.add_argument('--config', '-c', type=argparse.
FileType('r'),
                        help='config file')
    parser.add_argument('-o', dest='output', type=argparse.
FileType('w'),
                        help='output file',
                        default=sys.stdout)

    args = parser.parse_args()
    if args.config:
        config = configparser.ConfigParser()
        config.read_file(args.config)
        # Transforming values into integers
        args.n1 = int(config['ARGUMENTS']['n1'])
        args.n2 = int(config['ARGUMENTS']['n2'])

    main(args.n1, args.n2, args.output)
```

6. Run the result to check that it's sending the output to the defined file. Note that there's no output outside the result files:

```
$ python3 prepare_task_step6.py -n1 3 -n2 5 -o result.txt
$ cat result.txt
The result is 15
$ python3 prepare_task_step6.py -c config.ini -o result2.txt
$ cat result2.txt
The result is 35
```

How it works...

Note that the argparse module allows us to define files as parameters, with the argparse.FileType type, and opens them automatically. This is very handy and will raise an error if the file path leads to an invalid location.

Remember to open the file in the correct mode. In *step 5*, the config file is opened in read mode (r) and the output file in write mode (w), which will overwrite the file if it exists. You may find the append mode (a) useful, which will add the next piece of data at the end of an existing file.

configparser module allows us to use config files with ease. As demonstrated in *step 2*, the parsing of the file is simple, as follows:

```
config = configparser.ConfigParser()
config.read_file(file)
```

The config will then be accessible as a dictionary. This will have the sections of the config file as the keys, and inside another dictionary with each of the config values. So, the value n2 in the ARGUMENTS section is accessed as config['ARGUMENTS']['n2'].

Note that the values are always stored as strings, which are required to be transformed into other types, such as integers.

If you need to obtain Boolean values, do not perform value = bool(config[raw_value]), as any string will be transformed into True no matter what; for instance, the string False is a true string, as it's not empty. Using an empty string is a bad option as well, as they are very confusing. Use the .getboolean method instead, for example, value = config.getboolean(raw_value). There are similar getint() and getfloat() for integers and float values.

Python 3 allows us to pass a `file` parameter to the `print` function, which will write to that file. *Step 5* shows the usage to redirect all of the printed information to a file.

Note that the default parameter is `sys.stdout`, which will print the value to the terminal (standard output). This means that calling the script without an `-o` parameter will display the information on the screen, which is helpful when developing and debugging the script:

```
$ python3 prepare_task_step6.py -c config.ini
The result is 35
$ python3 prepare_task_step6.py -c config.ini -o result.txt
$ cat result.txt
The result is 35
```

There's more...

Please refer to the full documentation of `configparser` in the official Python documentation: `https://docs.python.org/3/library/configparser.html`.

In most cases, this configuration parser should be good enough, but if more power is needed, you can use YAML files as configuration files. YAML files (`https://learn.getgrav.org/advanced/yaml`) are very common as configuration files. They are well structured and can be parsed directly, taking into account of various data types:

1. Add PyYAML to the `requirements.txt` file:

    ```
    PyYAML==5.3
    ```

2. Install the requirements in the virtual environment:

    ```
    $ pip install -r requirements.txt
    ```

3. Create the `prepare_task_yaml.py` file:

    ```python
    import yaml
    import argpars
    import sys


    def main(number, other_number, output):
        result = number * other_number
        print(f'The result is {result}', file=output)
    ```

```python
if __name__ == '__main__':
    parser = argparse.ArgumentParser()
    parser.add_argument('-n1', type=int, help='A number',
default=1)
    parser.add_argument('-n2', type=int, help='Another
number', default=1)
    parser.add_argument('-c', dest='config', type=argparse.
FileType('r'),
 help='config file in YAML format',
 default=None)
    parser.add_argument('-o', dest='output', type=argparse.
FileType('w'),
                        help='output file',
                        default=sys.stdout)

    args = parser.parse_args()
    if args.config:
        config = yaml.load(args.config, Loader= yaml.
FullLoader)
        # No need to transform values
        args.n1 = config['ARGUMENTS']['n1']
        args.n2 = config['ARGUMENTS']['n2']

    main(args.n1, args.n2, args.output)
```

Note that the PyYAML yaml.load() function requires a
Loader parameter. This is to avoid arbitrary code execution if the
YAML file comes from an untrusted source. Always use yaml.
SafeLoader unless you need a set of YAML language features.
Never use loaders other than yaml.SafeLoader if any part of
the data coming from a YAML file comes from an untrusted source
(for example, user input). Refer to this article for more information:
https://github.com/yaml/pyyaml/wiki/PyYAML-yaml.
load(input)-Deprecation.

4. Define the config file, config.yaml:

```yaml
ARGUMENTS:
    n1: 7
    n2: 4
```

5. Then, run the following:

```
$ python3 prepare_task_yaml.py -c config.yaml
The result is 28
```

There's also the possibility of setting a default config file, as well as a default output file. This can be handy to create a task that requires no input parameters.

As a general rule, try to avoid creating too many input and configuration parameters if the task has a very specific objective in mind. Try to limit the input parameters to different executions of the task. A parameter that never changes is probably fine being defined as a **constant**. A high number of parameters will make config files or command-line arguments complicated and will create more maintenance in the long run. On the other hand, if your objective is to create a very flexible tool to be used in very different situations, then creating more parameters is probably a good idea. Try to find your own proper balance!

See also

*   The *Command-line arguments* recipe in *Chapter 1, Let's Begin Our Automation Journey*, to get more information about command-line arguments.
*   The *Sending email notifications* recipe, covered later in this chapter, to see a more fleshed-out example of an automated task.
*   The *Debugging with breakpoints* recipe in *Chapter 13, Debugging Techniques*, to learn how to debug the code before executing it automatically.

Setting up a cron job

Cron is an old-fashioned but reliable way of executing commands. It has been around since the 1970s in Unix, and it's an old favorite in system administration to perform maintenance tasks such as freeing up disk space, rotating log files, making backups, and other common, repetitive operations.

This recipe is Unix and Unix-like operating systems specific, so it will work in Linux and macOS. While it's possible to schedule a task in Windows, it's very different and uses Task Scheduler, which won't be described here. If you have access to a Linux server, this can be a good way of scheduling periodic tasks.

The main advantages are as follows:

*   It's present in virtually all Unix or Linux systems and configured to run automatically.
*   It's easy to use, although a little deceptive at first.

- It's well known. Almost anyone involved with admin tasks will have a general idea of how to use it.

- It allows for easy periodic commands, with good precision.

However, it also has some disadvantages, including the following:

- By default, it may not give much feedback. Retrieving the output, logging execution, and errors are critical.

- The task should be as self-contained as possible to avoid problems with environment variables, such as using the wrong Python interpreter, or what path should execute.

- It is Unix-specific.

- Only fixed periodic times are available.

- It doesn't control how many tasks run at the same time. Each time the countdown goes off, it creates a new task. For example, a task that takes 1 hour to complete, and that is scheduled to run once every 45 minutes, will have 15 minutes of overlap where two tasks will be running.

Don't understate the latest effect. Running multiple expensive tasks at the same time can have a bad effect on performance. Having expensive tasks overlapping may result in a race condition where each task stops the others from ever finishing! Allow ample time for your tasks to finish and keep an eye on them. Keep in mind that any other program running in the same host may have their performance affected, which can include any service, such as web servers, databases, and email. Check how loaded the host where the task will execute is so as to avoid surprises.

Getting ready

We will produce a script, called `cron.py`:

```python
import argparse
import sys
from datetime import datetime
import configparser


def main(number, other_number, output):
    result = number * other_number
    print(f'[{datetime.utcnow().isoformat()}] The result is
{result}',
```

```
        file=output)


if __name__ == '__main__':
    parser = argparse.ArgumentParser(formatter_class=argparse.
ArgumentDefaultsHelpFormatter)
    parser.add_argument('--config', '-c', type=argparse.
FileType('r'),
                        help='config file',
                        default='/etc/automate.ini')
    parser.add_argument('-o', dest='output', type=argparse.
FileType('w'),
                        help='output file',
                        default=sys.stdout)

    args = parser.parse_args()
    if args.config:
        config = configparser.ConfigParser()
        config.read_file(args.config)
        # Transforming values into integers
        args.n1 = int(config['ARGUMENTS']['n1'])
        args.n2 = int(config['ARGUMENTS']['n2'])

    main(args.n1, args.n2, args.output)
```

Note the following details:

1. The config file is, by default, /etc/automate.ini. Reuse config.ini from the previous recipe.

2. A timestamp has been added to the output. This will make it explicit when the task is run.

3. The result is being added to the file, as shown with the a mode where the file is open.

4. The ArgumentDefaultsHelpFormatter parameter automatically adds information about default values when printing the help using the -h argument.

Check that the task is producing the expected result and that you can log to a known file:

```
$ python3 cron.py
[2020-01-15 22:22:31.436912] The result is 35
$ python3 cron.py -o /path/automate.log
$ cat /path/automate.log
[2020-01-15 22:28:08.833272] The result is 35
```

How to do it...

1. Obtain the full path of the Python interpreter. This is the interpreter that's in your virtual environment:

    ```
    $ which python
    /your/path/.venv/bin/python
    ```

2. Prepare the cron job to be executed. Get the full path and check that it can be executed without any problems. Execute it a couple of times:

    ```
    $ /your/path/.venv/bin/python /your/path/cron.py -o /path/
    automate.log
    $ /your/path/.venv/bin/python /your/path/cron.py -o /path/
    automate.log
    ```

3. Check that the result is being added correctly to the result file:

    ```
    $ cat /path/automate.log
    [2020-01-15 22:28:08.833272] The result is 35
    [2020-01-15 22:28:10.510743] The result is 35
    ```

4. Edit the crontab file to run the task once every 5 minutes:

    ```
    $ crontab -e


    */5 * * * * /your/path/.venv/bin/python /your/path/cron.py -o /
    path/automate.log
    ```

    Note that this opens an editing terminal with your default command-line editor.

    If you haven't set up your default command-line editor, then, by default, it is likely to be Vim. This can be disconcerting if you don't have experience with Vim. Press *I* to start inserting text and *Esc* when you're done. Then, exit after saving the file with wq. For more information about Vim, refer to this introduction: https://null-byte.wonderhowto.com/how-to/intro-vim-unix-text-editor-every-hacker-should-be-familiar-with-0174674.

For information on how to change the default command-line editor, refer to the following link: `https://www.a2hosting.com/kb/developer-corner/linux/setting-the-default-text-editor-in-linux`.

5. Check the crontab contents. Note that this displays the crontab contents, but doesn't set it to edit:

```
$ contab -l
*/5 * * * * /your/path/.venv/bin/python /your/path/cron.py -o /
path/automate.log
```

6. Wait and check the result file to see how the task is being executed:

```
$ tail -F /path/automate.log
[2020-01-17 21:20:00.611540] The result is 35
[2020-01-17 21:25:01.174835] The result is 35
[2020-01-17 21:30:00.886452] The result is 35
```

How it works...

The crontab line consists of a line describing how often to run the task (the first six elements), plus the task. Each of the initial six elements means a different unit of time to execute. Most of them are stars, meaning *any*:

```
*  *  *  *  *  *
|  |  |  |  |  |
|  |  |  |  |  +-- Year              (range: 1900-3000)
|  |  |  |  +----- Day of the Week   (range: 1-7, 1 standing for Monday)
|  |  |  +------- Month of the Year (range: 1-12)
|  |  +--------- Day of the Month  (range: 1-31)
|  +----------- Hour               (range: 0-23)
+------------- Minute             (range: 0-59)
```

Therefore, our line, `*/5 * * * * *`, *means every time the minute is divisible by 5, in all hours, all days... all years.*

Here are some examples:

```
30   15 * * * * means "every day at 15:30"
30    * * * * * means "every hour, at 30 minutes"
0,30 * * * * * means "every hour, at 0 minutes and 30 minutes"
*/30 * * * * * means "every half hour"
0     0 * * 1 * means "every Monday at 00:00"
```

Do not try to guess too much. Use a cheat sheet such as `https://crontab.guru/` for examples and tweaks. Most of the common usages will be described there directly. You can also edit a formula and get a descriptive piece of text of how it's going to run.

After the description of how to run the cron job, include the line to execute the task, as prepared in *step 2* of the *How to do it...* section.

Note that the task is described with all of the full paths for every related file—the interpreter, the script, and the output file. This removes all ambiguity related to the paths and reduces the chances of possible errors. A very common error is for cron to not be able to determine one or more of these three elements.

There's more...

The description of the default output (standard output) can be a bit verbose. When calling `python3 cron.py -h`, it gets displayed as:

```
-o OUTPUT   output file (default: <_io.TextIOWrapper name='<stdout>'
mode='w' encoding='utf-8'>)
```

This is the description of the **standard output (stdout)**. The format of the parameter can be changed using the `formatter_class` argument in the `ArgumentParser`. This means that you can use a custom formatter inheriting from the available default ones to tweak the display of the value. Refer to the documentation at `https://docs.python.org/2/library/argparse.html#formatter-class`

If there's any problem in the execution of the crontab, you should receive a system mail. This will show up as a message in the terminal like this:

```
You have mail.
$
```

This can be read with mail:

```
$ mail
Mail version 8.1 6/6/93. Type ? for help.
"/var/mail/jaime": 1 message 1 new
>N 1 jaime@Jaimes-iMac-5K Fri Jun 17 21:15 20/914 "Cron <jaime@Jaimes-iM"
? 1
Message 1:
...
```

```
/usr/local/Cellar/python/3.8.1/Frameworks/Python.framework/Versions/3.8/
Resources/Python.app/Contents/MacOS/Python: can't open file 'cron.py':
[Errno 2] No such file or directory
```

In the next recipe, we will explore methods to capture the errors independently so that the task can run smoothly.

See also

- The *Adding command-line options* recipe in *Chapter 1, Let's Begin Our Automation Journey*, to understand the basic concepts of command-line options.
- The *Capturing errors and problems* recipe, next in this chapter, to learn how to store events happening during the execution.

Capturing errors and problems

An automated task's main characteristic is its *fire-and-forget* quality. We are not actively looking at the result, but making it run in the background.

Most of the recipes in this book deal with external information, such as web pages or other reports, so the likelihood of finding an unexpected problem when running it is high. This recipe will present an automated task that will safely store unexpected behaviors in a log file that can be checked afterward.

Getting ready

As a starting point, we'll use a task that will divide two numbers, as described in the command line.

This task is very similar to the one presented in *step 5 of How it works* for the *Preparing a task* recipe, earlier this chapter. However, instead of multiplying two numbers, we'll divide them.

How to do it...

1. Create the `task_with_error_handling_step1.py` file, as follows:

```python
import argparse
import sys

def main(number, other_number, output):
    result = number / other_number
```

```
    print(f'The result is {result}', file=output)


if __name__ == '__main__':
    parser = argparse.ArgumentParser()
    parser.add_argument('-n1', type=int, help='A number',
default=1)
    parser.add_argument('-n2', type=int, help='Another
number', default=1)
    parser.add_argument('-o', dest='output', type=argparse.
FileType('w'),
                            help='output file', default=sys.
stdout)


    args = parser.parse_args()


    main(args.n1, args.n2, args.output)
```

2. Execute it a couple of times to see that it divides two numbers:

```
$ python3 task_with_error_handling_step1.py -n1 3 -n2 2
The result is 1.5
$ python3 task_with_error_handling_step1.py -n1 25 -n2 5
The result is 5.0
```

3. Check that dividing by 0 produces an error, and that the error is not logged on the result file:

```
$ python task_with_error_handling_step1.py -n1 5 -n2 1 -o result.
txt
$ cat result.txt
The result is 5.0
$ python task_with_error_handling_step1.py -n1 5 -n2 0 -o result.
txt
Traceback (most recent call last):
 File "task_with_error_handling_step1.py", line 20, in <module>
 main(args.n1, args.n2, args.output)
 File "task_with_error_handling_step1.py", line 6, in main
 result = number / other_number
ZeroDivisionError: division by zero
$ cat result.txt
```

4. Create the `task_with_error_handling_step4.py` file:

```
import argparse
import sys
import logging


LOG_FORMAT = '%(asctime)s %(name)s %(levelname)s %(message)s'
LOG_LEVEL = logging.DEBUG


def main(number, other_number, output):
    logging.info(f'Dividing {number} between {other_number}')
    result = number / other_number
    print(f'The result is {result}', file=output)


if __name__ == '__main__':
    parser = argparse.ArgumentParser()
    parser.add_argument('-n1', type=int, help='A number',
default=1)
    parser.add_argument('-n2', type=int, help='Another
number', default=1)

    parser.add_argument('-o', dest='output', type=argparse.
FileType('w'),
                        help='output file', default=sys.
stdout)
    parser.add_argument('-l', dest='log', type=str, help='log
file',
                        default=None)

    args = parser.parse_args()
    if args.log:
        logging.basicConfig(format=LOG_FORMAT, filename=args.
log,
                            level=LOG_LEVEL)
    else:
        logging.basicConfig(format=LOG_FORMAT, level=LOG_
LEVEL)
```

```
    try:
        main(args.n1, args.n2, args.output)
    except Exception as exc:
        logging.exception("Error running task")
        exit(1)
```

5. Run it to check that it displays the proper INFO and ERROR logs, and that it stores it on the log file:

```
$ python3 task_with_error_handling_step4.py -n1 5 -n2 0
2020-01-19 14:25:28,849 root INFO Dividing 5 between 0
2020-01-19 14:25:28,849 root ERROR division by zero
Traceback (most recent call last):
  File "task_with_error_handling_step4.py", line 31, in <module>
    main(args.n1, args.n2, args.output)
  File "task_with_error_handling_step4.py", line 10, in main
    result = number / other_number
ZeroDivisionError: division by zero
$ python3 task_with_error_handling_step4.py -n1 5 -n2 0 -l error.
log
$ python3 task_with_error_handling_step4.py -n1 5 -n2 0 -l error.
log
$ cat error.log
2020-01-19 14:26:15,376 root INFO Dividing 5 between 0
2020-01-19 14:26:15,376 root ERROR division by zero
Traceback (most recent call last):
  File "task_with_error_handling_step4.py", line 33, in <module>
    main(args.n1, args.n2, args.output)
  File "task_with_error_handling_step4.py", line 11, in main
    result = number / other_number
ZeroDivisionError: division by zero
2020-01-19 14:26:19,960 root INFO Dividing 5 between 0
2020-01-19 14:26:19,961 root ERROR division by zero
Traceback (most recent call last):
  File "task_with_error_handling_step4.py", line 33, in <module>
    main(args.n1, args.n2, args.output)
  File "task_with_error_handling_step4.py", line 11, in main
```

```
    result = number / other_number
ZeroDivisionError: division by zero
```

How it works...

To properly capture any unexpected exceptions, the main function should be wrapped in a `try-except block`, as implemented in *step 4* of the *How to do it...* section. Compare this to how *step 1* does not wrap the code:

```
try:
    main(...)
except Exception as exc:
    # Something went wrong
    logging.exception("Error running task")
    exit(1)
```

Note that logging the exception is important for getting information on what went wrong.

This kind of exception is nicknamed Pokémon Exception because it can catch 'em all. It will capture any unexpected error at the highest level. Do not use it in other areas of the code, as capturing everything can hide unexpected errors. At the very least, any unexpected exception should be logged to allow for further analysis.

The extra step, to exit with status 1 by using the `exit(1)` call, informs the operating system that something went wrong with our script.

The `logging` module allows us to log. Note the basic configuration, which includes an optional file to store the logs, the format, and the level of the logs to display.

The available levels for logs are—from less critical to more critical—DEBUG, INFO, WARNING, ERROR, and CRITICAL. The logging level will set the minimum severity required to log the message. For example, an INFO log won't be stored if the severity is set to WARNING.

Creating logs is easy. You can do this by making a call to the `logging.<logging level>` method (where the logging level is DEBUG, INFO, and so on). For example:

```
>>> import logging
>>> logging.basicConfig(level=logging.INFO)
>>> logging.warning('a warning message')
WARNING:root:a warning message
>>> logging.info('an info message')
INFO:root:an info message
```

```
>>> logging.debug('a debug message')
>>>
```

Note how logs with a severity lower than INFO are not displayed. Use the level definition to tweak how much information to display. This may change, for example, how DEBUG logs may be used only while developing the task, but not be displayed when running it. Notice that task_with_error_handling_step4.py defines the logging level to be DEBUG, by default.

A good definition of log levels is key to displaying relevant information while reducing noise. It is not easy to set up sometimes, but especially if more than one person is involved, try to agree on exactly what WARNING versus ERROR means to avoid misinterpretations.

logging.exception() is a special case that will create an ERROR log, but it will also include information about the exception, such as the **stack trace**.

Remember to check logs to discover errors. A useful reminder is to add a note to the results file, like this:

```
try:
    main(args.n1, args.n2, args.output)
except Exception as exc:
    logging.exception(exc)
    print('There has been an error. Check the logs', file=args.
output)
```

There's more...

The Python logging module has many capabilities, including the following:

- It provides further tweaks to the format of the log, for example, including the file and line number of the log that was produced.
- It defines different logger objects, each one with its own configuration, such as logging level and format. This allows us to publish logs to different systems in different ways, though, normally, a single logger object is used to keep things simple.

- It sends logs to multiple places, such as the standard output and file, or even a remote logger.

- It automatically rotates logs, creating new log files after a certain time or size. This is handy for keeping logs organized by day or week. It also allows for the compression or removal of old logs. Logs take up space when they accumulate.

- It reads standard logging configurations from files.

Instead of creating complex rules on what to log, try to log extensively using the proper level for each, and then filter by level.

For comprehensive details, refer to the Python documentation of the module at `https://docs.python.org/3.8/library/logging.html`, or the tutorial at `https://docs.python.org/3.8/howto/logging.html`.

See also

- The *Adding command-line options* recipe in *Chapter 1*, *Let's Begin Our Automation Journey*, to describe the basic elements of the command-line options.

- The *Preparing a task* recipe, covered earlier in the chapter, to learn about the strategy to follow when designing an automated task.

Sending email notifications

Email has become an inescapable tool for everyday use. It's arguably the best place to send a notification if an automated task has detected something. On the other hand, email inboxes are already too full up with spam messages, so be careful.

Spam filters are also a reality. Be careful with whom to send emails to and the number of emails to be sent. An email server or address can be labeled as a `spam source`, and all emails may be quietly dropped by the internet.

This recipe will show you how to send a single email using an existing email account.

This approach is viable for spare emails sent to a couple of people, as a result of an automated task, but no more than that. Refer to *Chapter 9*, *Dealing with Communication Channels*, for more ideas on how to send emails, including groups.

Getting ready

For this recipe, we require a valid email account set up, which includes the following:

- A valid email server using SMTP; SMTP is the standard email protocol
- A port to connect to
- An address
- A password

These four elements should be enough to be able to send an email.

Some email services, for example, Gmail, will encourage you to set up 2FA, meaning that a password is not enough to send an email. Typically, they'll allow you to create a specific password for apps to use, bypassing the 2FA request. Check your email provider's information for options.

The email service you use should indicate what the SMTP server is and what port to use in their documentation. This can be retrieved from email clients as well, as they are the same parameters. Check your provider documentation. In the following example, we will use a Gmail account.

How to do it...

1. Create the `email_task.py` file, as follows:

```python
import argparse
import configparser

import smtplib
from email.message import EmailMessage


def main(to_email, server, port, from_email, password):
    print(f'With love, from {from_email} to {to_email}')

    # Create the message
    subject = 'With love, from ME to YOU'
    text = '''This is an example test'''
    msg = EmailMessage()
    msg.set_content(text)
    msg['Subject'] = subject
```

```
    msg['From'] = from_email
    msg['To'] = to_email

    # Open communication and send
    server = smtplib.SMTP_SSL(server, port)
    server.login(from_email, password)
    server.send_message(msg)
    server.quit()


if __name__ == '__main__':
    parser = argparse.ArgumentParser()
    parser.add_argument('email', type=str, help='destination
email')
    parser.add_argument('-c', dest='config', type=argparse.
FileType('r'),
                        help='config file', default=None)

    args = parser.parse_args()
    if not args.config:
        print('Error, a config file is required')
        parser.print_help()
        exit(1)

    config = configparser.ConfigParser()
    config.read_file(args.config)

    main(args.email,
         server=config['DEFAULT']['server'],
         port=config['DEFAULT']['port'],
         from_email=config['DEFAULT']['email'],
         password=config['DEFAULT']['password'])
```

2. Create a configuration file called email_conf.ini with the specifics of
   your email account. For example, for a Gmail account, fill in the following
   template. The template is available in GitHub at https://github.com/
   PacktPublishing/Python-Automation-Cookbook-Second-Edition/blob/
   master/Chapter02/email_conf.ini but be sure to fill it in with your data:

```
[DEFAULT]
email = EMAIL@gmail.com
```

```
server = smtp.gmail.com
port = 465
password = PASSWORD
```

3. Ensure that the file cannot be read or written by other users on the system, setting the permissions of the file to allow only our user. 600 permissions mean read and write access for the file owner, and no access to anyone else:

   ```
   $ chmod 600 email_conf.ini
   ```

4. Run the script to send a test email:

   ```
   $ python3 email_task.py -c email_conf.ini destination_email@
   server.com
   ```

5. Check the inbox of the destination email; an email should be received with the subject With love, from ME to YOU.

How it works...

There are two key steps in the preceding scripts—the generation of the message and the sending.

The message needs to contain mainly the To and From email addresses, as well as the Subject. If the content is pure text, as in this case, calling .set_content() is enough. The whole message can then be sent.

It is technically possible to send an email that is tagged as coming from a different email address than the one you used to send it. This is discouraged, though, as it can be considered by your email provider as trying to impersonate a different email. You can use the reply-to header to allow answering to a different account.

Sending the email requires you to connect to the specified server and start an SMTP connection. SMTP is the standard for email communication.

The steps are quite straightforward—configure the server, log into it, send the prepared message, and quit.

If you need to send more than one message, you can log in, send multiple emails, and then quit, instead of connecting each time.

There's more...

If the objective is a bigger operation, such as a marketing campaign, or even production emails, such as confirming a user's email, please refer to *Chapter 9, Dealing with Communication Channels*.

The email message content used in this recipe is very simple, but emails can be much more complicated than that.

The To field can contain multiple recipients. Separate them with commas, like this:

```
message['To'] = ','.join(recipients)
```

Emails can be defined in HTML, with an alternative plain text, and have attachments. The basic operation is to set up a MIMEMultipart and then attach each of the MIME parts that compose the email:

```
from email.mime.multipart import MIMEMultipart
from email.mime.text import MIMEText
from email.mime.image import MIMEImage

message = MIMEMultipart()
part1 = MIMEText('some text', 'plain')
message.attach(part1)
with open('path/image', 'rb') as image:
    part2 = MIMEImage(image.read())
message.attach(part2)
```

The most common SMTP connection is SMTP_SSL, which is more secure, as all communication with the server is encrypted and always requires a login and password. However, plain, unauthenticated SMTP exists—check your email provider documentation.

Remember that this recipe is aimed toward simple notifications. Emails can grow quite complex if attaching different information. If your objective is an email for customers or any general group, try to use the ideas in *Chapter 9, Dealing with Communication Channels*.

See also

- The *Adding command-line options* recipe in *Chapter 1, Let's Begin Our Automation Journey*, to understand the basic concepts of command-line options.
- The *Preparing a task* recipe, covered earlier in this chapter, to learn about the strategy to follow when designing an automated task.

3
Building Your First Web Scraping Application

The internet, and the **World Wide Web (WWW)**, is probably the most prominent source of information today. Most of that information is retrievable through HTTP. HTTP was invented originally to share pages of hypertext (hence the name **HyperText Transfer Protocol**), which started the WWW.

This process happens each time that we request a web page, so it should be familiar to almost everyone. But we can also perform these operations programmatically to retrieve and process information automatically. Python has in its standard library an HTTP client, but the fantastic `requests` module makes obtaining web pages very easy. In this chapter, we will see how.

In this chapter, we'll cover the following recipes:

- Downloading web pages
- Parsing HTML
- Crawling the web
- Subscribing to feeds
- Accessing web APIs
- Interacting with forms
- Using Selenium for advanced interaction
- Accessing password-protected pages
- Speeding up web scraping

Let's start with the basics of how to programmatically obtain an existing web page.

Downloading web pages

The basic ability to download a web page involves making an HTTP GET request against a URL. This is the basic operation of any web browser.

Let's quickly recap the different parts of this operation, as it has three distinct elements:

1. Using the HTTP protocol. This deals with the way the request is structured.
2. Using the GET method, which is the most common HTTP method. We'll see more in the *Accessing web APIs* recipe.
3. A full URL describing the address of the page, including the server (for example: mypage.com) and the path (for example: /page).

That request will be routed toward the server by the internet and processed by the server, then a response will be sent back. This response will contain a **status code**, typically 200 if everything went fine, and a body with the result, which will normally be text with an HTML page.

Most of this is handled automatically by the HTTP client used to perform the request. We'll see in this recipe how to make a simple request to obtain a web page.

 HTTP requests and responses can also contain headers. Headers contain important information about the request itself, such as the total size of the request, the format of the content, the date of the request, and what browser or server is used.

Getting ready

Using the fantastic requests module, getting web pages is super simple. Install the module:

```
$ echo "requests==2.23.0" >> requirements.txt
$ source .venv/bin/activate
(.venv) $ pip install -r requirements.txt
```

We'll download the page at http://www.columbia.edu/~fdc/sample.html because it is a straightforward HTML page that is easy to read in text mode.

How to do it...

1. Import the `requests` module:

   ```
   >>> import requests
   ```

2. Make a request to the server using the following URL, which will take a second or two:

   ```
   >>> url = 'http://www.columbia.edu/~fdc/sample.html'
   >>> response = requests.get(url)
   ```

3. Check the returned object status code:

   ```
   >>> response.status_code
   200
   ```

4. Check the content of the result:

   ```
   >>> response.text
   '<!DOCTYPE HTML PUBLIC "-//W3C//DTD HTML 4.01 Transitional//EN">\
   n<html>\n<head>\n

   ...

   FULL BODY

   ...

   <!-- close the <html> begun above -->\n'
   ```

5. Check the ongoing and returned headers:

   ```
   >>> response.request.headers
   {'User-Agent': 'python-requests/2.22.0', 'Accept-Encoding': 'gzip,
   deflate', 'Accept': '*/*', 'Connection': 'keep-alive'}
   >>> response.headers
   {'Date': 'Fri, 24 Jan 2020 19:04:12 GMT', 'Server': 'Apache',
   'Last-Modified': 'Wed, 11 Dec 2019 12:46:44 GMT', 'Accept-Ranges':
   'bytes', 'Vary': 'Accept-Encoding,User-Agent', 'Content-Encoding':
   'gzip', 'Content-Length': '10127', 'Keep-Alive': 'timeout=15,
   max=100', 'Connection': 'Keep-Alive', 'Content-Type': 'text/
   html', 'Set-Cookie': 'BIGipServer~CUIT~www.columbia.edu-80-
   pool=1311259520.20480.0000; expires=Sat, 25-Jan-2020 01:04:12 GMT;
   path=/; Httponly'}
   ```

How it works...

The operation of requests is very simple; perform the request, using the GET method in this case, over the URL. This returns a result object that can be analyzed. The main elements are the status_code and the body content, which can be presented as text.

The full request can be inspected in the request attribute:

```
>>> response.request
<PreparedRequest [GET]>
>>> response.request.url
http://www.columbia.edu/~fdc/sample.html'
```

The full requests module documentation can be found here: https://requests.readthedocs.io/en/master/.

Over the course of the chapter, we'll be showing more features of the requests library.

There's more...

All HTTP status codes can be seen at this web page: https://httpstatuses.com/. They are also described in the http.HTTPStatus enum with convenient constant names, such as OK, NOT_FOUND, or FORBIDDEN.

 The most famous error status code is arguably 404, which is returned when the resource described by a URL is not found. Try it out by doing requests.get(http://www.columbia.edu/invalid).

The general structure of the status code is:

- 1XX – Information on specifics about the protocol.

- 2XX – Success.

- 3XX – Redirection. For example: The URL is no longer valid and is available somewhere else. The new URL should be included.

- 4XX – Client error. There's some error in the information sent to the server (like a bad format) or in the client (for example, authentication is required to be able to access the URL).

5XX – Server error. There's an error on the server side; for example, the server might be unavailable or there might be a bug processing the request.

A request can use the **HTTPS (secure HTTP)** protocol. It is the same as HTTP but ensures that the contents of the request and response are private. `requests` handles it transparently.

 Any website that handles any private information should use HTTPS to ensure that the information has not leaked out. HTTP is vulnerable to someone eavesdropping. Use HTTPS where available.

See also

- The *Installing third-party packages* recipe in *Chapter 1, Let's Begin Our Automation Journey*, to learn the basics of installing external modules.

- The *Parsing HTML* recipe, later in this chapter, to find out how to treat the information returned from the server.

Parsing HTML

Downloading raw text or a binary file is a good starting point, but the main language of the web is HTML.

HTML is a structured language, defining different parts of a document such as headings and paragraphs. HTML is also hierarchical, defining sub-elements. The ability to parse raw text into a structured document is basically the ability to extract information automatically from a web page. For example, some text can be relevant if enclosed in certain HTML elements, such as a `class div` or after a heading `h3` tag.

Getting ready

We'll use the excellent `Beautiful Soup` module to parse HTML text into a memory object that can be analyzed. We need to use the latest version of the `beautifulsoup4` package to be compatible with Python 3. Add the package to your `requirements.txt` and install the dependencies in the virtual environment:

```
$ echo "beautifulsoup4==4.8.2" >> requirements.txt
$ pip install -r requirements.txt
```

How to do it...

1. Import `BeautifulSoup` and `requests`:

   ```
   >>> import requests
   >>> from bs4 import BeautifulSoup
   ```

2. Set up the URL of the page to download and retrieve it:

   ```
   >>> URL = 'http://www.columbia.edu/~fdc/sample.html'
   >>> response = requests.get(URL)
   >>> response
   <Response [200]>
   ```

3. Parse the downloaded page:

   ```
   >>> page = BeautifulSoup(response.text, 'html.parser')
   ```

4. Obtain the title of the page. See that it is the same as what's displayed in the browser:

   ```
   >>> page.title
   <title>Sample Web Page</title>
   >>> page.title.string
   'Sample Web Page'
   ```

5. Find all the `h3` elements in the page, to determine the existing sections:

   ```
   >>> page.find_all('h3')
   ```

   ```
   [<h3><a name="contents">CONTENTS</a></h3>, <h3><a name="basics">1.
   Creating a Web Page</a></h3>, <h3><a name="syntax">2. HTML
   Syntax</a></h3>, <h3><a name="chars">3. Special Characters</a></
   h3>, <h3><a name="convert">4. Converting Plain Text to HTML</
   a></h3>, <h3><a name="effects">5. Effects</a></h3>, <h3><a
   name="lists">6. Lists</a></h3>, <h3><a name="links">7. Links</
   a></h3>, <h3><a name="tables">8. Tables</a></h3>, <h3><a
   name="install">9. Installing Your Web Page on the Internet</a></
   h3>, <h3><a name="more">10. Where to go from here</a></h3>]
   ```

6. Extract the text on the section for *Special Characters*. Stop when you reach the next <h3> tag:

   ```
   >>> link_section = page.find('h3', attrs={'id': 'chars'})
   >>> section = []
   ```

```
>>> for element in link_section.next_elements:
...     if element.name == 'h3':
...         break
...     section.append(element.string or '')
...
>>> result = ''.join(section)
>>> result
```

'3. Special Characters\n\nHTML special "character entities"
start with ampersand (&&) and\nend with semicolon (;;), like
"€€" = "€". The\never-popular "no-break space" is
  . There are special\nentity names for accented Latin
letters and other West European special\ncharacters such as:\
n\n\n\n\nää\na-umlaut\n\xa0ä\xa0\n\nÄÄ\
nA-umlaut \n\xa0Ä\xa0\n\náá\na-acute \n\xa0á\xa0\
n\nàà\na-grave \n\xa0à\xa0\n\nññ\
nn-tilde \n\xa0ñ\xa0\n\nßß\nGerman double-s\n\
xa0ß\xa0\n\n\nþþ\nIcelandic thorn \n\xa0þ\xa0\n\xa0þ\
xa0\n\n\n\n\nExamples:\n\n\nFor SpanishSpanish you would need:\
nÁÁ (Á),\náá (á),\nÉÉ
(É),\néé (é),\nÍÍ (Í),\
níí (í),\nÓÓ (Ó),\nóó
(ó),\nÚÚ (ú),\núú (ú),\
nÑÑ (Ñ),\nññ (ñ);\n¿¿
(¿);\n¡¡ (¡).\nExample: Añorarán = Añora
ránAñorarán.\n\n\nFor GermanGerman you
would need:\nÄÄ (Ä),\nää (ä),\nÖÖ
(Ö),\nöö (ö),\nÜÜ (ü),\nüü (ü),\
nßß (ß).\nExample: Grüße aus Köln = Grüße
aus KölnGrüße aus Köln.\n\n\nCLICK
HERECLICK HERE\nfor a complete list. When the page encoding
is\nUTF-8UTF-8, which is\nrecommended, you can also enter any
character at all, Roman,\nCyrillic, Arabic, Hebrew, Greek.
Japanese,\netc, either as numeric entities or (if you have a way
to type them) directly\nfrom the keyboard.\n\n\n\nAnd remember:
if you want to\ninclude <<, &&,\nor >> literally in text to be
displayed, you have\nto write <<,\n&&, >>,
respectively.\n\n\n\n\n'

Notice that all the raw text is displayed, without including the enclosing HTML tags.

How it works...

The first step is to download the page. Then, the raw text can be parsed, as in *step 3*.
The resulting page object contains the parsed information.

 The html.parser parser is the default one, but for certain operations, it can have problems. For example, for big pages it can be slow, and it can have issues rendering highly dynamic web pages. You can use other parsers, such as lxml, which is much faster, or html5lib, which will be closer to how a browser operates. They are external modules that will need to be added to the requirements.txt file.

BeautifulSoup allows us to search for HTML elements. It can search for the first
occurrence of an HTML element with .find() or return a list with .find_all().
In *step 5*, it searched for a specific tag, <a>, that had a particular attribute, id=chars.
After that, it kept iterating on .next_elements until it found the next h3 tag, which
marks the end of the section.

The text of each element is extracted and finally composed into a single text. Note the
or that avoids storing None, returned when an element has no text.

 HTML is highly versatile and can have multiple structures. The case presented in this recipe is typical, but other options on dividing sections can be grouping related sections inside a big <div> tag or other elements, or even raw text. Some experimentation will be required until you find the specific process to extract the juicy bits on a web page. Don't be afraid to try!

There's more...

Regexes can be used as input in the .find() and .find_all() methods. For
example, this search uses the h2 and h3 tags:

```
>>> page.find_all(re.compile('^h(2|3)'))
```

```
[<h2>Sample Web Page</h2>, <h3 id="contents">CONTENTS</h3>, <h3
id="basics">1. Creating a Web Page</h3>, <h3 id="syntax">2. HTML Syntax</
h3>, <h3 id="chars">3. Special Characters</h3>, <h3 id="convert">4.
Converting Plain Text to HTML</h3>, <h3 id="effects">5. Effects</
h3>, <h3 id="lists">6. Lists</h3>, <h3 id="links">7. Links</h3>, <h3
id="tables">8. Tables</h3>, <h3 id="viewing">9. Viewing Your Web Page</
h3>, <h3 id="install">10. Installing Your Web Page on the Internet</h3>,
<h3 id="more">11. Where to go from here</h3>]
```

Another useful `find` parameter is including the CSS class with the `class_ parameter`. This will be shown later in the book.

The full Beautiful Soup documentation can be found here: `https://www.crummy. com/software/BeautifulSoup/bs4/doc/`.

See also

- The *Installing third-party packages* recipe in *Chapter 1, Let's Begin Our Automation Journey*, to learn about installing external modules.
- The *Downloading web pages* recipe, earlier in this chapter, to learn the basics of requesting web pages.

Crawling the web

Given the nature of hyperlink pages, starting from a known place and following links to other pages is a very important tool in your arsenal when scraping the web.

To do so, we crawl a page looking for a short phrase, and we print any paragraph that contains it. We will search only in pages that belong to a single site, for example: only URLs starting with `www.somesite.com`. We won't follow links to external sites.

Getting ready

This recipe builds on the concepts introduced so far, so it will involve downloading and parsing pages to search for links and then continue downloading.

When crawling the web, remember to set limits when downloading. It's very easy to crawl over too many pages. As anyone checking Wikipedia can confirm, the internet is potentially limitless.

We'll use a prepared example, available in the GitHub repo at `https://github. com/PacktPublishing/Python-Automation-Cookbook-Second-Edition/tree/ master/Chapter03/test_site`. Download the whole site and run the included script:

```
$ python simple_delay_server.py
```

This serves the site at the URL `http://localhost:8000`. You can find this in a browser. It's a simple blog with three entries.

Most of it is uninteresting, but we added a couple of paragraphs that contain the keyword `python`:

Figure 3.1: A screenshot of the blog

How to do it...

1. The full script, `crawling_web_step1.py`, is available on GitHub at the following link: `https://github.com/PacktPublishing/Python-Automation-Cookbook-Second-Edition/blob/master/Chapter03/crawling_web_step1.py`. The most relevant bits are displayed here:

   ```
   ...

   def process_link(source_link, text):
       logging.info(f'Extracting links from {source_link}')
       parsed_source = urlparse(source_link)
       result = requests.get(source_link)
       # Error handling. See GitHub for details
       ...
       page = BeautifulSoup(result.text, 'html.parser')
       search_text(source_link, page, text)
   ```

```
            return get_links(parsed_source, page)


    def get_links(parsed_source, page):
        '''Retrieve the links on the page'''
        links = []
        for element in page.find_all('a'):
            link = element.get('href')
            # Validate is a valid link. See GitHub for details
            ...
            links.append(link)
        return links
```

2. Search for references to `python` to return a list with URLs that contain it and the paragraph. Notice there are a couple of errors because of broken links:

```
$ python crawling_web_step1.py http://localhost:8000/ -p python
Link http://localhost:8000/: --> A smaller article , that contains
a reference to Python
Link http://localhost:8000/files/5eabef23f63024c20389c34b94d
ee593-1.html: --> A smaller article , that contains a reference to
Python
Link http://localhost:8000/files/33714fc865e02aeda2dabb9a42a78
7b2-0.html: --> This is the actual bit with a python reference
that we are interested in.
Link http://localhost:8000/files/archive-september-2018.html: -->
A smaller article , that contains a reference to Python
Link http://localhost:8000/index.html: --> A smaller article ,
that contains a reference to Python
```

3. Another good search term is `crocodile`. Try it out:

```
$ python crawling_web_step1.py http://localhost:8000/ -p crocodile
```

How it works...

Let's see each of the components of the script:

1. A loop that goes through all the found links, in the `main` function:

```
    def main(base_url, to_search):
        checked_links = set()
        to_check = [base_url]
        max_checks = 10
```

```
        while to_check and max_checks:
            link = to_check.pop(0)
            links = process_link(link, text=to_search)
            checked_links.add(link)
            for link in links:
                if link not in checked_links:
                    checked_links.add(link)
                    to_check.append(link)

        max_checks -= 1
```

Note that there's a retrieval limit of 10 pages, and the code here is checking that any new link to be added is not added already.

 Note that these two elements act as limits for the script. We won't download the same link twice and we'll stop at some point.

2. Downloading and parsing the link, in the process_link function:

```
    def process_link(source_link, text):
        logging.info(f'Extracting links from {source_link}')
        parsed_source = urlparse(source_link)
        result = requests.get(source_link)
        if result.status_code != http.client.OK:
            logging.error(f'Error retrieving {source_link}:
{result}')
            return []

        if 'html' not in result.headers['Content-type']:
            logging.info(f'Link {source_link} is not an HTML
page')
            return []

        page = BeautifulSoup(result.text, 'html.parser')
        search_text(source_link, page, text)

        return get_links(parsed_source, page)
```

The code here downloads the file and checks that the status is correct to skip errors such as broken links. This code also checks that the type (as described in `Content-Type`) is an HTML page to skip PDFs and other formats. Finally, it parses the raw HTML into a `BeautifulSoup` object.

The code also parses the source link using `urlparse`, so later, in *step 4*, it can skip all the references to external sources. `urlparse` divides a URL into its constituent elements:

```
>>> from urllib.parse import urlparse
>>> urlparse('http://localhost:8000/files/
b93bec5d9681df87e6e8d5703ed7cd81-2.html')
ParseResult(scheme='http', netloc='localhost:8000', path='/files/
b93bec5d9681df87e6e8d5703ed7cd81-2.html', params='', query='',
fragment='')
```

3. The code finds the text to search, in the `search_text` function:

```
def search_text(source_link, page, text):
    '''Search for an element with the searched text and print
it'''
    for element in page.find_all(text=re.compile(text,
flags=re.IGNORECASE)):
        print(f'Link {source_link}: --> {element}')
```

This searches the parsed object for the specified text. Note that the search is done as a `regex` and only in the text of the page. It prints the resulting matches, including `source_link`, referencing the URL where the match was found:

```
for element in page.find_all(text=re.compile(text)):
    print(f'Link {source_link}: --> {element}')
```

4. The `get_links` function retrieves all links on a page:

```
def get_links(parsed_source, page):
    '''Retrieve the links on the page'''
    links = []
    for element in page.find_all('a'):
        link = element.get('href')
        if not link:
            continue

        # Avoid internal, same page links
        if link.startswith('#'):
            continue
```

```
                   if link.startswith('mailto:'):
                       # Ignore other links like mailto
                       # More cases like ftp or similar may be included
        here
                       continue

                   # Always accept local links
                   if not link.startswith('http'):
                       netloc = parsed_source.netloc
                       scheme = parsed_source.scheme
                       path = urljoin(parsed_source.path, link)
                       link = f'{scheme}://{netloc}{path}'

                   # Only parse links in the same domain
                   if parsed_source.netloc not in link:
                       continue

                   links.append(link)

           return links
```

This searches in the parsed page for all `<a>` elements and retrieves the `href` elements, but only elements that have such `href` elements and that are a fully qualified URL (starting with `http`) or a local link. This removes links that are not a URL, such as a '#' link or links that are internal to the page.

> Keep in mind that some references could have other effects, for example, the `mailto:` scheme. There is a check to avoid `mailto:` schemes, but there could be cases like `ftp` or `irc`, though they are rare to see in practice.

An extra check is done to check that the links have the same source as the original link; only then are they registered as valid links. The `netloc` attribute detects whether a link comes from the same URL domain as the parsed URL generated in *step 2*.

We won't follow links that point to a different address (for example, an `http://www.google.com` one).

Finally, the links are returned, where they'll be added to the loop described in *step 1*.

There's more...

Further filters could be enforced; for example, all links that end in `.pdf` could be discarded, as they likely refer to PDF files:

```
# In get_links
if link.endswith('pdf'):
    continue
```

The use of `Content-Type` can also be determined to parse the returned object in different ways. Keep in mind that `Content-Type` won't be available without making the request, which means the code cannot skip links without requesting them. A PDF result (`Content-Type: application/pdf`) won't have a valid `response.text` object to be parsed, but a PDF result can be parsed in other ways. The same goes for other types, such as a CSV file (`Content-Type: text/csv`) or a ZIP file that may need to be decompressed (`Content-Type: application/zip`). We'll see how to deal with those later.

See also

- The *Downloading web pages* recipe, earlier in this chapter, to learn the basics of requesting web pages.
- The *Parsing HTML* recipe, earlier in this chapter, to learn how to parse elements in HTML.

Subscribing to feeds

RSS is probably the biggest secret of the internet. Its time in the spotlight seemed to be during the 2000s, and it enables easy subscription to websites. It is present in lots of websites and it's incredibly useful.

At its core, RSS is a way of presenting a succession of ordered references (typically articles, but also other elements such as podcast episodes or YouTube publications) and publishing times. This makes for a very natural way of learning what articles are new since the last check, as well as presenting some structured data about them, such as the title and a summary.

In this recipe, we will present the `feedparser` module and determine how to obtain data from an RSS feed.

RSS is not the only available feed format. There's also a format called Atom, but Atom and RSS are more or less the same. `feedparser` is also capable of parsing Atom, so both formats can be processed in the same way.

Getting ready

We need to add the `feedparser` dependency to our `requirements.txt` file and reinstall it:

```
$ echo "feedparser==5.2.1" >> requirements.txt
$ pip install -r requirements.txt
```

Feed URLs can be found on almost all pages that deal with publications, including blogs, news, podcasts, and so on. Sometimes they are very easy to find, but sometimes they are a little bit hidden. Search for `feed` or RSS.

Most newspapers and news agencies have their RSS feeds divided by themes. For our example, we'll parse the **New York Times** main page feed, `https://rss.nytimes.com/services/xml/rss/nyt/HomePage.xml`. There are more feeds available on the main feed page: `https://archive.nytimes.com/www.nytimes.com/services/xml/rss/index.html`.

Please note that the feeds may be subject to terms and conditions of use. In the case of the New York Times, the terms and conditions are described at the end of the main feed page.

Please note that this feed changes quite often, meaning that the linked entries will be different than the examples in this book.

How to do it...

1. Import the `feedparser` module, as well as `datetime`, `delorean`, and `requests`:

    ```
    >>> import feedparser
    >>> import datetime
    >>> import delorean
    >>> import requests
    ```

2. Parse the feed (it will be downloaded automatically) and check when it was last updated. Feed information, like the title of the feed, can be obtained in the `feed` attribute:

    ```
    >>> rss = feedparser.parse('http://rss.nytimes.com/services/xml/
    rss/nyt/HomePage.xml')
    >>> rss.channel.updated
    Friday, 24 Jan 2020 19:42:27 +0000'
    ```

3. Get the entries that are less or equal to 6 hours old:

    ```
    >>> time_limit = delorean.parse(rss.channel.updated) - datetime.
    timedelta(hours=6)
    >>> entries = [entry for entry in rss.entries if delorean.
    parse(entry.published) > time_limit]
    ```

4. Some of the returned entries will be older than 6 hours:

    ```
    >>> len(entries)
    28
    >>> len(rss.entries)
    54
    ```

5. Retrieve information about the entries, such as the `title`. The full entry URL is available as `link`. Explore the available information in this particular feed:

    ```
    >>> entries[18]['title']
    'These People Really Care About Fonts'
    >>> entries[18]['link']
    'https://www.nytimes.com/2020/01/24/style/typography-font-design.
    html?emc=rss&partner=rss'
    >>> requests.get(entries[18].link)
    <Response [200]>
    ```

How it works...

The parsed `feed` object contains the information of the entries, as well as general information about the `feed` itself, such as when it was updated. The `feed` information can be found in the `feed` attribute:

```
>>> rss.feed.title
'NYT > Top Stories'
```

Each of the entries works as a dictionary, so the fields are easy to retrieve. They can also be accessed as attributes, but treating them as keys allows us to get all the available fields:

```
>>> entries[5].keys()
dict_keys(['title', 'title_detail', 'links', 'link', 'id', 'guidislink',
'media_content', 'summary', 'summary_detail', 'media_credit', 'credit',
'content', 'authors', 'author', 'author_detail', 'published', 'published_
parsed', 'tags'])
```

The basic strategy when dealing with feeds is to parse them and go through the entries, performing a quick check on whether they are interesting or not, for example, by checking the *description* or *summary*. If the entry seems worth it, they can be fully downloaded through the `link` field. Then, to avoid rechecking entries, store the latest publication date and next time, only check newer entries.

There's more...

The full `feedparser` documentation can be found here: `https://pythonhosted.org/feedparser/`.

The information available can differ from feed to feed. In the New York Times example, there's a `tag` field with tag information, but this is not standard. As a minimum, entries will have a title, a description, and a link.

> RSS feeds are also a great way of curating your own selection of news sources. There are great feed readers for that.

See also

- The *Installing third-party packages* recipe in *Chapter 1, Let's Begin Our Automation Journey*, to learn the basics of installing external modules.

- The *Downloading web pages* recipe, earlier in this chapter, to learn more about making requests and obtaining remote pages.

Accessing web APIs

Rich interfaces can be created through the web, allowing powerful interactions through HTTP. The most common interface is through RESTful APIs using JSON. These text-based interfaces are easy to understand and to program, and use common technologies that are **language agnostic**, meaning they can be accessed in any programming language that has an HTTP `client` module, including, of course, Python.

> Formats other than JSON are used, such as XML. But JSON is a very simple and readable format that translates very well into Python dictionaries (and other language equivalents). JSON is, by far, the most common format in RESTful APIs at the moment. Learn more about JSON here: `https://www.json.org/`.

The strict definition of RESTful requires some specific characteristics, but an informal definition of RESTful is a system that describes resources through HTTP URLs. This means each URL represents a particular resource, such as an article in a newspaper or a property on a real estate site. Resources can then be manipulated through HTTP methods (`GET` to view, `POST` to create, `PUT`/`PATCH` to edit, and `DELETE` to delete).

> Proper RESTful interfaces need to have certain characteristics. They are a way of creating interfaces that is not strictly restricted to HTTP interfaces. You can read more about it here: `https://codewords.recurse.com/issues/five/what-restful-actually-means`.

Using `requests` is very easy with RESTful interfaces, as they include native JSON support.

Getting ready

To demonstrate how to operate RESTful APIs, we'll use the example site `https://jsonplaceholder.typicode.com/`. It simulates a common case with posts, comments, and other common resources. We will use posts and comments. The URLs to use will be as follows:

```
# The collection of all posts
/posts
# A single post. X is the ID of the post
/posts/X
# The comments of post X
/posts/X/comments
```

The site returns the correct result for each of them. Pretty handy!

 Because it is a test site, data won't be created, but the site will return all the correct responses.

How to do it...

1. Import `requests`:

   ```
   >>> import requests
   ```

2. Get a list of all posts and display the latest post:

   ```
   >>> result = requests.get('https://jsonplaceholder.typicode.com/posts')
   >>> result
   <Response [200]>
   >>> result.json()
   # List of 100 posts NOT DISPLAYED HERE
   >>> result.json()[-1]
   {'userId': 10, 'id': 100, 'title': 'at nam consequatur ea labore
   ea harum', 'body': 'cupiditate quo est a modi nesciunt soluta\
   nipsa voluptas error itaque dicta in\nautem qui minus magnam et
   distinctio eum\naccusamus ratione error aut'}
   ```

3. Create a new post. See the URL of the newly created resource. The call also returns the resource:

```
>>> new_post = {'userId': 10, 'title': 'a title', 'body':
'something something'}
>>> result = requests.post('https://jsonplaceholder.typicode.com/
posts',
                json=new_post)
>>> result
<Response [201]>
>>> result.json()
{'userId': 10, 'title': 'a title', 'body': 'something something',
'id': 101}
>>> result.headers['Location']
'http://jsonplaceholder.typicode.com/posts/101'
```

Notice that the POST request to create the resource returns 201, which is the proper status for created.

4. Fetch an existing post with GET:

```
>>> result = requests.get('https://jsonplaceholder.typicode.com/
posts/2')
>>> result
<Response [200]>
>>> result.json()
{'userId': 1, 'id': 2, 'title': 'qui est esse', 'body': 'est
rerum tempore vitae\nsequi sint nihil reprehenderit dolor beatae
ea dolores neque\nfugiat blanditiis voluptate porro vel nihil
molestiae ut reiciendis\nqui aperiam non debitis possimus qui
neque nisi nulla'}
```

5. Use PATCH to update its values. Check the returned resource:

```
>>> update = {'body': 'new body'}
>>> result = requests.patch('https://jsonplaceholder.typicode.com/
posts/2', json=update)
>>> result
<Response [200]>
>>> result.json()
{'userId': 1, 'id': 2, 'title': 'qui est esse', 'body': 'new
body'}
```

How it works...

Two kinds of resources are typically accessed – single resources (`https://jsonplaceholder.typicode.com/posts/X`) and collections (`https://jsonplaceholder.typicode.com/posts`)

- Collections accept GET to retrieve all the members of the collection and POST to create a new resource
- Single elements accept GET to get the element, PUT and PATCH to edit, and DELETE to remove elements

All the available HTTP methods can be called in `requests`. In the previous recipes, we used `.get()`, but `.post()`, `.patch()`, `.put()`, and `.delete()` are available.

The returned response object has a `.json()` method that decodes the result from JSON.

Equally, to send information, a `json` argument is available. This encodes a dictionary into JSON and sends it to the server. The data needs to follow the format of the resource or an error may be raised.

> GET and DELETE don't require data, while PATCH, PUT, and POST do require data to be sent through the body payload.

The referred-to resource will be returned, and its URL is available in the header. This is useful when creating a new resource, as its URL is not known beforehand.

> The difference between PATCH and PUT is that the latter replaces the whole resource, while the former does a partial update.

There's more...

RESTful APIs are very powerful but also have huge variability. Please check the documentation of the specific API to learn about its details.

See also

- The *Downloading web pages* recipe, earlier in this chapter, to learn the basics of requesting web pages
- The *Installing third-party packages* recipe in *Chapter 1, Let's Begin Our Automation Journey*, to learn the basics of installing external modules

Interacting with forms

A common element present in web pages is forms. Forms are a way of sending values to a web page, for example, to create a new comment on a blog post, or to submit a purchase.

Browsers present forms so you can input values and send them in a single action after pressing the submit or equivalent button. We'll see how to create this action programmatically in this recipe.

 Be aware that sending data to a site is normally a more delicate matter than receiving data from it. For example, sending automatic comments to a website is very much the definition of **spam**. This means that it can be more difficult to automate as it involves considering security measures. Double-check that what you're trying to achieve is a valid, ethical use case.

Getting ready

We'll work against the test server `https://httpbin.org/forms/post`, which allows us to send a test form and sends back the submitted information.

 Note that the URL `https://httpbin.org/forms/post` renders the form, but internally calls the URL `https://httpbin.org/post` to send the information. We'll use both URLs during this recipe.

The following is an example form to order a pizza:

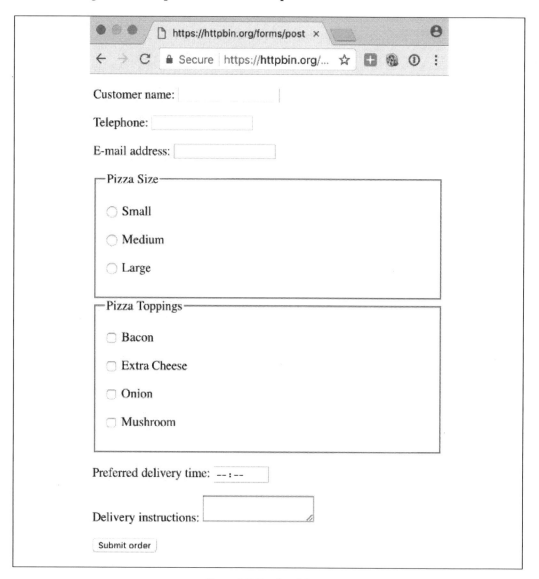

Figure 3.2: Rendered form

You can fill the form in manually and see it return the information in JSON format, including extra information such as the browser being used.

The following is the frontend of the web form that is generated:

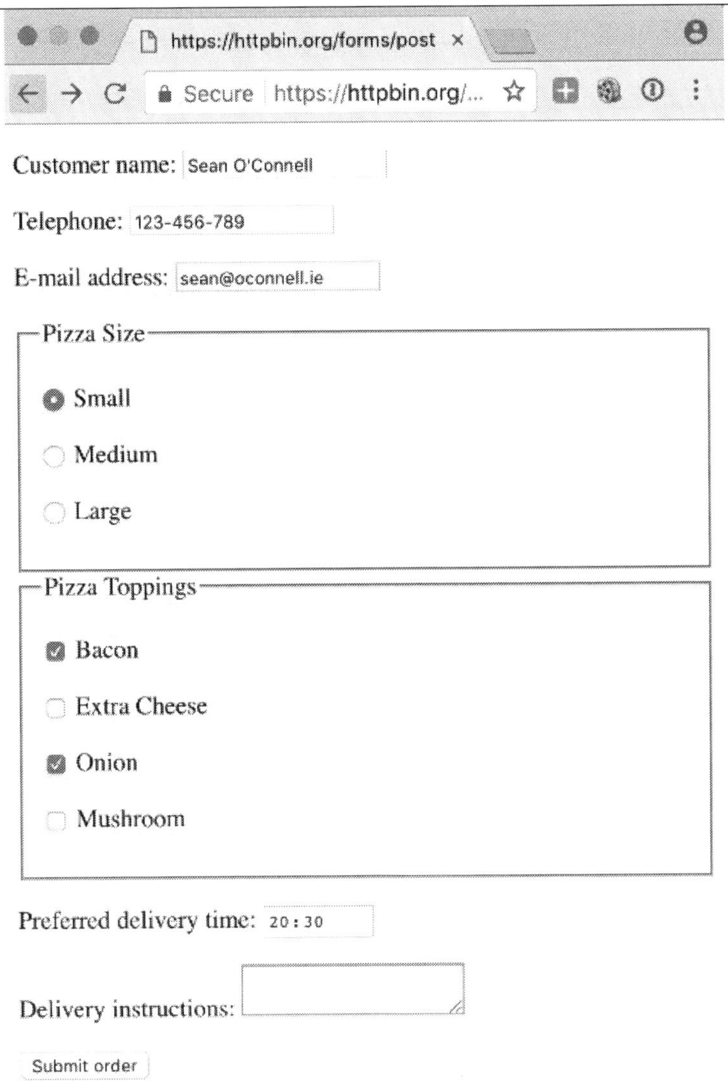

Figure 3.3: Filled-in form

The following screenshot shows the backend of the web form that is generated:

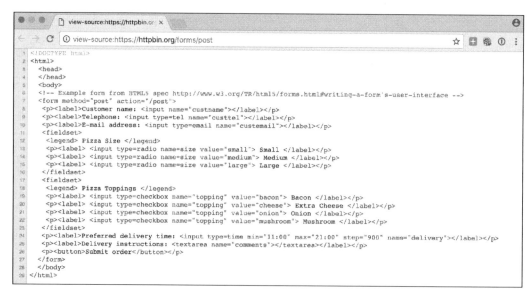

Figure 3.4: Returned JSON content

We need to analyze the HTML to see the accepted data for the form. The source code is as follows:

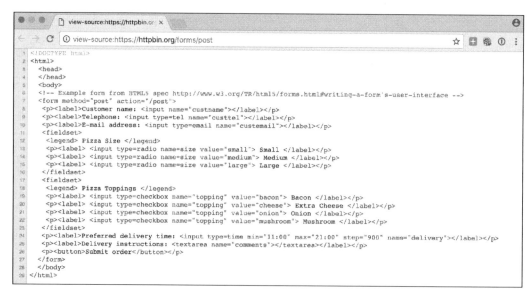

Figure 3.5: Source code

Check the names of the inputs, `custname`, `custtel`, `custemail`, `size` (a radio option), `topping` (a multiselection checkbox), `delivery` (time), and `comments`.

How to do it...

1. Import the `requests`, `BeautifulSoup`, and `re` modules:

   ```
   >>> import requests
   >>> from bs4 import BeautifulSoup
   >>> import re
   ```

2. Retrieve the form page, parse it, and print the input fields. Check that the posting URL is `/post` (not `/forms/post`):

   ```
   >>> response = requests.get('https://httpbin.org/forms/post')
   >>> page = BeautifulSoup(response.text)
   >>> form = page.find('form')
   >>> {field.get('name') for field in form.find_all(re.
   compile('input|textarea'))}
   {'delivery', 'topping', 'size', 'custemail', 'comments',
   'custtel', 'custname'}
   ```

   Note that `textarea` is a valid input and is defined in the HTML format.

3. Prepare the data to be posted as a dictionary. Check that the values are as defined in the form:

   ```
   >>> data = {'custname': "Sean O'Connell", 'custtel': '123-456-
   789', 'custemail': 'sean@oconnell.ie', 'size': 'small', 'topping':
   ['bacon', 'onion'], 'delivery': '20:30', 'comments': ''}
   ```

4. Post the values and check that the response is the same as returned in the browser:

   ```
   >>> response = requests.post('https://httpbin.org/post', data)
   >>> response
   <Response [200]>
   >>> response.json()
   {'args': {}, 'data': '', 'files': {}, 'form': {'comments': '',
   'custemail': 'sean@oconnell.ie', 'custname': "Sean O'Connell",
   'custtel': '123-456-789', 'delivery': '20:30', 'size': 'small',
   'topping': ['bacon', 'onion']}, 'headers': {'Accept': '*/*',
   'Accept-Encoding': 'gzip, deflate', 'Connection': 'close',
   'Content-Length': '140', 'Content-Type': 'application/x-www-
   form-urlencoded', 'Host': 'httpbin.org', 'User-Agent': 'python-
   requests/2.22.0'}, 'json': None, 'origin': '89.100.17.159', 'url':
   'https://httpbin.org/post'}
   ```

How it works...

`Requests` directly encodes and sends data in the configured format. By default, it sends `POST` data in the `application/x-www-form-urlencoded` format.

 Compare the action of requests with the *Accessing web APIs* recipe, where the data is explicitly sent in JSON format using the argument `json`. This means that the `Content-Type` is `application/json` instead of `application/x-www-form-urlencoded`.

The key aspect here is to respect the format of the form and the possible values that can return an error if incorrect, typically a 400 error, indicating a problem with the client.

There's more...

Other than following the format of forms and inputting valid values, the main problem when working with forms is the multiple ways of preventing spam and abusive behavior.

You will often have to ensure that you have downloaded a form before submitting it, to avoid submitting multiple forms or **Cross-Site Request Forgery (CSRF)**.

 CSRF, which means producing a malicious call from a page to a different one taking advantage of the fact that your browser is authenticated, is a serious problem – for example, you might think you were entering a site about adorable puppies, that in fact takes advantage of you being logged into your bank page to perform financial operations on your behalf: such as transferring your savings to a distant account. Here is a good description of CSRF: `https://stackoverflow.com/a/33829607`. New techniques in browsers help with these CSRF issues by default.

To obtain the specific token, you need to first download the form, as shown in the recipe, obtain the value of the CSRF token, and resubmit it. Note that the token can have different names; this is just an example:

```
>>> form.find(attrs={'name': 'token'}).get('value')
'ABCEDF12345'
```

See also

- The *Downloading web pages* recipe, earlier in this chapter, to learn the basics of requesting web pages.

- The *Parsing HTML* recipe, earlier in this chapter, to follow up on structuring the returned information from the server.

Using Selenium for advanced interaction

Sometimes, nothing short of the real thing will work. Selenium is a project to use to achieve automation in web browsers. It's conceived as a way of automatic testing, but it also can be used to automate interactions with a site.

Selenium can control Safari, Chrome, Firefox, Internet Explorer, or Microsoft Edge, though it requires installing a specific driver for each case. We'll use Chrome.

Getting ready

We need to install the right driver for Chrome, called `chromedriver`. It is available here: `https://sites.google.com/a/chromium.org/chromedriver/`. It is available for most platforms. It also requires that you have Chrome installed: `https://www.google.com/chrome/`.

Add the `selenium` module to `requirements.txt` and install it:

```
$ echo "selenium==3.141.0" >> requirements.txt
$ pip install -r requirements.txt
```

How to do it...

1. Import Selenium, start a browser and load the form page. A page will open reflecting the operations:

   ```
   >>> from selenium import webdriver
   >>> browser = webdriver.Chrome()
   >>> browser.get('https://httpbin.org/forms/post')
   ```

 Note the banner in Chrome showing it is being controlled by automated test software.

2. Add a value in the **Customer name** field. Remember that it is called `custname`:

```
>>> custname = browser.find_element_by_name("custname")
>>> custname.clear()
>>> custname.send_keys("Sean O'Connell")
```

The form will update:

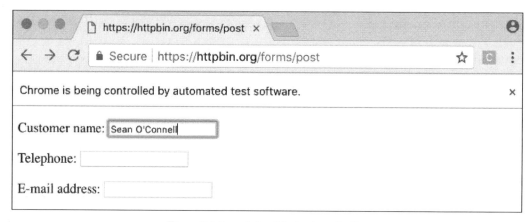

Figure 3.6: Form being filled automatically

3. Set the pizza size to `medium`:

```
>>> for size_element in browser.find_elements_by_name("size"):
...       if size_element.get_attribute('value') == 'medium':
...           size_element.click()
...
>>>
```

This will set the **Pizza Size** radio button.

4. Add `bacon` and `cheese`:

```
>>> for topping in browser.find_elements_by_name('topping'):
...       if topping.get_attribute('value') in ['bacon', 'cheese']:
...           topping.click()
...
>>>
```

Finally, the checkboxes will appear as marked:

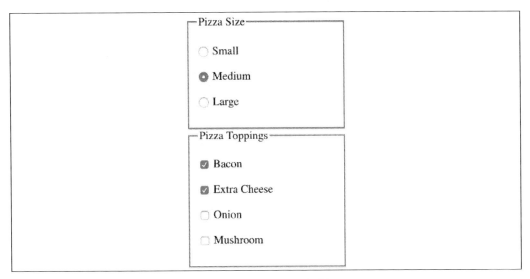

Figure 3.7: Form with checked boxes

5. Submit the form. The page will submit and the result will be displayed:

```
>>> browser.find_element_by_tag_name('form').submit()
```

The form will be submitted and the result from the server will be displayed:

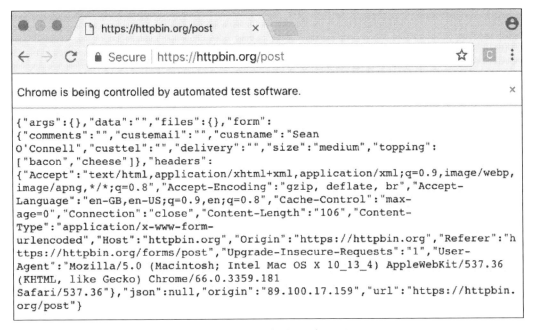

Figure 3.8: Returned JSON information

6. Close the browser:

```
>>> browser.quit()
```

How it works...

Step 1 in the *How to do it...* section shows how to create a Selenium page and go to a particular URL.

Selenium works in a similar way to Beautiful Soup: you select an element and then manipulate it. The selectors in Selenium work in a similar way to those in Beautiful Soup, with the most common ones being `find_element_by_id`, `find_element_by_class_name`, `find_element_by_name`, `find_element_by_tag_name`, and `find_element_by_css_selector`.

There are equivalent `find_elements_by_X` actions that return lists by other attributes other than the first found element (such as `find_elements_by_tag_name`, `find_elements_by_name`, and more). This is also useful when checking whether an element is there or not. If there are no elements, `find_element` will raise an error while `find_elements` will return an empty list.

Data on the elements can be obtained through `.get_attribute()` for HTML attributes (such as the values on the form elements) or `.text`.

Elements can be manipulated by simulating sending keystrokes to input text with the method `.send_keys()`, sending clicks with `.click()`, or submitting the form with `.submit()`. Note that `.click()` will select/deselect in the same way that a click of the mouse will.

Finally, *step 6* closes the browser.

There's more...

Here is the Python Selenium documentation: `http://selenium-python.readthedocs.io/`.

For each of the elements, there's extra information that can be extracted, such as `.is_displayed()` or `.is_selected()`. Text can be searched using `.find_element_by_link_text()` and `.find_element_by_partial_link_text()`.

Sometimes, opening a browser can be inconvenient. An alternative is to start the browser in headless mode and manipulate it from there, like this:

```
>>> from selenium.webdriver.chrome.options import Options
>>> chrome_options = Options()
```

```
>>> chrome_options.add_argument("--headless")
>>> browser = webdriver.Chrome(chrome_options=chrome_options)
>>> browser.get('https://httpbin.org/forms/post')
```

The page won't be displayed, but a screenshot can be saved anyway with the following line:

```
>>> browser.save_screenshot('screenshot.png')
```

See also

- The *Parsing HTML* recipe, earlier in this chapter, to learn how to parse elements in HTML.

- The *Interacting with forms* recipe, earlier in this chapter, to see alternatives to dealing with forms.

Accessing password-protected pages

Sometimes a web page is not open to the public but protected in some way. The simplest aspect of protection is to use basic HTTP authentication, which is integrated into virtually every web server and implements a user/password schema.

Getting ready

We can test this kind of authentication in `https://httpbin.org`.

It has a path, `/basic-auth/{user}/{password}`, which forces authentication, with the user and password stated. This is very handy for understanding how authentication works.

How to do it...

1. Import `requests`:

   ```
   >>> import requests
   ```

2. Make a GET request to the URL with the wrong credentials. Notice that we set the credentials on the URL to be `user` and `psswd`:

   ```
   >>> requests.get('https://httpbin.org/basic-auth/user/psswd',
                     auth=('user', 'psswd'))
   <Response [200]>
   ```

3. Use the wrong credentials to return a 401 status code (unauthorized):

```
>>> requests.get('https://httpbin.org/basic-auth/user/psswd',
                  auth=('user', 'wrong'))
<Response [401]>
```

4. The credentials can also be passed directly as part of the URL, separated by a colon and an @ symbol before the server, like this:

```
>>> requests.get('https://user:psswd@httpbin.org/basic-auth/user/
psswd')
<Response [200]>
>>> requests.get('https://user:wrong@httpbin.org/basic-auth/user/
psswd')
<Response [401]>
```

How it works...

As HTTP basic authentication is supported everywhere, support from `requests` is very easy.

Steps 2 and *4* in the *How to do it...* section show how to provide the proper password. *Step 3* shows what happens when the password is wrong.

 Remember to always use HTTPS to ensure that the sending of the password is kept secret. If you use HTTP, the password will be sent in the open over the internet, allowing it to be captured by listening elements.

There's more...

Adding the user and password to the URL works on the browser as well. Try to access the page directly to see a box asking for the username and password:

Figure 3.9: User credentials page

When using a URL containing the user and password, `https://user:psswd@httpbin.org/basic-auth/user/psswd`, the dialog does not appear, and it authenticates automatically.

If you need to access multiple pages, you can create a session in `requests` and set the authentication parameters to avoid having to input them everywhere:

```
>>> s = requests.Session()
>>> s.auth = ('user', 'psswd')
>>> s.get('https://httpbin.org/basic-auth/user/psswd')
<Response [200]>
```

See also

- The *Downloading web pages* recipe, earlier in this chapter, to learn the basics of requesting web pages.
- The *Accessing web APIs* recipe, earlier in this chapter, to learn how to access APIs that are behind an authentication wall.

Speeding up web scraping

Most of the time spent downloading information from web pages is usually spent waiting. A request goes from our computer to the remote server to process it, and until the response is composed and comes back to our computer, we cannot do much about it.

During the execution of the recipes in the book, you'll notice there's a wait involved in `requests` calls, normally of around one or two seconds. But computers can do other stuff while waiting, including making more requests at the same time. In this recipe, we will see how to download a list of pages in parallel and wait until they are all ready. We will use an intentionally slow server to show why it's worth getting this right.

Getting ready

We'll get code to crawl and search for keywords, making use of the `futures` capabilities of Python 3 to download multiple pages at the same time.

A `future` is an object that represents the promise of a value. This means that you immediately receive an object while the code is being executed in the background – only, when specifically requesting its `.result()`, the code waits until the result is available.

 If the result is already available at that point, that makes it faster. Think of the operation as putting something in the washing machine while doing other tasks. There's a chance that the laundry will be done by the time we finish the rest of our chores.

To generate a `future`, you need a background engine, called an **executor**. Once created, `submit` a function and parameters to it to retrieve a `future`. The retrieval of the result can be delayed as long as necessary, allowing the generation of several `futures` in a row; then we can wait until all are finished and execute them in parallel. This is an alternative to creating one, waiting until it finishes, creating another, and so on.

There are several ways to create an executor; in this recipe, we'll use `ThreadPoolExecutor`, which uses threads.

We'll use a prepared example, available at the following GitHub repo: `https://github.com/PacktPublishing/Python-Automation-Cookbook-Second-Edition/tree/master/Chapter03/test_site`. Download the whole site and run the included script:

```
$ python simple_delay_server.py -d 2
```

This serves the site at the URL http://localhost:8000. You can see it in a browser. It's a simple blog with three entries. Most of it is uninteresting, but we added a couple of paragraphs that contain the keyword python. The parameter -d 2 makes the server intentionally slow, simulating a bad connection.

How to do it...

1. Write the following script, speed_up_step1.py. The full code is available on GitHub at the Chapter03 directory (https://github.com/PacktPublishing/Python-Automation-Cookbook-Second-Edition/blob/master/Chapter03/speed_up_step1.py). Here are only the most relevant parts. It is based on crawling_web_step1.py:

```
...
def process_link(source_link, text):
    ...
    return source_link, get_links(parsed_source, page)
...


def main(base_url, to_search, workers):
    checked_links = set()
    to_check = [base_url]
    max_checks = 10

    with concurrent.futures.ThreadPoolExecutor(max_workers=workers) as executor:
        while to_check:
            futures = [executor.submit(process_link, url, to_search)
                       for url in to_check]
            to_check = []
            for data in concurrent.futures.as_completed(futures):
                link, new_links = data.result()

                checked_links.add(link)
                for link in new_links:
                    if link not in checked_links and link not in to_check:
                        to_check.append(link)
```

```
                    max_checks -= 1
                    if not max_checks:
                        return



        if __name__ == '__main__':
            parser = argparse.ArgumentParser()
            ...
            parser.add_argument('-w', type=int, help='Number of
        workers',
                                    default=4)
            args = parser.parse_args()

            main(args.u, args.p, args.w)
```

2. Notice the differences in the `main` function. Also, there's an extra parameter added (number of concurrent workers), and the function `process_link` now returns the source link.

3. Run the `crawling_web_step1.py` script to get a time baseline. Notice that the output has been removed here for clarity:

```
$ time python crawling_web_step1.py http://localhost:8000/
... REMOVED OUTPUT
real 0m12.221s
user 0m0.160s
sys 0m0.034s
```

4. Run the new script with one worker, which will make it slower than the original one:

```
$ time python speed_up_step1.py -w 1
... REMOVED OUTPUT
real 0m16.403s
user 0m0.181s
sys 0m0.068s
```

5. Increase the number of workers:

```
$ time python speed_up_step1.py -w 2
... REMOVED OUTPUT
real 0m10.353s
```

```
user 0m0.199s

sys 0m0.068s
```

6. Adding more workers decreases the time:

```
$ time python speed_up_step1.py -w 5

... REMOVED OUTPUT

real 0m6.234s

user 0m0.171s

sys 0m0.040s
```

How it works...

The main engine to create the concurrent requests is the main function. Notice that the rest of the code is basically untouched (other than returning the source link in the process_link function).

 This change is actually quite common when adapting for concurrency. Concurrent tasks need to return all the relevant data, as they cannot rely on an ordered context.

This is the relevant part of the code that handles the concurrent engine:

```
with concurrent.futures.ThreadPoolExecutor(max_
workers=workers) as executor:
    while to_check:
        futures = [executor.submit(process_link, url, to_
search)
                        for url in to_check]
        to_check = []
        for data in concurrent.futures.as_completed(futures):
            link, new_links = data.result()

            checked_links.add(link)
            for link in new_links:
                if link not in checked_links and link not in
to_check:
                    to_check.append(link)

            max_checks -= 1
```

```
if not max_checks:
    return
```

The `with` context creates a pool of workers, specifying how many. Inside, a list of futures containing all the URLs to retrieve is created. The `.as_completed()` function returns the futures that are finished, and then there's some work to do to obtain newly found links and check whether they need to be added to be retrieved or not. This process is similar to the one presented in the *Crawling the web* recipe.

The process starts again until enough links have been retrieved or there are no links to retrieve. Note that the links are retrieved in batches; the first time, the base link is processed and all links are retrieved. In the second iteration, all those links will be requested. Once they are all downloaded, a new batch will be processed.

 When dealing with concurrent requests, keep in mind that they can change order between two executions. If a request takes a little more or a little less time, that can affect the ordering of the retrieved information. Because we stop after downloading 10 pages, that also means that the 10 pages could be different.

There's more...

The full `futures` documentation in Python can be found here: `https://docs.python.org/3/library/concurrent.futures.html`.

 As you can see in *steps 4* and *5* in the *How to do it...* section, properly determining the number of workers can require some tests. Some numbers can make the process slower, due to the increase in management. Do not be afraid to experiment!

In the Python world, there are other ways to make concurrent HTTP requests. There's a native request module that allows us to work with `futures`, called `requests-futures`. It can be found here: `https://github.com/ross/requests-futures`.

Another alternative is to use asynchronous programming. This way of working has recently gotten a lot of attention, as it can be very efficient in situations that involve dealing with many concurrent calls, but the resulting way of coding is different from the traditional way and requires some time to get used to. Python includes the `asyncio` module to work that way, and there's a good module called `aiohttp` to work with HTTP requests. You can find more information about `aiohttp` here: `https://aiohttp.readthedocs.io/en/stable/client_quickstart.html`.

A good introduction to asynchronous programming can be found in this article: `https://djangostars.com/blog/asynchronous-programming-in-python-asyncio/`.

See also

- The *Crawling the web* recipe, earlier in this chapter, for the less efficient alternative to this recipe.
- The *Downloading web pages* recipe, earlier in this chapter, to learn the basics of requesting web pages.

4

Searching and Reading Local Files

In this chapter, we will introduce the basic operations to read information from files, starting with searching and opening files stored in different directories and subdirectories. Then, we'll describe some of the most common file types and how to read them, including formats such as raw text files, PDFs, and Word documents.

The last recipe will search for a word inside different kinds of files, recursively in a directory tree.

In this chapter, we'll cover the following recipes:

- Crawling and searching directories
- Reading text files
- Dealing with encodings
- Reading CSV files
- Reading log files
- Reading file metadata
- Reading images
- Reading PDF files
- Reading Word documents
- Scanning documents for a keyword

We will start by accessing all the files in a directory tree.

Crawling and searching directories

In this recipe, we'll learn how to scan a directory recursively to get all the files contained there. That will include all the files in subdirectories. The matched files can be of a particular kind, like text files, or every single one of them.

This is normally a starting operation when dealing with files, to detect all the existing ones.

Getting ready

Let's start by creating a test directory with some file information:

```
$ mkdir dir
$ touch dir/file1.txt
$ touch dir/file2.txt
$ mkdir dir/subdir
$ touch dir/subdir/file3.txt
$ touch dir/subdir/file4.txt
$ touch dir/subdir/file5.pdf
$ touch dir/file6.pdf
```

All the files will be empty; we will use them in this recipe only to discover them. Notice there are four files that have a `.txt` extension, and two that have a `.pdf` extension.

 The files are also available in the GitHub repository here: https://github.com/PacktPublishing/Python-Automation-Cookbook-Second-Edition/tree/master/Chapter04/documents/dir.

Enter the created `dir` directory

```
$ cd dir
```

How to do it...

1. Print all the filenames in the `dir` directory and subdirectories:

```
>>> import os
>>> for root, dirs, files in os.walk('.'):
...     for file in files:
```

```
...              print(file)
...
file1.txt
file2.txt
file6.pdf
file3.txt
file4.txt
file5.pdf
```

2. Print the full path of the files, joining with the `root`:

```
>>> for root, dirs, files in os.walk('.'):
...      for file in files:
...            full_file_path = os.path.join(root, file)
...            print(full_file_path)
...
./dir/file1.txt
./dir/file2.txt
./dir/file6.pdf
./dir/subdir/file3.txt
./dir/subdir/file4.txt
./dir/subdir/file5.pdf
```

3. Print only the `.pdf` files:

```
>>> for root, dirs, files in os.walk('.'):
...      for file in files:
...            if file.endswith('.pdf'):
...                  full_file_path = os.path.join(root, file)
...                  print(full_file_path)
...
./dir/file6.pdf
./dir/subdir/file5.pdf
```

4. Print only files that contain an even number:

```
>>> import re
>>> for root, dirs, files in os.walk('.'):
...      for file in files:
...            if re.search(r'[13579]', file):
```

```
...              full_file_path = os.path.join(root, file)
...              print(full_file_path)
...
./dir/file1.txt
./dir/subdir/file3.txt
./dir/subdir/file5.pdf
```

How it works...

`os.walk()` goes through a whole directory and all subdirectories under it, returning all the files. For each directory, it returns a tuple with the directory, any subdirectories under it, and all the files:

```
>>> for root, dirs, files in os.walk('.'):
...       print(root, dirs, files)
...
. ['dir'] []
./dir ['subdir'] ['file1.txt', 'file2.txt', 'file6.pdf']
./dir/subdir [] ['file3.txt', 'file4.txt', 'file5.pdf']
```

The `os.path.join()` function allows us to join two paths, such as the base path and the file.

As paths are returned as pure strings, any kind of filtering can be done, as in *step 3*. In *step 4*, the full power of regular expressions can be used to filter.

In the next recipe, we'll deal with the content of the files, and not just the filename.

There's more...

In this recipe, the returned files are not opened or modified in any way. This operation is read-only. Files can be opened as described in the following recipes.

 Be aware that changing the structure of the directory while walking over it may affect the results. If you need to carry out some file maintenance while walking through the tree, like copying or moving a file, it's a good idea to store it in a different directory.

The `os.path` module has other interesting functions. We talked about `.join()`, but other included utilities are:

- `os.path.abspath()`, which returns the absolute path of a file.
- `os.path.split()`, which splits the path between directory and file:

    ```
    >>> os.path.split('/a/very/long/path/file.txt')
    ('/a/very/long/path', 'file.txt')
    ```

- `os.path.exists()`, to return whether a file exists or not on the filesystem.

The full documentation about `os.path` can be found here: `https://docs.python.org/3/library/os.path.html`. Another module, `pathlib`, can be used for higher-level access, in an object-oriented way: `https://docs.python.org/3/library/pathlib.html`.

As demonstrated in *step 4*, multiple ways of filtering can be used. All of the string manipulations and tips shown in *Chapter 1, Let's Begin Our Automation Journey,* are available.

See also

- The *Introducing regular expressions* recipe in *Chapter 1, Let's Begin Our Automation Journey*, to learn how to filter using regular expressions.
- The *Reading text files* recipe, later in this chapter, to open the found files and read their context.

Reading text files

After searching for a particular file, the next typical action is to open it and read its content. Text files are very simple yet very powerful files. They store data in plain text, without complicated binary formats.

Text file support is provided natively in Python, and it's easy to consider it a collection of lines that can be represented as Python strings.

Getting ready

We'll read the `zen_of_python.txt` file, containing *The Zen of Python* by Tim Peters, which is a collection of aphorisms that very well describe the design principles behind Python.

It is available in the GitHub repository here: `https://github.com/PacktPublishing/Python-Automation-Cookbook-Second-Edition/blob/master/Chapter04/documents/zen_of_python.txt`:

```
Beautiful is better than ugly.
Explicit is better than implicit.
Simple is better than complex.
Complex is better than complicated.
Flat is better than nested.
Sparse is better than dense.
Readability counts.
Special cases aren't special enough to break the rules.
Although practicality beats purity.
Errors should never pass silently.
Unless explicitly silenced.
In the face of ambiguity, refuse the temptation to guess.
There should be one-- and preferably only one --obvious way to do it.
Although that way may not be obvious at first unless you're Dutch.
Now is better than never.
Although never is often better than *right* now.
If the implementation is hard to explain, it's a bad idea.
If the implementation is easy to explain, it may be a good idea.
Namespaces are one honking great idea -- let's do more of those!
```

The Zen of Python is described in PEP-20 here: `https://www.python.org/dev/peps/pep-0020/`.

 The Zen of Python will be displayed on any Python interpreter by typing `import this`.

How to do it...

1. Open and print the whole file, line by line (the result is not displayed):

```
>>> with open('zen_of_python.txt') as file:
...     for line in file:
...         print(line)
...

[RESULT NOT DISPLAYED]
```

2. Open the file and print any line containing the string should:

```
>>> with open('zen_of_python.txt', 'r') as file:
...     for line in file:
...         if 'should' in line.lower():
...             print(line)
...
Errors should never pass silently.


There should be one-- and preferably only one --obvious way to do
it.
```

3. Open the file and print the first line containing the word better:

```
>>> with open('zen_of_python.txt', 'rt') as file:
...     for line in file:
...         if 'better' in line.lower():
..              print(line)
...             break
...
Beautiful is better than ugly.
```

How it works...

To open a file, use the open() function. This returns a file object that then can be iterated over to return it line by line, as shown in *step 1* of the *How to do it...* section. Note it opens the file in text mode.

The with context manager is a very convenient way of dealing with files. It will close the file after finishing its use (leaving the block). It will do so even if an exception has been raised.

Step 2 shows how to iterate and filter the lines based on what lines are applicable for our tasks. The lines are returned as strings that can be filtered in multiple ways, as described in the recipes in *Chapter 1, Let's Begin Our Automation Journey* and *Chapter 3, Building Your First Web Scraping Application*.

Reading the whole file may not be required, as shown in *step 3*. Because iterating through the file line by line will be reading the file as you go, you can stop at any time, avoiding reading the rest of the file. For a small file such as our example, that's not very relevant, but for long files, this can reduce memory use and time.

There's more...

The `with` context manager is the preferred way of dealing with files, but it's not the only one. You may also open and close them manually, like this:

```
>>> file = open('zen_of_python.txt')
>>> content = file.read()
>>> file.close()
```

Note the `.close()` method, to ensure that the file is closed and to free resources related to opening a file. The `.read()` method reads the whole file in one go, instead of line by line.

> The `.read()` method also accepts a size parameter in bytes that limits the size of the data read. For example, `file.read(1024)` will return up to 1KB of information. The next call to `.read()` will continue from that point.

Files are opened in a particular mode. Modes define a combination of read/write, as well as whether to treat the data as text or binary data. By default, files are opened in read-only and text mode, which are described as `"r"` (*step 2*) or `"rt"` (*step 3*).

More modes will be explored in other recipes.

See also

- The *Crawling and searching directories* recipe, earlier in this chapter, to find files that will be read later.
- The *Dealing with encodings* recipe, later in this chapter, to learn how to deal with files encoded in a non-standard way.

Dealing with encodings

Text files can be present in different encodings. In recent years, the situation has greatly improved, as there are a few encodings that are pretty standard, but there are still compatibility problems when working with different systems.

There's a difference between raw data in a file and a string object in Python. The string object has been transformed from whatever encoding the file contained into a native Unicode string. Once it is in this format, it may need to be stored in different encodings. By default, Python works with the encoding defined by the OS, which in modern operating systems is UTF-8. This is a highly compatible encoding, but you may need to save files in a different one, depending on your specific requirements.

Getting ready

We prepared two files in the GitHub repository that store the string 20£ in two different encodings: one in the usual UTF-8 and another in ISO 8859-1, a different common encoding. These prepared files are available in GitHub under the Chapter04/documents directory, with the names example_iso.txt and example_utf8.txt: https://github.com/PacktPublishing/Python-Automation-Cookbook-Second-Edition/tree/master/Chapter04/documents.

We'll use the Beautiful Soup module, presented previously in the *Parsing HTML* recipe in *Chapter 3, Building Your First Web Scraping Application*.

How to do it...

1. Open the example_utf8.txt file and display its content:

```
>>> with open('example_utf8.txt') as file:
...     print(file.read())
..
20£
```

2. Try to open the example_iso.txt file, which will raise an exception:

```
>>> with open('example_iso.txt') as file:
...     print(file.read())
...
Traceback (most recent call last):
   ...
UnicodeDecodeError: 'utf-8' codec can't decode byte 0xa3 in
position 2: invalid start byte
```

3. Open the example_iso.txt file with the proper encoding:

```
>>> with open('example_iso.txt', encoding='iso-8859-1') as file:
...     print(file.read())
```

```
...
20£
```

4. Open the `utf8` file and save its content in an `iso-8859-1` file:

```
>>> with open('example_utf8.txt') as file:
...     content = file.read()
>>> with open('example_output_iso.txt', 'w',
encoding='iso-8859-1') as file:
...     file.write(content)
...
4
```

5. Finally, read from the new file in the proper format to ensure it is correctly saved:

```
>>> with open('example_output_iso.txt', encoding='iso-8859-1') as
file:
...     print(file.read())
...
20£
```

How it works...

Step 1 and *step 2* in the *How to do it...* section are very straightforward. In *step 3*, we add an extra parameter, `encoding`, to specify that the file needs to be opened in something different to UTF-8.

 Python accepts a lot of standard encodings right out of the box. Check here for all of them and their aliases: `https://docs.python.org/3/library/codecs.html#standard-encodings`.

In *step 4*, we create a new file in ISO-8859-1 and write to it as usual. Notice the "w" parameter, which specifies to open it for writing and in text mode.

Step 5 is a confirmation that the file is properly saved.

There's more...

This recipe assumes that we know the encoding a file is in. But sometimes, we're not sure about that. Beautiful Soup, a module used to parse HTML, can try to detect what encoding a particular file has.

 Automatically detecting what encoding a file has may be, well, impossible. There are potentially an infinite number of encodings! But a subset of usual encodings should cover 90% of real-world cases. Just remember that the easiest way of knowing for sure is to ask whomever created the file in the first place.

To do so, we'll need to open the file to read in binary format with the 'rb' parameter. And then, we'll pass the binary content to the UnicodeDammit module of Beautiful Soup, like this:

```
>>> from bs4 import UnicodeDammit
>>> with open('example_output_iso.txt', 'rb') as file:
...     content = file.read()
...
>>> suggestion = UnicodeDammit(content)
>>> suggestion.original_encoding
'iso-8859-1'
>>> suggestion.unicode_markup
'20£\n'
```

The encoding can then be inferred. Though .unicode_markup returns the decoded string, it's better to use this suggestion only to obtain the encoding, and then reopen the file in text mode with the proper encoding.

See also

- The *Manipulating strings* recipe in *Chapter 1, Let's Begin Our Automation Journey*, to learn more about how to edit strings.
- The *Parsing HTML* recipe in *Chapter 3, Building Your First Web Scraping Application*, to learn more about Beautiful Soup.

Reading CSV files

Some text files contain tabular data separated by commas. This is a convenient way of creating structured data, instead of using proprietary, more complex binary formats such as Excel or others. These files are called **Comma Separated Values** or **CSV** files, and most spreadsheet packages allow us to work directly with them.

Getting ready

We've prepared a CSV file using the data for the top 10 movies by theatre attendance, as described by this page: `http://www.mrob.com/pub/film-video/topadj.html`.

We copied the first 10 elements of the table into a spreadsheet program (Numbers) and exported the file as a CSV. The file is available in the GitHub repository in the `Chapter04/documents` directory as `top_films.csv`:

Figure 4.1: Content of the CSV file

How to do it...

1. Import the `csv` module:

    ```
    >>> import csv
    ```

2. Open the file, create a reader, and iterate through it to show the tabular data of all rows (only three rows are shown):

    ```
    >>> with open('top_films.csv') as file:
    ...     data = csv.reader(file)
    ```

```
...    for row in data:
...        print(row)
...
['Rank', 'Admissions\n(millions)', 'Title (year) (studio)',
'Director(s)']
['1', '225.7', 'Gone With the Wind (1939)\xa0(MGM)', 'Victor
Fleming, George Cukor, Sam Wood']
['2', '194.4', 'Star Wars (Ep. IV: A New Hope) (1977)\xa0(Fox)',
'George Lucas']
...
['10', '118.9', 'The Lion King (1994)\xa0(BV)', 'Roger Allers, Rob
Minkoff']
```

3. Open the file and use `DictReader` to structure the data, including the header:

```
>>> with open('top_films.csv') as file:
...        data = csv.DictReader(file)
...        structured_data = [row for row in data]
...
>>> structured_data[0]
{'Rank': '1', 'Admissions\n(millions)': '225.7', 'Title (year)
(studio)': 'Gone With the Wind (1939)\xa0(MGM)', 'Director(s)':
'Victor Fleming, George Cukor, Sam Wood'}
```

4. Each of the items in `structured_data` is a full dictionary that contains each of the values:

```
>>> structured_data[0].keys()
dict_keys(['Rank', 'Admissions\n(millions)', 'Title (year)
(studio)', 'Director(s)'])
>>> structured_data[0]['Rank']
'1'
>>> structured_data[0]['Director(s)']
'Victor Fleming, George Cukor, Sam Wood'
```

How it works...

Notice that the file needs to be read and that we use a `with` context block. This ensures that the file is closed at the end of the block.

As shown in *step 2* in the *How to do it...* section, the `csv.reader` class allows us to structure the returning lines of code by subdividing them as lists, following the format of the table data. Notice how all the values are described as strings. `csv.reader` does not understand whether the first line is a header or not.

For a more structured read of the file, in *step 3*, we used `csv.DictReader`. By default, it reads the first row as a header defining the applicable fields, and then converts each of the rows into dictionaries with those fields.

> Sometimes, like in this case, the names of the fields as described in the file can be a little verbose. Don't be afraid to translate the dictionary as an extra step into more manageable field names.

There's more...

A CSV has a very loosely defined file structure interpretation. There are several ways that the data can be stored. This is represented in the `csv` module as **dialects**. For example, the values can be delimited by commas, semicolons, or tabs. The list of default accepted dialects can be displayed by calling `csv.list_dialect()`.

> By default, the dialect will be Excel, which is the most common one. Even other spreadsheets will commonly use it.

Dialects can also be inferred from the file itself through the `Sniffer` class. The `Sniffer` class analyzes a sample of the file (or the whole file) and returns a `dialect` object to allow reading in the proper way.

Notice that the file is open with no new lines, to not make any assumptions about it:

```
>>> with open('top_films.csv', newline='') as file:
...     dialect = csv.Sniffer().sniff(file.read())
```

The dialect can then be used when opening the reader. Note the `newline` again, as the dialect will split the lines correctly:

```
>>> with open('top_films.csv', newline='') as file:
...     reader = csv.reader(file, dialect)
...     for row in reader:
...         print(row)
```

The full `csv` module documentation can be found here: `https://docs.python.org/3/library/csv.html`.

See also

- The *Dealing with encodings* recipe, earlier in this chapter, to learn how to deal with encodings.
- The *Reading text files* recipe, earlier in this chapter, to learn more about opening and reading files.

Reading log files

Another common structured text file format is **log files**. Log files consist of rows of logs, which are a line of text with a particular format, describing an event.

 Logs are structured only in the same file or type of file. Formats can be very different and there's no common structure or syntax for them. Each application can and will use a different format.

Typically, each one will have a time when the event occurred, so the file is an ordered collection of them.

Getting ready

The `example_log.log` file containing five sales logs can be obtained from the GitHub repository here: `https://github.com/PacktPublishing/Python-Automation-Cookbook-Second-Edition/blob/master/Chapter04/documents/example_logs.log`.

The format is:

```
[<Timestamp in iso format>] - SALE - PRODUCT: <product id> - PRICE:
$<price of the sale>
```

We'll use the `Chapter01/price_log.py` file to process each log into an object. There's a copy in the `Chapter04/documents` directory to simplify the import process.

How to do it...

1. Import `PriceLog`:

```
>>> from price_log import PriceLog
```

2. Open the log file and parse all logs:

```
>>> with open('example_logs.log') as file:
...       logs = [PriceLog.parse(log) for log in file]
...
>>> len(logs)
5
>>> logs[0]
<PriceLog (Delorean(datetime=datetime.datetime(2018, 6, 17, 22,
11, 50, 268396), timezone='UTC'), 1489, 9.99)>
```

3. Determine the total income by all sales:

```
>>> total = sum(log.price for log in logs)
>>> total
Decimal('47.82')
```

4. Determine how many units have been sold of each `product_id`:

```
>>> from collections import Counter
>>> counter = Counter(log.product_id for log in logs)
>>> counter
Counter({1489: 2, 4508: 1, 8597: 1, 3086: 1})
```

5. Filter the logs to find all occurrences of selling `product` ID `1489`:

```
>>> logs = [log for log in logs if log.product_id == 1489]
>>> len(logs)
2
>>> logs[0].product_id, logs[0].timestamp
(1489, Delorean(datetime=datetime.datetime(2018, 6, 17, 22, 11,
50, 268396), timezone='UTC'))
>>> logs[1].product_id, logs[1].timestamp
(1489, Delorean(datetime=datetime.datetime(2018, 6, 17, 22, 11,
50, 268468), timezone='UTC'))
```

How it works...

As each entry is a single line, we open the file and go one by one, parsing each of them. The parsing code is available in `price_log.py`. Check it for more details on the parsing process.

In *step 2* in the *How to do it...* section, we open the file and process each of the lines to create a log list with all our processed logs. Then, we can produce aggregation operations, as in the next steps.

Step 3 shows how to aggregate all values. In this case, summing the price of all items sold over the log file to get the total revenue.

Step 4 uses `Counter` to determine the amount of each item in the file log. This returns a dictionary-like object with the values to count and the number of times they appear.

Filtering can also be done in a line-by-line approach, as shown in *step 5*. This is similar to the other filtering we've done in the recipes of this chapter.

There's more...

Remember that you can stop processing a file as soon as you have all the data you need. This may be a good strategy if the file is very big, as is usually the case with log files.

`Counter` is a great tool to quickly count a list. See the Python documentation here for more details: `https://docs.python.org/3/library/collections. html#counter-objects`. You can get the ordered items by calling the following:

```
>>> counter.most_common()
[(1489, 2), (4508, 1), (8597, 1), (3086, 1)]
```

See also

- The *Using a third-party tool—parse* recipe in *Chapter 1, Let's Begin Our Automation Journey*.
- The *Reading text files* recipe, earlier in this chapter, to learn more about opening and reading files.

Reading file metadata

File metadata is everything associated with a particular file that is not the data content itself. The most obvious is the file name, but there are more parameters available such as the size of the file, the creation date, or its permissions.

Browsing through that data is important, for example, to filter files older than a date, or to find all files bigger than a value in KBs. In this recipe, we'll see how to access the file metadata in Python.

Getting ready

We'll use the `zen_of_python.txt` file, available in the GitHub repository (`https://github.com/PacktPublishing/Python-Automation-Cookbook-Second-Edition/blob/master/Chapter04/documents/zen_of_python.txt`). As you can see, by using the `ls` command, the file is `856` bytes, and, in this example, it was created on June 14:

```
$ ls -lrt zen_of_python.txt
-rw-r--r--@ 1 jaime staff 856 14 Jun 21:22 zen_of_python.txt
```

On your computer, the dates may vary, based on when you downloaded the code.

How to do it...

1. Import `os` and `datetime`:

    ```
    >>> import os
    >>> from datetime import datetime
    ```

2. Retrieve the stats of the `zen_of_python.txt` file:

    ```
    >>> stats = os.stat(('zen_of_python.txt'))
    >>> stats
    os.stat_result(st_mode=33188, st_ino=15822537, st_dev=16777224,
    st_nlink=1, st_uid=501, st_gid=20, st_size=856, st_
    atime=1529461935, st_mtime=1529007749, st_ctime=1529007757)
    ```

3. Get the size of the file, in bytes:

    ```
    >>> stats.st_size
    856
    ```

4. Obtain when the file was last modified:

    ```
    >>> datetime.fromtimestamp(stats.st_mtime)
    datetime.datetime(2018, 6, 14, 21, 22, 29)
    ```

5. Obtain when the file was last accessed:

```
>>> datetime.fromtimestamp(stats.st_atime)
datetime.datetime(2018, 6, 20, 3, 32, 15)
```

How it works...

`os.stats` returns a `stats` object that represents the metadata stored in the filesystem. The metadata includes:

- The size of the file, in bytes, as shown in *step 3* in the *How to do it...* section, using `st_size`.
- When the file content was last modified, as shown in *step 4*, using `st_mtime`.
- When the file was last read (accessed), as shown in *step 5*, using `st_atime`.

The times are returned as timestamps, so in *step 4* and *step 5*, we create a `datetime` object from the timestamps to better access the data.

All these values can be used to filter the files and access the meaningful ones.

 Notice you don't need to open the file with `open()` to read its metadata. Detecting whether a file has been changed after a known time by reading the modification time will be quicker than comparing its content, so you can take advantage of that for comparison.

There's more...

To obtain the stats one by one, there are also convenience functions available in `os.path`, which follow the pattern `get<value>`:

```
>>> os.path.getsize('zen_of_python.txt')
856
>>> os.path.getmtime('zen_of_python.txt')
1529531584.0
>>> os.path.getatime('zen_of_python.txt')
1529531669.0
```

The value is specified in the UNIX timestamp format (seconds since January 1, 1970).

Note that calling all of these three functions will be slower than making a single call to os.stats and processing the results. Also, returned stats can be inspected to detect the available metadata.

The values described in this recipe are available for all filesystems, but there are more values that can be used, depending on the particular platform.

For example, to obtain the creation date of a file, you can use the st_birthtime parameter for macOS or st_mtime in Windows.

 st_mtime is always available, but its meaning changes between systems. In Unix systems, it will change when the content is modified, so it's not a reliable time of creation.

os.stat will follow symbolic links. If you want to get the stats of a symbolic link, use os.lstat().

You can check the full documentation about all available stats here: https://docs.python.org/3/library/os.html - os.stat_result.

See also

- The *Reading text files* recipe, earlier in this chapter, to learn the basics of opening and reading files.
- The *Reading images* recipe, later in this chapter, to learn how to read and treat image files.

Reading images

Probably the most common data that is not text is image data. Images have their own set of specific metadata that can be read to filter values or perform other operations.

The main challenge is dealing with multiple formats and different metadata definitions. We'll show in this recipe how to get information from both a JPEG and a PNG, and how the same information can be encoded differently.

Getting ready

The best general toolkit for dealing with images in Python is, arguably, `Pillow`. This library allows you to easily read files in the most common formats, as well as perform operations on them. `Pillow` started as a fork of **PIL** (**Python Imaging Library**), a previous module that became stagnant some years ago.

We will also use the `xmltodict` module to transform some data from XML into a more convenient dictionary. We will add both modules to `requirements.txt` and reinstall them in the virtual environment:

```
$ echo "Pillow==7.0.0" >> requirements.txt

$ echo "xmltodict==0.12.0" >> requirements.txt

$ pip install -r requirements.txt
```

The metadata information in photo files is defined in the **EXIF** (**Exchangeable Image File**) format. EXIF is a standard for storing information about pictures, including things like what camera took the picture, when it was taken, GPS describing the location, exposure, focal length, color info, and so on.

 You can get a good summary here: `https://www.slrphotographyguide.com/what-is-exif-metadata/`. All the information is optional, but virtually all digital cameras and processing software will store some data. Because of the privacy concerns, parts of it, like the exact location, can be disabled.

The following images will be used for this recipe, and are available to download in the GitHub repository (`https://github.com/PacktPublishing/Python-Automation-Cookbook-Second-Edition/tree/master/Chapter04/images`):

- `photo-dublin-a1.jpg`
- `photo-dublin-a2.png`
- `photo-dublin-b.png`

Two of them, `photo-dublin-a1.jpg` and `photo-dublin-a2.png`, are the same scene, but while the first is the untouched picture, the second one has been retouched to slightly change the colors, and has also been scaled. Notice one is in JPEG format and the other in PNG. The other one, `photo-dublin-b.png`, is a different picture. Both pictures were taken in Dublin, with the same phone camera, on two different days.

While `Pillow` understands how JPG files store the EXIF info directly, PNG files store XMP info, a more generic standard that can contain EXIF data inside.

> More info about XMP can be obtained here: `https://www.adobe.com/devnet/xmp.html`. For the most part, it defines an XML tree structure that's relatively readable in `raw`.

To further complicate matters, XMP is encoded using RDF, which is a standard describing how to encode an XML tree.

> If EFIX, XMP, and RDF sound confusing, well, it's because they are. XMP stores the EXIF information using RDF. Ultimately, the differences between them are not very relevant, and the best approach is to find out the interesting bits and pieces. We can inspect the specifics of the names using Python introspection tools and check exactly how the data is structured, and what the name of the parameter we are looking for is.

As the GPS information is stored in different formats, we've included in the GitHub repository a file called `gps_conversion.py`: `https://github.com/PacktPublishing/Python-Automation-Cookbook-Second-Edition/blob/master/Chapter04/gps_conversion.py`. This includes the functions `exif_to_decimal` and `rdf_to_decimal`, which will transform both formats into decimals to compare them.

How to do it...

1. Import the modules and functions to use in this recipe:

   ```
   >>> from PIL import Image
   >>> from PIL.ExifTags import TAGS, GPSTAGS
   >>> import xmltodict
   >> from gps_conversion import exif_to_decimal, rdf_to_decimal
   ```

2. Open the first photo:

   ```
   >>> image1 = Image.open('images/photo-dublin-a1.jpg')
   ```

3. Get the width, height, and format of the file:

   ```
   >>> image1.height
   3024
   >>> image1.width
   ```

```
4032
>>> image1.format
'JPEG'
```

4. Retrieve the EXIF information of the image and transform it into a convenient dictionary. Show the camera, the lens used, and when it was taken:

```
>>> exif_info_1 = {TAGS.get(tag, tag): value
        for tag, value in image1._getexif().items()}
>>> exif_info_1['Model']
'iPhone X'
>>> exif_info_1['LensModel']
'iPhone X back dual camera 4mm f/1.8'
>>> exif_info_1['DateTimeOriginal']
'2018:04:21 12:07:55'
```

5. Open the second image and obtain the XMP info:

```
>>> image2 = Image.open('images/photo-dublin-a2.png')
>>> image2.height
1512
>>> image2.width
2016
>>> image2.format
'PNG'
>>> xmp_info = xmltodict.parse(image2.info['XML:com.adobe.xmp'])
```

6. Obtain the RDF description field, which contains all the values we are looking for. Retrieve the model (a TIFF value), the lens model (an EXIF value), and the creation date (an XMP value). Check the values are the same as in *step 4*, even if the file is different:

```
>>> rdf_info_2 = xmp_info['x:xmpmeta']['rdf:RDF']
['rdf:Description']
>>> rdf_info_2['tiff:Model']
'iPhone X'
>>> rdf_info_2['exifEX:LensModel']
'iPhone X back dual camera 4mm f/1.8'
>>> rdf_info_2['xmp:CreateDate']
'2018-04-21T12:07:55'
```

7. Obtain the GPS information in both pictures, transform them into an equivalent format, and check that they are the same. Notice that the resolution is not the same, but they match up to the fourth decimal point:

```
>>> gps_info_1 = {GPSTAGS.get(tag, tag): value
        for tag, value in exif_info_1['GPSInfo'].items()}
>>> exif_to_decimal(gps_info_1)
('N53.34690555555556', 'W6.247797222222222')
>>> rdf_to_decimal(rdf_info_2)
('N53.346905', 'W6.247796666666667')
```

8. Open the third image and obtain the creation date and GPS info, and check it doesn't match the other photo, although it is close (the second and third decimals are not the same):

```
>>> image3 = Image.open('photo-dublin-b.png')
>>> xmp_info = xmltodict.parse(image3.info['XML:com.adobe.xmp'])
>>> rdf_info_3 = xmp_info['x:xmpmeta']['rdf:RDF']
['rdf:Description']
>>> rdf_info_3['xmp:CreateDate']
'2018-03-08T18:16:57'
>>> rdf_to_decimal(rdf_info_3)
('N53.34984166666667', 'W6.260388333333333')
```

How it works...

`Pillow` is able to interpret files in most common image formats, as shown in *step 2* in the *How to do it…* section.

The `Image` object contains the basic information about the size and format of the file, and is displayed in *step 3*. The `info` property contains information that is dependent on the format.

The EXIF metadata for JPG files can be parsed with the `._getexif()` method, but then it needs to be translated properly, as it uses the raw binary definition. For example, the number 42,036 corresponds to the `LensModel` property. Fortunately, there's a definition of all tags in the `PIL.ExifTags` module. We translate the dictionary into readable tags in *step 4* to obtain a more readable dictionary.

Step 5 opens a PNG format, which has the same properties related to size, but the metadata is stored in XML/RDF format and needs to be parsed with the help of `xmltodict`. *Step 6* shows how to navigate this metadata to extract the same information that's in JPG format. The data is the same, as both files come from the same original picture, even if the images are different.

Xmltodict has some issues when trying to parse data that's not in XML format. Check that the input is valid XML.

Step 7 extracts the GPS information for both images, which is stored in different ways, and shows they are the same (although the precision is different because of the way it is encoded).

Not every image will necessarily have location information or other metadata. This information can be changed or removed, or stored differently, depending on the format and the camera generating the file.

Step 8 shows the information on a different photo.

There's more...

Pillow also has a lot of functionality around modifying pictures. It is very easy to resize or make simple modifications to a file, such as rotating it. You can find the complete Pillow documentation here: https://pillow.readthedocs.io.

Pillow allows a lot of operations with images. Not only simple operations such as resizing or transforming one format into another, but also things like cropping the image, applying color filters, or generating animated GIFs. If you're interested in image processing using Python, it is definitely the module to master.

The GPS coordinates in the recipe are stated in **DMS (Degrees, Minutes, Seconds)** and **DDM (Degrees, Decimal, Minutes)**, and transformed into **DD (Decimal, Degrees)**. You can find out more about the different GPS formats here: http://www.ubergizmo.com/how-to/read-gps-coordinates/. You'll also find out how to search the exact locations of the pictures there, in case you're curious.

A more advanced use of reading image files is to try to process them for **OCR (Optical Character Recognition)**. This means automatically detecting text in an image and extracting and processing it. The open source module tesseract allows you to do this, and it can be used with Python and Pillow.

You need to install tesseract on your system (https://github.com/tesseract-ocr/tesseract/wiki), and the pytesseract Python module (using pip install pytesseract).

You can download a file with clear text, called `photo-text.jpg`, from the GitHub repository at `https://github.com/PacktPublishing/Python-Automation-Cookbook-Second-Edition/blob/master/Chapter04/images/photo-text.jpg`:

```
>>> from PIL import Image
>>> import pytesseract
>>> pytesseract.image_to_string(Image.open('photo-text.jpg'))
'Automate!'
```

OCR can be difficult if the text is not very clear in the image, or it is mixed with images, or it uses a distinctive font. There's an example of that in the `photo-dublin-a-text.jpg` file, (available in the GitHub repository at `https://github.com/PacktPublishing/Python-Automation-Cookbook-Second-Edition/blob/master/Chapter04/images/photo-dublin-a-text.jpg`), which includes text over the picture:

```
>>> >>> pytesseract.image_to_string(Image.open('photo-dublin-a-text.jpg'))
'fl\n\nAutomat'
```

More information about Tesseract is available at the following links:

`https://github.com/tesseract-ocr/tesseract`

`https://github.com/madmaze/pytesseract`

 Properly importing files to OCR may require initial image processing for better results. Image processing is out of scope for the objectives of this book, but you may use OpenCV, which is more powerful than `Pillow`. You can process a file and then open it with `Pillow`: `http://opencv-python-tutroals.readthedocs.io/en/latest/py_tutorials/py_tutorials.html`.

See also

- The *Reading text files* recipe, earlier in this chapter, to learn the basics of opening and reading files.
- The *Reading file metadata* recipe, earlier in this chapter, to learn how to get extra information from files.
- The *Crawling and searching directories* recipe, earlier in this chapter, to learn how to search and find files in directories.

Reading PDF files

A common format for documents is **PDF** (**Portable Document Format**). It started as a format to describe a document for any printer, so PDF is a format that ensures that the document will be printed exactly as shown. It has become a powerful standard for sharing documents, especially documents that are final and intended to be read-only.

Getting ready

For this recipe, we are going to use the `PyPDF2` module. We need to add it to our virtual environment:

```
$ echo "PyPDF2==1.26.0" >> requirements.txt
$ pip install -r requirements.txt
```

In the GitHub directory `Chapter03/documents`, we have prepared two documents, `document-1.pdf` and `document-2.pdf`, to use in this recipe. Note they contain mostly Lorem Ipsum text, which is just placeholder.

 Lorem Ipsum text is commonly used in design to show text without needing to create the content before the design. You can learn more about it here: `https://loremipsum.io/`.

They are both the same test document, but the second one can only be opened with a password. The password is `automate`.

How to do it...

1. Import the module:

   ```
   >>> from PyPDF2 import PdfFileReader
   ```

2. Open the `document-1.pdf` file and create a PDF document object. Notice the file needs to be open for the whole reading:

   ```
   >>> file = open('document-1.pdf', 'rb')
   >>> document = PdfFileReader(file)
   ```

3. Get the number of pages of the document and check it is not encrypted:

```
>>> document.numPages
3
>>> document.isEncrypted
False
```

4. Get the creation date from the document info (2018-Jun-24 11:15:18) and discover that it has been created with a Mac Quartz PDFContext:

```
>>> document.documentInfo['/CreationDate']
"D:20180624111518Z00'00'"
>>> document.documentInfo['/Producer']
'Mac OS X 10.13.5 Quartz PDFContext'
```

5. Get the first page and read the text on it:

```
>>> document.pages[0].extractText()
'!A VERY IMPORTANT DOCUMENT \nBy James McCormac CEO Loose Seal Inc
'
```

6. Do the same operation for the second page (redacted here):

```
>>> document.pages[1].extractText()
'"!This is an example of a test document that is stored in PDF
format. It contains some \nsentences to describe what it is and
the it has lore ipsum text.\n!"\nLorem ipsum dolor sit amet,
consectetur adipiscing elit. ...$'
```

7. Close the file and open document-2.pdf:

```
>>> file.close()
>>> file = open('document-2.pdf', 'rb')
>>> document = PdfFileReader(file)
```

8. Check the document is encrypted (it requires a password) and raise an error if we try to access its content:

```
>>> document.isEncrypted
True
>>> document.numPages
...
PyPDF2.utils.PdfReadError: File has not been decrypted
```

9. Decrypt the file and access its content:

```
>>> document.decrypt('automate')
1
```

```
>>> document.numPages
3
>>> document.pages[0].extractText()
'!A VERY IMPORTANT DOCUMENT \nBy James McCormac CEO Loose Seal Inc
'
```

10. Close the file to clean up:

```
>>> file.close()
```

How it works...

Once the document is open, as shown in *step 1* and *step 2* in the *How to do it...* section, the `document` object provides access to the document.

Some useful properties are the number of pages, available in `.numPages`, and each of the pages, available in `.pages`, which can be accessed like a list.

Other data that's accessible is stored in `.documentInfo`, which stores metadata on the creator and when it was created.

 The information in `.documentInfo` is optional and sometimes not up to date. It depends greatly on the tool used to generate the PDF.

Each of the `page` objects can get its text by calling `.extractText()`, which will return all the text contained in the page, as done in *step 5* and *step 6*. This method tries to extract all text, but it has some limitations. For well-structured texts, such as our example, it works quite well, and the resulting text can be processed cleanly. When dealing with text in multiple columns or located in strange positions, it may complicate working with it.

 Notice that the PDF file needs to be open for the whole operation, instead of using a `with` context operator. After leaving the `with` block, the file is closed.

Step 8 and *step 9* show how to deal with encrypted files. You can detect whether a file is encrypted or not with `.isEncrypted`, and then decrypt it with the `.decrypt` method, providing the correct password.

There's more...

PDF is such a flexible format that it is widely used for a variety of purposes, but that also means that it can be difficult to parse and process.

While most PDF files contain text information, it is not uncommon that they contain images of text. This happens when a document has been scanned. In this case, the information is stored as a collection of images, instead of in structured text. This makes it difficult to extract the textual data; we may end up having to resort to methods such as OCR to parse the images into text.

PyPDF2 does not provide a good interface to deal with images. You may need to transform the PDF into a collection of images and then process the images with other tools like `Pillow`. See the *Reading images* recipe for ideas about OCR and the usage of `Pillow`. Most PDF readers can do it, or you can use a command-line tool such as `pdftoppm` (https://linux.die.net/man/1/pdftoppm) or QPDF (see the following).

Some methods of encrypting files may not be understood by PyPDF2. It will generate `NotImplementedError: only algorithm code 1 and 2 are supported`. If that happens, you need to decrypt the PDF externally and open it once it is decrypted. You can use QPDF to create a copy without the password, as follows:

```
$ qpdf --decrypt --password=PASSWORD encrypted.pdf output-decrypted.pdf
```

The full documentation for QPDF is available here: http://qpdf.sourceforge.net/files/qpdf-manual.html. QPDF is available in most package managers as well.

> QPDF is capable of doing a lot of transformations and analyzing PDFs in depth. There are also bindings in Python on a library called `pikepdf` (https://pikepdf.readthedocs.io/en/stable/). This package is more complicated to use than PyPDF2 and it's not as straightforward for text extraction, but it can be useful for other operations such as extracting images from a PDF.

See also

- The *Reading text files* recipe, earlier in this chapter, to learn the basics of opening and reading files.
- The *Crawling and searching directories* recipe, earlier in this chapter, to learn how to search and find files in directories.

Reading Word documents

Word documents (.docx) are another common kind of document that stores mainly text. They are typically generated with Microsoft Office, but other tools also produce compatible files. They are probably the most common format to share files that need to be editable, but they are also common for distributing documents.

We'll see in this recipe how to extract text information from a Word document.

Getting ready

We'll use the python-docx module to read and process Word documents:

```
$ echo "python-docx==0.8.10" >> requirements.txt
$ pip install -r requirements.txt
```

We have prepared a test file, available in the GitHub Chapter04/documents directory, called document-1.docx, which we'll use in this recipe. Note that this document follows the same Lorem Ipsum pattern that was described in the test document for the *Reading PDF files* recipe.

How to do it...

1. Import python-docx:

   ```
   >> import docx
   ```

2. Open the document-1.docx file:

   ```
   >>> doc = docx.Document('document-1.docx')
   ```

3. Check some of the metadata properties stored in core_properties:

   ```
   >> doc.core_properties.title
   'A very important document'
   >>> doc.core_properties.keywords
   'lorem ipsum'
   >>> doc.core_properties.modified
   datetime.datetime(2018, 6, 24, 15, 1, 7)
   ```

4. Check the number of paragraphs:

   ```
   >>> len(doc.paragraphs)
   58
   ```

5. Walk through the paragraphs to detect the ones that contain text. Notice not all text is displayed here:

```
>>> for index, paragraph in enumerate(doc.paragraphs):
...     if paragraph.text:
...         print(index, paragraph.text)
...
30 A VERY IMPORTANT DOCUMENT
31 By James McCormac
32 CEO Loose Seal Inc
34

...
56 TITLE 2
57 ...
```

6. Obtain the text for paragraphs 30 and 31, which correspond to the title and subtitle on the first page:

```
>>> doc.paragraphs[30].text
'A VERY IMPORTANT DOCUMENT'
>>> doc.paragraphs[31].text
'By James McCormac'
```

7. Each of the paragraphs has runs, which are sections of the text with different properties. Check that the first text paragraph and run is in bold and the second is in italics:

```
>>> doc.paragraphs[30].runs[0].italic
>>> doc.paragraphs[30].runs[0].bold
True
>>> doc.paragraphs[31].runs[0].bold
>>> doc.paragraphs[31].runs[0].italic
True
```

8. In this document, most of the paragraphs have only one run, but we have a good example of different runs in paragraph 48. Display its text and the different styles. For example, the word Word is in bold, and ipsum is in italics:

```
>>> [run.text for run in doc.paragraphs[48].runs]
['This is an example of a test document that is stored in ',
'Word', ' format', '. It contains some ', 'sentences', ' to
describe what it is and it has ', 'lore', 'm', ' ipsum', ' text.']
>>> run1 = doc.paragraphs[48].runs[1]
```

```
>>> run1.text
'Word'
>>> run1.bold
True
>>> run2 = doc.paragraphs[48].runs[8]
>>> run2.text
' ipsum'
>>> run2.italic
True
```

How it works...

The most important peculiarity of Word documents is that the data is structured in paragraphs, instead of in pages. The size of the font, line size, and other considerations may make the number of pages change.

Most of the paragraphs are also typically empty, or contain only new lines, tabs, or other whitespace characters. It is a good idea to check when a paragraph is empty and skip it.

In the *How to do it...* section, *step 2* opens the file and *step 3* shows how to access the core properties. These are properties that are defined in Word as document metadata, such as the author or creation date.

 This information needs to be taken with a grain of salt, as a lot of tools that produce Word documents (but not Microsoft Office) won't necessarily fill it. Double-check before using that information.

The paragraphs of the document can be iterated and have their text extracted in raw format, as shown in *step 6*. This is information that doesn't include styling information and is typically the most useful format for processing the data automatically.

If the styling information is required, the runs can be used, as in *step 7* and *step 8*. Each paragraph can contain one or more runs, which are smaller text units that share the same styling. For example, if a sentence is *Word1* word2 **word3**, there will be three runs, one with italicized text (Word1), another with underline (word2), and another with bold (word3). Furthermore, there can be intermediate runs with regular text that contain just whitespaces, making a total of five runs.

The styling can be detected individually for properties such as bold, italic, or underline.

> The division in runs can be quite complicated. Due to the way editors work, it is not uncommon to have `half-words`, a word split into two runs, sometimes with the same properties. Do not rely on the number of runs and analyze the content. In particular, double-check if you're trying to ensure if a part with a particular style is divided in two or more runs. A good example is the words `lore` and `m` (it should be a single word, `lorem`) in *step 8*.

Be aware that because Word documents are produced by so many sources, a lot of properties may not be set up, leaving it to the tool to specify the specifics to use. For example, it is very common to keep the default font, which may mean that the font information on the runs is left empty.

There's more...

Further style information can be found under the `font` attribute, such as `small_caps` or `size`:

```
>>> run2.font.cs_italic
True
>>> run2.font.size
152400
>>> run2.font.small_caps
```

Normally, focusing on the raw text, without paying attention to the style information, is the correct way of parsing. But sometimes, a bold word in a paragraph will have special significance. It may be the header or some particularly meaningful text. Because it's highlighted, it likely is what you're looking for! Keep that in mind when analyzing documents.

You can find the whole `python-docx` documentation here: `https://python-docx.readthedocs.io/en/latest/`.

See also

- The *Reading text files* recipe, earlier in this chapter, to learn the basics of opening and reading text files.
- The *Reading PDF files* recipe, earlier in this chapter, to learn how to process other kinds of document files.

Scanning documents for a keyword

In this recipe, we will apply all the lessons from the previous recipes and search all the files in the directory for a particular keyword. This is a recap of the rest of the recipes in this chapter and includes a script that searches different kinds of files.

Getting ready

Be sure to include the following modules in the `requirements.txt` file and install them into your virtual environment:

```
beautifulsoup4==4.8.2

Pillow==7.0.0

PyPDF2==1.26.0

python-docx==0.8.10
```

Check that the directory to search has the following files (all are available in `https://github.com/PacktPublishing/Python-Automation-Cookbook-Second-Edition/tree/master/Chapter04/documents/`. Note that `file5.pdf` and `file6.pdf` are copies of `document-1.pdf`, for simplicity. `file1.txt` to `file4.txt` are empty files:

```
├── dir
│   ├── file1.txt
│   ├── file2.txt
│   ├── file6.pdf
│   └── subdir
│       ├── file3.txt
│       ├── file4.txt
│       └── file5.pdf
├── document-1.docx
├── document-1.pdf
├── document-2-1.pdf
├── document-2.pdf
├── example_iso.txt
├── example_output_iso.txt
├── example_utf8.txt
├── top_films.csv
└── zen_of_python.txt
```

We've prepared a script, scan.py, that will search for a word in all the .txt, .csv, .pdf, and .docx files. The script is available in the Chapter04 directory of the GitHub repository.

How to do it...

1. Refer to help -h for how to use the scan.py script:

    ```
    $ python scan.py -h
    usage: scan.py [-h] [-w W]

    optional arguments:
     -h, --help show this help message and exit
     -w W Word to search
    ```

2. Search for the word the, which is present in most of the files:

    ```
    $ python scan.py -w the
    >>> Word found in ./documents/top_films.csv
    >>> Word found in ./documents/zen_of_python.txt
    >>> Word found in ./documents/document-1.pdf
    >>> Word found in ./documents/dir/file6.pdf
    >>> Word found in ./documents/dir/subdir/file5.pdf
    ```

3. Search for the word lorem, only present in the PDF and .docx files:

    ```
    $ python scan.py -w lorem
    >>> Word found in ./documents/document-1.pdf
    >>> Word found in ./documents/document-1.docx
    >>> Word found in ./documents/dir/file6.pdf
    >>> Word found in ./documents/dir/subdir/file5.pdf
    ```

4. Search for the word 20£, only present in the two ISO files, with different encodings, and in the UTF8 file:

    ```
    $ python scan.py -w 20£
    >>> Word found in ./documents/example_iso.txt
    >>> Word found in ./documents/example_output_iso.txt
    >>> Word found in ./documents/example_utf8.txt
    ```

5. The search is case-insensitive. Search for the word BETTER, only present in the zen_of_python.txt file:

    ```
    $ python scan.py -w BETTER
    >>> Word found in ./documents/zen_of_python.txt
    ```

How it works...

The `scan.py` file has the following elements:

1. An entry point that parses the input parameters and creates the help for the command line.
2. A main function that walks through the directory and analyzes each of the files found. Based on their extension, it decides whether there's an available function to process and search it.
3. An EXTENSION dictionary, which pairs the extensions with the function to search them.
4. The `search_txt`, `search_csv`, `search_pdf`, and `search_docx` functions, which process and search for the required word for each kind of file.

Keep in mind that file extensions are just file name endings and only a hint of the format of a file. So, they should be taken with a pinch of salt. In the Python standard library, there's the function `mimetypes.guess_type`, which can give an educated guess as to the type of a file. Check the Python documentation here: `https://docs.python.org/3.8/library/mimetypes.html`.

The comparison is case-insensitive, so the search word is transformed into lowercase and, in all comparisons, the text is transformed into lowercase.

Each of the search functions has its own peculiarities:

1. `search_txt` first opens the file to determine its encoding, using `UnicodeDammit`, then it opens the file and reads it line by line. As soon as the word is found, it stops and returns success.
2. `search_csv` opens the file in CSV, and iterates not only line by line, but also column by column. As soon as the word is found, it returns.
3. `search_pdf` opens the file and exits if it is encrypted. If not, it goes page by page, extracting the text and comparing it with the word. It returns as soon as it finds a match.
4. `search_docx` opens the file and iterates through all its paragraphs for a match. As soon as a match is found, the function returns.

There's more...

There are some extra ideas that could be implemented:

*   More search functions could be added. In this chapter, we went through log files and images, as well as text files.

- A similar structure could work for searching for files and returning only the last 10.

- `search_csv` is not sniffing to detect the dialect. This could be added as well.

- Reading is quite sequential. It should be possible to read the files in parallel, analyzing them for faster returns. Be aware that reading files in parallel can lead to sorting issues, as the files won't always be processed in the same order.

See also

- The *Crawling and searching directories* recipe, earlier in this chapter, to learn how to search and find files in directories.

- The *Reading text files* recipe, earlier in this chapter, to learn the basics of opening and reading basic text files.

- The *Dealing with encodings* recipe, earlier in this chapter, to learn how to open files in different encodings.

- The *Reading CSV files* recipe, earlier in this chapter, to learn how to read CSV files.

- The *Reading PDF files* recipe, earlier in this chapter, to learn how to open and read PDF documents.

- The *Reading Word documents* recipe, earlier in this chapter, to learn the basics of reading Word documents.

5

Generating Fantastic Reports

We'll see in this chapter how to write automated documents and perform associated operations, such as dealing with templates in different formats. We will cover simple options like plain text and also options that include richer possibilities, such as Markdown. We'll also cover standard formats such as Word and PDF. These two formats are arguably the most common way of sharing documents and reports across the globe.

In this chapter, we will cover the following recipes:

- Creating a simple report in plain text
- Using templates for reports
- Formatting text in Markdown
- Writing a basic Word document
- Styling a Word document
- Generating structure in Word documents
- Adding pictures to Word documents
- Writing a simple PDF document
- Structuring a PDF
- Aggregating PDF reports
- Watermarking and encrypting a PDF

We will start our report generation with a minimal text-only one.

Creating a simple report in plain text

The simplest possible way to create a report is to generate plain text and store it in a file. Though this may seem simplistic in comparison with other formats that we will see later, don't underestimate its utility. Plain text is the easiest format to share as it will work in virtually all environments, and textual information can go a long way in representing information.

Getting ready

For this recipe, we will generate a brief report in text format about the number of watched movies in the last month and total time. Internally, the original data to be represented will be in the shape of a Python dictionary. The report will include the generation date as well, for reference.

How to do it...

1. Import `datetime`:

   ```
   >>> from datetime import datetime
   ```

2. Create the template with the report in text format:

   ```
   >>> TEMPLATE = '''
   Movies report
   -------------

   Date: {date}
   Movies seen in the last 30 days: {num_movies}
   Total minutes: {total_minutes}
   '''
   ```

3. Create a dictionary with the values to store. Note that this is the data to be presented in the report:

   ```
   >>> data = {
       'date': datetime.utcnow(),
       'num_movies': 3,
       'total_minutes': 376,
   }
   ```

4. Compose the text of the report, adding the data to the template:

   ```
   >>> report = TEMPLATE.format(**data)
   ```

5. Create a new file with the current date and store the report:

```
>>> FILENAME_TMPL = "{date}_report.txt"
>>> filename = FILENAME_TMPL.format(date=data['date'].
strftime('%Y-%m-%d'))
>>> filename
2020-01-26_report.txt
>>> with open(filename, 'w') as file:
...     file.write(report)
```

6. Check the newly created report:

```
$ cat 2020-01-26_report.txt
Movies report
-------------


Date: 2020-01-26 23:40:08.737671
Movies seen in the last 30 days: 3
Total minutes: 376
```

How it works...

Step 2 and *step 3* in the *How to do it…* section set up a simple template and add a dictionary with all the data. Then, in *step 4*, those two are combined into the specific report.

 In *step 4*, the dictionary is combined with a template. Notice that the keys on the dictionary correspond to the parameters on the template. The trick here is to use the double star in the format call to unpack the dictionary, passing each of the keys as a parameter to format().

In *step 5*, the resulting report, a string, is stored in a newly created file. We use the with context manager paired with open(), as introduced in previous chapters. In this case, we generate a new file to write the data. After closing the with block, the file is properly closed and the data is stored on the disk.

 The open modes determine how to open a file, whether it is to read or write, and whether the file is in text or binary. The w mode opens the file to write it, overwriting it if it already exists. Be careful not to delete an existing file by mistake!

Step 6 checks that the file has been created with the proper data.

There's more...

The filename is created with a dynamic date to minimize the probability of overwriting existing files. The date format starting with the year and ending with the day has been selected so that the files are sorted in the correct order.

 The format YYYY-MM-DD for dates is covered in the ISO 8601 standard, which describes different ways to format dates and times. It is a standard format that's easily parsed and supported in Python.

The `with` context manager will close the file, even if there's an exception. In case of an error, the `write` call will raise an `IOError` exception.

 Some of the common problems when writing to disk are problems with permissions, no space left on the hard drive, or a path problem (for instance, trying to write in a non-existent directory).

Note that a file may not be fully committed to disk until it is closed or explicitly flushed. Generally, the operating system will take care of it, but keep this in mind if you're trying to open a file twice, one for read and one for write.

 This can produce an error if the program ends abruptly before being able to flush the data into the hard drive, making data apparently disappear. If required, call `file.flush()` to force the data to be committed to disk. This is useful when writing several times into the same file. Note that at the end of the `with` block, the file will be flushed and closed automatically.

See also

- The *Using templates for reports* recipe, later in this chapter, to learn about HTML templates.
- The *Formatting text in Markdown* recipe, later in this chapter, to learn about Markdown.
- The *Aggregating PDF reports* recipe, later in this chapter, to learn how to produce PDF reports.

Using templates for reports

While plain text can convey a lot of information, to generate better reports, we need a system where styling can be added to the text. Details such as bold text, bullet points, and images can make a difference. As all browsers work with HTML, generating reports in this format is a good option. Everyone is familiar with a browser rendering text.

HTML is a very flexible format that can be used to render rich text and reports. While an HTML template can be managed as pure plain text, doing so is very error prone and tedious. There are tools that allow you to add better handling of structured text and define templates.

This also detaches the template from the code, separating the generation of the data from the representation of that data. The styling of the template can be done separately by specialized designers, making it look great.

Getting ready

The tool used in this recipe, Jinja2, reads a file that contains the template and applies the context to it. The context contains the data to be displayed.

We should start by installing the module:

```
$ echo "jinja2==2.11.1" >> requirements.txt
$ pip install -r requirements.txt
```

Jinja2 uses its own syntax, which is a mixture of HTML and Python. It is aimed at HTML documents, so it easily performs operations such as correctly escaping special characters.

In the GitHub repository, `https://github.com/PacktPublishing/Python-Automation-Cookbook-Second-Edition/tree/master/Chapter05`, we've included a template file called `jinja_template.html` with the template to use.

How to do it...

1. Import the Jinja2 `Template` and `datetime`:

   ```
   >>> from jinja2 import Template
   >>> from datetime import datetime
   ```

2. Read the template from the files into memory:

   ```
   >>> with open('jinja_template.html') as file:
   ...     template = Template(file.read())
   ```

3. Create a context with the data to be displayed:

```
>>> context = {
...     'date': datetime.now(),
...     'movies': ['Casablanca', 'The Sound of Music', 'Vertigo'],
...     'total_minutes': 404,
... }
```

4. Render the template and write a new file, `report.html`, with the following result:

```
>>> with open('report.html', 'w') as file:
...     file.write(template.render(context))
```

5. Exit the Python interpreter and open the `report.html` file in a browser:

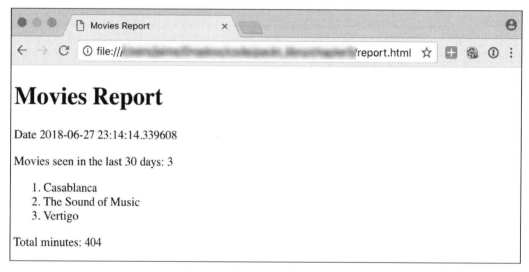

Figure 5.1: The rendered report.html

How it works...

Steps 2 and *4* in the *How to do it…* section are very straightforward: they read the template and render and save the resulting report.

As seen in *steps 3* and *4*, the main task is to create a context dictionary with the information to be displayed. The template then renders that information, as shown in *step 5*. Let's take a look at `jinja_template.html`:

```
<!DOCTYPE html>
<html lang="en">
```

```
<head>
    <title> Movies Report</title>
</head>
<body>
    <h1>Movies Report</h1>
    <p>Date {{date}}</p>
    <p>Movies seen in the last 30 days: {{movies|length}}</p>
    <ol>
        {% for movie in movies %}
        <li>{{movie}}</li>
        {% endfor %}
    </ol>
    <p>Total minutes: {{total_minutes}} </p>
</body>
</html>
```

Most of it is replacing the context values defined between curly brackets, such as {{total_minutes}}.

Note the tag, {% for ... %} / {% endfor %}, which defines a loop. That allows for a very Pythonic way to generate multiple rows or elements in a list.

Filters can be applied to the variables to modify them. In this case, the length filter is applied to the movies list to obtain the size using the pipe symbol, as shown in {{movies|length}}.

There's more...

Other than the {% for %} tag, there's also an {% if %} tag, allowing it to display conditionally:

```
{% if movies|length > 5 %}
  Wow, so many movies this month!
{% else %}
  Regular number of movies
{% endif %}
```

There are a good number of defined filters already (see the whole list here: http://jinja.pocoo.org/docs/2.11/templates/#list-of-builtin-filters). It is also possible to define custom ones.

Note that you can add a lot of processing and logic to the template using filters. While a little bit is fine, try to limit the amount of logic in the template. Most of the calculations for data to be displayed should be done beforehand, leaving the template to just display values. This makes the context very straightforward and simplifies the template, allowing for changes.

When dealing with HTML files, it is good to auto-escape the variables. This means that special characters could be interpreted as part as the HTML syntax instead of verbatim text; for example, the < character will be replaced by the equivalent HTML code to be properly displayed on an HTML page. To do so, create the template with the `autoescape` parameter. Check the difference here:

```
>>> Template('{{variable}}', autoescape=False).render({'variable': '<'})
'<'
>>> Template('{{variable}}', autoescape=True).render({'variable': '<'})
'&lt;'
```

Escaping can be applied to each variable with the `e` filter (meaning *escape*) and unapplied with the `safe` filter (meaning it is safe to render as it is).

Jinja2 templates are extensible, meaning that you can create a `base_template.html` file and then extend it, changing some of the elements. You can include other files as well, partitioning and separating different sections. Refer to the full documentation for further details.

 Jinja2 is very powerful and allows us to create complex HTML templates, and also in other formats such as LaTeX or JavaScript, though this requires configuring. I encourage you to read the whole documentation and have a look at all its capabilities!

The whole Jinja2 documentation can be found here: `http://jinja.pocoo.org/docs/2.11/`.

See also

- The *Creating a simple report in plain text* recipe, earlier in this chapter, to learn the basics of creating plain text reports.

- The *Formatting text in Markdown* recipe, later in this chapter, to learn Markdown, an alternative template format.

Formatting text in Markdown

Markdown is a very popular markup language used to create plain text that can be converted into styled HTML. It is a good way of structuring documents in a way that they are still easy to read in plain text format, while being able to properly style them in HTML.

In this recipe, we'll see how to transform a Markdown document into styled HTML using Python.

Getting ready

We should start by installing the `mistune` module, which will compile Markdown documents into HTML:

```
$ echo "mistune==0.8.4" >> requirements.txt
$ pip install -r requirements.txt
```

In the GitHub repository, there is a template file called `markdown_template.md` with a template of the report to generate.

How to do it...

1. Import `mistune` and `datetime`:

   ```
   >>> import mistune
   >>> from datetime import datetime
   ```

2. Read the template from the file:

   ```
   >>> with open('markdown_template.md') as file:
   ..      template = file.read()
   ```

3. Set up the context of the data to be included in the report:

   ```
   >>> context = {
   ...     'date': datetime.now(),
   ...     'pmovies': ['Casablanca', 'The Sound of Music', 'Vertigo'],
   ...     'total_minutes': 404,
   ... }
   ```

4. As movies need to be displayed as bullet points, we will transform the list into a suitable Markdown bullet list. Also, we will store the number of movies:

   ```
   >>> context['num_movies'] = len(context['pmovies'])
   >>> context['movies'] = '\n'.join('* {}'.format(movie) for movie
   in context['pmovies'])
   ```

5. Render the template and compile the resulting Markdown into HTML:

```
>>> md_report = template.format(**context)
>>> report = mistune.markdown(md_report)
```

6. Finally, store the resulting report in the `report.html` file:

```
>>> with open('report.html', 'w') as file:
...     file.write(report)
```

7. Open the `report.html` file in a browser to check the result:

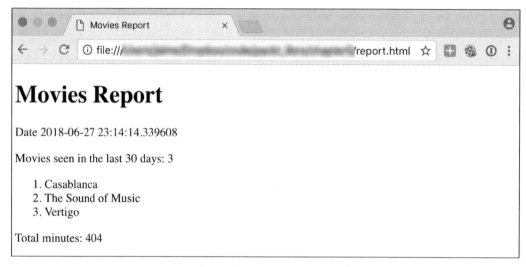

Figure 5.2: The rendered report, as seen in a browser

How it works...

Steps 2 and *3* in the *How do it...* section prepare the template and the data to be displayed. In *step 4*, extra information is produced—the number of movies, which is derivative from the `movies` element. The `movies` element is then transformed into a valid Markdown element from a Python list. Note the new lines and the initial `*`, which will be rendered as a bullet point:

```
>>> '\n'.join('* {}'.format(movie) for movie in context['pmovies'])
'* Casablanca\n* The Sound of Music\n* Vertigo'
```

In *step 5*, the template is generated in Markdown format. The format is very readable in this raw form, which is the strong point of Markdown:

```
Movies Report
=======


Date: 2018-06-29 20:47:18.930655


Movies seen in the last 30 days: 3


* Casablanca

* The Sound of Music

* Vertigo


Total minutes: 404
```

Then, using `mistune`, the report is transformed into HTML and stored in a file in *step 6*.

There's more...

Learning Markdown is extremely useful, as it is supported by many common web pages as a way of enabling text input that is easy to read and write and can render to a styled format. Some examples are GitHub, Stack Overflow, and most blogging platforms.

 There is actually more than one kind of Markdown. This is because the official definition was limited or ambiguous, and there was little interest in clarifying or extending it. This led to several implementations that are slightly different, such as GitHub Flavored Markdown, MultiMarkdown, and CommonMark.

The text in Markdown is quite readable, but in case you need to interactively see how it will look, you can use the Dillinger online editor at `https://dillinger.io/`.

`Mistune` full docs are available here: `http://mistune.readthedocs.io/en/latest/`.

The full Markdown syntax can be found at `https://daringfireball.net/projects/markdown/syntax`, and a good cheat sheet with the most frequently used elements can be found at `https://www.markdownguide.org/cheat-sheet/`.

See also

- The *Creating a simple report in pain text* recipe, earlier in this chapter, to learn the basics of creating plain text reports.

- The *Using templates for reports* recipe, earlier in this chapter, to learn how to create templates directly in HTML.

Writing a basic Word document

Microsoft (MS) Office is one of the most common pieces of software, and MS Word in particular is almost the de facto standard for editable documents. Generating docx documents is possible with automated scripts, which may help distribute reports in a format that's easily shared in many businesses.

In this recipe, we will learn how to generate a full Word document programmatically.

Getting ready

We'll use the python-docx module to process Word documents:

```
$ echo "python-docx==0.8.10" >> requirements.txt
$ pip install -r requirements.txt
```

How to do it...

1. Import python-docx and datetime:

```
>>> import docx
>>> from datetime import datetime
```

2. Define the context with the data to be stored in the report:

```
>>> context = {
...     'date': datetime.now(),
...     'movies': ['Casablanca', 'The Sound of Music', 'Vertigo'],
...     'total_minutes': 404,
... }
```

3. Create a new docx document and include a heading, Movies Report:

```
>>> document = docx.Document()
>>> document.add_heading('Movies Report', 0)
```

4. Add a paragraph describing the date, with the date in italics:

```
>>> paragraph = document.add_paragraph('Date: ')
>>> paragraph.add_run(str(context['date'])).italic = True
```

5. Add information about the number of movies seen in a different paragraph:

```
>>> paragraph = document.add_paragraph('Movies see in the last 30
days: ')
>>> paragraph.add_run(str(len(context['movies']))).italic = True
```

6. Add each of the movies as a bullet point:

```
>>> for movie in context['movies']:
...      document.add_paragraph(movie, style='List Bullet')
```

7. Add the total minutes and save the file, as follows:

```
>>> paragraph = document.add_paragraph('Total minutes: ')
>>> paragraph.add_run(str(context['total_minutes'])).italic = True
>>> document.save('word-report.docx')
```

8. Close the interpreter and open the word-report.docx file to check it:

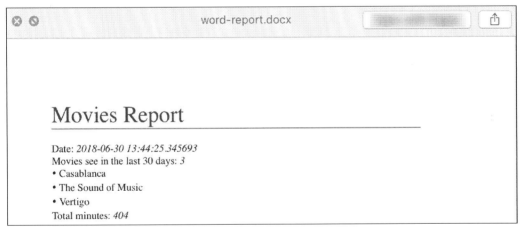

Figure 5.3: The content of word-report.docx

How it works...

The basics of a Word document is that it is divided into paragraphs, and each of the paragraphs is divided into runs. A run is a part of a paragraph that shares the same style.

Steps 1 and *2* in the *How to do it…* section are preparation for importing and defining the data that's going to be stored in the report.

In *step 3*, the document is created and a heading with the proper title is added. This automatically styles the text.

Dealing with paragraphs is introduced in *step 4*. A new paragraph is created based on the text with the default style, but new runs can be added to change it. Here, we added the first run with the text Date:, but another run is added after that with the specific time and the format changed to *italics*.

In *steps 5* and *6*, we can see information about the movies. The first part stores the number of movies, in a similar format to *step 4*. After that, the movies are added to the report one by one, and the style is set up to be bullet points with the style "*List Bullet*."

Finally, *step 7* stores the total run time of all movies, in a similar way to *step 4*, and stores the document in a file.

There's more...

If you need to introduce extra lines in the document for formatting purposes, add empty paragraphs.

Due to the way that the MS Word format works, there's no easy way of determining how many pages a document will have. You may need to run some tests on sizes, especially if you're generating dynamic documents.

 Even if you generate docx files, having MS Office is not necessary. There are other applications that can open and deal with these files, including free alternatives such as LibreOffice.

The whole python-docx documentation is available here: https://python-docx.readthedocs.io/en/latest/.

See also

- The *Styling a Word document* recipe, later in this chapter, to learn how format a document.
- The *Generating structure in Word documents* recipe, later in this chapter, to learn how to create sections and other separators in Word documents.

Styling a Word document

A Word document can contain text with almost no format, but we can also add styling to help us understand the displayed content. Word has a set of predefined styles that can be used to variate the document and highlight the important parts of it.

Getting ready

We'll use the `python-docx` module to process Word documents:

```
$ echo "python-docx==0.8.10" >> requirements.txt
$ pip install -r requirements.txt
```

How to do it...

1. Import the `python-docx` module:

    ```
    >>> import docx
    ```

2. Create a new document:

    ```
    >>> document = docx.Document()
    ```

3. Add a paragraph that highlights some words in different ways (*Italics*, **bold**, and <u>underline</u>):

    ```
    >>> p = document.add_paragraph('This shows different kinds of
    emphasis: ')
    >>> p.add_run('bold').bold = True
    >>> p.add_run(', ')
    <docx.text.run.Run object at ...>
    >>> p.add_run('italics').italic = True
    >>> p.add_run(' and ')
    <docx.text.run.Run object at ...>
    >>> p.add_run('underline').underline = True
    >>> p.add_run('.')
    <docx.text.run.Run object at ...>
    ```

4. Create some paragraphs and style them with default styles, such as `List Bullet`, `List Number`, or `Quote`:

    ```
    >>> document.add_paragraph('a few', style='List Bullet')
    <docx.text.paragraph.Paragraph object at ...>
    >>> document.add_paragraph('bullet', style='List Bullet')
    ```

```
<docx.text.paragraph.Paragraph object at ...>
>>> document.add_paragraph('points', style='List Bullet')
<docx.text.paragraph.Paragraph object at ...>
>>>
>>> document.add_paragraph('Or numbered', style='List Number')
<docx.text.paragraph.Paragraph object at ...>
>>> document.add_paragraph('that will', style='List Number')
<docx.text.paragraph.Paragraph object at ...>
>>> document.add_paragraph('that keep', style='List Number')
<docx.text.paragraph.Paragraph object at ...>
>>> document.add_paragraph('count', style='List Number')
<docx.text.paragraph.Paragraph object at ...>
>>>
>>> document.add_paragraph('And finish with a quote',
style='Quote')
<docx.text.paragraph.Paragraph object at 0x10d2336d8>
```

5. Create a paragraph in a different font and size. We'll use `Arial` font and a point size of `25`. The paragraph will be aligned to the right:

```
>>> from docx.shared import Pt
>>> from docx.enum.text import WD_ALIGN_PARAGRAPH
>>> p = document.add_paragraph('This paragraph will have a manual
styling and right alignment')
>>> p.runs[0].font.name = 'Arial'
>>> p.runs[0].font.size = Pt(25)
>>> p.alignment = WD_ALIGN_PARAGRAPH.RIGHT
```

6. Save the document:

```
>>> document.save('word-report-style.docx')
```

7. Open the `word-report-style.docx` document to verify its content:

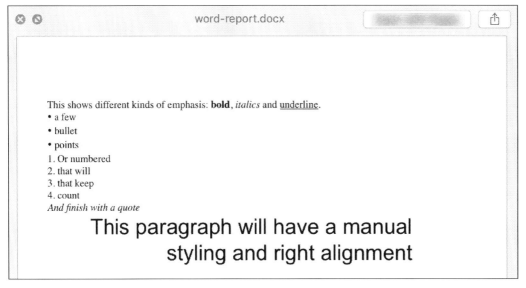

Figure 5.4: The final word-report-style.docx document

How it works...

After creating the document in *step 1*, *step 2* from the *How to do it...* section adds a paragraph with several runs. In Word, a paragraph can contain multiple runs, which are smaller parts that may have different styles. In general, any format change related to individual words will be applied to a run, while a change that affects the whole paragraph will be applied to the paragraph object.

Each of the runs are created, by default, with the Normal style. Any attribute of .bold, .italic, or .underline can be changed to True to set up whether the run should be in a proper style or a combination of these. A value of False will deactivate it, while a None value will apply the configured default.

Note that the proper word in this protocol is *italic*, and not *italics*. Setting the property to italics won't have any effect, but won't display an error either.

Step 4 shows how to apply some of the default styles for paragraphs; in this case, to show bullet points, numbered lists, and quotes. There are more included styles, and these can be found on this page of the following documentation: https:// python-docx.readthedocs.io/en/latest/user/styles-understanding. html?highlight=List%20Bullet#paragraph-styles-in-default-template. Try to find out which ones work best for your document.

The `.font` property of a run is shown in *step 5*. This allows you to manually set up a specific font and size. Note that the size needs to be specified using the proper `Pt` (points) object.

 Points are common on regular Word documents, but sometimes it can be difficult to know the exact size. Don't be afraid to perform some tests and experiment with them.

The alignment of the paragraph is set up in the `paragraph` object, and uses a constant to define whether it is left, right, center, or justified. All alignment options can be found here: `https://python-docx.readthedocs.io/en/latest/api/enum/WdAlignParagraph.html`.

Finally, *step 7* saves the file to the filesystem.

There's more...

The `font` attribute can also be used to set up more properties of the text, such as small caps, shadow, emboss, or strikethrough. The whole range of possibilities is shown in the following documentation: `https://python-docx.readthedocs.io/en/latest/api/text.html#docx.text.run.Font`.

Another available option is to change the color of the text:

```
>>> from docx.shared import RGBColor
>>> DARK_BLUE = RGBColor.from_string('1b3866')
>>> run.font.color.rbg = DARK_BLUE
```

The color can be described in the usual hex format from a string. Try to define all the colors as named constants to ensure they are all consistent, and limit yourself to a maximum of three colors in a report so as not to distract from the content.

You can use an online color picker, such as this one: `https://www.w3schools.com/colors/colors_picker.asp`. Remember to not use the # at the beginning. If you need to generate a palette, it's a good idea to use tools such as `https://coolors.co/` to generate good combinations.

The whole `python-docx` documentation is available here: `https://python-docx.readthedocs.io/en/latest/`.

See also

- The *Writing a basic Word document* recipe, earlier in this chapter, to learn the basics of how to create a Word document.

- The *Generating structure in Word documents* recipe, next, to learn how to create sections and other separators in Word documents.

Generating structure in Word documents

To create proper professional reports, they need to be properly structured. An MS Word document doesn't have the concept of *a page*, as it works in paragraphs. But we can introduce breaks and sections to properly divide a document.

We'll see in this recipe how to create a structured Word document, introducing breaks to create sections.

Getting ready

We'll use the `python-docx` module to process Word documents:

```
$ echo "python-docx==0.8.10" >> requirements.txt
$ pip install -r requirements.txt
```

How to do it...

1. Import the `python-docx` module:

```
>>> import docx
```

2. Create a new document:

```
>>> document = docx.Document()
```

3. Create a paragraph that has a line break:

```
>>> p = document.add_paragraph('This is the start of the
paragraph')
>>> run = p.add_run()
>>> run.add_break(docx.text.run.WD_BREAK.LINE)
>>> p.add_run('And now this in a different line')
>>> p.add_run(". Even if it's on the same paragraph.")
```

4. Create a page break and write a paragraph:

```
>>> document.add_page_break()
>>> document.add_paragraph('This appears in a new page')
```

5. Create a new section, which will be on landscape pages:

```
>>> section = document.add_section( docx.enum.section.WD_SECTION.
NEW_PAGE)
>>> section.orientation = docx.enum.section.WD_ORIENT.LANDSCAPE
>>> section.page_height, section.page_width = section.page_width,
section.page_height
>>> document.add_paragraph('This is part of a new landscape
section')
```

6. Create another section, reverting to portrait orientation:

```
>>> section = document.add_section( docx.enum.section.WD_SECTION.
NEW_PAGE)
>>> section.orientation = docx.enum.section.WD_ORIENT.PORTRAIT
>>> section.page_height, section.page_width = section.page_width,
section.page_height
>>> document.add_paragraph('In this section, recover the portrait
orientation')
```

7. Save the document:

```
>>> document.save('word-report-structure.docx')
```

8. Check the result by opening the document and checking the resulting sections:

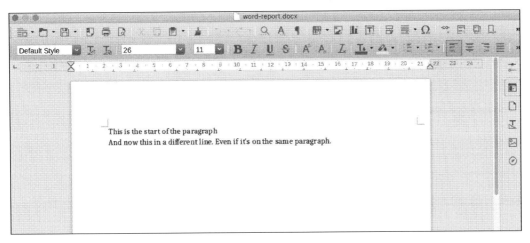

Figure 5.5: The rendered first page

Check the new page:

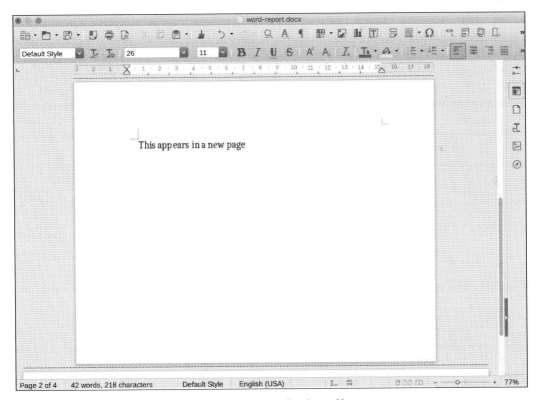

Figure 5.6: The rendered new file

Check for a landscape section:

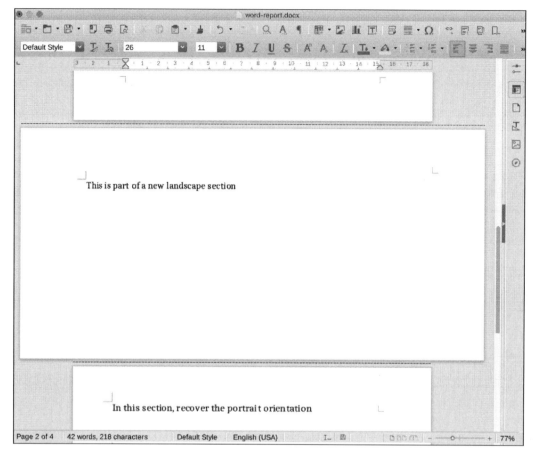

Figure 5.7: The rendered landscape section

Then, go back to portrait orientation:

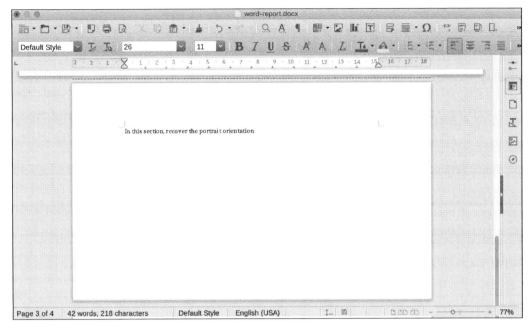

Figure 5.8: The new page, after going back to portrait orientation

How it works...

After creating the document in *step 2* in the *How to do it…* section, we add a paragraph for the first section. Notice that the document starts with a section. The paragraph introduces a line break in the middle of the paragraph.

> There is a small difference between a line break in a paragraph and a new paragraph, though for most uses, it is quite similar. Try to experiment with them.

A page break is introduced in *step 3*, without changing the section.

Step 4 creates a new section on a new page. *Step 5* also changes the orientation of the page to landscape in the section. In *step 6*, a new section is introduced, and the orientation reverts to portrait.

 Note that when changing the orientation, we also need to swap the width and height. Each new section inherits the properties from the previous one, so this swapping needs to happen in *step 6* as well.

Finally, the document is saved in *step 7*.

There's more...

A section mandates page composition, including the orientation and size of the page. The size of the page can be changed using the length options, such as Inches or Cm:

```
>>> from docx.shared import Inches, Cm
>>> section.page_height = Inches(10)
>>> section.page_width = Cm(20)
```

The page margins can also be defined in the same way:

```
>>> section.left_margin = Inches(1.5)
>>> section.right_margin = Cm(2.81)
>>> section.top_margin = Inches(1)
>>> section.bottom_margin = Cm(2.54)
```

Sections can also be forced to start not only on the next page, but on the next odd page, which will look better when printing on two sides:

```
>>> document.add_section( docx.enum.section.WD_SECTION.ODD_PAGE)
```

The whole python-docx documentation is available here: https://python-docx.readthedocs.io/en/latest/.

See also

- The *Writing a basic Word document* recipe, earlier in this chapter, to learn the basics of how to create a Word document.

- The *Styling a Word document* recipe, earlier in this chapter, to learn how to add format to the document.

Adding pictures to Word documents

Word documents can include images to show graphs or any other kind of extra information. Adding an image is a great way of creating rich reports.

> Any experienced Word user will know how frustrating it can be to properly position an image, as the surrounding environment can make it change. Keep in mind that, while positioning the image programmatically can help, as it will be included in a specific place, changing the surrounding paragraphs can change how it gets rendered.

In this recipe, we'll learn how to attach an existing image file to a Word document.

Getting ready

We'll use the `python-docx` module to process Word documents:

```
$ echo "python-docx==0.8.10" >> requirements.txt
$ pip install -r requirements.txt
```

We need to prepare an image to include in the document. We'll use the file in GitHub at `https://github.com/PacktPublishing/Python-Automation-Cookbook-Second-Edition/blob/master/Chapter04/images/photo-dublin-a1.jpg`, which shows a view of Dublin. You can download it on the command line, like this:

```
$ wget https://github.com/PacktPublishing/Python-Automation-Cookbook-Second-Edition/blob/master/Chapter04/images/photo-dublin-a1.jpg
```

How to do it...

1. Import the `python-docx` module:

    ```
    >>> import docx
    ```

2. Create a new document:

    ```
    >>> document = docx.Document()
    ```

3. Create a paragraph with some text:

    ```
    >>> document.add_paragraph('This is a document that includes a
    picture taken in Dublin')
    ```

4. Add the image:

    ```
    >>> image = document.add_picture('photo-dublin-a1.jpg')
    ```

5. Scale the image properly to fit on the page (14 x 10 cm):

    ```
    >>> from docx.shared import Cm
    >>> image.width = Cm(14)
    >>> image.height = Cm(10)
    ```

6. The image has been added to a new paragraph. Align it to the center and add descriptive text:

    ```
    >>> paragraph = document.paragraphs[-1]
    >>> from docx.enum.text import WD_ALIGN_PARAGRAPH
    >>> paragraph.alignment = WD_ALIGN_PARAGRAPH.CENTER
    >>> paragraph.add_run().add_break()
    >>> paragraph.add_run('A picture of Dublin')
    ```

7. Add a new paragraph with extra text, and save the document:

    ```
    >>> document.add_paragraph('Keep adding text after the image')
    <docx.text.paragraph.Paragraph object at XXX>
    >>> document.save('report.docx')
    ```

8. Check the result:

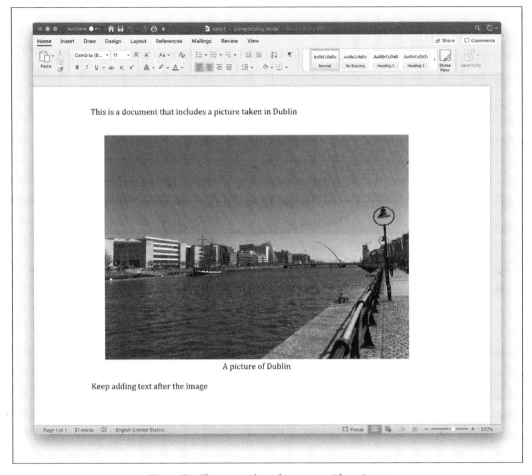

Figure 5.9: The report.docx document with a picture

How it works...

The first few steps (*steps 1* to *3* in the *How to do it…* section) create the document and add some text.

Step 4 adds the image from the file, while *step 5* resizes it into a manageable size. By default, the image is too big.

Keep in mind the proportion of the image when resizing. Note that you can also use other measures such as *Inch*, which is defined in *shared* as well.

Inserting the image creates a new paragraph as well, so the paragraph can be styled to align the image or to add more text, such as a reference or description. The paragraph is obtained in *step 6* through the `document.paragraph` property. The last paragraph is obtained and styled properly, aligning it to the center. A new line and a `run` with descriptive text are added.

Step 7 adds extra text after the image and saves the document.

There's more...

The size of the image can be changed, but as we saw previously, the proportion of the image needs to be calculated if it changes. The resizing may end up not being perfect if done by approximation, as in *step 5* from the *How to do it...* section.

 Notice that the image does not have a perfect ratio of 10:14. Instead, it is 10:13.33. For a photograph, that may be good enough, but for images sensitive to proportion changes, such as a chart, it may require extra care.

To obtain the proper ratio, divide the height by the width and then scale properly:

```
>>> image = document.add_picture('photo-dublin-a1.jpg')
>>> image.height / image.width
0.75
>>> RELATION = image.height / image.width
>>> image.width = Cm(12)
>>> image.height = Cm(12 * RELATION)
```

If you need to transform the values to a particular size, you can use the cm, inches, mm, or pt attributes:

```
>>> image.width.cm
12.0
>>> image.width.mm
120.0
>>> image.width.inches
```

```
4.724409448818897
>>> image.width.pt
340.15748031496065
```

The whole `python-docx` documentation is available here: `https://python-docx.readthedocs.io/en/latest/`.

See also

- The *Writing a basic Word document* recipe, earlier in this chapter, to learn the basics of working with Word documents.
- The *Styling a Word document* recipe, earlier in this chapter, to learn how to add rich format to the document.
- The *Generating structure in Word documents* recipe, earlier in this chapter, to learn how to add sections and other separators to the documents.

Writing a simple PDF document

PDF files are a common format for shared reports. The main characteristic of PDF documents is that they define exactly how the document is going to look and be printed, and they are read-only after being produced. This makes them very straightforward to use to transmit information.

In this recipe, we'll see how to write a simple PDF report using Python.

Getting ready

We'll use the `fpdf` module to create PDF documents:

```
$ echo "fpdf==1.7.2" >> requirements.txt
$ pip install -r requirements.txt
```

How to do it...

1. Import the `fpdf` module:

   ```
   >>> import fpdf
   ```

2. Create a document:

   ```
   >>> document = fpdf.FPDF()
   ```

3. Define the font and color for a title, and add the first page:

   ```
   >>> document.set_font('Times', 'B', 14)
   ```

```
>>> document.set_text_color(19, 83, 173)
>>> document.add_page()
```

4. Write the title of the document:

```
>>> document.cell(0, 5, 'PDF test document')
>>> document.ln()
```

5. Write a long paragraph:

```
>>> document.set_font('Times', '', 12)
>>> document.set_text_color(0)
>>> document.multi_cell(0, 5, 'This is an example of a long
paragraph. ' * 10)
[]
>>> document.ln()
```

6. Write another long paragraph:

```
>>> document.multi_cell(0, 5, 'Another long paragraph. Lorem ipsum
dolor sit amet, consectetur adipiscing elit.' * 20)
[]
```

7. Save the document:

```
>>> document.output('report.pdf')
''
```

8. Check the `report.pdf` document:

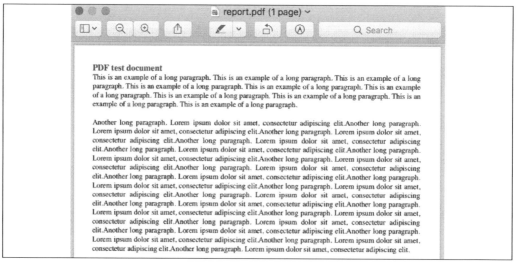

Figure 5.10: The content of report.pdf

How it works...

The `fpdf` module creates a PDF document and allows us to write in it.

> Due to the peculiarities of a PDF, the best way to think about it is to imagine a cursor writing in the document and moving to the next position, similar to a typewriter.

The first operations are to specify the font and size to use, and then add the first page. This is done in *step 3*. The first font is in bold (second argument, `'B'`) and in a bigger font than the rest of the document. This makes it a title. The color is also set up with `.set_text_color`, in RGB components.

> The text can also be styled in italics with *I* and underlined with <u>U</u>. You can combine them, so **BI** will produce text in both bold and italic.

The `.cell` call creates a box of text with the specified text. The first couple of parameters are the width and height. Width `0` uses the whole space up to the right margin. Height `5` (mm) is adequate for a size `12` font. The call to `.ln` introduces a new line.

To write a multiline paragraph, we use the `.multi_cell` method. Its parameters are the same as `.cell`. Two paragraphs are written in *steps 5* and *6*. Notice the change in font previously, to distinguish the title from the body of the report. `.set_text_color` is called with a single argument to set up the color in grayscale. In this case, it is in black using `0`.

> Using `cell` for long text will make it go over the margin and off the page. Use it only for text that will fit in a single line. You can find the size of a string with `.get_string_width`.

The document is saved to disk in *step 7*.

There's more...

Pages are added automatically if a `multi_cell` operation occupies all space available in a page. Calling `.add_page` will move to a new page.

You can use any of the default fonts (Courier, Helvetica, and Times), or add an extra font using .add_font. Check the documentation for more details: http://pyfpdf.readthedocs.io/en/latest/reference/add_font/index.html.

 The Symbol and ZapfDingbats fonts are also available, but represent symbols. This could be useful if you need to display special characters, but be sure to test the result before using them. The rest of the default fonts should include your necessities for serif, sans serif, and fixed-width cases. In PDFs, the fonts used will be embedded in the document, so they'll always be displayed correctly.

Keep the height consistent throughout the document, at least between text of the same size. Define a constant you're comfortable with, and use it for the whole content:

```
>>> BODY_TEXT_HEIGHT = 5
>>> document.multi_cell(0, BODY_TEXT_HEIGHT, text)
```

By default, the text will be justified, but that can be changed. Use the align argument with J (justified), C (center), R (right), or L (left). For example, this produces text aligned to the left:

```
>>> document.multi_cell(0, BODY_TEXT_HEIGHT, text, align='L')
```

The full FPDF documentation can be found here: http://pyfpdf.readthedocs.io/en/latest/index.html.

See also

- *Structuring a PDF*, next, to learn how to add separators to a PDF document.
- *Aggregating PDF reports*, later in this chapter, to learn how to merge different PDF documents into one.
- *Watermarking and encrypting a PDF*, later in this chapter, to learn how to add security measures to the document.

Structuring a PDF

Some elements can be automatically generated when creating a PDF to add a better look and structure to your elements. In this recipe, we'll see how to add a header and footer, and how to create links to other parts of the document.

Getting ready

We'll use the `fpdf` module to create PDF documents:

```
$ echo "fpdf==1.7.2" >> requirements.txt
$ pip install -r requirements.txt
```

How to do it...

The `structuring_pdf.py` script is available in GitHub here: `https://github.com/PacktPublishing/Python-Automation-Cookbook-Second-Edition/blob/master/Chapter05/structuring_pdf.py`. The most relevant bits are displayed here:

```python
import fpdf
from random import randint

class StructuredPDF(fpdf.FPDF):
    LINE_HEIGHT = 5

    def footer(self):
        self.set_y(-15)
        self.set_font('Times', 'I', 8)
        page_number = 'Page {number}/{{nb}}'.format(number=self.page_no())
        self.cell(0, self.LINE_HEIGHT, page_number, 0, 0, 'R')

    def chapter(self, title, paragraphs):
        self.add_page()
        link = self.title_text(title)
        page = self.page_no()
        for paragraph in paragraphs:
            self.multi_cell(0, self.LINE_HEIGHT, paragraph)
            self.ln()

        return link, page

    def title_text(self, title):
        self.set_font('Times', 'B', 15)
        self.cell(0, self.LINE_HEIGHT, title)
```

```python
        self.set_font('Times', '', 12)
        self.line(10, 17, 110, 17)
        link = self.add_link()
        self.set_link(link)
        self.ln()
        self.ln()

        return link

    def get_full_line(self, head, tail, fill):
        ...
    def toc(self, links):
        self.add_page()
        self.title_text('Table of contents')
        self.set_font('Times', 'I', 12)

        for title, page, link in links:
            line = self.get_full_line(title, page, '.')
            self.cell(0, self.LINE_HEIGHT, line, link=link)
            self.ln()


LOREM_IPSUM = ...

def main():
    document = StructuredPDF()
    document.alias_nb_pages()
    links = []
    num_chapters = randint(5, 40)
    for index in range(1, num_chapters):
        chapter_title = 'Chapter {}'.format(index)
        num_paragraphs = randint(10, 15)
        link, page = document.chapter(chapter_title,
```

```
                                    [LOREM_IPSUM] * num_
    paragraphs)
          links.append((chapter_title, page, link))


    document.toc(links)
    document.output('report.pdf')
```

1. Run the script. It will generate the `report.pdf` file, which contains some
    chapters and a table of contents. Note that the specific content it generates is
    somehow random, so the specific numbers will vary each time you run it:

    ```
    $ python3 structuring_pdf.py
    ```

    Check the result. Here is a sample:

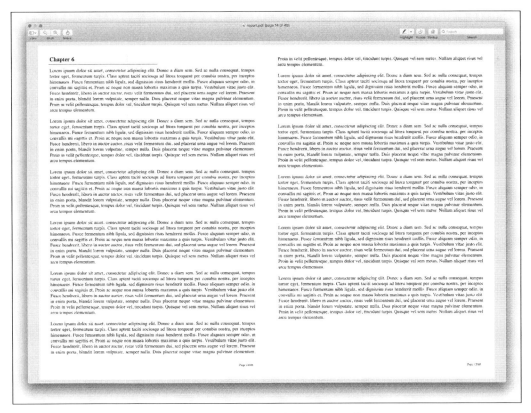

Figure 5.11: Two pages inside report.pdf

Check the table of contents at the end:

report.pdf (page 49 of 49)

Q Search

Table of contents

Page 49/49

Figure 5.12: The table of contents at the end of report.pdf

How it works...

Let's take a look at each of the elements of the script.

StructuredPDF defines a class that inherits from FPDF. This is useful to overwrite the footer method, which creates a footer for each of the pages at generation time. It also helps simplify the code in main.

The main function creates the document. It starts the document and adds each of the chapters, collecting their link information. Finally, it calls the toc method to generate a table of contents using the link information.

The text to be stored is generated by multiplying the LOREM_IPSUM text, which is a placeholder.

The chapter method first prints a title section, and then adds each of the paragraphs. It collects the page number the chapter starts on and the link returned by the title_ text method to return them.

The title_text method writes the text in bigger and bolder text. Then, it adds a line to separate the title from the body of the chapter. It generates and sets a link object pointing to the current page in the following lines:

```
link = self.add_link()
self.set_link(link)
```

This link will be used in the table of contents to add a clickable element that points to this chapter.

The footer method automatically adds a footer to each page. It sets a smaller font, and it adds text with the current page (obtained through page_no) and uses {nb}, which will be replaced with the total number of pages.

> The call to .alias_nb_pages() in main ensures {nb} is replaced when the document is generated.

Finally, the table of contents is generated in the toc method. It writes the title and adds all the referenced links that have been collected as the link, page, and chapter name, which is all the info required.

There's more...

Notice the use of randint to add a bit of randomness to the document. This call, available in Python's standard library, returns a random number between the defined maximum and minimum. Both are included.

The get_full_line method generates a properly sized line for the table of contents. It takes a start (the name of the chapter) and end (the page number), and adds the number of fill characters (dots) until the line has the proper width (120 mm).

To calculate the size of the text, the script calls get_string_width, which takes into account the font and the size.

Link objects can be used to point to a specific page, instead of the current one, and also not to the start of the page. To tweak the call, use set_link(link, y=place, page=num_page). Check the documentation at http://pyfpdf.readthedocs.io/ en/latest/reference/set_link/index.html.

Adjusting some of the elements can take a certain degree of trial and error; for example, to position the line. A slightly longer or shorter line can be a matter of taste. Don't be afraid to experiment and check until it produces the desired effect.

The full FPDF documentation can be found here: `http://pyfpdf.readthedocs.io/en/latest/index.html`.

See also

- The *Writing a simple PDF document* recipe, earlier in this chapter, to learn the basics of how to work with PDF documents.
- The *Aggregating PDF reports* recipe, later in this chapter, to learn how to merge multiple documents into a single one.
- The *Watermarking and encrypting a PDF* recipe, later in this chapter, to learn how to add security measures to the document.

Aggregating PDF reports

In this recipe, we'll see how to combine two PDFs into one. We will add the pages of one report at the end of the other.

Getting ready

We'll use the `PyPDF2` module. `Pillow` and `pdf2image` are also dependencies used by the scripts:

```
$ echo "PyPDF2==1.26.0" >> requirements.txt
$ echo "pdf2image==1.11.0" >> requirements.txt
$ echo "Pillow==7.0.0" >> requirements.txt
$ pip install -r requirements.txt
```

For `pdf2image` to properly work, it needs to install `pdftoppm`, so check here for instructions on how to install it for different platforms: `https://github.com/Belval/pdf2image#first-you-need-pdftoppm`.

We need two PDFs to combine them. For this recipe, we'll use two PDFs: a `report.pdf` file generated by the `structuring_pdf.py` script, available on GitHub: `https://github.com/PacktPublishing/Python-Automation-Cookbook-Second-Edition/blob/master/Chapter05/structuring_pdf.py`, and another (`report2.pdf`) after watermarking it through the following command:

```
$ python watermarking_pdf.py report.pdf -u automate_user -o report2.pdf
```

This uses the watermarking script, watermarking_pdf.py, described in the *Watermarking and encrypting a PDF* recipe, which is available on GitHub: https://github.com/PacktPublishing/Python-Automation-Cookbook-Second-Edition/blob/master/Chapter05/watermarking_pdf.py.

How to do it...

1. Import PyPDF2 and create the output PDF:

   ```
   >>> import PyPDF2
   >>> output_pdf = PyPDF2.PdfFileWriter()
   ```

2. Read the first file and create a reader:

   ```
   >>> file1 = open('report.pdf', 'rb')
   >>> pdf1 = PyPDF2.PdfFileReader(file1)
   ```

3. Append all pages to the output PDF:

   ```
   >>> output_pdf.appendPagesFromReader(pdf1)
   ```

4. Open the second file, create a reader, and append the pages to the output PDF:

   ```
   >>> file2 = open('report2.pdf', 'rb')
   >>> pdf2 = PyPDF2.PdfFileReader(file2)
   >>> output_pdf.appendPagesFromReader(pdf2)
   ```

5. Create the output file and save it:

   ```
   >>> with open('result.pdf', 'wb') as out_file:
   ...     output_pdf.write(out_file)
   ```

6. Close both source files:

   ```
   >>> file1.close()
   >>> file2.close()
   ```

7. Check the output file and confirm that it contains both PDF pages.

How it works...

PyPDF2 allows us to create a reader for each source file and add all its pages to a newly created PDF writer. Note that the files are opened in binary mode (rb).

The input files need to remain open until the result is saved. This is due to the way the copy of the pages works. If the file is open, the resulting file may be stored as an empty file.

The PDF writer is finally saved into a new file. Notice that the file needs to be open to write in binary mode (wb).

There's more...

`.appendPagesFromReader` is very convenient for adding all pages, but it's also possible to add a number of pages one by one with `.addPage`. For example, to add the third page, the code would look like this:

```
>>> page = pdf1.getPage(3)
>>> output_pdf.addPage(page)
```

The full documentation for PyPDF2 can be found here: `https://pythonhosted.org/PyPDF2/`.

See also

- The *Writing a simple PDF document* recipe, earlier in this chapter, to learn the basics of how to work with PDF documents.
- The *Structuring a PDF* recipe, earlier in this chapter, to learn how to add separators to a PDF document.
- The *Watermarking and encrypting a PDF* recipe, later in this chapter, to learn how to add security measures to the document.

Watermarking and encrypting a PDF

PDF files have some interesting security measures to limit the distribution of a document. We can encrypt the content, requiring users to input a password in order to be able to read it. We'll also see how to add a watermark to label the document clearly as not for public distribution and, if leaked, to know its origin.

Getting ready

We'll use the `pdf2image` module to transform PDF documents to PIL images. `Pillow` is a prerequisite. We'll also use PyPDF2:

```
$ echo "pdf2image==1.11.0" >> requirements.txt
$ echo "Pillow==7.0.0" >> requirements.txt
$ echo "PyPDF2==1.26.0" >> requirements.txt
$ pip install -r requirements.txt
```

For pdf2image to work properly, it needs to install pdftoppm, so check here for instructions on how to install it for different platforms: https://github.com/Belval/pdf2image#.

We also need a PDF file to watermark and encrypt. We'll use a report.pdf file generated by the structuring_pdf.py script, described in the *Structuring a PDF* recipe, which is available on GitHub: https://github.com/PacktPublishing/Python-Automation-Cookbook-Second-Edition/blob/master/Chapter05/structuring_pdf.py.

How to do it...

1. The script, watermarking_pdf.py, is available on GitHub here: https://github.com/PacktPublishing/Python-Automation-Cookbook-Second-Edition/blob/master/Chapter05/watermarking_pdf.py. The most relevant bits are displayed here:

    ```python
    def encrypt(out_pdf, password):
        output_pdf = PyPDF2.PdfFileWriter()

        in_file = open(out_pdf, "rb")
        input_pdf = PyPDF2.PdfFileReader(in_file)
        output_pdf.appendPagesFromReader(input_pdf)
        output_pdf.encrypt(password)

        # Intermediate file
        with open(INTERMEDIATE_ENCRYPT_FILE, "wb") as out_file:
            output_pdf.write(out_file)

        in_file.close()

        # Rename the intermediate file
        os.rename(INTERMEDIATE_ENCRYPT_FILE, out_pdf)


    def create_watermark(watermarked_by):
    ```

```python
        mask = Image.new('L', WATERMARK_SIZE, 0)
        draw = ImageDraw.Draw(mask)
        font = ImageFont.load_default()
        text = 'WATERMARKED BY {}\n{}'.format(watermarked_by,
    datetime.now())
        draw.multiline_text((0, 100), text, 55, font=font)

        watermark = Image.new('RGB', WATERMARK_SIZE)
        watermark.putalpha(mask)
        watermark = watermark.resize((1950, 1950))
        watermark = watermark.rotate(45)
        # Crop to only the watermark
        bbox = watermark.getbbox()
        watermark = watermark.crop(bbox)

        return watermark

    def apply_watermark(watermark, in_pdf, out_pdf):
        # Transform from PDF to images
        images = convert_from_path(in_pdf)
        ...
        # Paste the watermark in each page
        for image in images:
            image.paste(watermark, position, watermark)

        # Save the resulting PDF
        images[0].save(out_pdf, save_all=True, append_
    images=images[1:])
```

2. Watermark the PDF file with the following command:

```
$ python watermarking_pdf.py report.pdf -u automate_user -o out.
pdf
Creating a watermark
Watermarking the document
```

3. Check that the document added a watermark with `automate_user` and a timestamp to all the pages of `out.pdf`:

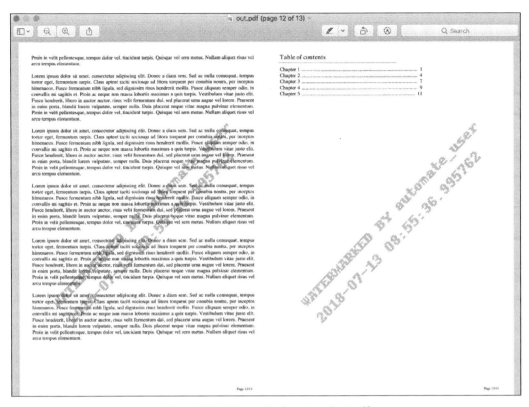

Figure 5.13: Watermarked content of out.pdf

4. Watermark and encrypt with the following command. Note that encrypting may take a little bit of time:

```
$ python watermarking_pdf.py report.pdf -u automate_user -o out.
pdf -p secretpassword
```

```
Creating a watermark
```

```
Watermarking the document
```

```
Encrypting the document
```

5. Open the resulting `out.pdf` file and check that it requires you to input the `secretpassword` password. The timestamp will also be new.

How it works...

The `watermarking_pdf.py` script first obtains the parameters from the command line using `argparse`, and then passes it to a `main` function that calls the other three functions, `create_watermark`, `apply_watermark`, and, if a password is used, `encrypt`.

`create_watermark` generates an image with the watermark. It uses the Pillow `Image` class to create a gray image (mode `L`) and draw the text. Then, this image gets applied as an alpha channel to a new image, making the image semi-transparent so that it will show the text to watermark.

> The alpha channel makes fully transparent anything in white (color 0) and fully opaque anything in black (color 255). In this case, the background is white (fully transparent) and the color of the text is 55, making it semi-transparent.

The image is then rotated 45 degrees and cropped to reduce the transparent background that may have appeared. This centers the image and allows for better positioning.

In the next step, `apply_watermark` transforms the PDF into a sequence of PIL `Images` using the `pdf2image` module. It calculates the position to apply the watermark, and then pastes the watermark.

> The image needs to be located by its top-left corner. This is located in the half of the document, minus half of the watermark, in both height and width. Note that the script assumes that all the pages of the document have the same size.

Finally, the result is saved to a PDF. Notice the `save_all` parameter, which allows us to save a multipage PDF.

If a password is passed, the `encrypt` function is called. It opens the output PDF using `PdfFileReader` and creates a new intermediate PDF with `PdfFileWriter`. All the pages of the output PDF are added to the new PDF, the PDF is encrypted, and then the intermediate PDF is renamed as the output PDF using `os.rename`.

There's more...

As part of the watermarking process, notice that the pages are transformed, from text into image. This adds extra protection as the text won't be extractable directly as text. When protecting a file, this is a good idea, as it will stop copying/pasting directly.

> This is not a huge security measure, though, as the text may be extracted through OCR tools. But it protects against casual extraction of the text. The output file size is also much bigger, about 30 MB. This also makes it slower to encrypt and decrypt.

The default font from PIL can be a little rough. Another font, if the `TrueType` or `OpenType` file is available, can be added and used by calling the following:

```
font = ImageFont.truetype('my_font.ttf', SIZE)
```

Note that this may require installing the `FreeType` libraries, normally available as part of the `libfreetype` package. Further documentation is available at `https://www.freetype.org/`. Depending on the font and size, you may need to adjust the sizes.

The full `pdf2image` documentation can be found at `https://github.com/Belval/pdf2image`, the full documentation for `PyPDF2` at `https://pythonhosted.org/PyPDF2/`, and the full documentation for `Pillow` at `https://pillow.readthedocs.io/en/5.2.x/`.

See also

- The *Writing a simple PDF document* recipe, earlier in this chapter, to learn how to add separators to a PDF document.

- The *Structuring a PDF* recipe, earlier in this chapter, to learn how to add separators to a PDF document.

- The *Aggregating PDF reports* recipe, earlier in this chapter, to learn how to merge multiple documents into a single one.

6
Fun with Spreadsheets

Spreadsheets are one of the most versatile and omnipresent tools in the world of computing. Their intuitive approach of sheets and cells is used by virtually everyone that uses a computer as part of their day-to-day operations. But they allow you to apply complex operations, including the use of macro languages. There's even a running joke that whole complex businesses are managed and described within a single spreadsheet, somewhere. They are incredibly powerful tools.

This makes the ability to automate reading from and writing to spreadsheets so interesting. We'll see in this chapter how to process spreadsheets, mainly in the most common format, Excel. The final recipe will cover a free alternative, LibreOffice, and in particular, how to use Python as a scripting language inside it.

Python presents advantages over using specific tools included in spreadsheet suites. First, it is more versatile than custom tools like VBA, which only work on a single suite of applications. You can also take advantage of its vast available library to perform operations, both in terms of capacity (for example, using a statistical library or a specialized mathematical library) and in terms of performance. Also, in Python, the code is readable and easy to understand compared to other alternatives. In *Chapter 7, Cleaning and Processing Data*, we'll go through some techniques that can help you increase the productivity of dealing with spreadsheet files and processes.

In this chapter, we will cover the following recipes:

- Writing a CSV spreadsheet
- Updating CSV files

- Reading an Excel spreadsheet
- Updating an Excel spreadsheet
- Creating new sheets in an Excel spreadsheet
- Creating charts in Excel
- Working with cell formats in Excel
- Creating a macro in LibreOffice

Let's start by taking a look at CSV files.

Writing a CSV spreadsheet

CSV files are simple spreadsheets in a highly compatible format. They are text files with tabular data, separated by commas (hence the name Comma-Separated Values), in a simple table format. CSV files can be created using Python's standard library and can be read by all kinds of spreadsheet software.

Getting ready

For this recipe, only the standard library of Python is required. Everything is ready out of the box!

How to do it...

1. Import the `csv` module:

```
>>> import csv
```

2. Define the header with how the data will be ordered and the data to store:

```
>>> HEADER = ('Admissions', 'Name', 'Year')
>>> DATA = [
... (225.7, 'Gone With the Wind', 1939),
... (194.4, 'Star Wars', 1977),
... (161.0, 'ET: The Extra-Terrestrial', 1982)
... ]
```

3. Write the data into a CSV file:

```
>>> with open('movies.csv', 'w', newline='') as csvfile:
...     movies = csv.writer(csvfile)
...     movies.writerow(HEADER)
...     for row in DATA:
...         movies.writerow(row)
```

4. Check the resulting CSV file in a spreadsheet. In the following screenshot, the file is displayed using the LibreOffice software:

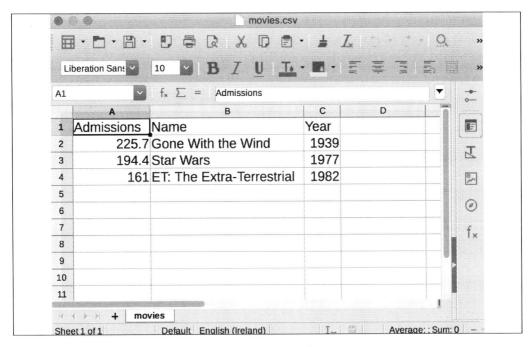

Figure 6.1: Contents of the `movies.csv` file

How it works...

After the preparation work in *steps 1* and *2* in the *How to do it…* section, *step 3* is the part that saves the `movies.csv` file.

It opens a new file, `movies.csv`, in write (w) mode. The file handle object in `csvfile` references the file, which the `CSV.writer()` function uses to create the CSV file. All this happens in a `with` block, so it closes the file when the block is complete.

Note the `newline=''''` parameter. This is done to make the `writer` be in control of the `newline` format and avoid incompatibility issues, such as adding a newline twice. This won't normally be a problem, but sometimes the CSV format may require the newline to be a specific character, different from the default one. This can happen, for example, if working with a file to be used on a different operating system. It's better to handle it explicitly in the CSV configuration.

The `writer` writes the elements row by row using the `.writerow()` method. The first row is the HEADER, and the remaining rows are the lines of data.

There's more...

The code presented stores the data in the default CSV dialect. The CSV dialect defines what character divides the data on each row (commas or other characters), how to escape characters, newline characters (also known as line terminators) defining a new entry, and so on.

> Escape is the process of storing characters that could be interpreted as part of the syntax; for example, storing a column with a text that includes a comma or a quote. The dialect will determine how to store it in that case, normally by adding a special character, for example, \, for a verbatim comma.

In case the dialect needs to be tweaked, each of these parameters can be defined in the `writer` call. Refer to the following link for a list of all the parameters that can be defined: `https://docs.python.org/3/library/csv.html#dialects-and-formatting-parameters`.

> CSV files are better when simple. If the data to be stored is complicated, maybe the best alternative is not a CSV file. But CSV files are extremely useful when dealing with tabular data. They can be understood by virtually all programs, and even dealing with them at a low level is easy.

The full `csv` module documentation can be found here: `https://docs.python.org/3/library/csv.html`.

See also

- The *Reading CSV files* recipe in *Chapter 4, Searching and Reading Local Files*.
- The *Updating CSV files* recipe in the following section.

Updating CSV files

Given that CSV files are simple text files, the best solution to update their content is to read them, process them into internal Python objects, make the changes, and then overwrite the result back in the same format. In this recipe, we will see how to do this.

Getting ready

In this recipe, we will use the `movies.csv` file that is available on GitHub at
`https://github.com/PacktPublishing/Python-Automation-Cookbook-Second-`
`Edition/blob/master/Chapter06/movies.csv`. It contains the following data:

Admissions	Name	Year
225.7	Gone With the Wind	1939
194.4	Star Wars	1968
161.0	ET: The Extra-Terrestrial	1982

Figure 6.2: Movie data

Notice that the `Year` of `Star Wars` is incorrect (the movie was released in 1977). We'll
change it in this recipe.

How to do it...

1. Import the `csv` module and define the filename:

```
>>> import csv
>>> FILENAME = 'movies.csv'
```

2. Read the content of the file using `DictReader` and transform this content into
a list of ordered rows:

```
>>> with open(FILENAME, newline='') as file:
...     data = [row for row in csv.DictReader(file)]
```

3. Check the obtained data. Change the proper value from 1968 to 1977:

```
>>> data
[{'Admissions': '225.7', 'Name': 'Gone With the Wind', 'Year':
'1939'}, {'Admissions': '194.4', 'Name': 'Star Wars', 'Year':
'1977'}, {'Admissions': '161.0', 'Name': 'ET: The Extra-
Terrestrial', 'Year': '1982'}]
>>> data[1]['Year']
'1968'
>>> data[1]['Year'] = '1977'
```

4. Open the file again and store the values:

```
>>> HEADER = data[0].keys()
>>> with open(FILENAME, 'w', newline='') as file:
...     writer = csv.DictWriter(file, fieldnames=HEADER)
...     writer.writeheader()
...     writer.writerows(data)
```

5. Check the result in spreadsheet software. The result is similar to that displayed in *step 4* of the *Writing a CSV spreadsheet* recipe.

How it works...

After importing the `csv` module in *step 2* of the *How to do it...* section, we extract all the data from the file. The file is opened in a `with` block. `DictReader` conveniently transforms it into a list of dictionaries, with the headers as keys and the content of the cell as the values.

The conveniently formatted data can then be manipulated and modified. We changed the data to fix the `Year` problem in *step 3*.

> In this recipe, we change the value by directly accessing a row number, but searching the specific row or rows to change may be required in a more general case.

Step 4 overwrites the file and, using `DictWriter`, stores the data. `DictWriter` requires us to define the fields on the columns by requiring the `fieldnames`. To obtain them, we retrieve the keys of one of the rows and store them in `HEADER`.

The file is opened again in `w` mode to overwrite it. `DictWriter` first stores the header with `.writeheader` and then stores all the rows with a single call to `.writerows()`.

> The rows can also be added one by one by calling the `.writerow()` method.

After closing the `with` block, the file is stored and can be checked to verify it is correct.

There's more...

For familiar data sources, the dialect of the CSV file is typically known, but this may not always be the case, especially if the file comes from an unknown source. In that case, the `Sniffer` class can help. It analyzes a sample of the file (or the whole file) and returns a guessed `dialect` object:

```
>>> with open(FILENAME, newline='') as file:
...     dialect = csv.Sniffer().sniff(file.read())
```

The dialect can then be passed to the `DictReader` class when opening the file. The file will need to be opened twice for reading.

 Remember to use the dialect on the `DictWriter` class as well to save the file in the same format.

The full documentation for the `csv` module can be found here: `https://docs.python.org/3.7/library/csv.html`.

See also

* The *Reading CSV files* recipe in *Chapter 4*, *Searching and Reading Local Files*.
* The *Writing a CSV spreadsheet* recipe earlier in the chapter.

Reading an Excel spreadsheet

MS Office is arguably the most common office suite software, making its formats pretty much standard. MS Excel is probably the most common spreadsheet application and the Excel format is the most common spreadsheet format, mirrored by many other spreadsheet applications.

In this recipe, we'll see how to obtain information from an Excel spreadsheet using the `openpyxl` module in Python.

Getting ready

We will use the `openpyxl` module. We should install the module, adding it to our `requirements.txt` file as follows:

```
$ echo "openpyxl==3.0.3" >> requirements.txt
$ pip install -r requirements.txt
```

In the GitHub repository, there's an Excel spreadsheet named `movies.xlsx` that contains information on the top 10 movies by attendance. The file can be found here: `https://github.com/PacktPublishing/Python-Automation-Cookbook-Second-Edition/blob/master/Chapter06/movies.xlsx`.

The source of the information can be found at `http://www.mrob.com/pub/film-video/topadj.html`.

How to do it...

1. Import the `openpyxl` module:

```
>>> import openpyxl
```

2. Load the file into memory:

```
>>> xlsfile = openpyxl.load_workbook('movies.xlsx')
```

3. List all sheets and get the first one, which is the only one that contains data:

```
>>> xlsfile.sheetnames
['Sheet1']
>>> sheet = xlsfile['Sheet1']
```

4. Obtain the value of cells B4 and D4 (admissions and director of E.T.):

```
>>> sheet['B4'].value
161
>>> sheet['D4'].value
'Steven Spielberg'
```

5. Obtain the size in rows and columns. Any cell out of that range will return None as a value:

```
>>> sheet.max_row
11
>>> sheet.max_column
4
>>> sheet['A12'].value
>>> sheet['E1'].value
```

How it works...

After importing the module in *step 1*, *step 2* in the *How to do it...* section loads the file into memory in a `Workbook` object. Each workbook can contain one or more sheets, each of them containing cells.

To determine the available sheets, in *step 3*, we obtain all the sheet names (there's a single one in this example) and then access the sheet like a dictionary to retrieve a `Worksheet` object.

`Worksheet` can then access all the cells directly by their names, such as A4 or C3. Each of them will return a `Cell` object. The `.value` attribute stores the value in the cell.

In the rest of the recipes in this chapter, we will see more attributes of `Cell` objects. Keep reading!

Obtaining the area where the data is stored is possible with `max_columns` and `max_rows`. This allows us to search within the limits of the data.

 Excel defines the columns as letters (A, B, C, and so on) and rows as numbers (1, 2, 3, and so on). Remember to always set the column, and then the row (`D1`, and not `1D`), or an error will be raised.

Cells outside the area are accessible but won't return data. They are available to write new data.

There's more...

Cells can also be retrieved with `sheet.cell(column, row)`. Both elements start their index at `1`.

All the cells within the data area iterate from the sheet, for example:

```
>>> for row in sheet:
...     for cell in row:
...         # Do stuff with cell
```

This will return a list of lists with all cells, row by row: A1, A2, A3 ... B1, B2, B3, and so on.

 You can retrieve the cell's column with columns iterating through `sheet.columns`: A1, B1, C1, and so on, A2, B2, C2, and so on.

When retrieving a cell, you can find its position with `.coordinate`, `.row`, and `.column`:

```
>>> cell.coordinate
'D4'
>>> cell.column
```

```
'D'
>>> cell.row
4
```

The full openpyxl documentation can be found here: https://openpyxl.
readthedocs.io/en/stable/index.html.

See also

- The *Updating an Excel spreadsheet* recipe in the following section.
- The *Creating new sheets in an Excel spreadsheet* recipe later on in the chapter.
- The *Creating charts in Excel* recipe later on in the chapter.
- The *Working with cell formats in Excel* recipe later on in the chapter.

Updating an Excel spreadsheet

In this recipe, we'll see how to update an existing Excel spreadsheet. This will
include changing raw values in cells and setting up formulas that will be evaluated
when the spreadsheet is open. We'll also see how to add comments to cells.

Getting ready

We will use the openpyxl module. We should install the module, adding it to our
requirements.txt file as follows:

```
$ echo "openpyxl==3.0.3" >> requirements.txt
$ pip install -r requirements.txt
```

In the GitHub repository, there's an Excel spreadsheet named movies.xlsx that
contains information on the top 10 movies by attendance.

The file can be found here: https://github.com/PacktPublishing/Python-
Automation-Cookbook-Second-Edition/blob/master/Chapter06/movies.xlsx.

How to do it...

1. Import the openpyxl module and the Comment class:

   ```
   >>> import openpyxl
   >>> from openpyxl.comments import Comment
   ```

2. Load the file into memory and get the sheet:

```
>>> xlsfile = openpyxl.load_workbook('movies.xlsx')
>>> sheet = xlsfile['Sheet1']
```

3. Obtain the value of cell D4 (director of E.T):

```
>>> sheet['D4'].value
'Steven Spielberg'
```

4. Change the value to just `Spielberg`:

```
>>> sheet['D4'].value = 'Spielberg'
```

5. Add a comment to that cell:

```
>>> sheet['D4'].comment = Comment('Changed text automatically',
'User')
```

6. Add a new element that obtains the total of all values in the `Admission` column:

```
>>> sheet['B12'] = '=SUM(B2:B11)'
```

7. Save the spreadsheet to the `movies_comment.xlsx` file:

```
>>> xlsfile.save('movies_comment.xlsx')
```

8. Check the resulting file, which includes the comment and the calculation of the total of column B in A12:

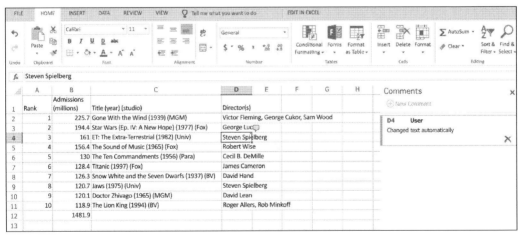

Figure 6.3: The cell now shows a comment

How it works...

In the *How to do it...* section, after making the imports in *step 1* and reading the spreadsheet in *step 2*, we select the cell to be changed in *step 3*.

Updating the value is done in *step 4* with an assignment. A comment in the cell is added, overwriting the *.comment* attribute with a new *Comment* class instance. Note that the name of the user making the comment is required.

Values can also include descriptions of formulas. In *step 6*, we add a new formula to cell *B12*. The value is calculated and displayed when the file is opened in *step 8*.

The value of a formula is not calculated in Python, but in Excel. This means that the formula could contain errors or display unexpected results through bugs in the resulting spreadsheet. Be sure to double-check that the formulas are correct.

Finally, in *step 7*, the spreadsheet is saved to disk by calling the `.save` method of the XLSX file object. The name of the resulting file can be the same one as the input file to overwrite it.

The comment and values can be viewed by externally accessing the file.

There's more...

You can store data as multiple data types, and it will be translated into the proper types for Excel. For example, storing `datetime` will store it in the proper date format. The same is true with `float` or other numeric formats.

If you don't need to change any value in the spreadsheet, you can open it in read-only mode:

```
>>> xlsfile = openpyxl.load_workbook('movies.xlsx', read_only=True)
>>> xlsfile['Sheet1']['A1'].value = '37%'
...
AttributeError: Cell is read only
```

Adding comments to automatically generated cells can help review the resulting file, making it clear how each specific value was generated.

While it is possible to add formulas to automatically generate Excel files, debugging the results can be tricky. When generating a result, generally, it's better to make the calculations in Python and store the result in a raw format.

The `data_only` parameter for `load_workbook` will load all the formulas as the resulting data. This can be useful if the result for formulas is expected to perform further calculations.

The full `openpyxl` documentation can be found here: `https://openpyxl.readthedocs.io/en/stable/index.html`.

See also

- The *Reading an Excel spreadsheet* recipe earlier in the chapter.
- The *Creating new sheets in an Excel spreadsheet* recipe in the following section.
- The *Creating charts in Excel* recipe later in the chapter.
- The *Working with cell formats in Excel* recipe later in the chapter.

Creating new sheets in an Excel spreadsheet

In this recipe, we'll demonstrate how to create a new Excel spreadsheet from scratch and deal with multiple sheets within that spreadsheet, including creating them.

Getting ready

We will use the `openpyxl` module. We should install the module, adding it to our `requirements.txt` file as follows:

```
$ echo "openpyxl==3.0.3" >> requirements.txt
$ pip install -r requirements.txt
```

We'll store it in the new file information about the movies with the most attendance. The data is extracted from here: `http://www.mrob.com/pub/film-video/topadj.html`.

How to do it...

1. Import the `openpyxl` module:

   ```
   >>> import openpyxl
   ```

2. Create a new Excel file. This creates a default sheet, called `Sheet`:

   ```
   >>> xlsfile = openpyxl.Workbook()
   >>> xlsfile.sheetnames
   ```

```
['Sheet']
>>> sheet = xlsfile['Sheet']
```

3. Add data about the number of attendees to this sheet from the source. Only the first three are added for simplicity:

```
>>> data = [
...      (225.7, 'Gone With the Wind', 'Victor Fleming'),
...      (194.4, 'Star Wars', 'George Lucas'),
...      (161.0, 'ET: The Extraterrestrial', 'Steven Spielberg'),
... ]
>>> for row, (admissions, name, director) in enumerate(data, 1):
...      sheet['A{}'.format(row)].value = admissions
...      sheet['B{}'.format(row)].value = name
```

4. Create a new sheet:

```
>>> sheet = xlsfile.create_sheet("Directors")
>>> sheet
<Worksheet "Directors">
>>> xlsfile.sheetnames
['Sheet', 'Directors']
```

5. Add the name of the director for each movie:

```
>>> for row, (admissions, name, director) in enumerate(data, 1):
...      sheet['A{}'.format(row)].value = director
...      sheet['B{}'.format(row)].value = name
```

6. Save the file as movie_sheets.xlsx:

```
>>> xlsfile.save('movie_sheets.xlsx')
```

7. Open the movie_sheets.xlsx file to check that it has two sheets with the proper information, as shown in the following screenshot:

Figure 6.4: Content of `movie_sheets.xlsx`

How it works...

In the *How to do it...* section, after importing the module in *step 1*, we create a new spreadsheet in *step 2*. This is a new spreadsheet that contains just the default sheet.

The data to be stored is defined in *step 3*. Note that it contains information that will go on both sheets (name in both; the admissions in the first sheet and the director's name in the second). In this step, the first sheet is filled.

 Note how the value is stored. The proper cell is defined as column A or B and the proper row (rows start at 1). The `enumerate` function returns a tuple with the first element as the index and the second as the enumerated parameter (in this case, a tuple with three values).

After that, the new sheet is created in *step 4*, using the name `Directors`. `.create_sheet` returns the new sheet.

The information in the `Directors` sheet is stored in *step 5* and the file is saved in *step 6*.

There's more...

The name of an existing sheet can be changed through the `.title` property:

```
>>> sheet = xlsfile['Sheet']
>>> sheet.title = 'Admissions'
>>> xlsfile.sheetnames
['Admissions', 'Directors']
```

Be careful, as it won't be possible to access the sheet with `xlsfile['Sheet']`. That name doesn't exist anymore!

The active sheet, the sheet that will be displayed when the file is opened, can be obtained through the `.active` property and changed with `._active_sheet_index`. The index starts at `0` for the first sheet:

```
>> xlsfile.active
<Worksheet "Admissions">
>>> xlsfile._active_sheet_index
0
>>> xlsfile._active_sheet_index = 1
>>> xlsfile.active
<Worksheet "Directors">
```

The sheet can also be copied using `.copy_worksheet`. Be aware that some data, for example, charts, won't be carried over. All the cell data will be duplicated:

```
new_copied_sheet = xlsfile.copy_worksheet(source_sheet)
```

If you need to copy charts, keep in mind that you can replicate them by code multiple times, if necessary.

The full `openpyxl` documentation can be found here: `https://openpyxl.readthedocs.io/en/stable/index.html`.

See also

- The *Reading an Excel spreadsheet* recipe earlier in the chapter.
- The *Updating an Excel spreadsheet* recipe earlier in the chapter.
- The *Creating charts in Excel* recipe in the following section.
- The *Working with cell formats in Excel* recipe later in the chapter.

Creating charts in Excel

Spreadsheets include a lot of tools to deal with data, including presenting the data in colorful charts. Let's see how to append a chart programmatically to an Excel spreadsheet.

Getting ready

We will use the openpyxl module. We should install the module, adding it to our requirements.txt file as follows:

```
$ echo "openpyxl==3.0.3" >> requirements.txt
$ pip install -r requirements.txt
```

We'll store it in the new file information about the movies with the most attendance. The data is extracted from here: http://www.mrob.com/pub/film-video/topadj.html.

How to do it...

1. Import the openpyxl module and create a new Excel file:

   ```
   >>> import openpyxl
   >>> from openpyxl.chart import BarChart, Reference
   >>> xlsfile = openpyxl.Workbook()
   ```

2. Add data about the number of attendees in this sheet from the source. Only the first three are added for simplicity:

   ```
   >>> data = [
   ...     ('Name', 'Admissions'),
   ...     ('Gone With the Wind', 225.7),
   ...     ('Star Wars', 194.4),
   ...     ('ET: The Extraterrestrial', 161.0),
   ... ]
   >>> sheet = xlsfile['Sheet']
   >>> for row in data:
   ...     sheet.append(row)
   ```

3. Create a BarChart object and fill it with basic information:

   ```
   >>> chart = BarChart()
   >>> chart.title = "Admissions per movie"
   >>> chart.y_axis.title = 'Millions'
   ```

4. Create a reference to the `data` and append the `data` to the chart:

```
>>> data = Reference(sheet, min_row=2, max_row=4, min_col=1, max_
col=2)
>>> chart.add_data(data, from_rows=True, titles_from_data=True)
```

5. Add the chart to the sheet and save the file:

```
>>> sheet.add_chart(chart, "A6")
>>> xlsfile.save('movie_chart.xlsx')
```

6. Check the resulting chart in the spreadsheet, as shown in the following screenshot:

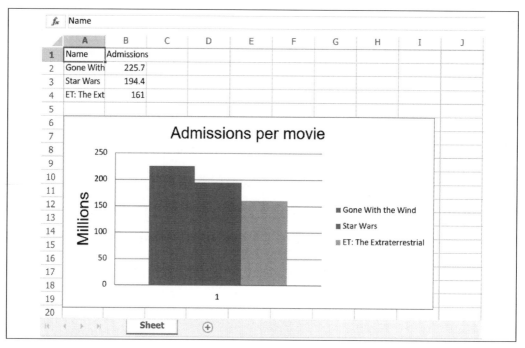

Figure 6.5: Displayed chart

How it works...

In the *How to do it...* section, after preparing the data in *steps 1* and *2*, the data is ready in the range A1:B4. Note that A1 and B1 both contain a header that should not be used in the chart.

In *step 3*, we set up the new chart and include the basic data, such as a title and the units of the *y-axis*.

Step 4 creates a reference box through a `Reference` object, from row 2 column 1 to row 4 column 2, which is the area where our data lives, excluding the header. The data is added to the chart with the `.add_data()` method. The `from_rows` argument makes each row a different data series. Another argument, `titles_from_data`, uses the first column to name the series.

The chart is added to cell A6 in *step 5* and saved to disk.

There's more...

Numerous charts can be created, including bar charts, line charts, area charts (line charts that fill the area between the line and the axis), pie charts, or scatter charts (XY charts where one value is plotted against the other). Each kind of chart has an equivalent class, for example, `PieChart` or `LineChart`.

Each one, at the same time, can have different types. For example, the default type for `BarChart` is column, printing the bars vertically, but they can also be printed vertically by selecting a different type:

```
>>> chart.type = 'bar'
```

Check the `openpyxl` documentation to see all available combinations.

- Instead of extracting the *x-axis* labels from the data, they can be set explicitly with `set_categories`. For example, compare *step 4* with the following code:

```
data = Reference(sheet, min_row=2, max_row=4, min_col=2, max_col=2)
labels = Reference(sheet, min_row=2, max_row=4, min_col=1, max_col=1)
chart.add_data(data, from_rows=False, titles_from_data=False)
chart.set_categories(labels)
```

The range, instead of using a `Reference` object, can also be input with text labels describing the region:

```
chart.add_data('Sheet!B2:B4', from_rows=False, titles_from_data=False)
chart.set_categories('Sheet!A2:A4')
```

This way of describing it may be more difficult to deal with if the range of data needs to be created programmatically.

Defining charts in Excel correctly can be difficult sometimes. The way Excel extracts the data from a particular range can be baffling. Remember to allow time for trial and error, and to deal with differences. For example, in *step 4*, we defined three series with one data point, while in the preceding code, we defined a single series with three data points. Most of those differences are subtle. Finally, the most important point is how the end chart looks. Try different chart types and learn the differences.

The full openpyxl documentation can be found here: `https://openpyxl.readthedocs.io/en/stable/index.html`.

See also

- The *Reading an Excel spreadsheet* recipe earlier in the chapter.
- The *Updating an Excel spreadsheet* recipe earlier in the chapter.
- The *Creating new sheets in an Excel spreadsheet* recipe in the previous section.
- The *Working with cell formats in Excel* recipe in the following section.

Working with cell formats in Excel

Presenting information in spreadsheets is not just a matter of organizing it into cells or displaying it graphically in charts. It also involves changing the format to highlight the important details. In this recipe, we'll see how to manipulate the format of cells to enhance the results and present the data in the best way.

Getting ready

We will use the openpyxl module. We should install the module, adding it to our `requirements.txt` file as follows:

```
$ echo "openpyxl==3.0.3" >> requirements.txt
$ pip install -r requirements.txt
```

We'll store it in the new file information about the movies with the most attendance. The data is extracted from here: `http://www.mrob.com/pub/film-video/topadj.html`.

How to do it...

1. Import the `openpyxl` module and create a new Excel file:

```
>>> import openpyxl
>>> from openpyxl.styles import Font, PatternFill, Border, Side
>>> xlsfile = openpyxl.Workbook()
```

2. Add data about the number of attendees in this sheet from the source. Only the first four are added, for simplicity:

```
>>> data = [
...     ('Name', 'Admissions'),
...     ('Gone With the Wind', 225.7),
...     ('Star Wars', 194.4),
...     ('ET: The Extraterrestrial', 161.0),
...     ('The Sound of Music', 156.4),
]
>>> sheet = xlsfile['Sheet']
>>> for row in data:
...     sheet.append(row)
```

3. Define the colors to use for styling the spreadsheet:

```
>>> BLUE = '0033CC'
>>> LIGHT_BLUE = 'E6ECFF'
>>> WHITE = 'FFFFFF'
```

4. Define the header in a blue background and a white font:

```
>>> header_font = Font(name='Tahoma', size=14, color=WHITE)
>>> header_fill = PatternFill("solid", fgColor=BLUE)
>>> for row in sheet['A1:B1']:
...     for cell in row:
...         cell.font = header_font
...         cell.fill = header_fill
```

5. Define an alternate pattern for the columns and a border on each row after the header:

```
>>> white_side = Side(border_style='thin', color=WHITE)
>>> blue_side = Side(border_style='thin', color=BLUE)
>>> alternate_fill = PatternFill("solid", fgColor=LIGHT_BLUE)
>>> border = Border(bottom=blue_side, left=white_side,
```

```
right=white_side)
>>> for row_index, row in enumerate(sheet['A2:B5']):
...        for cell in row:
...               cell.border = border
...               if row_index % 2:
...                     cell.fill = alternate_fill
```

6. Save the file as `movies_format.xlsx`:

```
>>> xlsfile.save('movies_format.xlsx')
```

7. Check the resulting file:

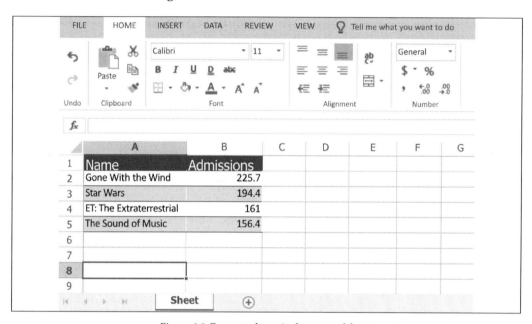

Figure 6.6: Formatted movie data spreadsheet

How it works...

- In the *How to do it…* section, in *step 1*, we import the openpyxl module and create a new Excel file. In *step 2*, we add the data to the first sheet. *Step 3* is also a preparation step to define the colors to be used. The colors are defined in hex format, which is common in the web design world.

To find the definition of colors, there are plenty of color pickers online or even embedded in the OS. A tool like `https://coolors.co/` can be useful to define a palette to work with.

In *step 4*, we prepare the format to define the header. The header will have a different font (Tahoma), a bigger size (14pt), and it will be white on a blue background. To do this, we prepare a `Font` object with the font, size, and foreground color, and a `PatternFill` with the background color.

The loop after creating `header_font` and `header_fill` applies the font and fill to the proper cells.

 Note that iterating over a range always returns the row, and then cells, even if only one row is involved.

In *step 5*, a border to the rows and an alternate background is applied. The border is defined with blue top and bottom and white left and right. The fill is created in a similar way to *step 4*, but in a light blue. The background is only applied to even rows.

 Note that the top border of a cell is the bottom of the one above, and vice versa. This means that it's possible to overwrite the border in a loop.

The file is finally saved in *step 6*.

There's more...

There are multiple options available to style the text, such as bold, italic, strikeout, or underline. Define the font and reassign it if you need to change any of its elements. And remember to check that the font is available in the system.

There are also various ways of creating a fill. `PatternFill` accepts several patterns, but the most useful one is `solid`. `GradientFill` can also be used to apply a two-color gradient.

It's best to limit yourself to solid fills using `PatternFill`. You can tweak the color to best represent what you want. Remember to include `style='solid'`, or the color may not appear.

It's also possible to define conditional formatting, but for an automatically generated spreadsheet, it's less complicated to try to define the logic in Python and then apply the proper static formatting based on the result.

Number formatting can be set up properly, for example:

```
cell.style = 'Percent'
```

This will display the value `0.37` as `37%`.

The full `openpyxl` documentation can be found here: `https://openpyxl.readthedocs.io/en/stable/index.html`.

See also

- The *Reading an Excel spreadsheet* recipe earlier in the chapter.
- The *Updating an Excel spreadsheet* recipe earlier in the chapter.
- The *Creating new sheets in an Excel spreadsheet* recipe earlier in the chapter.
- The *Creating charts in Excel* recipe in the previous section.

Creating a macro in LibreOffice

LibreOffice is a free productivity suite that's an alternative to MS Office and other office packages. It includes, among others, a text editor called `writer` and a spreadsheet program called `Calc`. Calc understands the regular Excel formats, and it's also totally scriptable internally through its UNO API. The UNO interface allows programmatic access to the suite, and it's accessible in different languages, such as Java.

One of these available languages is Python, making it very easy to generate very complex applications in a suite format, as this enables the use of the full Python standard library.

Using the full Python standard library provides access to elements such as cryptography, opening external files (including zip files), and connecting to remote databases. Also, you can take advantage of the Python syntax and avoid dealing with LibreOffice BASIC.

We'll see in this recipe how to add an external Python file as a macro that will change the contents of a spreadsheet.

Getting ready

LibreOffice needs to be installed. It is available at `https://www.libreoffice.org/`.

Once downloaded and installed, it needs to be configured to allow the execution of macros:

1. Go to **Settings | Security** to find the **Macro Security** details:

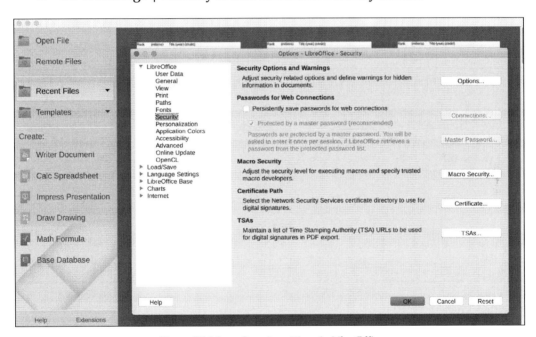

Figure 6.7: Macro Security settings in LibreOffice

2. Open **Macro Security** and select **Medium** to allow the execution of our macros. This will display a warning before allowing us to run a macro:

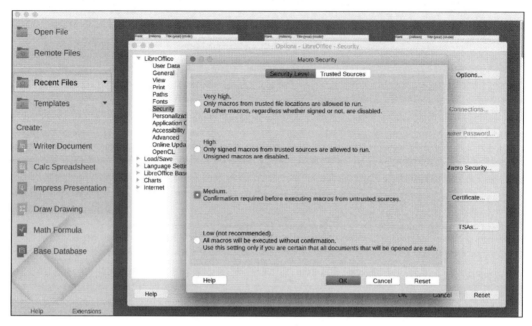

Figure 6.8: Setting macro security level to Medium

To insert the macro into the file, we'll use a script called `include_macro.py`, which is available at `https://github.com/PacktPublishing/Python-Automation-Cookbook-Second-Edition/blob/master/Chapter06/include_macro.py`.

The script with the macro is also available as `libreoffice_script.py` here: `https://github.com/PacktPublishing/Python-Automation-Cookbook-Second-Edition/blob/master/Chapter06/libreoffice_script.py`.

The file to put the script into, called `movies.ods`, is also available here: `https://github.com/PacktPublishing/Python-Automation-Cookbook-Second-Edition/blob/master/Chapter06/movies.ods`.

It contains, in `.ods` format (LibreOffice format), a table with the 10 movies with the highest admissions. The data was extracted from here: `http://www.mrob.com/pub/film-video/topadj.html`.

How to do it...

1. Use the `include_macro.py` script to attach the `libreoffice_script.py` file to the `movies.ods` macrofile:

```
$ python include_macro.py -h
usage: It inserts the macro file "script" into the file
"spreadsheet" in .ods format. The resulting file is located in the
macro_file directory, that will be created
        [-h] spreadsheet script

positional arguments:
  spreadsheet File to insert the script
  script Script to insert in the file

optional arguments:
  -h, --help show this help message and exit

$ python include_macro.py movies.ods libreoffice_script.py
```

2. Open the resulting file, `macro_file/movies.ods`, in LibreOffice. Notice that it shows a warning to enable the macros (click on **Enable**). Go to **Tools | Macros | Run Macro**:

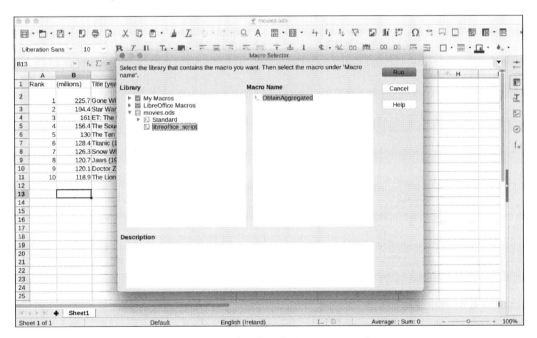

Figure 6.9: Running the `ObtainAggregated` macro

3. Select `ObtainAggregated` under `movies.ods | libreoffice_script` and click on **Run**. This calculates the aggregated admissions and stores them in cell `B12`. It adds a `Total` label in `A15`:

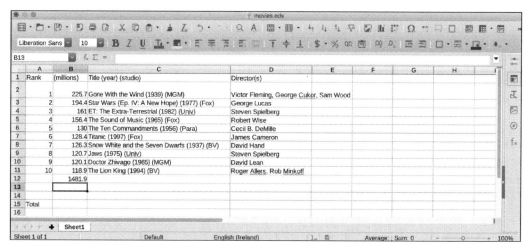

Figure 6.10: Aggregated admissions calculated in cell B12

4. Repeat *steps 2* and *3* to run it again. Now it runs all the aggregations, but adds `B12` and gets the result in `B13`:

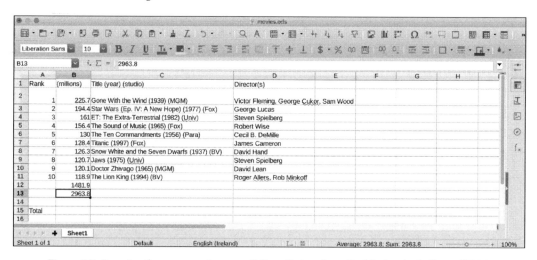

Figure 6.11: Running the macro again sums all the cells in column B, this time including cell B12

How it works...

The main work in *step 1* is done in the `include_macro.py` script. It copies the file into the `macro_file` subdirectory to avoid modifying the input.

Internally, an `.ods` file is a zip file with a certain structure. The script takes advantage of the zip file Python module to add the script to the proper subdirectory internally. It also modifies the `manifest.xml` file to allow LibreOffice to know there's a script inside the file.

The macro that is executed in *step 3* is defined in `libreoffice_script.py` and contains a single function:

```python
def ObtainAggregated(*args):
    # get the doc from the scripting context
    # which is made available to all scripts
    desktop = XSCRIPTCONTEXT.getDesktop()
    model = desktop.getCurrentComponent()
    # get the first sheet
    sheet = model.Sheets.getByIndex(0)

    # Find the admissions column
    MAX_ELEMENT = 20
    for column in range(0, MAX_ELEMENT):
        cell = sheet.getCellByPosition(column, 0)
        if 'Admissions' in cell.String:
            break
    else:
        raise Exception('Admissions not found')

    accumulator = 0.0
    for row in range(1, MAX_ELEMENT):
        cell = sheet.getCellByPosition(column, row)
        value = cell.getValue()
        if value:
            accumulator += cell.getValue()
        else:
            break

    cell = sheet.getCellByPosition(column, row)
    cell.setValue(accumulator)
```

```
cell = sheet.getCellRangeByName("A15")
cell.String = 'Total'
return None
```

The XSCRIPTCONTEXT variable is created automatically and allowed to get the current component, and from there, the first Sheet. After that, the sheet is iterated to find the Admissions column through .getCellByPosition and obtain the string value with the .String attribute. With the same method, it aggregates all the values in the column, extracting them through .getValue to get their numerical values.

As the loop iterates through the column until finding an empty cell, the second time it's executed, it will aggregate the value in B12, which is the aggregated value in the previous execution. This is done on purpose to show that macros can be executed multiple times, with different results.

Cells can also be referenced by their string position through .getCellRangeByName, to store Total in cell A15.

There's more...

The Python interpreter is embedded into LibreOffice, meaning that the specific version can change if LibreOffice changes. In the latest version of LibreOffice at the time of writing this book (6.4.0), the version included was Python 3.7.6.

The UNO interface is very complete and allows you to access a lot of advanced elements. Unfortunately, the documentation is not great, and achieving it can be complicated and time consuming. The documentation is defined in Java or C++, and there are examples in LibreOffice BASIC or other languages, but few for Python. The full documentation can be found at https://api.libreoffice.org/, and the reference is here: https://api.libreoffice.org/docs/idl/ref/index.html.

For example, it is possible to create complex charts or even interactive dialogs that ask for and process responses from the user. There's a lot of information in forums and old answers. The code in BASIC is also adaptable to Python most of the time.

LibreOffice is a fork of a previous project called OpenOffice. UNO is already available at the time of forking, meaning that some references will be found when searching for OpenOffice on the Internet.

Remember that LibreOffice is capable of reading and writing Excel files. Some features may not be 100% compatible. For example, there may be formatting issues.

 For the same reason, it is totally possible to generate a file in Excel format with the tools described in other recipes of this chapter and open it with LibreOffice. That can be a good approach as the documentation is better for openpyxl.

Debugging can also be tricky on occasion. Remember to ensure that a file is fully closed before reopening it with new code.

UNO is also capable of working with other parts of the LibreOffice suite, such as for creating other kinds of documents such as text documents in writer (analogous to MS Word).

See also

- The *Writing a CSV spreadsheet* recipe earlier in the chapter.
- The *Updating an Excel spreadsheet* recipe earlier in the chapter.

7
Cleaning and Processing Data

Some automated tasks will require dealing with large amounts of data. As data grows, two new and distinct problems appear. Processing the task takes too long and input data quality issues cause more problems.

Both problems are well known in the realm of data science dealing with big quantities of data, but the problems can appear even at a smaller scale.

The quality of input data is highly related to the number of sources of the data. In general, data from a single source will be more consistent, but using a single source is limiting. Even if the data comes from the same source, it could still contain inconsistencies or errors.

 Some examples of differences could be regional, such as date formats or currencies, extra information, different names for the same concept (including spelling differences), typos, general bad quality of data with errors... The list is huge!

To compare apples with apples, the input data will probably need to be cleaned. This can be a difficult task and require multiple iterations until the process is refined, particularly if the data changes over time. We will look at some techniques to approach this task.

Regarding time, for some automated cases, this is not a problem. It makes no difference if an automated background emailer, composing and sending a daily update email during the night hours to be read as people come into the office, takes two hours or two minutes. But if someone is waiting for timely results, this can be highly inefficient.

In particular, the waiting time during actual code development and testing is critical as it will not only use up time that could be spent on developing features but also destroys your focus and concentration, which are key to the development process.

There are several tips and techniques to speed up code execution. The main two are: avoid performing the same operation multiple times; and parallelize the task by dividing it into smaller chunks.

The best general advice on to reduce time for your computer tasks is to learn computer science, in particular, algorithms and data structures. This is out of scope for this book, and it can be a long journey. But don't be afraid to ask a fellow programmer for help! Even online!

Chapter 3, Building Your First Web Scraping Application, introduced parallelization of code as part of the *Speeding up web scraping* recipe. We will continue with the concept during this chapter.

In this chapter, we will cover the following recipes:

- Preparing a CSV spreadsheet
- Appending currency based on location
- Standardizing the date format
- Aggregating results
- Processing data in parallel
- Processing data with Pandas

Let's start by getting the base information ready in a tabular file.

Preparing a CSV spreadsheet

As we saw in the previous chapter, CSV files are files containing tabular data defined as a collection of rows with defined columns, separated by commas. They are a very common format for all kinds of data. We will see in this recipe how to extract data from log files and store the information in a CSV file.

Getting ready

We will use a similar log format as the one introduced in the *Extracting data from structured strings* recipe in *Chapter 1, Let's Begin Our Automation Journey*:

```
[<Timestamp>] - SALE - PRODUCT: <product id> - PRICE: <price>
```

Each line will represent a sale log.

We will use the `parse` module. We should install the module, adding it to our `requirements.txt` file as follows:

```
$ echo "parse==1.14.0" >> requirements.txt
$ pip install -r requirements.txt
```

In the GitHub repository, there are some log files to process with the following structure:

```
sale_logs/
    OH
        logs.txt
    ON
        logs.txt
```

The code can be found in the GitHub repository at https://github.com/PacktPublishing/Python-Automation-Cookbook-Second-Edition/tree/master/Chapter07.

How to do it...

1. Check the contents of the `sale_logs/OH/logs.txt` file:

```
$ head sale_logs/OH/logs.txt
[08-27-2019 18:39:41] - SALE - PRODUCT: 12346 - PRICE: 02.99
[08-27-2019 19:39:41] - SALE - PRODUCT: 12346 - PRICE: 02.99
[08-27-2019 20:39:41] - SALE - PRODUCT: 12346 - PRICE: 02.99
[08-27-2019 21:39:41] - SALE - PRODUCT: 12346 - PRICE: 02.99
[08-27-2019 22:39:41] - SALE - PRODUCT: 12345 - PRICE: 09.99
[08-27-2019 23:39:41] - SALE - PRODUCT: 12345 - PRICE: 07.99
[08-28-2019 00:39:41] - SALE - PRODUCT: 12346 - PRICE: 02.99
[08-28-2019 01:39:41] - SALE - PRODUCT: 12346 - PRICE: 02.99
[08-28-2019 02:39:41] - SALE - PRODUCT: 12346 - PRICE: 02.99
[08-28-2019 03:39:41] - SALE - PRODUCT: 12346 - PRICE: 02.99
```

2. Import the data and transform it into a CSV file using the `logs_to_csv.py` script. The script adds the location as input:

```
$ python logs_to_csv.py sale_logs/OH/logs.txt output_1_OH.csv -l
OH
```

3. Check the resulting CSV file in a spreadsheet. In the following screenshot, the file is displayed using the LibreOffice software:

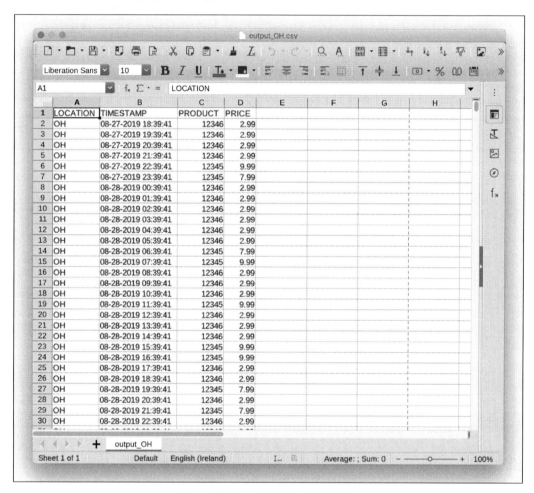

Figure 7.1: Screenshot of product data

Notice how the CSV includes the location, which is stated as OH. Notice also the format of the timestamp.

How it works...

Let's take a look at the `logs_to_csv.py` script, used in *step 2*.

It imports from the `price_log.py` file, which contains the parsing of the logs. This is similar to the code in the *Extracting data from structured strings* recipe in *Chapter 1, Let's Begin Our Automation Journey*. The code adds a header with all the rows and adds a location column. Let's take a look:

```python
class PriceLog(object):

    def __init__(self, location, timestamp, product_id, price):
        self.timestamp = timestamp
        self.product_id = product_id
        self.price = price
        self.location = location

    @classmethod
    def parse(cls, location, text_log):
        '''
        Parse from a text log with the format
        [<Timestamp>] - SALE - PRODUCT: <product id> - PRICE: <price>
        to a PriceLog object

        It requires a location
        '''
        def price(string):
            return Decimal(string)

        FORMAT = ('[{timestamp}] - SALE - PRODUCT: {product:d} - '
                  'PRICE: {price:price}')

        formats = {'price': price}
        result = parse.parse(FORMAT, text_log, formats)

        return cls(location=location, timestamp=result['timestamp'],
                   product_id=result['product'],
        price=result['price'])

    @classmethod
    def header(cls):
```

```
        return ['LOCATION', 'TIMESTAMP', 'PRODUCT', 'PRICE']

    def row(self):
        return [self.location, self.timestamp, self.product_id,
self.price]
```

The file is converted into CSV format by the `log_to_csv` function in the `logs_to_csv.py` file:

```
def log_to_csv(input_file, output_file, location):
    logs = [PriceLog.parse(location, line) for line in input_file]

    # Save into csv format
    writer = csv.writer(output_file)
    writer.writerow(PriceLog.header())
    writer.writerows(l.row() for l in logs)
```

The rest of the `logs_to_csv.py` file deals with the parsing of arguments, which was described in detail in *Chapter 2, Automating Tasks Made Easy*.

The resulting file contains the same information, but CSV is an easier format to understand, process, and add extra information to, as we will see in the following recipes.

There's more...

The main objective in this recipe is to import data from a text file into a CSV without imposing any formatting restrictions on the raw data. For example, the date is in a particular format. The timestamp format will change from file to file, as we will see in the following recipes.

The description of the location is also left deliberately open, as we will use it to set different kinds of locations in the following recipes.

If the log files are very big, reading the whole file and then saving it could be memory-inefficient. In that case, you can process one line at a time, in the following way:

```
def log_to_csv(input_file, output_file, location):
    writer = csv.writer(output_file)
    writer.writerow(PriceLog.header())

    # Read and save line by line
    for line in input_file:
```

```
        log = PriceLog.parse(location, line)
        writer.writerow(log.row())
```

This approach can also be done in batches, reading and writing several lines at a time. This can increase the throughput, though a bit of experimentation could be required to find the optimal solution.

See also

- The *Reading CSV files* recipe in *Chapter 4, Searching and Reading Local Files.*
- The *Extracting data from structured strings* recipe from *Chapter 1, Let's Begin Our Automation Journey.*
- The *Preparing a task* recipe in *Chapter 2, Automating Tasks Made Easy.*

Appending currency based on location

The resulting CSV file from the previous recipe doesn't contain currency information, even though the location can indicate different places with different currencies. In this recipe, we will process a CSV file to add extra information: the currency the prices are in, and a conversion into US dollars.

Getting ready

We will use the resulting CSV file from the previous recipe that receives and transforms logs to the following format:

`[<Timestamp>] - SALE - PRODUCT: <product id> - PRICE: <price>`

Each line will represent a sale log.

We will use the `parse` module. We should install the module, adding it to our `requirements.txt` file as follows:

`$ echo "parse==1.14.0" >> requirements.txt`

`$ pip install -r requirements.txt`

In the GitHub repository, there are some log files to process with the following structure:

```
sale_logs/
  OH
    logs.txt
  ON
```

```
logs.txt
```

The code can be found in the GitHub repository, at `https://github.com/` `PacktPublishing/Python-Automation-Cookbook-Second-Edition/tree/` `master/Chapter07`.

How to do it...

1. Import the data and transform it into a CSV file using the `logs_to_csv.py` script. The script adds the location as input. Create the files for both the OH and OT logs:

   ```
   $ python logs_to_csv.py sale_logs/OH/logs.txt output_1_OH.csv -l
   OH
   ```

   ```
   $ python logs_to_csv.py sale_logs/ON/logs.txt output_1_ON.csv -l
   ON
   ```

2. Process both resulting files using the `location_price.py` script:

   ```
   $ python location_price.py output_1_OH.csv output_2_OH.csv
   ```

   ```
   $ python location_price.py output_1_ON.csv output_2_ON.csv
   ```

3. Check the resulting CSV files in a spreadsheet. In the following screenshots, the files are displayed using the LibreOffice software:

	A	B	C	D	E	F	G
1	LOCATION	TIMESTAMP	PRODUCT	PRICE	COUNTRY	CURRENCY	USD
2	ON	2018-08-27 19:05:55+00:00	12346	3.99	CANADA	CAD	3
3	ON	2018-08-27 20:05:55+00:00	12346	3.99	CANADA	CAD	3
4	ON	2018-08-27 21:05:55+00:00	12346	3.99	CANADA	CAD	3
5	ON	2018-08-27 22:05:55+00:00	12345	10.5	CANADA	CAD	8
6	ON	2018-08-27 23:05:55+00:00	12346	3.99	CANADA	CAD	3
7	ON	2018-08-28 00:05:55+00:00	12346	3.99	CANADA	CAD	3
8	ON	2018-08-28 01:05:55+00:00	12346	3.99	CANADA	CAD	3
9	ON	2018-08-28 02:05:55+00:00	12346	3.99	CANADA	CAD	3
10	ON	2018-08-28 03:05:55+00:00	12346	3.99	CANADA	CAD	3
11	ON	2018-08-28 04:05:55+00:00	12346	3.99	CANADA	CAD	3
12	ON	2018-08-28 05:05:55+00:00	12345	10.5	CANADA	CAD	8
13	ON	2018-08-28 06:05:55+00:00	12346	3.99	CANADA	CAD	3
14	ON	2018-08-28 07:05:55+00:00	12346	3.99	CANADA	CAD	3
15	ON	2018-08-28 08:05:55+00:00	12345	13.5	CANADA	CAD	10
16	ON	2018-08-28 09:05:55+00:00	12346	3.99	CANADA	CAD	3
17	ON	2018-08-28 10:05:55+00:00	12345	10.5	CANADA	CAD	8
18	ON	2018-08-28 11:05:55+00:00	12346	3.99	CANADA	CAD	3
19	ON	2018-08-28 12:05:55+00:00	12346	3.99	CANADA	CAD	3
20	ON	2018-08-28 13:05:55+00:00	12346	3.99	CANADA	CAD	3
21	ON	2018-08-28 14:05:55+00:00	12346	3.99	CANADA	CAD	3
22	ON	2018-08-28 15:05:55+00:00	12346	3.99	CANADA	CAD	3

Figure 7.2a: Screenshot of Canadian product data

	A	B	C	D	E	F	G
1	LOCATION	TIMESTAMP	PRODUCT	PRICE	COUNTRY	CURRENCY	USD
2	OH	08-27-2019 18:39:41	12346	2.99	US	USD	2.99
3	OH	08-27-2019 19:39:41	12346	2.99	US	USD	2.99
4	OH	08-27-2019 20:39:41	12346	2.99	US	USD	2.99
5	OH	08-27-2019 21:39:41	12346	2.99	US	USD	2.99
6	OH	08-27-2019 22:39:41	12345	9.99	US	USD	9.99
7	OH	08-27-2019 23:39:41	12345	7.99	US	USD	7.99
8	OH	08-28-2019 00:39:41	12346	2.99	US	USD	2.99
9	OH	08-28-2019 01:39:41	12346	2.99	US	USD	2.99
10	OH	08-28-2019 02:39:41	12346	2.99	US	USD	2.99
11	OH	08-28-2019 03:39:41	12346	2.99	US	USD	2.99
12	OH	08-28-2019 04:39:41	12346	2.99	US	USD	2.99
13	OH	08-28-2019 05:39:41	12346	2.99	US	USD	2.99
14	OH	08-28-2019 06:39:41	12345	7.99	US	USD	7.99
15	OH	08-28-2019 07:39:41	12345	9.99	US	USD	9.99
16	OH	08-28-2019 08:39:41	12346	2.99	US	USD	2.99
17	OH	08-28-2019 09:39:41	12346	2.99	US	USD	2.99
18	OH	08-28-2019 10:39:41	12346	2.99	US	USD	2.99
19	OH	08-28-2019 11:39:41	12345	9.99	US	USD	9.99
20	OH	08-28-2019 12:39:41	12346	2.99	US	USD	2.99
21	OH	08-28-2019 13:39:41	12346	2.99	US	USD	2.99
22	OH	08-28-2019 14:39:41	12346	2.99	US	USD	2.99

Figure 7.2b: Screenshot of US product data

Notice how the currency changes depending on the location where the product was sold, either Ohio (US) or Ontario (Canada). The prices are displayed in their equivalent US Dollar value for comparison.

How it works...

Let's take a look at the location_price.py script, used in *step 2*.

The end of the script file deals with the parsing of arguments, which was described in detail in *Chapter 2, Automating Tasks Made Easy*.

The main function reads the input CSV and calls the add_price_by_location function for each of the rows. It then saves the file:

```
def main(input_file, output_file):
    reader = csv.DictReader(input_file)
    result = [add_price_by_location(row) for row in reader]

    # Save into csv format
    header = result[0].keys()
    writer = csv.DictWriter(output_file, fieldnames=header)
    writer.writeheader()
    writer.writerows(result)
```

It uses the CSV DictReader class to transform each of the rows into a dictionary. The dictionary is then passed for processing. The resulting rows are stored in the output CSV file using a DictWriter class. The header for the fields of the output file is obtained from the keys in the dictionary of the first output row.

The usage of DictReader and DictWriter was already described in *Chapter 6, Fun with Spreadsheets*.

The most interesting code is in add_price_by_location. This code will detect the country (USA or Canada) based on their location code. Let's take a look:

```
US_LOCATIONS = ['AL', 'AK', …, 'WY', 'DC']
CAD_LOCATIONS = ['AB', 'BC', … , 'NU', 'YT']
CAD_TO_USD = Decimal(0.76)


def add_price_by_location(row):
    location = row['LOCATION']
    if location in US_LOCATIONS:
        row['COUNTRY'] = 'USA'
        row['CURRENCY'] = 'USD'
        row['USD'] = Decimal(row['PRICE'])
    elif location in CAD_LOCATIONS:
        row['COUNTRY'] = 'CANADA'
        row['CURRENCY'] = 'CAD'
        row['USD'] = Decimal(row['PRICE']) * CAD_TO_USD
    else:
        raise Exception('Location not found')


    return row
```

Based on the location, it derives the currency. Note that the two-letter codes for Canadian provinces and territories and for US states are described in two lists. The full description of each is in the CAD_LOCATIONS and US_LOCATIONS arrays. If the detected location is a US state, the currency is set to US dollars, and it's set to Canadian dollars for all the provinces and territories in Canada.

It's very convenient that US states and Canadian provinces have different unique codes, making them easy to distinguish. In other systems, this may be more complicated.

It adds a new key to the dictionary for the country, the currency, and the US-dollar equivalent of the price. These three keys are then added as columns to the output CSV.

 Since Python 3.7, the dictionaries keep the insertion order. This means that the last added key to the dictionary will be retrieved last when keys are presented. This wasn't the case in previous versions, where we had to rely on OrderedDict, a specific kind of dictionary that preserves key order. We take advantage of this behavior regarding the generation of the header, as any new element introduced will be stored as a new column at the end, keeping the order of the old ones.

The resulting file provides information on each sale log in a common currency, making comparisons easier.

There's more...

As we commented before, processing and distinguishing location and currency may not be as straightforward as presented here. Different countries may have different ways of presenting places, and in some cases, codes used to represent locations from different countries may overlap.

The country is added as a column to have available later on.

The currency exchange rate is defined as a constant, but that's only an approximation. It may be necessary to obtain it from an external source. For example, www.exchangerate-api.com offers a free API to integrate exchange rate conversions, as follows:

```
>>> import requests
>>> result = requests.get('https://api.exchangerate-api.com/v4/latest/CAD')
>>> result.json()['rates']['USD']
0.755081
```

More complicated setups may require access to specific exchange rate sources or to be able to retrieve the historic information on rates.

 Most exchange rate sources have a limit on the number of calls, or charge per access. Be sure to avoid constant polling for data and store the rates for local usage.

See also

- The *Preparing a CSV spreadsheet* recipe from the previous section.
- The *Reading CSV files* recipe in *Chapter 4, Searching and Reading Local Files*.
- The *Preparing a task* recipe in *Chapter 2, Automating Tasks Made Easy*.

Standardizing the date format

The date time format in the logs is different depending on the location. In the Canadian logs, the format is the standard ISO 8601 in the format YYYY-MM-DD. The logs coming from the USA use the format MM-DD-YYYY. In this recipe, we will append a new column with a standard format to unify both dates.

Getting ready

We will use the resulting CSV file from the previous recipe that receives and transforms logs in the following format:

```
[<Timestamp>] - SALE - PRODUCT: <product id> - PRICE: <price>
```

Each line will represent a sale log.

We will use the `parse` module. We should install the module, adding it to our `requirements.txt` file as follows:

```
$ echo "parse==1.14.0" >> requirements.txt
$ pip install -r requirements.txt
```

In the GitHub repository, there are some log files to process with the following structure:

```
sale_logs/
  OH
    logs.txt
  ON
    logs.txt
```

The code can be found in the GitHub repository at https://github.com/PacktPublishing/Python-Automation-Cookbook-Second-Edition/tree/master/Chapter07.

How to do it...

1. Import the data and transform it into a CSV file using the `logs_to_csv.py` script. The script adds the location as input. Create the files for both the OH and OT logs:

```
$ python logs_to_csv.py sale_logs/OH/logs.txt output_1_OH.csv -l
OH
```

```
$ python logs_to_csv.py sale_logs/ON/logs.txt output_1_ON.csv -l
ON
```

2. Process both resulting files using the `location_price.py` script:

```
$ python location_price.py output_1_OH.csv output_2_OH.csv
```

```
$ python location_price.py output_1_ON.csv output_2_ON.csv
```

3. Process both files using the `standard_date.py` script:

```
$ python standard_date.py output_2_OH.csv output_3_OH.csv
```

```
$ python standard_date.py output_2_ON.csv output_3_ON.csv
```

4. Check the resulting CSV files in a spreadsheet. In the following screenshots, the files are displayed using the LibreOffice software:

	A	B	C	D	E	F	G	H
1	LOCATION	TIMESTAMP	PRODUCT	PRICE	COUNTRY	CURRENCY	USD	STD_TIMESTAMP
2	OH	08-27-2019 18:39:41	12346	2.99	USA	USD	2.99	2019-08-27T17:39:41+00:00
3	OH	08-27-2019 19:39:41	12346	2.99	USA	USD	2.99	2019-08-27T18:39:41+00:00
4	OH	08-27-2019 20:39:41	12346	2.99	USA	USD	2.99	2019-08-27T19:39:41+00:00
5	OH	08-27-2019 21:39:41	12346	2.99	USA	USD	2.99	2019-08-27T20:39:41+00:00
6	OH	08-27-2019 22:39:41	12345	9.99	USA	USD	9.99	2019-08-27T21:39:41+00:00
7	OH	08-27-2019 23:39:41	12345	7.99	USA	USD	7.99	2019-08-27T22:39:41+00:00
8	OH	08-28-2019 00:39:41	12346	2.99	USA	USD	2.99	2019-08-27T23:39:41+00:00
9	OH	08-28-2019 01:39:41	12346	2.99	USA	USD	2.99	2019-08-28T00:39:41+00:00
10	OH	08-28-2019 02:39:41	12346	2.99	USA	USD	2.99	2019-08-28T01:39:41+00:00
11	OH	08-28-2019 03:39:41	12346	2.99	USA	USD	2.99	2019-08-28T02:39:41+00:00
12	OH	08-28-2019 04:39:41	12346	2.99	USA	USD	2.99	2019-08-28T03:39:41+00:00
13	OH	08-28-2019 05:39:41	12346	2.99	USA	USD	2.99	2019-08-28T04:39:41+00:00
14	OH	08-28-2019 06:39:41	12345	7.99	USA	USD	7.99	2019-08-28T05:39:41+00:00
15	OH	08-28-2019 07:39:41	12345	9.99	USA	USD	9.99	2019-08-28T06:39:41+00:00
16	OH	08-28-2019 08:39:41	12346	2.99	USA	USD	2.99	2019-08-28T07:39:41+00:00
17	OH	08-28-2019 09:39:41	12346	2.99	USA	USD	2.99	2019-08-28T08:39:41+00:00
18	OH	08-28-2019 10:39:41	12346	2.99	USA	USD	2.99	2019-08-28T09:39:41+00:00
19	OH	08-28-2019 11:39:41	12345	9.99	USA	USD	9.99	2019-08-28T10:39:41+00:00
20	OH	08-28-2019 12:39:41	12346	2.99	USA	USD	2.99	2019-08-28T11:39:41+00:00
21	OH	08-28-2019 13:39:41	12346	2.99	USA	USD	2.99	2019-08-28T12:39:41+00:00
22	OH	08-28-2019 14:39:41	12346	2.99	USA	USD	2.99	2019-08-28T13:39:41+00:00

	A	B	C	D	E	F	G	H
1	LOCATION	TIMESTAMP	PRODUCT	PRICE	COUNTRY	CURRENCY	USD	STD_TIMESTAMP
2	ON	2018-08-27 19:05:55+00:00	12346	3.99	CANADA	CAD	3	2018-08-27 19:05:55+00:00
3	ON	2018-08-27 20:05:55+00:00	12346	3.99	CANADA	CAD	3	2018-08-27 20:05:55+00:00
4	ON	2018-08-27 21:05:55+00:00	12346	3.99	CANADA	CAD	3	2018-08-27 21:05:55+00:00
5	ON	2018-08-27 22:05:55+00:00	12345	10.5	CANADA	CAD	8	2018-08-27 22:05:55+00:00
6	ON	2018-08-27 23:05:55+00:00	12346	3.99	CANADA	CAD	3	2018-08-27 23:05:55+00:00
7	ON	2018-08-28 00:05:55+00:00	12346	3.99	CANADA	CAD	3	2018-08-28 00:05:55+00:00
8	ON	2018-08-28 01:05:55+00:00	12346	3.99	CANADA	CAD	3	2018-08-28 01:05:55+00:00
9	ON	2018-08-28 02:05:55+00:00	12346	3.99	CANADA	CAD	3	2018-08-28 02:05:55+00:00
10	ON	2018-08-28 03:05:55+00:00	12346	3.99	CANADA	CAD	3	2018-08-28 03:05:55+00:00
11	ON	2018-08-28 04:05:55+00:00	12346	3.99	CANADA	CAD	3	2018-08-28 04:05:55+00:00
12	ON	2018-08-28 05:05:55+00:00	12345	10.5	CANADA	CAD	8	2018-08-28 05:05:55+00:00
13	ON	2018-08-28 06:05:55+00:00	12346	3.99	CANADA	CAD	3	2018-08-28 06:05:55+00:00
14	ON	2018-08-28 07:05:55+00:00	12346	3.99	CANADA	CAD	3	2018-08-28 07:05:55+00:00
15	ON	2018-08-28 08:05:55+00:00	12345	13.5	CANADA	CAD	10	2018-08-28 08:05:55+00:00
16	ON	2018-08-28 09:05:55+00:00	12346	3.99	CANADA	CAD	3	2018-08-28 09:05:55+00:00
17	ON	2018-08-28 10:05:55+00:00	12345	10.5	CANADA	CAD	8	2018-08-28 10:05:55+00:00
18	ON	2018-08-28 11:05:55+00:00	12346	3.99	CANADA	CAD	3	2018-08-28 11:05:55+00:00
19	ON	2018-08-28 12:05:55+00:00	12346	3.99	CANADA	CAD	3	2018-08-28 12:05:55+00:00
20	ON	2018-08-28 13:05:55+00:00	12346	3.99	CANADA	CAD	3	2018-08-28 13:05:55+00:00
21	ON	2018-08-28 14:05:55+00:00	12346	3.99	CANADA	CAD	3	2018-08-28 14:05:55+00:00
22	ON	2018-08-28 15:05:55+00:00	12346	3.99	CANADA	CAD	3	2018-08-28 15:05:55+00:00

Figure 7.3: Screenshots of consistent standardized timestamps

Notice how the times in the **STD_TIMESTAMP** column are formatted in the same way, while those in the **TIMESTAMP** column are not.

How it works...

Let's take a look at the `standard_date.py` script, used in *step 3*.

The end of the script file deals with the parsing of arguments, which was described in detail in *Chapter 2, Automating Tasks Made Easy*.

The main function reads the input CSV and calls the `add_std_timestamp` function for each of the rows. It then writes the results in the output file:

```
def main(input_file, output_file):
    reader = csv.DictReader(input_file)
    result = [add_price_by_location(row) for row in reader]

    # Save into csv format
    header = result[0].keys()
    writer = csv.DictWriter(output_file, fieldnames=header)
    writer.writeheader()
    writer.writerows(result)
```

It uses the CSV `DictReader` class to transform each of the rows into a dictionary, which is then passed for processing. The output CSV file stores the resulting rows using `DictWriter`. The output file field headers are obtained from the keys in the dictionary of the first output row.

The usage of `DictReader` and `DictWriter` was already described in *Chapter 6, Fun with Spreadsheets*.

Each of the rows is modified in the `add_std_timestamp` function, depending on the country the log was written in. Let's take a look:

```
def add_std_timestamp(row):
    country = row['COUNTRY']
    if country == 'USA':
        # No change
        row['STD_TIMESTAMP'] = american_format(row['TIMESTAMP'])
    elif country == 'CANADA':
        # No change
        row['STD_TIMESTAMP'] = row['TIMESTAMP']
    else:
        raise Exception('Country not found')

    return row
```

Based on the country of origin, this function transforms the date and creates a new standardized timestamp.

Note that the country has been inserted into the data in the previous recipe, having been derived from the location codes. Storing the country explicitly in the previous stage of processing allows us to simplify the script for the date, as the data has been already calculated. This may look straightforward in this example, but duplicating operations in different stages while processing data is quite common as the focus while developing is generally only on a small part of the code, and not the code as a whole.

The function adds a new key to the dictionary with a standard timestamp in ISO 8601 format. The logs produced in Canada already have this format, but the ones generated in the United States need to be translated. The translation is done in the `american_format` function:

```
def american_format(timestamp):
    '''
```

```
    Transform from MM-DD-YYYY HH:MM:SS to iso 8601
    '''
    FORMAT = '%m-%d-%Y %H:%M:%S'

    parsed_tmp = datetime.strptime(timestamp, FORMAT)
    time_with_tz = parsed_tmp.astimezone(timezone.utc)
    isotimestamp = time_with_tz.isoformat()

    return isotimestamp
```

The timestamp is parsed using the standard Python library with `datetime.strptime` with the format `"%m-%d-%Y %H:%M:%S"`, which corresponds to MM-DD-YYYY HH:MM:SS. The resulting `datetime` object is then added to the UTC time zone, transformed into an ISO 8601 valid string, and then returned.

 Remember that since Python 3.7, the dictionaries keep the insertion order.

The resulting file allows us to compare times in the same format.

There's more...

In some cases, the detection of the timestamp format may not be dependent on other parameters such as the country and will require you to try several formats to see which one fits. When working with many sources, this can actually become a problem, as a single row may not contain enough information. For example, a date 05-06-2019 could be June 5th in international format, or May 6th in US format. An analysis of the whole file may be required or even taking a guess and validating it afterward.

The time in all the log files for the recipe is stored in UTC time, but that's not necessarily true in every case. It can be stored in different time zones.

In our example, the time zones in Ohio and Ontario are the same, but the time zones may be different depending on the location. Depending on the logs, this may require an adjustment.

The ISO 8601 format may include the time zone. For example, the ending in +00:00 shows the time zone is UTC. Don't assume that the time format will always include time zone information. If it's not present, it may lead to inconsistent times in your data. Always include the time zone, or use the times in UTC when combining different sources to avoid confusion.

If different time zones are used, the `delorean` module, introduced in *Chapter 1*, *Let's Begin Our Automation Journey*, helps define the times and match equivalent times in an easy way:

```
>>> import delorean
>>> timestamp = delorean.parse('2018-08-28 20:05:55+00:00')
>>> timestamp_EST = timestamp.shift('US/Eastern')
>>> timestamp_EST.datetime.isoformat()
'2018-08-28T16:05:55-04:00'
```

The full Delorean documentation can be found online at `https://delorean.readthedocs.io/`.

Notice how the old timestamps are still present in the CSV file, instead of being overwritten by the new timestamp column. Unless there's a clear need to save space, it's best to keep it for reference and to detect possible problems later. It also allows us to know easily when this stage has been applied to the given CSV file.

See also

- The *Appending currency based on location* recipe in the previous section.
- The *Reading CSV files* recipe in *Chapter 4*, *Searching and Reading Local Files*.
- The *Preparing a task* recipe in *Chapter 2*, *Automating Tasks Made Easy*.

Aggregating results

Once the data is cleaned, we can process the results. For our example, we will calculate the average sale price by both location and day, as well as the total sales by both location and day in the data range. As our data is stored by location, this will be done in two steps. First, we'll create the files per location, and then by date, using the date on the location results.

Getting ready

We will use the resulting CSV file from the previous recipe that receives and transforms logs in the following format:

```
[<Timestamp>] - SALE - PRODUCT: <product id> - PRICE: <price>
```

Each line will represent a sale log.

We will use the `parse` module and the `delorean` module. We should install the modules, adding them to our `requirements.txt` file as follows:

```
$ echo "parse==1.14.0" >> requirements.txt
$ echo "delorean==1.0.0" >> requirements.txt
$ pip install -r requirements.txt
```

In the GitHub repository, there are some log files to process with the following structure:

```
sale_logs/
    OH
        logs.txt
    ON
        logs.txt
```

The code can be found in the GitHub repository, at https://github.com/PacktPublishing/Python-Automation-Cookbook-Second-Edition/tree/master/Chapter07.

How to do it...

1. Import the data and transform it into a CSV file using the `logs_to_csv.py` script. The script adds the location as input. Create the files for both the OH and OT logs:

   ```
   $ python logs_to_csv.py sale_logs/OH/logs.txt output_1_OH.csv -l OH
   $ python logs_to_csv.py sale_logs/ON/logs.txt output_1_ON.csv -l ON
   ```

2. Process both resulting files using the `location_price.py` script:

   ```
   $ python location_price.py output_1_OH.csv output_2_OH.csv
   $ python location_price.py output_1_ON.csv output_2_ON.csv
   ```

3. Process both files using the `standard_date.py` script:

```
$ python standard_date.py output_2_OH.csv output_3_OH.csv
$ python standard_date.py output_2_ON.csv output_3_ON.csv
```

4. Process both resulting files using the `aggregate_by_location.py` script:

```
$ python aggregate_by_location.py output_3_ON.csv aggregate_ON.csv
$ python aggregate_by_location.py output_3_OH.csv aggregate_OH.csv
```

5. Check the resulting CSV files in a spreadsheet. In the following screenshots, the files are displayed using the LibreOffice software:

	A	B	C	D
1	DATE	TOTAL USD	NUMBER	AVERAGE
2	2019-08-27	32.93	7	4.7
3	2019-08-28	114.76	24	4.78
4	2019-08-29	111.76	24	4.66
5	2019-08-30	113.76	24	4.74
6	2019-08-31	135.76	24	5.66
7	2019-09-01	112.76	24	4.7
8	2019-09-02	126.76	24	5.28
9	2019-09-03	114.76	24	4.78
10	2019-09-04	115.76	24	4.82
11	2019-09-05	100.76	24	4.2
12	2019-09-06	119.76	24	4.99

	A	B	C	D
1	DATE	TOTAL USD	NUMBER	AVERAGE
2	2018-08-27	20	5	4
3	2018-08-28	113	24	4.71
4	2018-08-29	120	24	5
5	2018-08-30	120	24	5
6	2018-08-31	115	24	4.79
7	2018-09-01	106	24	4.42
8	2018-09-02	126	24	5.25
9	2018-09-03	159	24	6.62
10	2018-09-04	114	24	4.75
11	2018-09-05	134	24	5.58
12	2018-09-06	94	24	3.92

Figure 7.4: Screenshots of aggregated results

Let's take a look at the `aggregate_by_location.py` script, used in *step 6*.

The final part of the script file deals with the parsing of arguments, which was described in detail in *Chapter 2, Automating Tasks Made Easy*.

The `main` function reads the input CSV and calls the `calculate_results` function to generate the aggregated reports. It then writes the results in the output file. The usage of `DictReader` and `DictWriter` was already described in *Chapter 6, Fun with Spreadsheets*.

In the `calculate_results` function, the aggregation takes place. Each line is analyzed to check its date, and all the entries with the same date are aggregated:

```
def calculate_results(reader):
    result = []
    last_date = None
    total_usd = 0
    number = 0

    for row in reader:
        date = parse_iso(row['STD_TIMESTAMP'])
        if not last_date:
            last_date = date

        if last_date < date:
            # New day!
            result.append(line(date, total_usd, number))
            total_usd = 0
            number = 0
            last_date = date

        number += 1
        total_usd += Decimal(row['USD'])

    # Final results
    result.append(line(date, total_usd, number))
    return result
```

The code takes note of the latest date and keeps aggregating until it changes. Every time there's a change in date, the line is appended to the `result` array.

Note that this takes advantage of the fact that the data is sorted by
timestamp. In this example, the timestamps in the logs are sorted
by origin, but there may be scenarios where it is necessary to
perform some ordering and/or filtering. Use the same techniques
we described in this chapter, and create an extra step with the
sorting process if necessary.

To obtain the date, the input ISO format is parsed using the `delorean` module:

```
def parse_iso(timestamp):
    # Parse the ISO format
    total = delorean.parse(timestamp, dayfirst=False)
    # Keep only the date
    return total.date
```

The `dayfirst=False` parameter ensures that the timestamp is correctly interpreted.

The new (as yet unreleased) version of `delorean` will include
a specific `isofirst` parameter to explicitly parse ISO 8601.
This version hasn't been released at the time of writing, but it's
displayed in the documentation.

Each new line is configured in dictionary format on the `line` function, which is as
follows:

```
def line(date, total_usd, number):
    data = {
        'DATE': date,
        'TOTAL USD': total_usd,
        'NUMBER': number,
        # Round to two decimal places
        'AVERAGE': round(total_usd / number, 2),
    }
    return data
```

Each of the lines has the date, the total USD from sales, the number of sales, and an
average price per item.

Storing the aggregated total and the number of events that comprise this total allows us to aggregate the values further and calculate the average. Just the average on its own cannot be aggregated further, but the aggregated total and the number of events can, and the average can easily be calculated from them.

The aggregated file is stored in CSV format, after `calculate_results` returns the value to `main`.

There's more...

A careful examination of the input dates will show that they are not exactly identical. While the format in the `output_3_OH.csv` file is YYYY-MM-DDTHH:MM:SS+00:00, the format in the file `output_3_ON.csv` is YYYY-MM-DD HH:MM:SS+00:00. Note the space where the T is. The ISO 8601 format uses the T character to separate the date from the time, but it's quite common to see it separated with a space, as described in RFC3339 (`https://tools.ietf.org/html/rfc3339`), so most software tools will be able to parse it, including `delorean`.

 Noticing at a later stage that the data is not completely standardized is actually a common problem. Be forgiving with the input data and try to be as strict as possible with the data output.

The full `delorean` documentation can be found online at `https://delorean.readthedocs.io/`.

The average price per sale is rounded to two decimal places, which keeps it up to the penny and makes sense in this specific case. This is done through the built-in `round` function that accepts an extra parameter with the number of decimal places to round to:

```
>>> round(3.14159)
3
>>> round(3.14159, 4)
3.1416
```

If you need more control to round either up or down to the next integer, you can use the `math.ceil` and `math.floor` functions:

```
>>> import math
>>> math.ceil(3.14159)
```

4

```
>>> math.floor(3.14159)
```

3

For more general statistical operators other than the average, the Python module in the `statistics` standard library has functions such as `median()` and `quantiles()`. Check the documentation at `https://docs.python.org/3/library/statistics.html`.

While not required for the average, some of these measurements (such as the mode or median) may require working with the full data set in memory. This limits the amount of data that can be processed, especially for very big sets of data.

The debate over what exactly is *big data* is difficult, as there's not a single point where regular data becomes big. While an in-depth discussion about big data is out of scope for this book, its main characteristic is that it is data that cannot be contained in a single computer, requiring distributed processing in different computers. This complicates the operation a lot, to the point of requiring specialized skills to deal with it. Before moving to that area, think about whether the data could fit on a specific server with as much memory as possible and if that could be helpful. This approach of "throwing hardware at a problem" can go a long way, and it's typically cheaper than the work involved in re-architecting the code.

Please note that calculating statistics can be a difficult challenge requiring specific knowledge to avoid problems such as outliers modifying the average, or more subtle issues such as unrepresentative sampling of the data. When calculating something complicated, double check your assumptions and verify that the result correctly represents the desired measure. This may seem like an easy task to do, but it can be trickier than expected.

See also

- The *Standardizing the date format* recipe from the previous section.
- The *Reading CSV files* recipe in *Chapter 4*, *Searching and Reading Local Files*.
- The *Preparing a task* recipe in Chapter 2, *Automating Tasks Made Easy*.

Process data in parallel

The processing presented in the previous recipe works well. But it needs to process each file one by one. When we have a small number of files, this may be fine, but with huge numbers of files to handle, this will not be efficient. Each time we will be using a single CPU core, which is not the best for this type of number crunching task.

In this recipe, we will see how to process the files in parallel, making use of all the cores of the computer to speed up the process and greatly increase the throughput.

Getting ready

We will use the resulting CSV file from the previous recipe that receives and transforms logs in the following format:

```
[<Timestamp>] - SALE - PRODUCT: <product id> - PRICE: <price>
```

Each line will represent a sale log.

We will use the `parse` module and the `delorean` module. We should install the modules, adding them to our `requirements.txt` file as follows:

```
$ echo "parse==1.14.0" >> requirements.txt
$ echo "delorean==1.0.0" >> requirements.txt
$ pip install -r requirements.txt
```

In the GitHub repository, there are some log files to process with the following structure:

```
sale_logs/
   OH
      logs.txt
   ON
      logs.txt
```

The code can be found in the GitHub repository at `https://github.com/PacktPublishing/Python-Automation-Cookbook-Second-Edition/tree/master/Chapter07`.

How to do it...

1. Import the data and transform it into a CSV file using the `logs_to_csv.py` script. The script adds the location as input. Create the files for both the OH and OT logs:

```
$ python logs_to_csv.py sale_logs/OH/logs.txt output_1_OH.csv -l
OH

$ python logs_to_csv.py sale_logs/ON/logs.txt output_1_ON.csv -l
ON
```

2. Process both resulting files using the `location_price.py` script:

```
$ python location_price.py output_1_OH.csv output_2_OH.csv

$ python location_price.py output_1_ON.csv output_2_ON.csv
```

3. Process both files using the `standard_date.py` script:

```
$ python standard_date.py output_2_OH.csv output_3_OH.csv

$ python standard_date.py output_2_ON.csv output_3_ON.csv
```

4. Process all the files in a single call to `aggregate_by_location_parallel.py` specifying the files to process:

```
$ python aggregate_by_location_parallel.py "output_3_*.csv"

Processing output_3_ON.csv

Processing output_3_OH.csv

Done with output_3_ON.csv => aggregate_ON.csv

Done with output_3_OH.csv => aggregate_OH.csv
```

5. Check the resulting CSV files in a spreadsheet. In the following screenshots, the files are displayed using the LibreOffice software:

	A	B	C	D
1	DATE	TOTAL USD	NUMBER	AVERAGE
2	2019-08-28	32.93	7	4.7
3	2019-08-29	114.76	24	4.78
4	2019-08-30	111.76	24	4.66
5	2019-08-31	113.76	24	4.74
6	2019-09-01	135.76	24	5.66
7	2019-09-02	112.76	24	4.7
8	2019-09-03	126.76	24	5.28
9	2019-09-04	114.76	24	4.78
10	2019-09-05	115.76	24	4.82
11	2019-09-06	100.76	24	4.2
12	2019-09-07	119.76	24	4.99

	A	B	C	D
1	DATE	TOTAL USD	NUMBER	AVERAGE
2	2018-08-28	20	5	4
3	2018-08-29	113	24	4.71
4	2018-08-30	120	24	5
5	2018-08-31	120	24	5
6	2018-09-01	115	24	4.79
7	2018-09-02	106	24	4.42
8	2018-09-03	126	24	5.25
9	2018-09-04	159	24	6.62
10	2018-09-05	114	24	4.75
11	2018-09-06	134	24	5.58
12	2018-09-07	94	24	3.92

Figure 7.5: The results of the recipe

How it works...

Let's take a look at the `aggregate_by_location_parallel.py` script, used in *step 6*.

The final part of the script file deals with the parsing of arguments, which was described in detail in *Chapter 2, Automating Tasks Made Easy*.

The `main` function detects the input files to aggregate and then processes them in parallel:

```
def main(input_glob):
    input_files = [filename for filename in glob.glob(input_glob)]

    with concurrent.futures.ProcessPoolExecutor(max_workers=4) as
    executor:
        futures = [executor.submit(aggregate_filename, filename)
                for filename in input_files]
        concurrent.futures.wait(futures)
```

The function first uses the input glob to filter the related files and stores them in the `input_files` variable. This is done through the `glob.glob` function, which returns the filenames that match the glob.

Globs are patterns commonly encountered to match groups of filenames with wildcard characters, normally `*`. For example, `glob *.txt` will match any filename that has the extension `txt`.

Python includes a glob module as part of its standard library. You can check the full documentation at `https://docs.python.org/3/library/glob.html`.

The glob pattern searches by default in the current directory. Keep this in mind in case it requires tweaking.

The next step is to make a call using a parallel executor for each of the files to the `aggregate_filename` function. We will describe this function shortly, but let's take a look at the executor first:

```
with concurrent.futures.ProcessPoolExecutor(max_workers=4) as
executor:
    futures = [executor.submit(aggregate_filename, filename)
            for filename in input_files]
    concurrent.futures.wait(futures)
```

First, we define the executor using a `with` statement and a call to `ProcessPoolExecutor`. `ProcessPoolExecutor` creates a number of process workers that will run the submitted calls to the executor in the background.

`ProcessPoolExecutor` uses independent processes created in the background, instead of threads. You can use `ThreadPoolExecutor` as well.

Due to some limitations arising from how Python is structured internally, using threads is not optimal for workloads that are CPU intensive, such as numerical operations. Threads are adequate for I/O operations including calling external APIs and reading from disk.

For this particular workload that relies on crunching numbers, the number of processes (and therefore workers) should be the same as the number of cores in the CPU used. We assumed four for this example, which is a common number in desktop computers.

The next step is to create a future for each filename. The future is an object that references the call that will be executed in the background by the executor. When it's done, the future object will store the result.

> You can think of a future object as a ticket for a valet car cleaning. You submit the task, get a ticket, and can go do other things. When you're done, you hand back the ticket and may need to wait until it's finished, if there's still some work pending.

The last step is to wait until all futures are completed by calling concurrent. futures.wait. Note that there's no result to check for the futures in this specific example.

We introduced futures and executors in the *Speeding up web scraping* recipe in *Chapter 3, Building Your First Web Scraping Application*. In that recipe, we used a thread-based future.

The task to be executed wraps the aggregation of the file. Let's take a look:

```python
from aggregate_by_location import main as main_by_file


def aggregate_filename(filename):
    try:
        print(f'Processing {filename}')
        # Obtain the location
        match = re.match(r'output_3_(.*).csv', filename)
        location = match.group(1)
        output_file = f'aggregate_{location}.csv'

        with open(filename) as in_file, open(output_file, 'w') as out_file:
            main_by_file(in_file, out_file)

        print(f'Done with {filename} => {output_file}', flush=True)
    except Exception as exc:
        print(f'Unexpected exception {exc}')
```

At the core of it, there's a call to main_by_file. This method is imported directly from the *Aggregating results* recipe from the previous section. It receives an input file and produces an output file. These files are opened with read and write access using the with statement.

The names of the files are determined beforehand. The input file is a parameter of the function, but the output file is obtained from it. It uses the regex output_3_(.*). csv file to extract the location from the filename in a match group:

```
match = re.match(r'output_3_(.*).csv', filename)
location = match.group(1)
output_file = f'aggregate_{location}.csv'
```

The input filename and the resulting output file are printed to provide feedback while they are executing.

Working with regexes was described in more detail in the *Introducing regular expressions* and *Going deeper with regular expressions* recipes in *Chapter 1, Let's Begin Our Automation Journey*.

The resulting file is the same as the one produced in the previous *Aggregating results* recipe, but in this case, we process the files in parallel, up to four at the same time. This speeds up the process significantly.

There's more...

Working with parallel tasks has multiple advantages, but there are also some caveats that need to be taken into account.

Executing multiple tasks may make exceptions for stopping the execution of the whole script, as would happen with single-task runs. In our example, the aggregate_filename function contains a try/except block that will capture any possible issues and log the error. The rest of the files will continue, but at least the error can be noticed and won't be silently ignored.

> This is actually part of the Zen of Python, available by calling import this.
>
> *Errors should never pass silently.*
>
> *Unless explicitly silenced.*

The script could also include an extra check to see whether a particular file has already been created, after determining the output filename. This can be checked with the os.path.isfile function:

```
import os.path
...
output_file = f'aggregate_{location}.csv'
if os.path.isfile(output_file):
```

```
        # File already exists, do not overwrite
        Return

    with open(filename) as in_file ...
```

When dealing with large numbers of files, to repeat the execution of the script without starting from the beginning is a great advantage. A common problem is to process a gigantic amount of data, to have an error when processing is 80% complete, and then to restart the script from the beginning, having to redo all the work.

If possible, invest a bit of time in saving partial results to disk or other storage places, so they can be skipped over, thereby speeding up the processing.

 Keep the working dataset small for the purpose of development. It will allow you to iterate quickly and limits distractions. Also, store already processed data on disk.

One of the `print` statements to produce feedback adds the `flush` parameter:

```
print(f'Done with {filename} => {output_file}', flush=True)
```

The `flush` parameter will use the `print` statement to display the message immediately. If `flush` is not set, or if it's set to `False`, the message won't be printed instantly on screen, but goes to an intermediate buffer. The buffer will be printed when the operating system decides to do it, usually after a newline.

This may cause a small delay. That delay can be noticeable in certain cases, such as in the last task executed. In that case, the print buffer might hold information, but the program exits before the information is printed. In a single-task program, before exiting, the buffer is printed, but that's not guaranteed in multitask applications.

The parallel nature of the multitask application may also mean that the order of the files being processed is not consistent from one run to the next. To avoid problems, each of the tasks should be independent of each other to avoid introducing dependencies.

To learn more about `futures` and `executors`, check the Python documentation at https://docs.python.org/3/library/concurrent.futures.html.

See also

- The *Aggregating Results* recipe from the previous section.
- The *Reading CSV files* recipe in *Chapter 4, Searching and Reading Local Files*.
- The *Preparing a task* recipe in *Chapter 2, Automating Tasks Made Easy*.
- The *Speeding up web scraping* recipe in *Chapter 3, Building Your First Web Scraping Application*.

Process data with Pandas

For some operations, simple calculations are not enough. Sometimes, operations may have some nuances in the way they are calculated and have problems with precision due to using certain kinds of types.

 Python allows us to use big numbers automatically, but in certain languages, adjusting to big numbers could be a challenge. Numbers in computing have limitations such as limited precision or ranges where they are accurate. These limitations may not be obvious at first glance.

Even more so, Python is known not to have an amazing number-crunching performance. Complicated mathematical operations will take longer compared to a compiled language such as C++ or even Java.

That's why using a specialized package can greatly help. They deal with a lot of complexities of the treatment of data, and also produce better performance, as they're optimized for that.

In this recipe, we will see how to process the files using the Pandas library, which is an easy-to-use data analysis library for Python that's widely used by the scientific community.

Getting ready

We will use the resulting CSV file from the previous recipe that receives and transforms logs in the following format:

```
[<Timestamp>] - SALE - PRODUCT: <product id> - PRICE: <price>
```

Each line will represent a sale log.

We will use the `pandas` module. We should install the module, adding it to our `requirements.txt` file as follows:

```
$ echo "pandas==1.0.1" >> requirements.txt
$ pip install -r requirements.txt
```

In the GitHub repository, there are some log files to process with the following structure:

```
sale_logs/
    OH
        logs.txt
    ON
        logs.txt
```

The code can be found in the GitHub repository at `https://github.com/PacktPublishing/Python-Automation-Cookbook-Second-Edition/tree/master/Chapter07`.

How to do it...

1. Import the data and transform it into a CSV file using the `logs_to_csv.py` script. The script adds the location as input. Create the files for both the OH and OT logs:

    ```
    $ python logs_to_csv.py sale_logs/OH/logs.txt output_1_OH.csv -l OH
    $ python logs_to_csv.py sale_logs/ON/logs.txt output_1_ON.csv -l ON
    ```

2. Process both resulting files using the `location_price.py` script:

    ```
    $ python location_price.py output_1_OH.csv output_2_OH.csv
    $ python location_price.py output_1_ON.csv output_2_ON.csv
    ```

3. Process both files using the `standard_date.py` script:

    ```
    $ python standard_date.py output_2_OH.csv output_3_OH.csv
    $ python standard_date.py output_2_ON.csv output_3_ON.csv
    ```

4. Process all the files in a single call to `aggregate_by_location_pandas.py`, specifying the files to process:

```
$ python aggregate_by_location_by_pandas.py output_3_OH.csv
aggregate_pd_OH.csv
```

```
$ python aggregate_by_location_by_pandas.py output_3_ON.csv
aggregate_pd_ON.csv
```

5. Check the resulting CSV files, `aggregate_pd_OH.csv` and `aggregate_pd_ON.csv`, in a spreadsheet. In the following screenshots, the files are displayed using the LibreOffice software:

	A	B	C	D
1	DATE	TOTAL USD	NUMBER	AVERAGE
2	2018-08-28	20	5	4
3	2018-08-29	113	24	4.71
4	2018-08-30	120	24	5
5	2018-08-31	120	24	5
6	2018-09-01	115	24	4.79
7	2018-09-02	106	24	4.42
8	2018-09-03	126	24	5.25
9	2018-09-04	159	24	6.62
10	2018-09-05	114	24	4.75
11	2018-09-06	134	24	5.58
12	2018-09-07	94	24	3.92

	A	B	C	D
1	DATE	TOTAL USD	NUMBER	AVERAGE
2	2018-08-28	20	5	4
3	2018-08-29	113	24	4.71
4	2018-08-30	120	24	5
5	2018-08-31	120	24	5
6	2018-09-01	115	24	4.79
7	2018-09-02	106	24	4.42
8	2018-09-03	126	24	5.25
9	2018-09-04	159	24	6.62
10	2018-09-05	114	24	4.75
11	2018-09-06	134	24	5.58
12	2018-09-07	94	24	3.92

Figure 7.6: Checking the results of the recipe

How it works...

Let's take a look at the `aggregate_by_location_pandas.py` script, used in *step 6*.

> This recipe is equivalent to the *Aggregating results* recipe in this same chapter.

The final part of the script file deals with the parsing of arguments, which was described in detail in *Chapter 2, Automating Tasks Made Easy*.

In Pandas, the basic data model is called a `DataFrame`, which, in essence, is a representation of a table with rows and columns. Most of the operations are related to mutating the `DataFrame`.

The main function reads the input CSV and calls the `calculate_results` function to generate the aggregated reports. The usage of `DictReader` was already described in the *Updating CSV spreadsheets* recipe in *Chapter 6, Fun with Spreadsheets*. `Calculate_results` returns a `DataFrame`:

```python
def main(input_file, output_file):
    reader = csv.DictReader(input_file)
    result = calculate_results(reader)

    # Save into csv format
    output_file.write(result.to_csv())
```

The write operation to the output file uses the `.to_csv()` function that's available in Pandas for a `DataFrame`. This generates a text result that's equivalent to the CSV format. The data is written using the low-level `output.write()` call.

In the `calculate_results` function, the aggregation takes place. The aggregation takes places in three phases. First, the data is imported into a `DataFrame`, then the values are aggregated. Finally, the data is rounded to two decimal positions for compatibility. Let's take a look at the code:

```python
def pandas_format(row):
    row['DATE'] = pd.to_datetime(row['STD_TIMESTAMP'])
    row['USD'] = pd.to_numeric(row['USD'])

    return row
```

```
def calculate_results(reader):
    # Load the data, formatting
    data = pd.DataFrame(pandas_format(r) for r in reader)

    by_usd = data.groupby(data['DATE'].dt.date)['USD']
    result = by_usd.agg(['sum', 'count', 'mean'])

    # Round to 2 digital places
    result = result.round(2)

    # Rename columns
    result = result.rename(columns={
        'sum': 'TOTAL USD',
        'count': 'NUMBER',
        'mean': 'AVERAGE',
    })

    return result
```

The first line imports the data into a Pandas `DataFrame`. The `pandas_format`
function adds the `DATE` column, transforming the standard timestamp into
a `datetime` object, and transforms the `USD` column into a numeric format. This
is all laying the groundwork to allow Pandas to work with these columns.

The core of the aggregation happens in these two lines:

```
    by_usd = data.groupby(data['DATE'].dt.date)['USD']
    result = by_usd.agg(['sum', 'count', 'mean'])
```

The first line transforms the `DataFrame` to group the results by the `DATE` column
(which is a full `datetime` object) but only by its date, without hour information.
This aggregates the results by whole days. The grouped values are only presented
for the `USD` column.

The second line aggregates the results, in three different ways: `sum` is used to get
the total results, `count` to get the number of events, and `mean` for the average value.
They all refer to the `USD` column, selected previously.

The rest of the `calculate_results` function is more straightforward. It first rounds
the results to two digital positions with `.round(2)`. It then changes the names of
the columns to be consistent with the previous recipes. The `.rename` function uses
a dictionary to define the input and output results.

The resulting CSV file is equivalent to the one presented in the *Aggregating results* recipe, except for minimal format differences.

There's more...

The pattern shown in `calculate_results` when applying changes and overwriting the results is very common in Pandas:

```
result = by_usd.agg(['sum', 'count', 'mean'])
result = result.round(2)
result = result.rename(...)
```

This process can also be concatenated easily into the following:

```
result = by_usd.agg(['sum', 'count', 'mean']).round(2).rename(...)
```

This way of working means that for each operation, a copy of the data is generated. For very big collections of data, this may not be efficient. You can perform most operations without making a copy by using the `inplace` argument. This will mutate them without using extra memory space or copying data around.

Consider the following, for example:

```
result.rename(columns={
        'sum': 'TOTAL USD',
        'count': 'NUMBER',
        'mean': 'AVERAGE',
    }, inplace=True)
```

The preceding code will replace the columns without making a copy. It will return None instead. This doesn't allow us to use chained operations and it's generally considered bad practice. Use this only when having problems with memory.

Pandas is a big, complex package that has a lot of usages, from statistical analysis to plotting to complex mathematical applications. It is widely used in the data science community. Pandas uses the approach of describing the desired result, instead of the operations to perform.

 This approach is known as *declarative*, as opposed to imperative. *Declarative* languages aim at describing the result, the *WHAT*, while imperative languages describe the *HOW*. The most common example of a declarative language is the SQL language, used to interact with databases. Python is mainly an imperative language, but as we see in Pandas, the declarative approach can be used as well.

Pandas is very commonly used with Jupyter Notebook. This application allows users to create rich Python sessions that mix code execution, documentation, and graphs for a rich environment in the form of notebooks that can be accessed via a web browser. It's capable of automatically presenting data from modules such as Pandas or Matplotlib.

The aim of this project is to allow the exploration of data, instead of following a more repetitive process as when using an automated tool, but it's a fantastic tool to know how to use.

The notebook can be tested online at `https://jupyter.org/try`. Go to the main web page at `https://jupyter.org/` to check how to install it locally and read the whole documentation.

Here is an example session displaying some data:

Figure 7.7: The Jupyter Notebook

You can find the complete Pandas documentation at `https://pandas.pydata.org/docs/user_guide/index.html`.

See also

- The *Aggregating results* recipe from earlier in the chapter.
- The *Reading CSV files* recipe in *Chapter 4, Searching and Reading Local Files*.
- The *Preparing a task* recipe in *Chapter 2, Automating Tasks Made Easy*.

8
Developing Stunning Graphs

Graphs and images are fantastic ways of presenting complex data in an easy and understandable way. In this chapter, we will make use of the powerful `matplotlib` library to learn how to create all kinds of graphs. `matplotlib` is a library that's aimed at displaying data in multiple ways, and it can create stunning plots that help transmit and display information in the best way possible.

 `matplotlib` is well known and interacts well with other tools in the Python ecosystem. For example, `matplotlib` graphs can also be automatically displayed by Jupyter Notebooks as introduced in *Chapter 7, Cleaning and Processing Data.*

The graphs we'll cover will go from simple bar graphs to line or pie charts, and combine multiple plots in the same graph, annotate them, or even draw geographical maps.

The following recipes will be covered in this chapter:

- Plotting a simple sales graph
- Drawing stacked bars
- Plotting pie charts
- Displaying multiple lines
- Drawing a scatter plot
- Visualizing maps
- Adding legends and annotations

- Combining graphs
- Saving charts

Let's start by creating our first graph.

Plotting a simple sales graph

In this recipe, we'll see how to draw a sales graph by drawing bars proportional to sales in different periods.

Getting ready

We can install matplotlib in our virtual environment using the following commands:

```
$ echo "matplotlib==3.2.1" >> requirements.txt
$ pip install -r requirements.txt
```

In some OSes, this may require us to install additional packages; for example, in Ubuntu, it may require us to run apt-get install python3-tk. Check the matplolib documentation for details.

If you are using macOS, it's possible that you'll get an error like this: **RuntimeError: Python is not installed as a framework**. Refer to the matplotlib documentation on how to fix it: https://matplotlib.org/faq/osx_framework.html.

How to do it...

1. Import matplotlib:

   ```
   >>> import matplotlib.pyplot as plt
   ```

2. Prepare the data to be displayed on the graph:

   ```
   >>> DATA = (
   ...     ('Q1 2017', 100),
   ...     ('Q2 2017', 150),
   ...     ('Q3 2017', 125),
   ...     ('Q4 2017', 175),
   ... )
   ```

3. Split the data into usable formats for the graph. This is a preparation step:

   ```
   >>> POS = list(range(len(DATA)))
   ```

```
>>> VALUES = [value for label, value in DATA]
>>> LABELS = [label for label, value in DATA]
```

4. Create a bar graph with the data:

```
>>> plt.bar(POS, VALUES)
<BarContainer object of 4 artists>
>>> plt.xticks(POS, LABELS)
<REDACTED>
>>> plt.ylabel('Sales')
Text(0, 0.5, 'Sales')
```

5. Display the graph:

```
>>> plt.show()
```

6. The result will be displayed as follows in a new window:

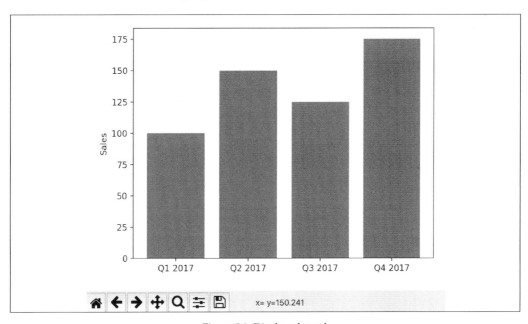

Figure 8.1: Displayed graph

How it works...

After importing the module, the data is presented in *step 2* of the *How to do it...*
section in a useable structure.

Because of the way `matplotlib` works, it requires an *X* component, as well as a *Y* component. In this case, our *X* component is just a sequence of increasing numbers, as many as there are data points. We store that in the variable POS. This positions each of the *Y* values and works as a temporal series. In VALUES, we store the numeric value of the sales as a sequence, and in LABELS, we store the associated label for each data point. All that preparation work is done in *step 3*.

Step 4 creates the bar graph with the sequences *X* (POS) and *Y* (VALUES). These define our bars. To specify the period it refers to, we put labels on the *x-axis* for each value with `.xticks` in the same way. To clarify the meaning, we add a label with `.ylabel`.

To display the resulting graph, *step 5* calls `.show`, which opens a new window with the result.

> Calling `.show` blocks the execution of the program. The program will resume when the window is closed.

There's more...

You may want to change the format in which the values are presented. In our example, maybe the numbers represent millions of dollars. To do so, you can add a formatter to the *y-axis*, so the values represented there will have it applied to them:

```
>>> from matplotlib.ticker import FuncFormatter

>>> def value_format(value, position):
...     return '$ {}M'.format(int(value))

>>> axes = plt.gca()
>>> axes.yaxis.set_major_formatter(FuncFormatter(value_format))
```

`value_format` is a function that returns a value based on the value and position of the data. Here, it will return the value 100 as $100M.

Values will be retrieved as floats, requiring you to transform them into integers for display.

To apply the formatter, we need to retrieve the `axis` object with `.gca` (get current axes). Then, the `.yaxi` attribute sets up the formatter for the *y-axis* labels.

The color of the bars can also be determined with the `color` parameter. Colors can be specified in multiple formats, as described at `https://matplotlib.org/api/colors_api.html`, but my favorite is following the XKCD color survey using the `xkcd:` prefix (no space after the colon):

```
>>> plt.bar(POS, VALUES, color='xkcd:moss green')
```

The full survey can be found here: `https://xkcd.com/color/rgb/`.

Most common colors, such as blue and red, are also available for quick tests. They tend to be a little bright and harsh to be used in good-looking reports, though.

Combining the color with formatting the axis gives us the following result:

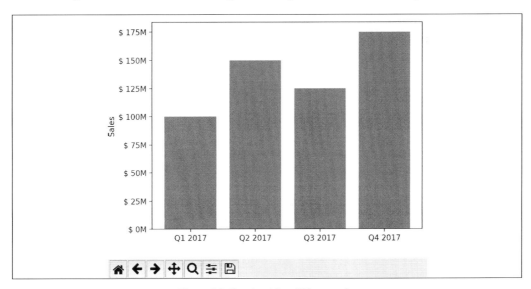

Figure 8.2: Graph with a different color

Bar graphs don't need to display information in a temporal way. As we've seen, matplotlib requires us to specify the *X* parameter of each bar. It's a powerful tool used to generate all kinds of graphs.

 For example, the bars can be arranged to display a histogram, such as for displaying people of a certain height. The bars will start at a low height, increase to the average size, and then drop back. Don't limit yourself to just spreadsheet charts!

The full matplotlib documentation can be found here: https://matplotlib.org/.

See also

- The *Drawing stacked bars* recipe, next in this chapter, to learn how to plot more accumulated information on each bar.

- The *Adding legends and annotations* recipe, later in this chapter, to learn how to add context information to a graph.

- The *Combining graphs* recipe, later in this chapter, to learn how to combine multiple plots into a single graph.

Drawing stacked bars

A powerful way of displaying different categories is to present them as stacked bars so that each of the categories and the total are displayed. We'll see how to do that in this recipe.

Getting ready

We need to install matplotlib in our virtual environment:

```
$ echo "matplotlib==3.2.1" >> requirements.txt
$ pip install -r requirements.txt
```

If you are using macOS, you may get an error like this: **RuntimeError: Python is not installed as a framework**. See the matplotlib documentation on how to fix it: https://matplotlib.org/faq/osx_framework.html.

How to do it...

1. Import `matplotlib`:

```
>>> import matplotlib.pyplot as plt
```

2. Prepare the data. This represents two products' sales; an established one and a new one:

```
>>> DATA = (
...         ('Q1 2017', 100, 0),
...         ('Q2 2017', 105, 15),
...         ('Q3 2017', 125, 40),
...         ('Q4 2017', 115, 80),
... )
```

3. Process the data to prepare the expected format:

```
>>> POS = list(range(len(DATA)))
>>> VALUESA = [valueA for label, valueA, valueB in DATA]
>>> VALUESB = [valueB for label, valueA, valueB in DATA]
>>> LABELS = [label for label, value1, value2 in DATA]
```

4. Create the bar plot. Two plots are required:

```
>>> plt.bar(POS, VALUESB)
<BarContainer object of 4 artists>
>>> plt.bar(POS, VALUESA, bottom=VALUESB)
<BarContainer object of 4 artists>
>>> plt.ylabel('Sales')
Text(0, 0.5, 'Sales')
>>> plt.xticks(POS, LABELS)
<REDACTED>
```

5. Display the graph:

```
>>> plt.show()
```

6. The result will be displayed in a new window, as follows:

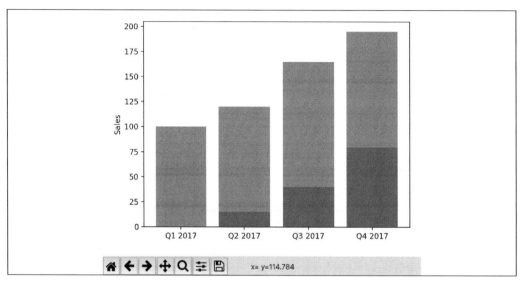

Figure 8.3: Stacked bars

How it works...

After importing the module, the data is presented in *step 2* in a useable structure.

In *step 3*, the data is prepared in three sequences, VALUESA, VALUESB, and LABELS. A POS increasing sequence is added so that the bars are positioned over the *x-axis*, one after the other.

Step 4 creates the bar graph with the sequences X (POS) and Y (VALUESB). The second bar sequence, VALUESA, is added on top of the previous one using the bottom=VALUESB argument. This process stacks both bars, positioning the full VALUESA bar on top of the VALUESB bar.

 Notice that we stack the second value, VALUESB, first. The second value represents a new product that was introduced to the market. VALUESA represents the established product and is more stable. This graph shows the growth of the new product better.

Each of the periods is labeled on the *x-axis* with .xticks. To clarify the meaning, we add a label with .ylabel.

To display the resulting graph, *step 5* calls .show, which opens a new window with the result.

Calling `.show` blocks the execution of the program. The program will resume when the window is closed.

There's more...

Another way of presenting stacked bars is by adding them as percentages so that the total doesn't change, only the relative sizes compared to each other.

To do that, VALUESA and VALUEB need to be calculated relative to the percentages in this way:

```
>>> VALUESA = [100 * valueA / (valueA + valueB) for label, valueA, valueB
in DATA]
>>> VALUESB = [100 * valueB / (valueA + valueB) for label, valueA, valueB
in DATA]
```

This makes each value equal to the percentage of the total, and the total always adds up to 100. This produces the following graphic:

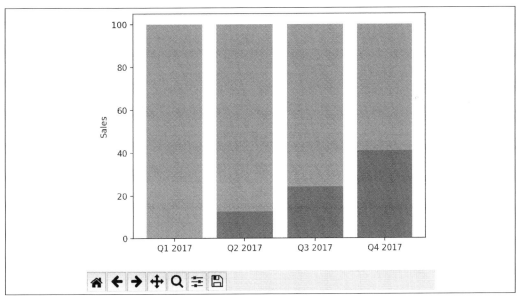

Figure 8.4: Stacking percentages

The bars don't necessarily need to be stacked. Sometimes, it may be interesting to present the bars one against the other for comparison.

To do that, we need to move the position of the second bar sequence. We'll also need to set thinner bars to allow spaces:

```
>>> WIDTH = 0.3
>>> plt.bar([p - WIDTH / 2 for p in POS], VALUESA, width=WIDTH)
>>> plt.bar([p + WIDTH / 2 for p in POS], VALUESB, width=WIDTH)
```

Note how the width of the bar is set to a third of the space since our reference space is 1 between the bars. The first bar is moved to the left, while the second bar is moved to the right to center them. The `bottom` argument has been deleted so that the bars aren't stacked:

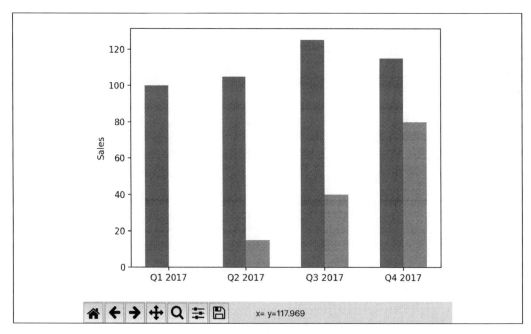

Figure 8.5: Independent bars

The full `matplotlib` documentation can be found here: https://matplotlib.org/.

See also

- The *Plotting a simple sales graph* recipe, earlier in this chapter, to learn the basics of drawing bar graphs.

- The *Adding legends and annotations* recipe, later in this chapter, to learn how to add context information to a graph.

- The *Combining graphs* recipe, later in this chapter, to learn how to add multiple plots to a single graph.

Plotting pie charts

Pie charts! A Business 101 favorite, and a common way of presenting percentages. We'll see in this recipe how to plot a pie chart, with different slices representing proportions.

Getting ready

We need to install `matplotlib` in our virtual environment using the following commands:

```
$ echo "matplotlib==3.2.1" >> requirements.txt
$ pip install -r requirements.txt
```

If you are using macOS, you may get an error like this: **RuntimeError: Python is not installed as a framework**. See the `matplotlib` documentation on how to fix it: `https://matplotlib.org/faq/osx_framework.html`.

How to do it...

1. Import `matplotlib`:

   ```
   >>> import matplotlib.pyplot as plt
   ```

2. Prepare the data. This represents several lines of products:

   ```
   >>> DATA = (
   ...      ('Common', 100),
   ...      ('Premium', 75),
   ...      ('Luxurious', 50),
   ...      ('Extravagant', 20),
   ... )
   ```

3. Process the data to prepare the expected format:

   ```
   >>> VALUES = [value for label, value in DATA]
   >>> LABELS = [label for label, value in DATA]
   ```

4. Create the pie chart:

   ```
   >>> plt.pie(VALUES, labels=LABELS, autopct='%1.1f%%')
   <REDACTED>
   >>> plt.gca().axis('equal')
   (-1.1113861431510297, 1.1005422098873965, -1.125031021533458,
   1.1221350517711501)
   ```

5. Display the graph:

```
>>> plt.show()
```

6. The result will be displayed in a new window, as follows:

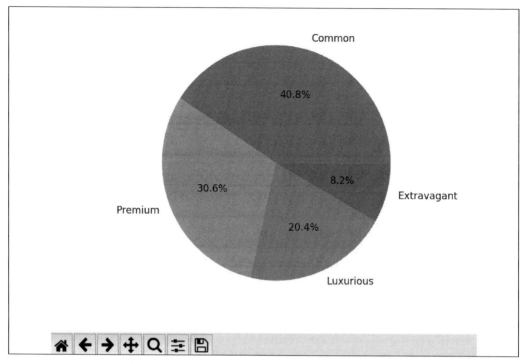

Figure 8.6: Pie chart

How it works...

The module is imported in *step 1* of the *How to do it…* section, and the data to present is imported in *step 2*. The data is separated into two components, a list of VALUES and a list of LABELS, in *step 3*.

The chart is created in *step 4* by adding VALUES and LABELS. The autopct parameter formats the value so it displays it as a percentage to a single decimal place.

The call to axis('equals') ensures the pie chart will look round, instead of having a bit of perspective and appearing as an oval.

To display the resulting graph, *step 5* calls .show, which opens a new window with the result.

Calling .show blocks the execution of the program. The program will resume when the window is closed.

There's more...

Pie charts are a little overused in business graphs. Most of the time, a bar chart with percentages or values will be a better way of visualizing the data, especially if more than two or three options are displayed. Try to limit the use of pie charts in your reports and data presentations.

Rotating the start of the wedges is possible with the startangle parameter, and the direction to set up the wedges is defined by counterclock (defaults to True):

```
>>> plt.pie(VALUES, labels=LABELS, startangle=90, counterclock=False)
```

The format inside the label can be set by a function. As the value inside the pie is defined as a percentage, finding the original value can be a little tricky. The following snippet creates a dictionary indexing by its percentage as an integer, so we can retrieve the referenced value. Please note that this assumes that no percentage gets repeated. If that's the case, the labels may be slightly incorrect. In that case, we may need to use up to the first decimal place for better precision:

```
>>> from matplotlib.ticker import FuncFormatter

>>> total = sum(value for label, value in DATA)
>>> BY_VALUE = {int(100 * value / total): value for label, value in DATA}

>>> def value_format(percent, **kwargs):
...     value = BY_VALUE[int(percent)]
...     return '{}'.format(value)
```

One or more wedges can also be separated using the explode parameter. This specifies how separated the wedge is from the center:

```
>>> explode = (0, 0, 0.1, 0)
>>> plt.pie(VALUES, labels=LABELS, explode=explode, autopct=value_format,
            startangle=90, counterclock=False)
```

By combining all these options, we get the following result when calling `plt. show()`:

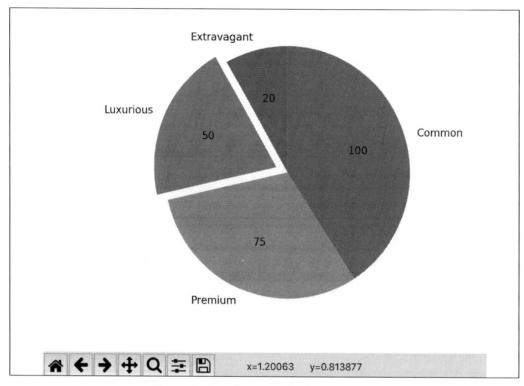

Figure 8.7: Highlighting a wedge by separating it

The full `matplotlib` documentation can be found here: `https://matplotlib.org/`.

See also

- The *Plotting a simple sales graph* recipe, earlier in this chapter, to learn the basics of plotting bar graphs.
- The *Drawing stacked bars* recipe, from the previous section, to learn how to plot accumulated values as bars.

Displaying multiple lines

This recipe will show you how to display multiple lines in a graph.

Getting ready

We need to install `matplotlib` in our virtual environment:

```
$ echo "matplotlib==3.2.1" >> requirements.txt
$ pip install -r requirements.txt
```

If you are using macOS, you may get an error like this: **RuntimeError: Python is
not installed as a framework**. See the `matplotlib` documentation on how to fix it:
`https://matplotlib.org/faq/osx_framework.html`.

How to do it...

1. Import `matplotlib`:

   ```
   >>> import matplotlib.pyplot as plt
   ```

2. Prepare the data. This represents two products' sales:

   ```
   >>> DATA = (
   ...     ('Q1 2017', 100, 5),
   ...     ('Q2 2017', 105, 15),
   ...     ('Q3 2017', 125, 40),
   ...     ('Q4 2017', 115, 80),
   ... )
   ```

3. Process the data to prepare the expected format:

   ```
   >>> POS = list(range(len(DATA)))
   >>> VALUESA = [valueA for label, valueA, valueB in DATA]
   >>> VALUESB = [valueB for label, valueA, valueB in DATA]
   >>> LABELS = [label for label, value1, value2 in DATA]
   ```

4. Create the line plot. Two lines are required:

   ```
   >>> plt.plot(POS, VALUESA, 'o-')
   [<matplotlib.lines.Line2D object at 0x12e78a2b0>]
   >>> plt.plot(POS, VALUESB, 'o-')
   [<matplotlib.lines.Line2D object at 0x12e7afcd0>]
   >>> plt.ylabel('Sales')
   Text(0, 0.5, 'Sales')
   >>> plt.xticks(POS, LABELS)
   <REDACTED>
   ```

5. Display the graph:

    ```
    >>> plt.show()
    ```

6. The result will be displayed in a new window:

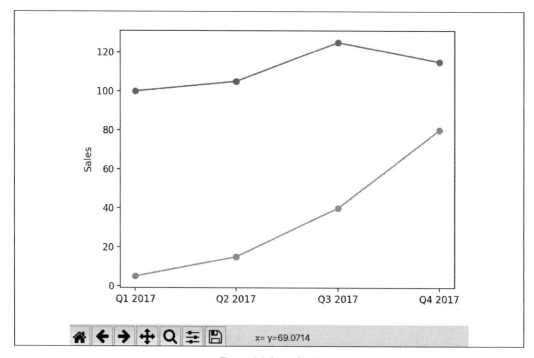

Figure 8.8: Line chart

How it works...

In the *How to do it...* section, *step 1* imports the module and *step 2* shows the data to be plotted in a formatted way.

In *step 3*, the data is prepared in three sequences, VALUESA, VALUEB, and LABELS. A POS increasing sequence is used to locate each of the points along the *x-axis*.

Step 4 creates the graph with the sequences X (POS) and Y (VALUESA), and then POS and VALUESB. The value 'o-' is added to draw a circle on each of the data points and a full line between them.

By default, the plot will display a solid line, with no marker on each point. If only the marker is used (that is, `'o'`), there'll be no line.

Each of the periods is labeled on the *x-axis* with `.xticks`. To clarify the meaning, we add a label with `.ylabel`.

To display the resulting graph, *step 5* calls `.show`, which opens a new window with the result.

 Calling `.show` blocks the execution of the program. The program will resume when the window is closed.

There's more...

Graphs with lines are deceptively simple and able to create a lot of interesting representations. It is probably the most convenient when showing mathematical graphs. For example, we can display a graph showing Moore's Law in a few lines of code.

 Moore's Law is an observation by Gordon Moore that the number of components in an integrated circuit doubles every 2 years. It was first described in 1965 and then corrected in 1975. It seems to be quite close to the historic rate of technological advancement over the last 40 years.

We first create a line describing the theoretical line, with data points from 1970 to 2013. Starting with 1,000 transistors, we double it every 2 years, up to 2013:

```
>>> POS = [year for year in range(1970, 2013)]
>>> MOORES = [1000 * (2 ** (i * 0.5)) for i in range(len(POS))]
>>> plt.plot(POS, MOORES)
[<matplotlib.lines.Line2D object at 0x12b7c27c0>]
```

Following some documentation, we extract a few examples of commercial CPUs, their year of release, and their number of integrated components from here: http://mercury.pr.erau.edu/~siewerts/cec320/documents/Papers/ AHistoryofMicroprocessorTransistorCount.pdf.

Due to the big numbers, we'll use the notation of `1_000_000` for 1 million, which is available in Python 3:

```
>>> DATA = (
...     ('Intel 4004', 2_300, 1971),
...     ('Motorola 68000', 68_000, 1979),
...     ('Pentium', 3_100_000, 1993),
...     ('Core i7', 731_000_000, 2008),
... )
```

Draw a line with markers to display those points at the proper places. The `'v'` mark will display a triangle:

```
>>> data_x = [x for label, y, x in DATA]
>>> data_y = [y for label, y, x in DATA]
>>> plt.plot(data_x, data_y, 'v')
[<matplotlib.lines.Line2D object at 0x12b7c2d60>]
```

For each data point, append a label in the proper place with the name of the CPU:

```
>>> for label, y, x in DATA:
...     plt.text(x, y, label)
Text(1971, 2300, 'Intel 4004')
Text(1979, 68000, 'Motorola 68000')
Text(1993, 3100000, 'Pentium')
Text(2008, 731000000, 'Core i7')
```

Finally, growth doesn't make sense displayed in a linear graph, so we change the scale to be logarithmic, which makes exponential growth look like a straight line. But to keep the sense of dimension, we add a grid. Call `.show` to display the graph:

```
>>> plt.gca().grid()
>>> plt.yscale('log')
```

The resulting graph will be displayed when calling `plt.show()`:

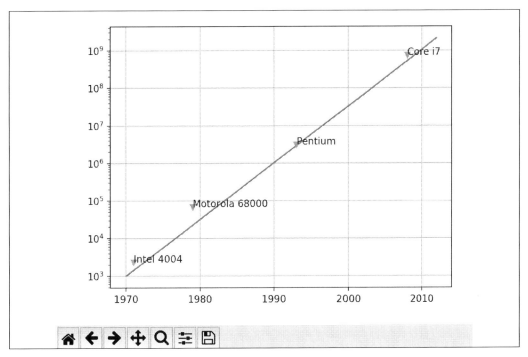

Figure 8.9: Moore's Law graph

Note how the straight line follows the duplication of transistors in the logarithmic scale and the processors are close. You can see that the real processors look pretty similar to the prediction done by Moore!

The full `matplotlib` documentation can be found here: `https://matplotlib.org/`. In particular, check the available formats for the lines (solid, dashed, dotted, and so on) and markers (dot, circle, triangle, star, and so on) here: `https://matplotlib.org/api/_as_gen/matplotlib.pyplot.plot.html`.

See also

- The *Adding legends and annotations* recipe, later in this chapter, to learn how to add context information to a graph.
- The *Combining graphs* recipe, later in this chapter, to learn how to add multiple plots to a single graph.

Drawing a scatter plot

A scatter plot is one where the information is displayed as dots with *X* and *Y* values. They are very useful when presenting data with two dimensions (as opposed to a temporal series seen previously) and to see whether there's any relationship between two variables. In this recipe, we'll display a graph plotting time spent on a website against money spent to see whether we can see a pattern.

Getting ready

We need to install `matplotlib` in our virtual environment:

```
$ echo "matplotlib==3.2.1" >> requirements.txt
$ pip install -r requirements.txt
```

If you are using macOS, you may get an error like this: **RuntimeError: Python is not installed as a framework**. See the `matplotlib` documentation on how to fix it: `https://matplotlib.org/faq/osx_framework.html`.

As we're going to be working with data points, we'll use the `scatter.csv` file to read the data. This file is available on GitHub at `https://github.com/PacktPublishing/Python-Automation-Cookbook-Second-Edition/blob/master/Chapter08/scatter.csv`.

How to do it...

1. Import `matplotlib`, `csv`, and `FuncFormatter` (to format the axes later):

    ```
    >>> import csv
    >>> import matplotlib.pyplot as plt
    >>> from matplotlib.ticker import FuncFormatter
    ```

2. Prepare the data, reading from the file using the `csv` module:

    ```
    >>> with open('scatter.csv') as fp:
    ...     reader = csv.reader(fp)
    ...     data = list(reader)
    ```

3. Prepare the data for plotting, and then plot it:

    ```
    >>> data_x = [float(x) for x, y in data]
    >>> data_y = [float(y) for x, y in data]
    >>> plt.scatter(data_x, data_y)
    <matplotlib.collections.PathCollection object at 0x11ccbda30>
    ```

4. Improve the context by formatting the axes:

```
>>> def format_minutes(value, pos):
...     return '{}m'.format(int(value))
>>> def format_dollars(value, pos):
...     return '${}'.format(value)
>>> plt.gca().xaxis.set_major_formatter(FuncFormatter(format_
minutes))
>>> plt.xlabel('Time in website')
Text(0.5, 0, 'Time in website')
>>> plt.gca().yaxis.set_major_formatter(FuncFormatter(format_
dollars))
>>> plt.ylabel('Spending')
Text(0, 0.5, 'Spending')
```

5. Show the graph:

```
>>> plt.show()
```

6. The result will be displayed in a new window:

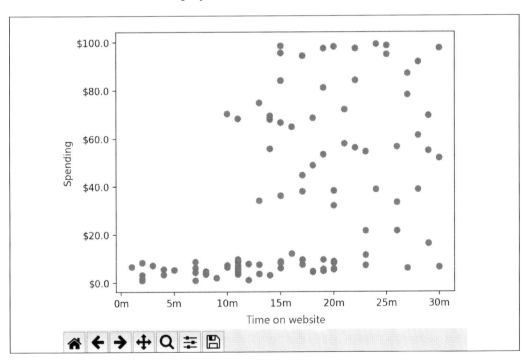

Figure 8.10: Scatter plot

How it works...

Step 1 of the *How to do it...* section imports the modules we'll use later.

Step 2 reads the data from the CSV file. The data is transformed into a list to allow us to iterate through it several times, as that's necessary for *step 3*.

Step 3 prepares the data in two arrays and then uses `.scatter` to plot them. The parameters for `.scatter`, as with other methods of `matplotlib`, require an array of *X* and *Y* values. They both need to be the same size. The data is converted into a `float` from the file format to ensure the number format.

Step 4 refines the way the data is presented on each axis. For each axis, a function is created that defines how the values on that axis should be displayed (in dollars or in minutes). The function accepts the value to display and the position as inputs. Typically, the position will be ignored. The axis formatter will be overwritten with `.set_major_formatter`. Notice that both axes are returned with `.gca` (get current axes).

A label is added to the axes with `.xlabel` and `.ylabel`.

Finally, *step 5* displays the graph in a new window. Analyzing the result, we can say that there seems to be two kinds of users, ones who spend less than 10 minutes and never spend more than $10, and users who spend more time and also have a higher chance of spending up to $100.

> Note that the data presented is synthetic, and it has been generated with the result in mind. Real-life data will probably look more spread out. Statistical analysis can be used to determine trends and patterns with a higher degree of sophistication.

There's more...

A scatter plot can display not only points in two dimensions, but also add a third (area) and even a fourth dimension (color).

To add those elements, use the parameters s for `size` and c for `color`.

> `size` is defined as the diameter of a ball in points squared. So, for a ball of diameter 10, 100 will be used. `color` can use any of the usual definitions of color in `matplotlib`, such as hex color, RGB, and so on. See the documentation for more details: `https://matplotlib.org/users/colors.html`.

For example, we can generate a random graph using the four dimensions in the following way:

```
>>> import matplotlib.pyplot as plt
>>> import random
>>> NUM_POINTS = 100
>>> COLOR_SCALE = ['#FF0000', '#FFFF00', '#FFFF00', '#7FFF00', '#00FF00']
>>> data_x = [random.random() for _ in range(NUM_POINTS)]
>>> data_y = [random.random() for _ in range(NUM_POINTS)]
>>> size = [(50 * random.random()) ** 2 for _ in range(NUM_POINTS)]
>>> color = [random.choice(COLOR_SCALE) for _ in range(NUM_POINTS)]
>>> plt.scatter(data_x, data_y, s=size, c=color, alpha=0.5)
<matplotlib.collections.PathCollection object at 0x123552ee0>
>>> plt.show()
```

COLOR_SCALE goes from green to red, and the size of each of the points will be between 0 and 50 points in diameter. The result should be something like this:

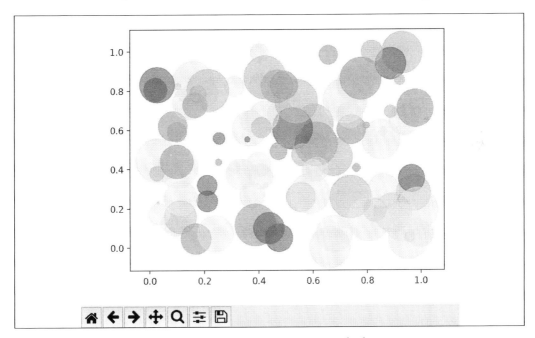

Figure 8.11: Displaying points, sizes, and colors

Note that the values are random, so each time the code is run it will generate a different graph.

The `alpha` value makes each of the points semitransparent, allowing us to see where they overlap. The higher this value is, the less transparent the points will be. This parameter will affect the displayed color as it will blend the point in with the background.

 Even though it's possible to display two independent values in terms of size and color, they can also be related to any of the other values. For example, making the color dependent on the size will make all the points of the same size the same color, which may help us distinguish between the data. Remember that the ultimate goal of a graph is to make data easy to understand. Try different approaches to improve this.

The full `matplotlib` documentation can be found here: `https://matplotlib.org/`.

See also

- The *Displaying multiple lines* recipe, earlier in this chapter, to learn how to plot multiple lines that follow a temporal series.
- The *Adding legends and annotations* recipe, later in this chapter, to learn how to add context information to a graph.

Visualizing maps

To best way to show information that changes from region to region is to create a map that presents the information, while at the same time giving a regional sense of location for the data.

In this recipe, we'll make use of the `Fiona` module to import GIS information, as well as `matplotlib` to display the information. We will display a map of Western Europe and display the population of each country with a color grade. The darker the color, the larger the population.

Getting ready

We need to install `matplotlib` and `Fiona` in our virtual environment:

```
$ echo "matplotlib==3.2.1" >> requirements.txt
$ echo "Fiona==1.8.13" >> requirements.txt
$ pip install -r requirements.txt
```

If you are using macOS, you may get an error like this: **RuntimeError: Python is not installed as a framework**. See the `matplotlib` documentation on how to fix it: `https://matplotlib.org/faq/osx_framework.html`.

The map data needs to be downloaded. Fortunately, there's a lot of freely available data for geographic information. A search on Google should quickly return almost everything you need, including detailed information on regions, counties, rivers, or any other kind of data.

 GIS information is available in different formats from a lot of public organizations. `Fiona` is capable of understanding most common formats and treating them in equivalent ways, but there are small differences. Read the `Fiona` documentation for more details.

The data we'll use in this recipe, covering all European countries, is available on GitHub at the following URL: `https://github.com/leakyMirror/map-of-europe/blob/master/GeoJSON/europe.geojson`. Note that it is in GeoJSON, which is an easy standard to work with.

How to do it...

1. Import the modules:

```
>>> import matplotlib.pyplot as plt
>>> import matplotlib.cm as cm
>>> import fiona
```

2. Load the population of the countries to display:

```
>>> COUNTRIES_POPULATION = {
...         'Spain': 47.2,
...         'Portugal': 10.6,
...         'United Kingdom': 63.8,
...         'Ireland': 4.7,
...         'France': 64.9,
...         'Italy': 61.1,
...         'Germany': 82.6,
...         'Netherlands': 16.8,
...         'Belgium': 11.1,
...         'Denmark': 5.6,
...         'Slovenia': 2,
...         'Austria': 8.5,
```

```
...        'Luxembourg': 0.5,
...        'Andorra': 0.077,
...        'Switzerland': 8.2,
...        'Liechtenstein': 0.038,
... }
>>> MAX_POPULATION = max(COUNTRIES_POPULATION.values())
>>> MIN_POPULATION = min(COUNTRIES_POPULATION.values())
```

3. Prepare the `colormap`, which will determine the color each country will be displayed in (differing shades of green). Calculate which color corresponds to each country:

```
>>> colormap = cm.get_cmap('Greens')
>>> COUNTRY_COLOUR = {
...        country_name: colormap(
...            (population - MIN_POPULATION) / (MAX_POPULATION - MIN_
POPULATION)
...        )
...        for country_name, population in COUNTRIES_POPULATION.
items()
... }
```

4. Open the file and read the data, filtering by the countries we defined the population in *step 1*:

```
>>> with fiona.open('europe.geojson') as fd:
>>>        full_data = [data for data in fd
...                    if data['properties']['NAME'] in COUNTRIES_
POPULATION]
```

5. Plot each of the countries in the proper color:

```
>>> for data in full_data:
...        country_name = data['properties']['NAME']
...        color = COUNTRY_COLOUR[country_name]
...        geo_type = data['geometry']['type']
...        if geo_type == 'Polygon':
...            data_x = [x for x, y in data['geometry']
['coordinates'][0]]
...            data_y = [y for x, y in data['geometry']
['coordinates'][0]]
...            plt.fill(data_x, data_y, c=color)
...        elif geo_type == 'MultiPolygon':
```

```
...              for coordinates in data['geometry']['coordinates']:
...                  data_x = [x for x, y in coordinates[0]]
...                  data_y = [y for x, y in coordinates[0]]
...                  plt.fill(data_x, data_y, c=color)
```

6. Display the result:

```
>>> plt.show()
```

7. The result will be displayed in a new window, as follows:

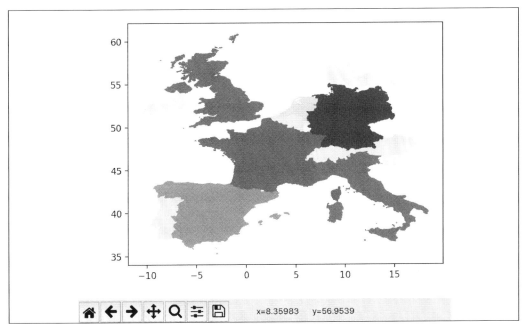

Figure 8.12: Displaying a map

How it works...

After importing the modules in *step 1* from the *How to do it…* section, the data to be displayed is defined in *step 2*. Note that the names need to be in the same format as they'll be in the GEO file. The minimum and maximum populations are calculated to properly balance the range later.

The population has been rounded to a significant number, and it's defined in millions. Only a few countries have been defined for this recipe, but there are more available in the GIS file.

Step 3 describes a `colormap` defining the color range in shades of green (`Greens`). This is one standard `colormap` in `matplotlib`, but we can use others, such as oranges, reds, or plasma for a more cold-to-hot approach. More details are available in the documentation: `https://matplotlib.org/examples/color/colormaps_reference.html`.

The `COUNTRY_COLOUR` dictionary stores the color defined by `colormap` for each country. The population is normalized to a number from 0.0 (least population) to 1.0 (most), and passed to `colormap` to retrieve the color at the scale it corresponds to.

The GIS information is then retrieved in *step 4*. `fiona` reads the `europe.geojson` file and the data is copied so we can use it in the next steps. It also filters to only deal with the countries we defined the population of, which means no extra countries are plotted.

The loop in *step 5* goes over the country information list in `data_list`, and then each country's geometry is plotted using `.fill`, which plots a polygon. The geometry of each country is either a single polygon (`Polygon`) or more than one (`MultiPolygon`). In each case, the proper polygons are drawn, all in the same color. This means `MultiPolygon` is drawn several times.

> GIS information is stored as points for coordinates describing the latitude and longitude of the point. Areas, such as countries, have a list of coordinates that describe an area within them. Some maps are more precise and have more points defining areas. Multiple polygons may be required to define a country, as some parts may be separated from each other, with islands being the most obvious case, but there are also exclaves. Exclaves are regions of countries detached from the main body, like Alaska.

Finally, the data is displayed by calling `.show`.

There's more...

Taking advantage of the information contained in the GIS file, we can add extra information to the map. The `properties` object contains information about the name of the country, but also its ISO name, FID code, and central location as LON and LAT. We can use this information to display the name of the country using `.text`:

```
long, lat = data['properties']['LON'], data['properties']['LAT']
iso3 = data['properties']['ISO3']
plt.text(long, lat, iso3, horizontalalignment='center')
```

This code will live inside the loop in *step 6* in the *How to do it...* section.

 If you analyze the file, you'll see that the `properties` object contains information about the population, stored as `POP2005`, so you can draw the population information directly from the map. That is left as an exercise. Different map files contain different information, so be sure to play around to unleash all the possibilities.

Also, you may notice that the map may be distorted in some cases. `matplotlib` will try to present it in a square box, and if the map is not roughly square, this will be evident. For example, try to display only Spain, Portugal, Ireland, and the UK. We can force the graph to present 1 point of latitude with the same space as 1 point of longitude, which is a good approach if we are not drawing something near the poles. This is achieved by calling `.set_aspect` in the axes. Current axes can be obtained through `.gca` (**get current axes**):

```
>>> axes = plt.gca()
>>> axes.set_aspect('equal', adjustable='box')
```

Also, to improve the look of the map, we can set up a background color that helps to differentiate between the background and the foreground, and remove the labels in the axes, as printing the latitude and longitude is probably distracting. Removing the labels on the axes is achieved by setting empty labels with `.xticks` and `.yticks`. The background color is mandated by the foreground color of the axes:

```
>>> plt.xticks([])
([], <a list of 0 Text major ticklabel objects>)
>>> plt.yticks([])
([], <a list of 0 Text major ticklabel objects>)
>>> axes = plt.gca()
>>> axes.set_facecolor('xkcd:light blue')
```

Finally, to better differentiate between the different regions, a line surrounding each area can be added. This can be done by drawing a thin line with the same data as `.fill`, right after. Notice that this code is repeated twice in *step 2*:

```
>>> plt.fill(data_x, data_y, c=color)
[<matplotlib.patches.Polygon object at 0x1161a49d0>]
>>> plt.plot(data_x, data_y, c='black', linewidth=0.2)
[<matplotlib.lines.Line2D object at 0x1161a4b80>]
```

After applying all these elements to the map, it now looks like this:

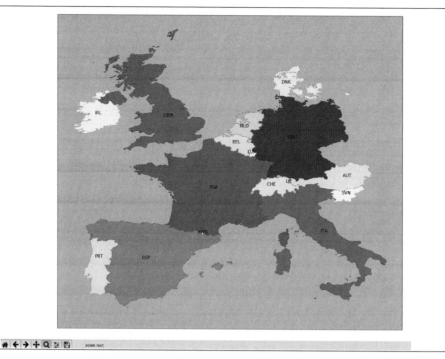

Figure 8.13: Map with colored countries and background color

The resulting code is available on GitHub here: `https://github.com/PacktPublishing/Python-Automation-Cookbook-Second-Edition/blob/master/Chapter08/visualising_maps.py`.

 As we've seen, maps are drawn as general polygons. Don't be afraid to include other geometrical forms. You can define your own polygons and print them with `.fill` or some extra labels. For example, far away regions may need to be transported to avoid having too large a map. Or, rectangles can be used to print extra information on top of parts of the map.

The full `Fiona` documentation can be found here: `https://fiona.readthedocs.io/`. The full `matplotlib` documentation can be found here: `https://matplotlib.org/`.

See also

- The *Adding legends and annotations* recipe, next in this chapter, to learn how to add context information to a graph.

- The *Combining graphs* recipe, later in this chapter, to learn how to add multiple plots to a single graph.

Adding legends and annotations

When drawing graphs with dense information, a legend may be required to display relevant information to improve the understanding of the data presented, like what color is assigned to what concept. In matplotlib, legends can be pretty rich and there are multiple ways of presenting them. Annotations to draw attention to specific points are also useful to help the reader understand the information displayed on the graph.

In this recipe, we'll create a graph with three different components and display a legend with information to better understand it, as well as annotating the most interesting points on our graph.

Getting ready

We need to install matplotlib in our virtual environment:

```
$ echo "matplotlib==3.2.1" >> requirements.txt
$ pip install -r requirements.txt
```

If you are using macOS, you may get an error like this: **RuntimeError: Python is not installed as a framework**. See the matplotlib documentation on how to fix it: https://matplotlib.org/faq/osx_framework.html.

How to do it...

1. Import matplotlib:

   ```
   >>> import matplotlib.pyplot as plt
   ```

2. Prepare the data to be displayed on the graph and the legends that should be displayed. Each of the lines is composed of the time label, sales of ProductA, sales of ProductB, and sales of ProductC:

   ```
   >>> LEGEND = ('ProductA', 'ProductB', 'ProductC')
   >>> DATA = (
   ...      ('Q1 2017', 100, 30, 3),
   ```

```
...        ('Q2 2017', 105, 32, 15),
...        ('Q3 2017', 125, 29, 40),
...        ('Q4 2017', 115, 31, 80),
... )
```

3. Split the data into usable formats for the graph. This is a preparation step:

```
>>> POS = list(range(len(DATA)))
>>> VALUESA = [valueA for label, valueA, valueB, valueC in DATA]
>>> VALUESB = [valueB for label, valueA, valueB, valueC in DATA]
>>> VALUESC = [valueC for label, valueA, valueB, valueC in DATA]
>>> LABELS = [label for label, valueA, valueB, valueC in DATA]
```

4. Create a bar graph with the data:

```
>>> WIDTH = 0.2
>>> plt.bar([p - WIDTH for p in POS], VALUESA, width=WIDTH)
<BarContainer object of 4 artists>
>>> plt.bar([p for p in POS], VALUESB, width=WIDTH)
<BarContainer object of 4 artists>
>> plt.bar([p + WIDTH for p in POS], VALUESC, width=WIDTH)
<BarContainer object of 4 artists>
>>> plt.ylabel('Sales')
Text(0, 0.5, 'Sales')
>>> plt.xticks(POS, LABELS)
<REDACTED>
```

5. Add an annotation displaying the maximum growth in the chart:

```
>>> plt.annotate('400% growth', xy=(1.2, 18), xytext=(1.3, 40),
                 horizontalalignment='center',
                 arrowprops=dict(facecolor='black', shrink=0.05))
Text(1.3, 40, '400% growth')
```

6. Add the legend:

```
>>> plt.legend(LEGEND)
<matplotlib.legend.Legend object at 0x1153d1e80>
```

7. Display the graph:

```
>>> plt.show()
```

8. The result will be displayed in a new window:

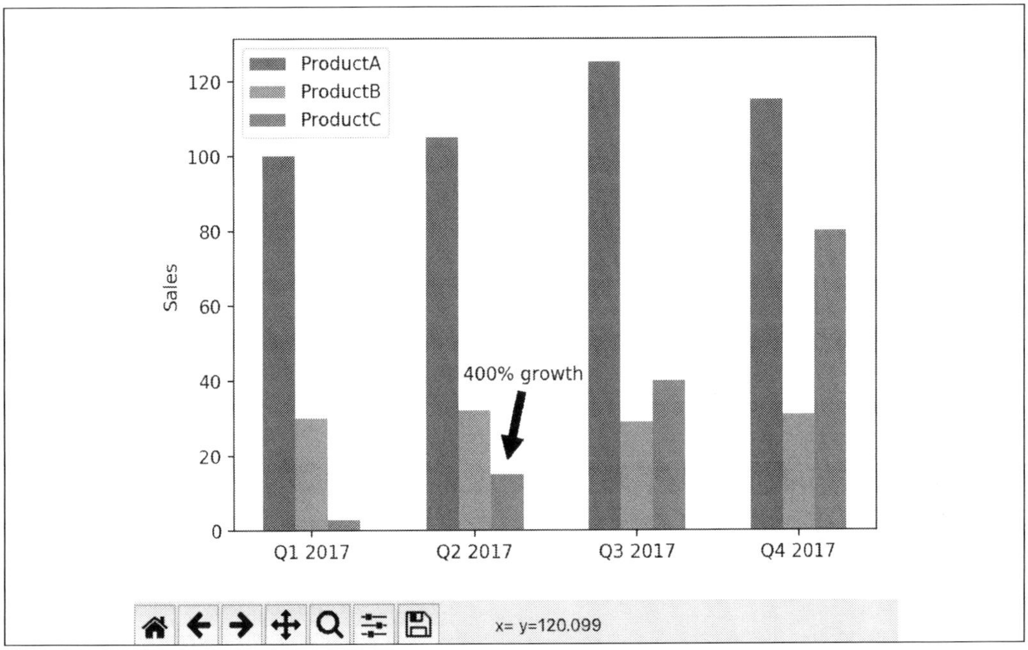

Figure 8.14: Pointing to interesting parts of the graph

How it works...

Steps 1 and *2* of the *How to do it...* section prepare the imports and the data that will be displayed by the bar chart. In *step 3*, the data is split into different arrays to prepare the input for `matplotlib`. Basically, each data sequence is stored in a different array.

Step 4 draws the data. Each data sequence gets a call to `.bar`, specifying its position and values. Labels do the same as `.xticks`. To separate each of the bars around the labels, the first one is displaced to the left and the third to the right.

An annotation is added above the bar for `ProductC` in the second quarter. Note that the annotation includes the point in `xy` and the text location in `xytext`.

In *step 6*, the legend is added. Notice that the labels need to be added to the data in the same order as the data was inputted. The legend is located automatically in an area that doesn't cover any data. `Arrowprops` tells the arrow to point to the data.

Finally, the graph is drawn in *step 7* by calling `.show`.

 Calling `.show` blocks the execution of the program. The program will resume when the window is closed.

There's more...

Legends will be displayed automatically in most cases with just a call to `.legend`. If you need to customize the order in which they appear, you may refer each label to a specific element. For example, this way (note it calls `ProductA` the `valueC` series):

```
>>> valueA = plt.bar([p - WIDTH for p in POS], VALUESA, width=WIDTH)
>>> valueB = plt.bar([p for p in POS], VALUESB, width=WIDTH)
>>> valueC = plt.bar([p + WIDTH for p in POS], VALUESC, width=WIDTH)
>>> plt.legend((valueC, valueB, valueA), LEGEND)
<matplotlib.legend.Legend object at 0x112273fa0>
```

The location of the legend can also be changed manually, through the `loc` parameter. By default, it is `best` and it will draw the legend over an area where there's the least overlap of data (ideally none). But values such as `right`, `upper`, `left`, and so on can be used, or a specific `(X, Y)` tuple.

Another option is to plot the legend outside of the graph using the `bbox_to_anchor` option. In this case, the legend is attached to the `(X, Y)` of the bounding box, where `0` is the bottom-left corner of the graph and `1` is the upper-right corner. This may cause the legend to be clipped by the external border, so you may need to adjust where the graph starts and ends with `.subplots_adjust`:

```
>>> plt.legend(LEGEND, title='Products', bbox_to_anchor=(1, 0.8))
<matplotlib.legend.Legend object at 0x11963b910>
>>> plt.subplots_adjust(right=0.80)
```

Adjusting the `bbox_to_anchor` and `.subplots_adjust` parameters requires a little bit of trial and error in producing the expected result.

`.subplots_adjust` references the positions as the position of the axis where it will be displayed. This means that `right=0.80` will leave 20% of the screen on the right of the plot, while the default for left is `0.125`, meaning it leaves 12.5% of the space on the left of the plot. See the documentation for further details: `https://matplotlib.org/api/_as_gen/matplotlib.pyplot.subplots_adjust.html`.

The annotations can be done in different styles and can be tweaked with different options regarding the way to connect and so on. For example, this code will create an arrow with the `fancy` style connecting with a curve. The result is displayed here:

```
plt.annotate('400% growth', xy=(1.2, 18), xytext=(1.3, 40),
        horizontalalignment='center',
        arrowprops={'facecolor': 'black',
                    'arrowstyle': "fancy",
                    'connectionstyle': "angle3",
                })
```

In our recipe, we did not annotate to the end of the bar (point (`1.2, 15`)), but slightly above it, to give a little bit of breathing space.

 Adjusting the exact point to annotate and where to locate the text will require a bit of testing. The text was also positioned by looking for the best place to not overlap the text with the bars. The font size and color can be changed using the `fontsize` and `color` parameters in both the `.legend` and `.annotate` calls.

Applying all these elements, the graph may look similar to the following graph. This graph can be replicated by calling the `adding_legend_and_annotation.py` script, available in GitHub here: `https://github.com/PacktPublishing/Python-Automation-Cookbook-Second-Edition/blob/master/Chapter08/adding_legend_and_annotations.py`:

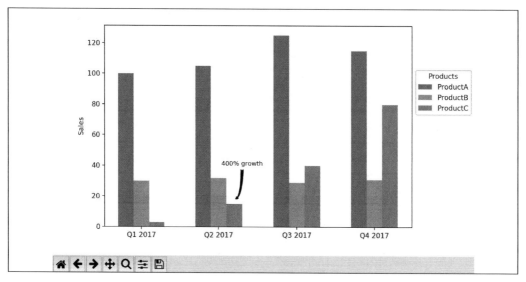

Figure 8.15: Legend adding context to each bar

The full `matplotlib` documentation can be found here: `https://matplotlib.org/`. In particular, the guide for legends can be found here: `https://matplotlib.org/users/legend_guide.html#plotting-guide-legend`. The guide for annotations can be found here: `https://matplotlib.org/users/annotations.html`.

See also

- The *Drawing stacked bars* recipe, earlier in this chapter, to learn how to plot accumulated values as bars that will benefit from a legend.

- The *Combining graphs* recipe, next in this chapter, to learn how to add multiple plots to a single graph.

Combining graphs

More than one plot can be combined in the same graph. In this recipe, we'll see how to present data in the same plot, on two different axes, and how to add more plots to the same graph.

Getting ready

We need to install `matplotlib` in our virtual environment:

```
$ echo "matplotlib==3.2.1" >> requirements.txt
$ pip install -r requirements.txt
```

If you are using macOS, you may get an error like this: **RuntimeError: Python is not installed as a framework**. See the `matplotlib` documentation on how to fix it: `https://matplotlib.org/faq/osx_framework.html`.

How to do it...

1. Import `matplotlib`:

```
>>> import matplotlib.pyplot as plt
```

2. Prepare the data to be displayed on the graph and the legends that should be displayed. Each of the lines is composed of the time label, sales of `ProductA`, and sales of `ProductB`. Notice how `ProductB` has a much higher value than A:

```
>>> DATA = (
...     ('Q1 2017', 100, 3000, 3),
...     ('Q2 2017', 105, 3200, 5),
...     ('Q3 2017', 125, 2900, 7),
...     ('Q4 2017', 115, 3100, 3),
... )
```

3. Prepare the data in independent arrays:

```
>>> POS = list(range(len(DATA)))
>>> VALUESA = [valueA for label, valueA, valueB, valueC in DATA]
>>> VALUESB = [valueB for label, valueA, valueB, valueC in DATA]
>>> VALUESC = [valueC for label, valueA, valueB, valueC in DATA]
>>> LABELS = [label for label, valueA, valueB, valueC in DATA]
```

Note that this expands and creates a list for each of the values.

 The values can also be expanded with this: LABELS, VALUESA, VALUESB, VALUESC = ZIP(*DATA).

4. Create the first subplot:

```
>>> plt.subplot(2, 1, 1)
<matplotlib.axes._subplots.AxesSubplot object at 0x115a91cd0>
```

5. Create a bar graph with information about VALUESA:

```
>>> valueA = plt.bar(POS, VALUESA)
```

```
>>> plt.ylabel('Sales A')
Text(0, 0.5, 'Sales A')
```

6. Create a different *y-axis*, and add information about VALUESB as a line plot:

```
>>> plt.twinx()
<matplotlib.axes._subplots.AxesSubplot object at 0x118b0c160>
>>> valueB = plt.plot(POS, VALUESB, 'o-', color='red')
>>> plt.ylabel('Sales B')
Text(0, 0.5, 'Sales B')
>>> plt.xticks(POS, LABELS)
<REDACTED>
```

7. Create another subplot and fill it with VALUESC:

```
>>> plt.subplot(2, 1, 2)
<matplotlib.axes._subplots.AxesSubplot object at 0x115abdfd0>
>>> plt.plot(POS, VALUESC)
[<matplotlib.lines.Line2D object at 0x118c7c0d0>]
>>> plt.gca().set_ylim(ymin=0)
(0.0, 7.2)
>>> plt.xticks(POS, LABELS)
<REDACTED>
```

8. Display the graph:

```
>>> plt.show()
```

9. The result will be displayed in a new window:

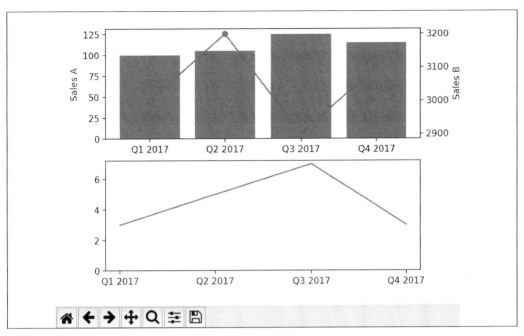

Figure 8.16: Multiple plots in the same graph

How it works...

In *Step 1* of the *How to do it…* section, all the required imports for the module are called.

Step 2 presents the data in a useable format.

Step 3 is a preparation step that splits the data into different arrays for the next steps.

Step 4 creates a new `.subplot`. This splits the full drawing into two elements. The parameters are number of rows, columns, and the selected subplot. So, we create two subplots in a column and draw in the first one.

Step 5 prints a `.bar` plot in this subplot using VALUESA data, and labels the *y-axis* with `Sales A` using `.ylabel`.

Step 6 creates a new *y-axis* with `.twinx`, drawing VALUESB as a line plot through `.plot`. The label is marked with `.ylabel` as `Sales B`. The *x-axis* is labeled using `.xticks`.

> The VALUESB plot is set to red to avoid both plots having the same color. By default, the first color is the same in both cases, and that will lead to confusion. The data points are marked with the `'o'` option.

In *step 7*, we changed to the second subplot using `.subplot`. The plot prints VALUESC as a line, and again puts the labels on the x-axis with `.xticker` and sets the minimum of the y-axis to 0. The graph is then displayed in *step 8*.

There's more...

Plots with multiple axes are complicated to read as a general rule. Use them only when there's a good reason to do so and the data is highly correlated.

> By default, the y-axis in line plots will try to present information between the minimum and maximum Y values. Truncating the axis is normally not the best way to present information, as it can distort the perceived differences. For example, changing values in the range from 10 to 11 can look like a huge deal if the graph goes from 10 to 11, but this is less than 10%. Setting the y-axis minimum to 0 with `plt.gca().set_ylim(ymin=0)` is a good idea, especially with two different axes.

The call to select the subplot will first go by row, then by column, so `.subplot(2, 2, 3)` will select the subplot in the first column, second row.

The divided subplot grid can be changed. A first call to `.subplot(2, 2, 1)` and `.subplot(2, 2, 2)`, and then calling `.subplot(2, 1, 2)`, will create a structure with two small plots in the first row and a wider one in the second. Going back will overwrite previously drawn subplots.

The full `matplotlib` documentation can be found here: `https://matplotlib.org/`. In particular, the guide for legends can be found here: `https://matplotlib.org/users/legend_guide.html#plotting-guide-legend`. The guide for annotations can be found here: `https://matplotlib.org/users/annotations.html`.

See also

- The *Drawing multiple lines* recipe, earlier in this chapter, which shows alternatives to displaying multiple values in a single graph.

- The *Visualizing maps* recipe, earlier in this chapter, to learn how to display other kinds of rich graphs with multiple data.

Saving charts

Once a chart is ready, we can store it on the hard drive so it can be referenced in other documents. In this recipe, we'll see how to save charts in different formats.

Getting ready

We need to install `matplotlib` in our virtual environment:

```
$ echo "matplotlib==3.2.1" >> requirements.txt
$ pip install -r requirements.txt
```

If you are using macOS, you may get an error like this: **RuntimeError: Python is not installed as a framework**. See the `matplotlib` documentation on how to fix it: `https://matplotlib.org/faq/osx_framework.html`.

How to do it...

1. Import `matplotlib`:

   ```
   >>> import matplotlib.pyplot as plt
   ```

2. Prepare the data to be displayed on the graph and split it into different arrays:

   ```
   >>> DATA = (
   ...     ('Q1 2017', 100),
   ...     ('Q2 2017', 150),
   ...     ('Q3 2017', 125),
   ...     ('Q4 2017', 175),
   ... )
   >>> POS = list(range(len(DATA)))
   >>> VALUES = [value for label, value in DATA]
   >>> LABELS = [label for label, value in DATA]
   ```

3. Create a bar graph with the data:

```
>>> plt.bar(POS, VALUES)
<BarContainer object of 4 artists>
>>> plt.xticks(POS, LABELS)
<REDACTED>
>>> plt.ylabel('Sales')
Text(0, 0.5, 'Sales')
```

4. Save the graph to the hard drive:

```
>>> plt.savefig('data.png')
```

5. Open the new file data.png to show the graph, as follows:

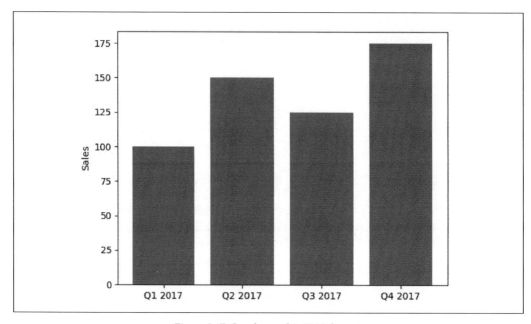

Figure 8.17: Graph saved in PNG format

How it works...

After importing and preparing the data in *steps 1* and *2* in the *How to do it...* section, the graph is generated in *step 3* by calling `.bar`. A `.ylabel` is added and the x-axis is labelled with the proper time description through `.xticks`.

Step 4 saves the file to the hard drive with the name `data.png`.

There's more...

The resolution of the image can be determined through the `dpi` parameter. This will affect the size of the file. Use resolutions between `72` and `300`. Lower ones will be difficult to read, while higher ones won't make sense unless the size of the graph is humongous:

```
>>> plt.savefig('data.png', dpi=72)
```

`matplotlib` understands how to store the most common file formats, such as JPEG, PDF, and PNG. It will be used automatically when the filename has the proper extension.

 Unless you have a specific requirement, use PNG. It is very efficient at storing graphs with limited colors compared to other formats. If you need to find all the supported files, you can call `plt.gcf().canvas.get_supported_filetypes()`.

The full `matplotlib` documentation can be found here: `https://matplotlib.org/`. In particular, the guide for legends can be found here: `https://matplotlib.org/users/legend_guide.html#plotting-guide-legend`. The guide for annotations can be found here: `https://matplotlib.org/users/annotations.html`.

See also

- The *Plotting a simple sales graph* recipe, earlier in this chapter, to learn the basics of plotting a bar graph.
- The *Adding legends and annotations* recipe, earlier in this chapter, to learn how to add context information to graphs.

9
Dealing with Communication Channels

Dealing with communication channels is where automating things can produce big gains. In this chapter, we'll see how to work with two of the most common communication channels—emails, including newsletters, and sending and receiving text messages by phone.

During the years, there has been a fair amount of abuse in both channels, like spam or unsolicited marketing messages, making it necessary for senders to use external tools to avoid messages being rejected by automated filters. We will present the proper caveats where applicable. The presented tools have a lot of features that will help you with your specific task. They also have excellent documentation, so do not be afraid to read it.

In this chapter, we will cover the following recipes:

- Working with email templates
- Sending an individual email
- Reading an email
- Adding subscribers to an email newsletter
- Sending notifications via email
- Producing SMS
- Receiving SMS
- Creating a Telegram bot

We will start by understanding how to use templates to generate good emails.

Working with email templates

To send an email, we first need to generate its content. In this recipe, we'll see how to generate a proper template, in both text-only style and HTML.

Getting ready

We should start by installing the `mistune` module, which will compile Markdown documents into HTML. We will also use the `jinja2` module to combine HTML with our text:

```
$ echo "mistune==0.8.4" >> requirements.txt
$ echo "jinja2==2.11.1" >> requirements.txt
$ pip install -r requirements.txt
```

In this book's GitHub repository, there are a couple of templates we will use— `email_template.md` at `https://github.com/PacktPublishing/Python-Automation-Cookbook-Second-Edition/blob/master/Chapter09/email_template.md` and a template for styling, `email_styling.html`, at `https://github.com/PacktPublishing/Python-Automation-Cookbook-Second-Edition/blob/master/Chapter09/email_styling.html`.

How to do it...

1. Import the modules:

   ```
   >>> import mistune
   >>> import jinja2
   ```

2. Read both templates from disk:

   ```
   >>> with open('email_template.md') as md_file:
   ...     markdown = md_file.read()

   >>> with open('email_styling.html') as styling_file:
   ...     styling = styling_file.read()
   ```

3. Define the `data` to include in the template. The template is quite simple and accepts only a single `name` parameter:

```
>>> data = {'name': 'Seamus'}
```

4. Render the Markdown template. This produces the text-only version of the data:

```
>>> text = markdown.format(**data)
```

5. Render the Markdown and add the styling:

```
>>> html_content = mistune.markdown(text)
>>> html = jinja2.Template(styling).render(content=html_content)
```

6. Save the text and the HTML version to disk to check them:

```
>>> with open('text_version.txt', 'w') as fp:
...     fp.write(text)
164
>>> with open('html_version.html', 'w') as fp:
...     fp.write(html)
4085
```

7. Exit the interpreter and check the text version:

```
$ cat text_version.txt
Hi Seamus:

This is an email talking about **things**

### Very important info

1. One thing
2. Other thing
3. Some extra detail

Best regards,

   *The email team*
```

8. Check the HTML version in a browser:

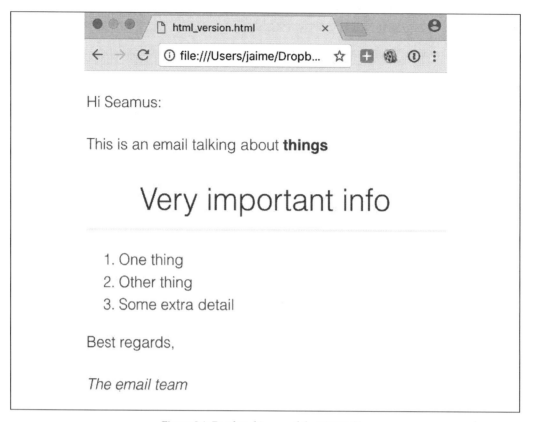

Figure 9.1: Rendered image of the HTML file

How it works...

Step 1 imports the modules that will be used later, and *step 2* reads the two templates that will be rendered. `email_template.md` is the basis of the content, and it's a Markdown template. `email_styling.html` is an HTML template that contains the basic HTML surrounding and CSS styling information.

The basic strategy is to create the content in Markdown format. This is a readable plain text file, which can be sent as part of the email. That content can then be converted into HTML and surrounded with some styling to assemble the complete, styled HTML file. The styling file `email_styling.html` has a content area where we can put the rendered HTML from Markdown.

Step 3 defines the data that will render in `email_template.md`. It is a very simple template that only requires a parameter called `name`.

In *step 4*, the Markdown template gets rendered with the `data`. This produces the plain text version of the email.

The `HTML` version is rendered in *step 5*. The plain text version is rendered to `HTML` using `mistune`, and then wrapped in `email_styling.html` using a `jinja2` template. The final version is a self-contained HTML document.

Finally, we save both versions, plain text (as `text`) and HTML (as `html`), to a file in *step 6*. *Steps 7* and *8* check the stored values. The information is the same, but in the `HTML` version, it is better styled.

There's more...

Using Markdown makes emails that contain a version in both plain text and HTML easy to generate. Markdown is quite readable in text format, and renders very naturally into HTML. That said, it is possible to generate a totally different HTML version, which will allow for more customization and taking advantage of HTML's features.

The full Markdown syntax can be found at `https://daringfireball.net/projects/markdown/syntax`, and a good cheat sheet with the most commonly used elements can be found at `https://www.markdownguide.org/cheat-sheet`.

While making a plain text version of an email is not strictly necessary, it is a good practice and shows you care about who reads the email. Most email clients accept HTML, but it's not totally universal.

For an HTML email, note that the whole stylesheet information should be contained in the email. This means that the CSS needs to be embedded into the HTML. Avoid making external references to resources that could lead the email to not render properly in some email clients, or even be qualified as spam.

The styling in `email_styling.html` is based on the modest stylesheet, which can be found here: `http://markdowncss.github.io/`. There are more CSS stylesheets that can be used, and a search using Google should find more. Remember to remove any external references, as discussed previously.

Images can be included in HTML by encoding the image in `base64` format so it can be embedded directly in the HTML `img` tag, instead of adding a reference:

```
>>> import base64
>>> with open("image.png",'rb') as file:
...     encoded_data = base64.b64encode(file)
>>> print "<img src='data:image/png;base64,{data}'/>".
format(data=encoded_data)
```

You can find more information about this technique in this article: `https://css-tricks.com/data-uris/`.

The `mistune` full documents are available at `http://mistune.readthedocs.io/en/latest/`, and the `jinja2` documentation can be found at `https://jinja.palletsprojects.com/en/2.11.x/`.

See also

- The *Formatting text in Markdown* recipe in *Chapter 5, Generating Fantastic Reports*, to learn more about Markdown
- The *Using templates for reports* recipe in *Chapter 5, Generating Fantastic Reports*, to learn more about Jinja2 templates
- The *Sending an individual email* recipe, later in this chapter, to follow up on how to send the composed email

Sending an individual email

The most basic way of sending an email is by using the standard **Simple Mail Transfer Protocol (SMTP)**. SMTP is one of the oldest protocols on the Internet. Although newer proprietary protocols exist, SMTP is the standard used by all email providers to communicate with each other and is one of the pillars of electronic communications.

SMTP allows you to send rich emails with multiple sections containing different kinds of data. These sections can be used to add attachments, or to generate alternative sections, such as a plain text and HTML version of the same message, to display on compatible email clients.

Given SMTP is such a strong standard, it is easy to use, and virtually all languages and operating systems support it. This ease of usage is also a weakness as the amount of spam email is huge, and big players in the email domain have strong incentives to disallow emails coming from non-verified sources, like a Python script.

This is why SMTP is only recommended for very sporadic use and simple purposes such as sending a few emails a day to controlled addresses.

 Do not use this method to send emails in bulk to distribution lists or to customers from random email addresses. You risk being banned from your service provider due to anti-spam rules.

Getting ready

For this recipe, we'll need an email account with a service provider. There are small differences based on the provider you'll use, but we'll be using a Gmail account as they are very common and free to access.

Due to Gmail's security, we'll need to create a specific app password that can be used to send an email. Follow the instructions here: `https://support.google.com/accounts/answer/185833`. This will help you generate a password for the purpose of this recipe. Remember to create it for mail access. You can delete the password afterward to remove it.

We'll use the `smtplib` module, which is part of Python's standard library.

How to do it...

1. Import the `smtplib` and `email` modules:

    ```
    >>> import smtplib
    >>> from email.mime.multipart import MIMEMultipart
    >>> from email.mime.text import MIMEText
    ```

2. Set up the credentials, replacing these with your own ones. For testing purposes, we'll send to the same email, but feel free to use a different address:

    ```
    >>> USER = 'your.account@gmail.com'
    >>> PASSWORD = 'YourPassword'
    >>> sent_from = USER
    >>> send_to = [USER]
    ```

3. Define the data to be sent. Notice the two alternatives, a plain text one and an HTML one:

    ```
    >>> text = "Hi!\nThis is the text version linking to https://www.
    packtpub.com/\nCheers!"
    >>> html = """<html><head></head><body>
    ... <p>Hi!<br>
    ... This is the HTML version linking to <a href="https://www.
    packtpub.com/">Packt</a><br>
    ... </p>
    ... </body></html>
    """
    ```

4. Compose the message as a MIME multipart, including `subject`, `to`, and `from`:

    ```
    >>> msg = MIMEMultipart('alternative')
    >>> msg['Subject'] = 'An interesting email'
    >>> msg['From'] = sent_from
    >>> msg['To'] = ', '.join(send_to)
    ```

5. Fill in the data content parts of the email:

    ```
    >>> part_plain = MIMEText(text, 'plain')
    >>> part_html = MIMEText(html, 'html')
    >>> msg.attach(part_plain)
    >>> msg.attach(part_html)
    ```

6. Send the email using the `SMTP SSL` protocol:

    ```
    >>> with smtplib.SMTP_SSL('smtp.gmail.com', 465) as server:
    ...      server.login(USER, PASSWORD)
    ...      server.sendmail(sent_from, send_to, msg.as_string())
    ```

7. The email should have been sent. Check your email account for the message. Checking the *original email*, you will see the full raw email, with elements in both HTML and plain text. The email has been redacted in the following screenshot:

```
Return-Path: <            @gmail.com>
Received: from         .local ([        .159])
      by smtp.gmail.com with ESMTPSA id 1                            .45.01
      for <        @gmail.com>
      (version=TLS1_2 cipher=ECDHE-RSA-AES128-GCM-SHA256 bits=128/128);
      Thu, 09 Aug 2018 13:45:01 -0700 (PDT)
Message-ID: <5b6ca7cd.            .85cd@mx.google.com>
Date: Thu, 09 Aug 2018 13:45:01 -0700 (PDT)
Content-Type: multipart/alternative; boundary="===============4673407806445885785=="
MIME-Version: 1.0
Subject: An interesting email
From:             @gmail.com
To:          @gmail.com

--===============4673407806445885785==
Content-Type: text/plain; charset="us-ascii"
MIME-Version: 1.0
Content-Transfer-Encoding: 7bit

Hi!
This is the text version linking to https://www.packtpub.com/
Cheers!
--===============4673407806445885785==
Content-Type: text/html; charset="us-ascii"
MIME-Version: 1.0
Content-Transfer-Encoding: 7bit


<html>
  <head></head>
  <body>
    <p>Hi!<br>
       This is the HTML version linking to <a href="https://www.packtpub.com/">Packt</a><br>
    </p>
  </body>
</html>

--===============4673407806445885785==--
```

Figure 9.2: Email in both plain text and HTML format

How it works...

After *step 1*, making the pertinent imports from `stmplib` and `email`, *step 2* defines the credentials obtained from Gmail.

Step 3 shows the HTML and text that is going to be sent. They are alternatives, so they should present the same information, but in different formats.

The basic message information is set up in *step 4*. It specifies the subject of the email, as well as the *from* and *to*. *Step 5* adds multiple parts, each with the proper `MIMEText` type.

 The last part that's added is the preferred alternative, according to the `MIME` format, so we add the `HTML` part last.

Step 6 sets up the connection with the server, logs in using the credentials, and sends the message. It uses a `with` context to get the connection. Note the address `smtp.gmail.com` and port `465` are specific for Gmail.

If there's an error with the credentials, it will raise an exception with the username and password not accepted.

There's more...

Note that `send_to` is a list of addresses. You can send an email to more than one address. The only caveat is in *step 4*, where it needs to be specified as a list of comma-separated values for all addresses.

 Although it is possible to label `sent_from` as a different address than the address used to send the email, it is not recommended. This can be interpreted as an indication of trying to fake the origin of the email and provokes labeling the email as spam.

The server used here, `smtp.gmail.com`, is the one specified by Gmail, and the defined port for SMTPS (secure SMTP) is `465`. Gmail also accepts port `587`, which is the standard, but requires you to specify the kind of session by calling `.starttls`, as shown in the following code:

```
with smtplib.SMTP('smtp.gmail.com', 587) as server:
    server.starttls()
    server.login(USER, PASSWORD)
    server.sendmail(sent_from, send_to, msg.as_string())
```

If you are interested in more details about these differences and both protocols, you can find more information in this article: `https://www.fastmail.com/help/technical/ssltlsstarttls.html`.

The full `smtplib` documentation can be found at `https://docs.python.org/3/library/smtplib.html`, and the `email` module, with information on the different formats for emails, including examples on `MIME` types, can be found here: `https://docs.python.org/3/library/email.html`. `MIME` types can be used to add binary attachments to emails.

See also

- The *Working with email templates* recipe, earlier in this chapter, to see how to compose the body of the email
- The *Sending notifications via email* recipe, later in this chapter, to learn how to send bulk emails

Reading an email

In this recipe, we'll see how to read emails from an account. We'll use the `IMAP4` standard, which is the most commonly used standard for reading emails.

Once read, the email can be processed and analyzed automatically to generate actions such as smart automated responses, forwarding the email to a different target, aggregating the results for monitoring, and so on. The options are unlimited!

Getting ready

For this recipe, we'll need an email account with a service provider. There are small differences based on the provider you use, but we'll use a Gmail account, as it is very common and free to access.

Due to Gmail's security, we'll need to create a specific app password to use to send an email. Follow the instructions here: `https://support.google.com/accounts/answer/185833`. This will generate a password for the purpose of this recipe. Remember to create it for mail. You can delete the password afterward to remove it.

We'll use the `imaplib` module, which is part of Python's standard library.

This recipe will read the last received email, so you can use it for better control over what's going to be read. We'll send a short email that looks like it was sent to the support team.

How to do it...

1. Import the `imaplib` and `email` modules:

```
>>> import imaplib
>>> import email
>>> from email.parser import BytesParser, Parser
>>> from email.policy import default
```

2. Set up the credentials, replacing the following with your own ones:

```
>>> USER = 'your.account@gmail.com'
>>> PASSWORD = 'YourPassword'
```

3. Connect to the email server:

```
>>> mail = imaplib.IMAP4_SSL('imap.gmail.com')
>>> mail.login(USER, PASSWORD)
```

4. Select the inbox folder:

```
>>> mail.select('inbox')
```

5. Read all email UIDs and retrieve the latest received email:

```
>>> result, data = mail.uid('search', None, 'ALL')
>>> latest_email_uid = data[0].split()[-1]
>>> result, data = mail.uid('fetch', latest_email_uid, '(RFC822)')
>>> raw_email = data[0][1]
```

6. Parse the email into a Python object:

```
>>> email_message = BytesParser(policy=default).parsebytes(raw_
email)
```

7. Display the subject and sender of the email:

```
>>> email_message['subject']
'[Ref ABCDEF] Subject: Product A'
>>> email.utils.parseaddr(email_message['From'])
('Sender name', 'sender@gmail.com')
```

8. Retrieve the payload of the text:

```
>>> email_type = email_message.get_content_maintype()
>>> if email_type == 'multipart':
...     for part in email_message.get_payload():
...         if part.get_content_type() == 'text/plain':
```

```
...               payload = part.get_payload()
... elif email_type == 'text':
...        payload = email_message.get_payload()
>>> print(payload)
Hi:


    I'm having difficulties getting into my account. What was the
URL, again?


    Thanks!
      A confused customer
```

How it works...

After importing the modules that will be used and defining the credentials, we connect to the server in *step 3*.

Step 4 connects to `inbox`. This is a default folder in Gmail that contains the received email.

 Of course, you may need to read a different folder. You can get a list of all folders by calling `mail.list()`.

In *step 5*, first, a list of UIDs is retrieved for all the emails in the inbox by calling `.uid('search', None, "ALL")`. The last email received is then retrieved again from the server through a `fetch` action with `.uid('fetch', latest_email_uid, '(RFC822)')`. This retrieves the email in RFC822 format, which is the standard. Note that retrieving the email marks it as read.

 The `.uid` command allows us to call IMAP4 commands, returning a tuple with the result (OK or NO) and the data. If there's an error, it will raise the proper exception.

The `BytesParser` module is used to transform the raw `RFC822` email into a Python object. This is done in *step 6*.

The metadata, including details such as the subject, the sender, and the timestamp, can be accessed like a dictionary, as shown in *step 7*. The addresses can be parsed from raw text format to separate the part with `email.utils.parseaddr`.

Finally, the content can be unfolded and extracted. If the type of the email is multipart, each of the parts can be extracted by iterating through `.get_payload()`. The one that's easier to deal with is `plain/text`, so assuming it is present, the code in *step 8* will extract it.

The email's body is stored in the `payload` variable.

There's more...

In *step 5*, we retrieved all the emails from the inbox, but that's not necessary. The search command can be parameterized with filter criteria, for example, by retrieving only the last day's emails:

```
import datetime
since = (datetime.date.today() - datetime.timedelta(days=1)).
strftime("%d-%b-%Y")
result, data = mail.uid('search', None, f'(SENTSINCE {since})')
```

This will search according to the date of the email. Notice that the resolution is in days.

There are more actions that can be done through IMAP4. Check RFC 3501 at `https://tools.ietf.org/html/rfc3501` and RFC 6851 at `https://tools.ietf.org/html/rfc6851` for further details.

> The preceding RFCs describe the IMAP4 protocol and can be a little arid. Checking the available commands in the RFCs' indexes will give you an idea of the capabilities of the protocol, and then you can search for examples on how to implement the specific command.

The subject and body of the email, as well as other metadata such as date, to, from, and so on, can be parsed and processed. For example, the subject retrieved in this recipe can be processed in the following way:

```
>>> import re
>>> re.search(r'\[Ref (\w+)] Subject: (\w+)', '[Ref ABCDEF] Subject:
Product A').groups()
('ABCDEF', 'Product')
```

See also

- *Chapter 1*, *Let's Begin Our Automation Journey*, for more information about regular expressions and other ways of parsing information.

Adding subscribers to an email newsletter

A common marketing tool is email newsletters. They are convenient ways of sending information to multiple targets. A good newsletter system is difficult to implement, and the recommended way is to use ones available on the market. A well-known one is **MailChimp** (`https://mailchimp.com/`).

MailChimp has a lot of possibilities, but the interesting one in regard to this book is its API, which can be scripted to automate tools. This RESTful API can be accessed through Python. In this recipe, we will see how to add more subscribers to an existing list.

Getting ready

As we will use MailChimp, we need to have an account with them. You can create a free account at `https://login.mailchimp.com/signup/`.

After creating the account, be sure to at least have a list that we can add subscribers to. As part of the registration process, it may have been created for you. It will appear under **Audience -> Manage Audience -> View Audience**:

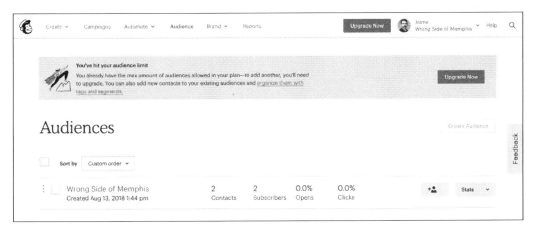

Figure 9.3: Audiences in MailChimp

The **Audience** will contain the subscribed users.

For the API, we'll need an API key. Go to **Account** -> **Extras** -> **API keys** and create a new one:

Figure 9.4: A screenshot of API keys in MailChimp

We will use the `requests` module to access the API. Add it to your virtual environment:

```
$ echo "requests==2.23" >> requirements.txt
$ pip install -r requirements.txt
```

The MailChimp API uses the concept of the **data center** (DC) that your account uses. This can be obtained from the last 4 digits of your API key or from the start of the URL from the MailChimp admin site. For example, `us19`.

How to do it...

1. Import the `requests` module:

   ```
   >>> import requests
   ```

2. Define the authentication and base URLs. The base URL requires your dc at the start (such as us19):

```
>>> API_KEY = 'your secret key'
>>> BASE = 'https://<dc>.api.mailchimp.com/3.0'
>>> auth = ('user', API_KEY)
```

3. Obtain all your lists:

```
>>> url = f'{BASE}/lists'
>>> response = requests.get(url, auth=auth)
>>> result = response.json()
```

4. Filter your lists to obtain the href for the required list:

```
>>> LIST_NAME = 'Your list name'
>>> this_list = [l for l in result['lists'] if l['name'] == LIST_
NAME][0]
>>> list_url = [l['href'] for l in this_list['_links'] if l['rel']
== 'self'][0]
```

5. With the list URL, you can obtain the URL for the members of the list:

```
>>> response = requests.get(list_url, auth=auth)
>>> result = response.json()
>>> result['stats']
{'member_count': 1, 'unsubscribe_count': 0, 'cleaned_count': 0,
...}
>>> members_url = [l['href'] for l in result['_links'] if l['rel']
== 'members'][0]
```

6. The list of members can be retrieved through a GET request to members_url:

```
>>> response = requests.get(members_url, auth=auth)
>>> result = response.json()
>>> len(result['members'])
1
```

7. Append a new member to the list:

```
>>> new_member = {
    'email_address': 'test@test.com',
    'status': 'subscribed',
}
>>> response = requests.post(members_url, json=new_member,
auth=auth)
```

8. Retrieving the list of users with a GET obtains both users:

```
>>> response = requests.get(members_url, auth=auth)
>>> result = response.json()
>>> len(result['members'])
2
```

How it works...

After importing the `requests` module in *step 1*, we define the basic values to connect in *step 2*: the base URL and the credentials. Note that for authentication, we only require the API key as the password, and any user (as described by the MailChimp documentation: `https://developer.mailchimp.com/documentation/mailchimp/guides/get-started-with-mailchimp-api-3/`).

Step 3 retrieves all the lists, calling the proper URL. The result is returned in JSON format. The call includes the `auth` parameter with the defined credentials. All subsequent calls will be made with this `auth` parameter for authentication purposes.

Step 4 shows how to filter the returned list to grab the URL of the list of interest. Each of the returned calls includes a list of `_links` with related information, making it possible to walk through the API.

The URL for the list is called in *step 5*. This returns information for the list, including the basic stats. By applying a similar filtering to *step 4*, we retrieve the URL for the members.

> Due to size constraints and to show relevant data, not all of the retrieved elements have been displayed. Feel free to analyze them interactively and find out about them. The data is well constructed and follows the RESTful principles of discoverability. Python's introspection makes it quite readable and understandable.

Step 6 retrieves the list of members, making a GET request to `members_url`, which can be seen as a single user. This can be seen in the *Getting ready* section, in the web interface.

Step 7 creates a new user and posts on `members_url` with the information passed in the `json` parameter so that it gets translated into JSON format. The updated data is retrieved in *step 7*, showing that there's a new user in the list.

There's more...

The full MailChimp API is quite powerful and can perform a large number of tasks. Go to the full MailChimp documentation to discover all the possibilities: `https://developer.mailchimp.com/`.

 As a brief note, and a little out of scope of this book, please be aware of the legal implications of adding subscribers to an automated list. Spam is a serious concern and there are new regulations in place to protect the rights of customers, such as GDPR. Ensure that you have the permission of users to email them. The good thing is that MailChimp automatically implements tools to help with this, such as automatic unsubscribe buttons.

The general MailChimp documentation is also quite interesting and shows a lot of possibilities. MailChimp is capable of managing newsletter and general distribution lists, but it can also be tailored to generate flows, schedule the sending of emails, and automatically send messages to your audience based on parameters such as their birthday.

See also

- The *Sending an individual email* recipe, earlier in this chapter, to see the differences between sending an email directly without this kind of tool
- The *Sending notification emails* recipe, next, to learn how to send emails tailored to a specific user for an action

Sending notifications via email

In this recipe, we will cover how to send emails to customers. Transactional emails are sent in response to an action by a user, such as confirmation or alert emails. Due to spam protection and other limitations, it is better to implement this kind of email with the help of external tools.

In this recipe, we will use **Mailgun** (`https://www.mailgun.com`), which is able to send these kinds of emails, as well as communicate responses.

Getting ready

We'll need to create an account with Mailgun. Go to `https://signup.mailgun.com` to create one. Notice that the credit card information is optional.

Once registered, go to **Domains** to see there's a sandbox environment. We can use it to test Mailgun's functionality, although it will only send emails to registered test email accounts. The API credentials will be displayed there:

Figure 9.5: Domain information in Mailgun

We need to register the account so we'll receive the email as an *authorized recipient.* You can add it here:

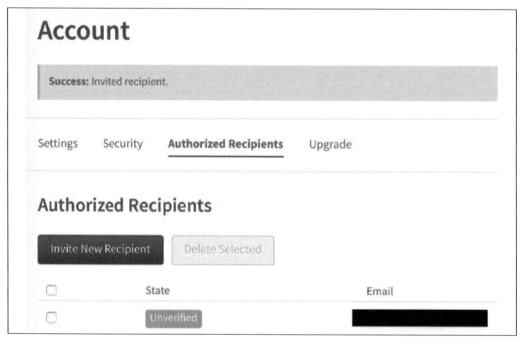

Figure 9.6: Verifying an account using Mailgun

To verify the account, check the email of the authorized recipient and confirm it. The email address is now ready to receive test emails:

Figure 9.7: The account is ready to receive test emails

We will use the `requests` module to connect to the Mailgun API. Install it in the virtual environment:

```
$ echo "requests==2.23" >> requirements.txt
$ pip install -r requirements.txt
```

Everything is ready to send emails, but notice that you can only send emails to authorized recipients. Being able to send emails everywhere requires us to set up a domain. Follow the Mailgun documentation for that: `https://documentation.mailgun.com/en/latest/quickstart-sending.html#verify-your-domain`.

How to do it...

1. Import the `requests` module:

   ```
   >>> import requests
   ```

2. Prepare the credentials, as well as the to and from emails. Note we're using a mock from:

   ```
   >>> KEY = 'YOUR-SECRET-KEY'
   >>> DOMAIN = 'YOUR-DOMAIN.mailgun.org'
   >>> TO = 'YOUR-AUTHORISED-RECEIVER'

   >>> FROM = f'sender@{DOMAIN}'
   >>> auth = ('api', KEY)
   ```

3. Prepare the email to be sent. Here, there is an HTML version and an alternative plain text one:

```
>>> text = "Hi!\nThis is the text version linking to https://www.
packtpub.com/\nCheers!"
>>> html = '''<html><head></head><body>
...     <p>Hi!<br>
...         This is the HTML version linking to <a href="https://
www.packtpub.com/">Packt</a><br>
...     </p>
...     </body></html>'''
```

4. Set up the data to send to Mailgun:

```
>>> data = {
...     'from': f'Sender <{FROM}>',
...     'to': f'Jaime Buelta <{TO}>',
...     'subject': 'An interesting email!',
...     'text': text,
...     'html': html,
... }
```

5. Make the call to the API:

```
>>> response = requests.post(f"https://api.mailgun.net/v3/
{DOMAIN}/messages", auth=auth, data=data)
>>> response.json()
{'id': '<YOUR-ID.mailgun.org>', 'message': 'Queued. Thank you.'}
```

6. Retrieve the events and check the email has been delivered:

```
>>> response_events = requests.get(f'https://api.mailgun.net/v3/
{DOMAIN}/events', auth=auth)
>>> response_events.json()['items'][0]['recipient'] == TO
True
>>> response_events.json()['items'][0]['event']
'delivered'
```

7. The email should appear in your inbox. As it was sent through the sandbox environment, be sure to check your spam folder if it doesn't show up directly.

How it works...

Step 1 imports the `requests` module to be used later. The credentials and the basic information in the message are defined in *step 2*, and should be extracted from the Mailgun web interface, as shown previously.

Step 3 defines the email that will be sent. *Step 4* structures the information in the way Mailgun expects. Notice the `html` and `text` fields. By default, it will set HTML as the preferred option and the plain text option as an alternative. The format for TO and FROM should be in the `Name <address>` format. You can use commas to separate multiple recipients in TO.

The call to the API is made in *step 5*. It is a POST call to the messages endpoint. The data is transferred in the standard way, and basic authentication is used with the `auth` parameter. Notice the definition in *step 2*. All calls to Mailgun should include this `auth` parameter. It returns a message, notifying you that it was successful, and then the message is queued.

In *step 6*, a call to retrieve the events through a GET request is made. This will show the latest actions performed, the last of which will be the recent send. Information about delivery status can also be found here.

There's more...

To send emails, you'll need to set up the domain with which to send it, instead of using the sandbox environment. You can find the instructions on how to do this here: `https://documentation.mailgun.com/en/latest/quickstart-sending.html#verify-your-domain`. This requires you to change your DNS records to verify that you are the legitimate owner of the domain. This also increases the deliverability of emails.

The emails can include attachments in the following way:

```
attachments = [
    ("attachment",
        ("attachment1.jpg", open("image.jpg","rb").read())
    ),
    ("attachment",
        ("attachment2.txt", open("text.txt","rb").read())
    )]
response = requests.post(f"https://api.mailgun.net/v3/{DOMAIN}/
messages",
                         auth=auth, files=attachments, data=data)
```

Notice the structure of `("attachment", (<filename>, <binary data>))`.

The data can include the usual information such as `cc` or `bcc`, but you can also delay the delivery for up to three days with the `o:deliverytime` parameter:

```python
import datetime
import email.utils
delivery_time = datetime.datetime.now() + datetime.timedelta(days=1)
data = {
    ...
    'o:deliverytime': email.utils.format_datetime(delivery_time),
}
```

Mailgun can also be used to receive emails and to trigger processes when they arrive; for example, forwarding them based on rules. Check the Mailgun documentation to find out more.

The full Mailgun documentation can be found here: `https://documentation.mailgun.com/en/latest/quickstart.html`. Be sure to check their *Best Practices* section at (`https://documentation.mailgun.com/en/latest/best_practices.html#email-best-practices`) to understand the world of sending emails and how to avoid them being labeled as spam.

See also

- The *Working with email templates* recipe, earlier in this chapter, to learn how to style emails using templates

- The *Sending an individual email* recipe, earlier in this chapter, to learn how to send emails directly from Python, instead of using an external service

Producing SMS messages

One of the most widely available communication channels is text messages. Text messages are very convenient to use to distribute information.

 SMS messages can be used for marketing purposes, but also as a way of alerting or sending notifications, or, very common recently, as a way of implementing two-factor authentication systems.

We will use **Twilio**, a service that exposes APIs to send SMS easily.

Getting ready

We need to create an account for Twilio at `https://www.twilio.com/`. Go to the page and register a new account.

You'll need to follow the instructions and set up a phone number to receive messages. You will need to input a code sent to this phone or receive a call to verify the phone line is correct.

Create a new project and check the dashboard. From there, you'll be able to create your first phone number so that you can receive and send SMS:

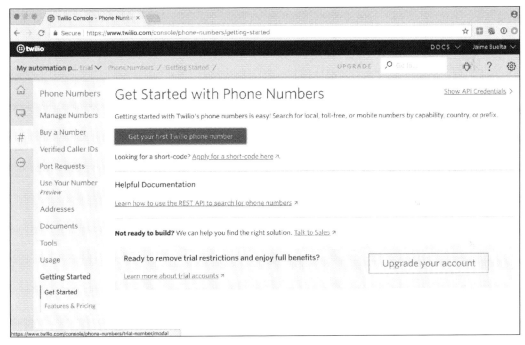

Figure 9.8: Setting up phone numbers using Twilio

Once the number has been configured, it will appear in the **Active Numbers** section in **All Products and Services** -> **Phone Numbers**.

On the main dashboard, check `ACCOUNT SID` and `AUTH TOKEN`. They'll be used later. Notice you'll need to display the auth token.

We'll also need to install the `twilio` module. Add it to your virtual environment:

```
$ echo "twilio==6.37.0" >> requirements.txt
$ pip install -r requirements.txt
```

Notice that the receiver phone number can only be a verified number with a trial account. You can verify more than one number; follow the documentation at `https://support.twilio.com/hc/en-us/articles/223180048-Adding-a-Verified-Phone-Number-or-Caller-ID-with-Twilio`.

How to do it...

1. Import `Client` from the `twilio` module:

   ```
   >>> from twilio.rest import Client
   ```

2. Set up the authentication credentials obtained from the dashboard previously. Also, set your Twilio phone number; as an example, here, we set `+353 12 345 6789`, a fake Irish number. It will be local to your country:

   ```
   >>> ACCOUNT_SID = 'Your account SID'
   >>> AUTH_TOKEN = 'Your secret token'
   >>> FROM = '+353 12 345 6789'
   ```

3. Start the `client` to access the API:

   ```
   >>> client = Client(ACCOUNT_SID, AUTH_TOKEN)
   ```

4. Send a message to your authorized phone number. Notice the underscore at the end of `from_`:

   ```
   >>> message = client.messages.create(body='This is a test message from Python!',
                                         from_=FROM,
                                         to='+your authorised number')
   ```

5. You'll receive an SMS on your phone:

Figure 9.9: Test message from Python

How it works...

The use of the Twilio client to send messages is very straightforward.

In *step 1*, we import Client. We prepare the credentials and configure the phone number in *step 2*.

Step 3 creates the client with the proper authentication, and the message is sent in *step 4*.

Note that the `to` number needs to be one of the authenticated numbers while you're working in a trial account, or it will produce an error. You can add more authenticated numbers; check the Twilio documentation.

All the messages that are sent from a trial account will include that detail in the SMS, as you can see in *step 5*.

There's more...

In certain regions (US and Canada, at the time of writing this), SMS numbers have the ability to send MMS messages, including images. To attach images to the message, add the `media_url` parameter and the URL of the image to send:

```
client.messages.create(body='An MMS message',
                       media_url='http://my.image.com/image.png',
                       from_=FROM,
                       to='+your authorised number')
```

The client is based on a RESTful API, and allows you to perform multiple operations, such as creating a new phone number or obtaining an available number first and then purchasing it:

```
available_numbers = client.available_phone_numbers("IE").local.
list()
number = available_numbers[0]
new_number = client.incoming_phone_numbers.create(phone_
number=number.phone_number)
```

Check the documentation for more available actions; most of the dashboard point-and-click actions can be performed programmatically.

Twilio is also capable of performing other phone services, such as phone calls and text-to-speech. Check it out in the full documentation.

The full Twilio documentation is available here: `https://www.twilio.com/docs/`.

See also

- The *Receiving SMS* recipe, next, to learn how to receive messages, as well as send them
- The *Creating a Telegram bot* recipe, later in this chapter, to further your knowledge

Receiving SMS

SMS can also be received and processed automatically. This enables services such as delivering information on request (for instance, send INFO GOALS to receive the results from the Soccer League), but also more complex flows such as in bots, which can have simple conversations with users that enable rich services such as remotely configuring a thermostat.

Each time Twilio receives an SMS to one of your registered phone numbers, it performs a request to a publicly available URL. This is configured in the Twilio service, meaning the code to execute when accessing the URL should be under your control. This creates the problem of having this URL available on the internet. That means that just your local computer won't work, as it's very unlikely that it is addressable externally from your local network. We will use Heroku (`http://heroku.com`) to deliver an available service, but there are other alternatives. The Twilio documentation provides examples of using `ngrok`, which allows for local development by creating a tunnel between a public address and your local development environment. See here for more details: `https://www.twilio.com/blog/2013/10/test-your-webhooks-locally-with-ngrok.html`.

This way of operating is common in communication APIs. It should be noted that Twilio has a beta API for WhatsApp, which works in a similar way. Check the docs for more information at `https://www.twilio.com/docs/sms/whatsapp/quickstart/python`.

Getting ready

We need to create an account for Twilio at `https://www.twilio.com/`. Refer to the *Getting ready* section in the *Producing SMS* recipe for detailed instructions.

For this recipe, we will also need to set up a web service in Heroku (`https://www.heroku.com/`) to be able to create a webhook capable of receiving SMS addressed to Twilio. Because the main objective of this recipe is the SMS part, we will be concise when setting up Heroku, but you can refer to its excellent documentation. It is quite easy to use:

1. Create an account in Heroku.

2. You'll need to install the command-line interface for Heroku (instructions for all platforms can be found at `https://devcenter.heroku.com/articles/getting-started-with-python#set-up`) and then log in to the command line:

   ```
   $ heroku login
   Enter your Heroku credentials.
   Email: your.user@server.com
   Password:
   ```

3. Download a basic Heroku template from `https://github.com/datademofun/heroku-basic-flask`. We will use it as a base for our server.

4. Add the `twilio` client to the `requirements.txt` file:

   ```
   $ echo "twilio" >> requirements.txt
   ```

    Replace the python interpreter with the newest supported version of python in the file `runtime.txt`. At the time of the writing, this was `3.8.3`. Check the heroku documentation `https://devcenter.heroku.com/articles/python-support#specifying-a-python-version`

5. Replace `app.py` with the one in GitHub at `https://github.com/PacktPublishing/Python-Automation-Cookbook-Second-Edition/blob/master/Chapter09/app.py`. The key part of this is to obtain the body of the request and send it back with some extra information. The code is displayed later in the *How it works…* section.

You can keep the existing `app.py` to check the template example and how Heroku works. Check out the README at `https://github.com/datademofun/heroku-basic-flask`.

6. Once done, commit the changes to Git:

```
$ git add .
$ git commit -m 'first commit'
```

7. Create a new service in Heroku. It will generate a new service name randomly (we used `service-name-12345` here). This URL is accessible:

```
$ heroku create

Creating app... done, ● SERVICE-NAME-12345

https://service-name-12345.herokuapp.com/ | https://git.heroku.com/service-name-12345.git
```

8. Deploy the service. In Heroku, deploying a service pushes the code to the remote Git server:

```
$ git push heroku master

...

remote: Verifying deploy... done.

To https://git.heroku.com/service-name-12345.git

 b6cd95a..367a994 master -> master
```

9. Check that the service is up and running at the webhook URL. Note it is displayed as output in the previous step. You can also check it in a browser:

```
$ curl https://service-name-12345.herokuapp.com/

All working!
```

How to do it...

1. Go to Twilio and access the **PHONE NUMBER** section. Configure the webhook URL. This will make the URL be called on each received SMS. Go to the **Active Numbers** section in **All Products** and **Services -> Phone Numbers** and fill in the webhook. Note /sms at the end of the webhook. Click on **Save**:

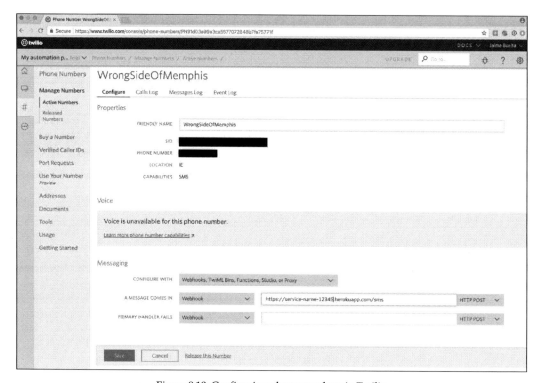

Figure 9.10: Configuring phone numbers in Twilio

2. The service is now up and running and can be used. Send an SMS to your Twilio phone number; you should get an automated response:

Figure 9.11: SMS from Twilio trial account

Note the blurred parts should be replaced with your information.

If you have a trial account, you can only send messages back to one of your authorized phone numbers, so you'll need to send the text from them.

How it works...

Step 1 sets up the webhook, so Twilio calls your Heroku app when receiving an SMS on the phone line.

Let's take a look at the code in app.py to see how this works. Here it is, redacted for clarity; check the full file at https://github.com/PacktPublishing/Python-Automation-Cookbook-Second-Edition/blob/master/Chapter09/app.py:

```python
from flask import Flask, request
from twilio.twiml.messaging_response import MessagingResponse

app = Flask(__name__)

@app.route('/')
def homepage():
    return 'All working!'

@app.route("/sms", methods=['GET', 'POST'])
def sms_reply():
    from_number = request.form['From']
    body = request.form['Body']
    resp = MessagingResponse()
    msg = (f'Awwwww! Thanks so much for your message {from_number},
           f'"{body}" to you too.')

    resp.message(msg)
    return str(resp)

if __name__ == '__main__':
    app.run()
```

app.py can be divided into three parts:

- The Python imports at the start of the file and startup of the Flask app at the end, which is just setting up Flask
- The call to homepage, which is generated to test that the server is working
- sms_reply, which is where the magic happens

The `sms_reply` function obtains the phone number that sends the SMS, as well as the body of the message, from the `request.form` dictionary. Then, compose a response in `msg`, attach it to a new `MessagingResponse`, and return it.

 We are using the message from the user as a whole, but remember all the techniques to parse text mentioned in *Chapter 1, Let's Begin Our Automation Journey*. They are all applicable here for detecting predefined actions or any other text processing.

The returned value will be sent back by Twilio to the sender, producing the result seen in *step 2*.

There's more...

To be able to generate automated conversations, the state of the conversation should be stored. For an advanced state, it should probably be stored in a database, generating a flow, but for simple cases, storing information in `session` may be enough. The session is able to store information in cookies that are persistent between the same combination of to and from phone numbers, allowing you to retrieve it between messages.

For example, this modification will return not only the send body, but the previous one as well. Only the relevant parts have been included:

```
app = Flask(__name__)
app.secret_key = b'somethingreallysecret!!!!'
...

@app.route("/sms", methods=['GET', 'POST'])
def sms_reply():
    from_number = request.form['From']
    last_message = session.get('MESSAGE', None)
    body = request.form['Body']
    resp = MessagingResponse()
    msg = (f'Awwwww! Thanks so much for your message {from_number}, '

        f'"{body}" to you too. ')
    if last_message:
        msg += f'Not so long ago you said "{last_message}" to me..'
    session['MESSAGE'] = body
    resp.message(msg)
    return str(resp)
```

The previous body is stored in the MESSAGE key of the session, which is carried over. Notice the requirement to define a secret key to be able to use the session data. Read this for information about it: https://flask.palletsprojects.com/en/1.1.x/quickstart/#sessions. More information about the handling of cookies in Twilio can be found here: https://support.twilio.com/hc/en-us/articles/223136287-How-do-Twilio-cookies-work-.

 To deploy the new version in Heroku, commit the new app.py file to Git, and then use `git push heroku master`. The new version will be deployed automatically!

Because the main objective of this recipe is to demonstrate how to reply, Heroku and Flask are not described in detail, but they both have excellent documentation. The full documentation for Heroku can be found at https://devcenter.heroku.com/categories/reference, and the documentation for Flask is here: http://flask.pocoo.org/docs/.

 Remember, the use of Heroku and Flask is just a convenience for this recipe. They're great and easy tools to use, but there are multiple alternatives to them, as long as you are able to expose a URL so that Twilio can call it. Also, check the security measures to ensure that requests to this endpoint come from Twilio: https://www.twilio.com/docs/usage/security#validating-requests.

The full documentation for Twilio can be found here: https://www.twilio.com/docs/.

See also

- The *Producing SMS* recipe, earlier in this chapter, to get to grips with the fundamentals of Twilio and how to receive messages.

- The *Creating a Telegram bot* recipe, next, to further your knowledge and apply it to similar elements.

Creating a Telegram bot

Telegram Messenger is an instant messaging app that has good support for creating bots. Bots are small applications that aim to produce automatic conversations. The big promise of bots is that, as machines, they can create any kind of conversation, totally indistinguishable from a conversation with a human being, and pass the *Turing Test*, but that objective is quite ambitious and not realistic for the most part.

 The Turing Test was proposed by Alan Turing in 1951. Two participants, a human and an **Artificial Intelligence (AI)** machine/ software program, communicate via text (like in an instant messaging app) with a human judge that decides which one is human and which one is not. If the judge can only guess correctly 50% of the time, it can't be easily differentiated and therefore the AI passes the test. This was one of the first attempts to measure AI.

But bots can be very useful for a more limited approach, similar to phone systems where you need to press 2 to check your account and press 3 to report a missing card. In this recipe, we'll see how to generate a simple bot that will display offers and events for a company.

Getting ready

We need to create a new bot for Telegram. This is done through an interface called the **BotFather**, which is a Telegram special channel that allows us to create a new bot. You can access the channel here: `https://telegram.me/botfather`. Access it through your Telegram account.

Run `/start` to start the interface and then create a new bot with `/newbot`. The interface will ask you for the name of the bot and a username, which should be unique.

Once it's set up, it will give you the following:

- The Telegram channel of your bot: `https:/t.me/<yourusername>`.
- A token to allow access to the bot. Copy it as it will be used later.

 You can generate a new token if you lose an existing token. Read the BotFather's documentation for more information.

We also need to install the Python module `telepot`, which wraps the RESTful interface from Telegram:

```
$ echo "telepot==12.7" >> requirements.txt
$ pip install -r requirements.txt
```

Download the `telegram_bot.py` script from GitHub at `https://github.com/PacktPublishing/Python-Automation-Cookbook-Second-Edition/blob/master/Chapter09/telegram_bot.py`.

How to do it...

1. Set up your generated token in the `telegram_bot.py` script on the TOKEN constant in line 6:

   ```
   TOKEN = '<YOUR TOKEN>'
   ```

2. Start the bot:

   ```
   $ python telegram_bot.py
   ```

3. Open the Telegram channel on your phone using the URL and start it. You can use the `help`, `offers`, and `events` commands:

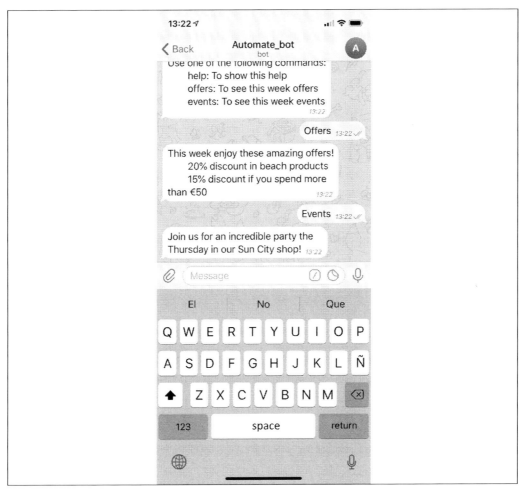

Figure 9.12: Marketing offers sent by SMS

How it works...

Step 1 sets the token to use for your specific channel. In *step 2*, we start the bot locally.

Let's see how the code in `telegram_bot.py` is structured:

```python
# IMPORTS

# TOKEN

# Define the information to return per command
def get_help():
def get_offers():
def get_events():
COMMANDS = {
    'help': get_help,
    'offers': get_offers,
    'events': get_events,
}

class MarketingBot(telepot.helper.ChatHandler):
...


# Create and start the bot
```

The `MarketingBot` class creates an interface to handle the communication with Telegram:

- When the channel is started, the `open` method will be called
- When a message is received, the `on_chat_message` method will be called
- If there's no answer in a while, `on_idle` will be called

In each case, the `self.sender.sendMessage` method is used to send a message back to the user. Most of the interesting bits happen in `on_chat_message`:

```python
def on_chat_message(self, msg):
    # If the data sent is not test, return an error
    content_type, chat_type, chat_id = telepot.glance(msg)
    if content_type != 'text':
        self.sender.sendMessage("I don't understand you. "
                                "Please type 'help' for options")
        return
```

```
# Make the commands case insensitive
command = msg['text'].lower()

if command not in COMMANDS:
    self.sender.sendMessage("I don't understand you. "
                            "Please type 'help' for options")

    return

message = COMMANDS[command]()
self.sender.sendMessage(message)
```

First, it checks whether the received message is text and returns an error message if it's not. It analyzes the received text, and if it's one of the defined commands, it executes the corresponding function to retrieve the text to return.

Then, it sends the message back to the user.

Step 3 shows how this works from the user's point of view, who is interacting with the bot.

There's more...

You can add more information, an avatar picture, and so on to your Telegram channel using the BotFather interface.

To simplify our interface, we can create a custom keyboard to simplify the bot. Create it after defining the commands, around line 44 of the script:

```
from telepot.namedtuple import ReplyKeyboardMarkup, KeyboardButton
keys = [[KeyboardButton(text=text)] for text in COMMANDS]
KEYBOARD = ReplyKeyboardMarkup(keyboard=keys)
```

Notice it is creating a keyboard with three rows, each with one of the commands. Then, add the resulting KEYBOARD as the reply_markup on each of the sendMessage calls, as follows:

```
message = COMMANDS[command]()
self.sender.sendMessage(message, reply_markup=KEYBOARD)
```

This replaces the keyboard with only the defined buttons, making the interface very obvious:

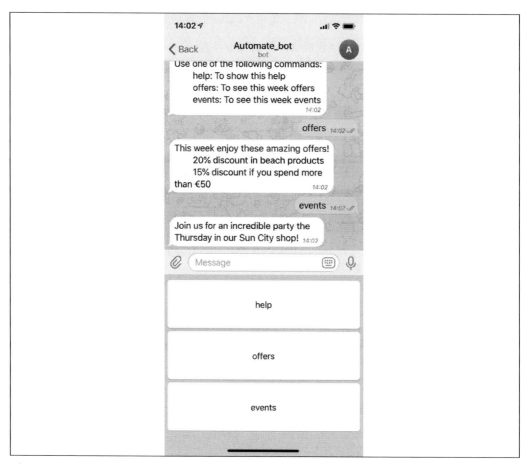

Figure 9.13: SMS with three buttons

These changes can be downloaded from the `telegram_bot_custom_keyboard.py` file, available in GitHub here: `https://github.com/PacktPublishing/Python-Automation-Cookbook-Second-Edition/blob/master/Chapter09/telegram_bot_custom_keyboard.py`.

You can create other kinds of custom interfaces, such as inline buttons or even a platform for creating games. Check the Telegram API docs for more information.

Interacting with Telegram can also be done through webhooks, in a similar way as presented in the *Receiving SMS* recipe. Check the example for Flask in the `telepot` documentation here: `https://github.com/nickoala/telepot/tree/master/examples/webhook`.

 Setting up a Telegram webhook can be done through `telepot`. It requires that your service is behind an HTTPS address to ensure the communication is private. This can be tricky to do with simple services. You can check the documentation on setting up a webhook in the Telegram docs: `https://core.telegram.org/bots/api#setwebhook`.

The full Telegram API for bots can be found here: `https://core.telegram.org/bots`.

The documentation for the `telepot` module can be found here: `https://telepot.readthedocs.io/en/latest/`.

See also

- The *Producing SMS* recipe, earlier in this chapter, to learn about the fundamentals of Twilio and how to receive SMS messages.

- The *Receiving SMS* recipe, earlier in this chapter, to learn how to receive SMS messages using Twilio.

10

Why Not Automate Your Marketing Campaign?

In this chapter, we will cover the following recipes, which are related to a marketing campaign:

- Detecting opportunities
- Creating personalized coupon codes
- Sending a notification to a customer on their preferred channel
- Preparing sales information
- Generating a sales report

Introduction

In this chapter, we will create a marketing campaign and go through each of the automatic steps we'll take. We will use concepts and recipes throughout this book in a single project that will require different steps.

Let's look at an example. For our project, our company wishes to set up a marketing campaign to improve engagement and sales. A very laudable effort. To do so, we can divide this into several tasks:

1. We want to detect the best moment to launch the campaign, so we will be notified from different sources about keywords that will help us make an informed decision

2. The campaign will include the generation of individual codes to be sent to potential customers

3. We will send these codes directly to users over their preferred channel, text message or email

4. To monitor the result of the campaign, we will compile the sales information

5. And finally, a sales report will be generated

This chapter will go through each of these tasks and present a combined solution based on modules and techniques that have been introduced in this book.

> While these examples have been created with real-life requirements in mind, take into account that your specific environment will always surprise you. Don't be afraid to experiment, tweak, and improve your system as you learn more about it. Iterating is the way to create great systems.

Let's get to it!

Detecting opportunities

In this chapter, we are presenting a marketing campaign divided into several tasks:

1. **Detect the best moment to launch the campaign**
2. Generate individual codes to be sent to potential customers
3. Send the codes directly to users over their preferred channel, text message or email
4. Collect the results of the campaign
5. Generate a sales report with an analysis of the results

This recipe covers *task 1*.

Our first task is to detect the best time to launch a campaign. To do so, we will monitor a list of news sites, searching for news containing one of our defined keywords. We add any article that matches these keywords to a report and send it in an email.

Getting ready

In this recipe, we will use several external modules previously presented in this book, `delorean`, `requests`, and `BeautifulSoup`. We need to add them to our virtual environment if they're not already there:

```
$ echo "delorean==1.0.0" >> requirements.txt
$ echo "requests==2.23.0" >> requirements.txt
$ echo "beautifulsoup4==4.8.2" >> requirements.txt
$ echo "feedparser==5.2.1" >> requirements.txt
$ echo "jinja2==2.11.1" >> requirements.txt
$ echo "mistune==0.8.4" >> requirements.txt
$ pip install -r requirements.txt
```

You need to make a list of RSS feeds, from which we will retrieve our data.

In our example, we're using the following feeds, which are all technology feeds of well-known news sites:

- `http://feeds.reuters.com/reuters/technologyNews`
- `https://rss.nytimes.com/services/xml/rss/nyt/Technology.xml`
- `https://feeds.bbci.co.uk/news/science_and_environment/rss.xml`

Download the `search_keywords.py` script, which will perform the actions, from GitHub at `https://github.com/PacktPublishing/Python-Automation-Cookbook-Second-Edition/blob/master/Chapter10/search_keywords.py`. You also need to download the email templates, which can be found at `https://github.com/PacktPublishing/Python-Automation-Cookbook-Second-Edition/blob/master/Chapter10/email_styling.html` and `https://github.com/PacktPublishing/Python-Automation-Cookbook-Second-Edition/blob/master/Chapter10/email_template.md`. There is a config template at `https://github.com/PacktPublishing/Python-Automation-Cookbook-Second-Edition/blob/master/Chapter10/config-opportunity.ini`.

You need a valid username and password for an email service. Check the `Sending an individual email` recipe in *Chapter 9, Dealing with Communication Channels.*

How to do it...

1. Create a `config-opportunity.ini` file, which should be in the following format. Remember to fill it with your details:

```
[SEARCH]
keywords = keyword, keyword
feeds = feed, feed
```

```
[EMAIL]
user = <YOUR EMAIL USERNAME>
password = <YOUR EMAIL PASSWORD>
from = <EMAIL ADDRESS FROM>
to = <EMAIL ADDRESS TO>
```

You can use the template from GitHub at `https://github.com/PacktPublishing/Python-Automation-Cookbook-Second-Edition/blob/master/Chapter10/config-opportunity.ini` to search for the keyword `cpu` and some test feeds. Remember to fill in the `EMAIL` fields with your own account details.

2. Call the script to produce the email and report:

   ```
   $ python search_keywords.py config-opportunity.ini
   ```

3. Check the `to` email; you should receive a report with the articles found. Keep in mind that it will be different depending on the daily news, but it should be something similar to this:

Hi!

This is an automated email checking articles published last week containing the *keywords*: cpu in the following feeds: http://feeds.reuters.com/reuters/technologyNews http://rss.nytimes.com/services/xml/rss/nyt/Technology.xml http://feeds.bbci.co.uk/news/science_and_environment/rss.xml

List of articles:

- **As Nvidia expands in artificial intelligence, Intel defends turf | Reuters** Nvidia Corp dominates chips for training computers to think like humans, but it faces an entrenched competitor in a major avenue for expansion in the artificial intelligence chip market: Intel Corp .<div class="feedflare"> <a href="http://feeds.reuters.com/~ff/reuters/technologyNews?a=A1okGChaZls:tKET_rJFBi0:yll2AUoC8zA"><img src="http://feeds.feedburner.com/~ff/reuters/technologyNews?d=yll2AUoC8zA" border="0"></img></a> <a href="http://feeds.reuters.com/~ff/reuters/technologyNews?a=A1okGChaZls:tKET_rJFBi0:V_sGLiPBpWU"><img src="http://feeds.feedburner.com/~ff/reuters/technologyNews?a=A1okGChaZls:tKET_rJFBi0:V_sGLiPBpWU" border="0"></img></a> <a href="http://feeds.reuters.com/~ff/reuters/technologyNews?a=A1okGChaZls:tKET_rJFBi0:-BTjWOF_DHI"><img src="http://feeds.feedburner.com/~ff/reuters/technologyNews?i=A1okGChaZls:tKET_rJFBi0:-BTjWOF_DHI" border="0"></img></a> </div><img src="http://feeds.feedburner.com/~r/reuters/technologyNews/~4/A1okGChaZls" height="1" width="1" alt=""/>: http://feeds.reuters.com/~r/reuters/technologyNews/~3/A1okGChaZls/as-nvidia-expands-in-artificial-intelligence-intel-defends-turf-idUSKBN1L2051
- **Give Your Old Computer New Life - The New York Times** If you're not ready to buy a whole new system, you might be able to add new parts and upgrade your aging machine for less than a few hundred dollars.: https://www.nytimes.com/2018/08/17/technology/personaltech/give-your-old-computer-new-life.html?partner=rss&emc=rss

Enjoy the read!

Figure 10.1: A list of articles containing the keyword `cpu`

How it works...

After creating the proper configuration for the script in *step 1*, web scraping and sending an email with the results is done in *step 2* by calling `search_keywords.py`.

Let's take a look at the `search_keywords.py` script. The code is structured into the following parts:

- The `IMPORTS` section makes available all the Python modules to be used later. It also defines `EmailConfig namedtuple` to help with handling the email parameters.

- `READ TEMPLATES` retrieves the email templates and stores them for later use in the `EMAIL_TEMPLATE` and `EMAIL_STYLING` constants.

- The `__main__` block starts the process by getting the configuration parameters, parsing the config file, and then calling the `main` function.

- The `main` function combines the other functions. First, it retrieves the articles, and then it obtains the body and sends the email.

- `get_articles` walks through all the feeds and discards any article that is over 1 week old. For the remaining articles, it searches for a match on the keywords. All the matched articles are returned, including information about the link and a summary.

- `compose_email_body` uses the email templates to compile the email body. Notice that the template is in Markdown and it gets parsed into HTML, to give the same information in plain-text and in HTML.

- `send_email` gets the body information, as well as required information such as the username/password, and sends the email.

There's more...

One of the main challenges in retrieving information from different sources is to parse the text in all cases. Some feeds may return information in different formats.

For instance, in our example, you can see that the Reuters feed summary includes HTML information that gets rendered in the resulting email. If you have that kind of problem, you may need to process the returned data further, until it becomes consistent. This may be highly dependent on the expected quality of the resulting report.

 When developing automatic tasks, especially when dealing with multiple input sources, expect to spend a lot of time cleaning the input to make it consistent. However, find a balance and keep in mind the final recipient. If the email is to be received, for example, by yourself or a friend, you can be a little more permissive than with an important client.

Another possibility is to increase the complexity of the match. In this recipe, the check is done with a simple `in operator`. Remember that all the techniques in *Chapter 1, Let's Begin Our Automation Journey*, are available for you to use, including all the regular expression's capabilities.

 This script is automatable through a cron job, as described in *Chapter 2, Automating Tasks Made Easy*. Try to run it every week!

See also

- The *Adding command-line arguments* recipe in *Chapter 1, Let's Begin Our Automation Journey*, to learn the details about the command-line arguments.

- The *Introducing regular* expressions recipe in *Chapter 1, Let's Begin Our Automation Journey*, to learn about how to use regular expressions.

- The *Preparing a task* recipe in *Chapter 2, Automating Tasks Made Easy*, to check the structure for a good automated task.

- The *Setting up a cron job* recipe in *Chapter 2, Automating Tasks Made Easy*, to learn how to repeat a job automatically.

- The *Parsing HTML* recipe in *Chapter 3, Building Your First Web Scraping Application*, to learn how to parse returned HTML.

- The *Crawling the web recipe* in *Chapter 3, Building Your First Web Scraping Application*, to learn how to follow up links when retrieving information on the web.

- The *Subscribing to feeds* recipe in *Chapter 3, Building Your First Web Scraping Application*, to learn the basics about dealing with RSS feeds.

- The *Sending an individual email* recipe in *Chapter 9, Dealing with Communication Channels*, to learn how to send emails using Python.

Creating personalized coupon codes

In this chapter, we are presenting a marketing campaign divided into several tasks:

1. Detect the best moment to launch the campaign

2. **Generate individual codes to be sent to potential customers**

3. Send the codes directly to users over their preferred channel, text message or email

4. Collect the results of the campaign

5. Generate a sales report with an analysis of the results

This recipe shows *task 2* of the campaign.

After an opportunity has been detected, we decide to generate a campaign for all customers. To direct promotions and avoid duplication, we will generate 1 million unique coupons, divided into three batches:

- Half of the codes will be printed and distributed in a marketing action.

- 300,000 codes will be reserved to be used later if the campaign hits some goals.

- The remaining 200,000 will be directed to customers through SMS and emails.

These coupons can be redeemed in the online system. Our task will be to generate the proper codes, which should meet the following requirements:

- The codes need to be unique.

- The codes need to be printable and easy to read, as some customers will be dictating them over the phone.

- There should be a quick way to discard fake codes. This will avoid attacks with random codes that could overload the system.

- The codes should be presented in CSV format for printing.

Getting ready

Download the `create_personalised_coupons.py` script, which will generate the coupons in CSV files, from GitHub at `https://github.com/PacktPublishing/Python-Automation-Cookbook-Second-Edition/blob/master/Chapter10/create_personalised_coupons.py`.

How to do it...

1. Call the `create_personalised_coupons.py` script. It will take a minute or two to run, depending on your processor speed. It will display the generated codes onscreen:

```
$ python create_personalised_coupons.py
Code: HWLF-P9J9E-U3
Code: EAUE-FRCWR-WM
Code: PMW7-P39MP-KT
...
```

2. Check it has created three CSV files, `codes_batch_1.csv`, `codes_batch_2.csv`, and `codes_batch_3.csv`, each with the proper number of codes:

```
$ wc -l codes_batch_*.csv
  500000 codes_batch_1.csv
  300000 codes_batch_2.csv
  200000 codes_batch_3.csv
 1000000 total
```

3. Check that each of the batch files contains unique codes. Your codes will be unique and different from the ones displayed here:

```
$ head codes_batch_2.csv
9J9F-M33YH-YR
7WLP-LTJUP-PV
WHFU-THW7R-T9
...
```

How it works...

Step 1 calls the script that generates all the codes, and *step 2* checks that the results are correct. *Step 3* shows the format in which the codes are stored. Let's analyze the `create_personalised_coupons.py` script.

In summary, it has the following structure:

```
# IMPORTS
...
# FUNCTIONS
def random_code(digits)
    ...
def checksum(code1, code2)
    ...
def check_code(code)
    ...
def generate_code()
    ...


# SET UP TASK
...
# GENERATE CODES
...
```

```
# CREATE AND SAVE BATCHES
...
```

The different functions work together to create a code. `random_code` generates a combination of random letters and numbers, taken from CHARACTERS. This string contains all the valid characters to choose from.

> The selection of characters is defined as symbols that are easy to print and cannot be mistaken for each other. For example, it will be difficult to distinguish between a letter O and the number 0, or the number 1 and the letter I, depending on the font. This may depend on the specifics of the typeface and the printing process, so check printing tests if necessary to adjust the characters. But avoid using all letters and numbers in printing form, as it may cause confusion. Increase the length of the codes if necessary; for example, if many more codes are required or if the number of easily recognizable symbols is smaller.

The `checksum` function generates, based on two codes, an extra digit that is derived from the two codes. This process is called **hashing**, and it's a well-known process in computing, especially for cryptography.

> The basic functionality of hashing is to produce an output from an input that is smaller and is not reversible, meaning it's very difficult to guess unless the input is known. Hashing has a lot of common applications in computing, normally under the hood. For example, Python dictionaries make extensive use of hashing.

In our recipe, we'll use SHA256, a well-known fast hashing algorithm included in the Python `hashlib` module:

```
def checksum(code1, code2):
    m = hashlib.sha256()
    m.update(code1.encode())
    m.update(code2.encode())
    checksum = int(m.hexdigest()[:2], base=16)
    digit = CHARACTERS[checksum % len(CHARACTERS)]
    return digit
```

Both codes are concatenated as input, and the resulting two hex digits of the resulting hash string are used to pick the corresponding character from CHARACTERS.

The hash digits get transformed into a base 10 number (as they are in base 16) and we apply the `modulo` operator to obtain one of the available characters.

The objective of this checksum is to be able to quickly check whether a code looks like it is correct and discard possible spam. We can produce the operation again over a code to see whether the checksum is the same. Note that this is not a cryptographic hash, as no secret is required at any point of the operation. Given this specific use case, this (low) level of security is probably fine for our purposes.

> `Cryptography` is a much bigger theme and ensuring that security is strong can be difficult. The main strategy in cryptography involving hashing is probably to store just the hash to avoid storing passwords in a readable format. You can read a quick introduction to that technique here: https://crackstation.net/hashing-security.htm.

The `generate_code` function then produces a random code, composed of four digits, then five digits, and then two digits of the checksum, divided by dashes. The first checksum digit is generated with the first nine digits in right-to-left order (using the four-character block as `code1` and the five-character block as `code2`). The second checksum digit is generated by reversing them (the five-character block as `code1` and the four-character block as `code2`).

The `check_code` function reverses the process and returns `True` if the code is correct, and `False` otherwise.

With the basic elements in place, the script starts by defining the required batches: 500,000, 300,000, and 200,000.

All the codes are generated in the same pool, called `codes`. This is to avoid duplicates between batches. Note that, due to the randomness of the process, we can't rule out the possibility of generating duplicated code, though such a possibility is small. We are allowed to retry up to three times to avoid generating duplicated code. The codes are stored in a set accumulator to guarantee their uniqueness and to speed up the process of checking whether a code is already there.

> `Sets` is another of the places where Python uses hashing under the hood, so it hashes the element to be added and compares it with the hashes of the elements already there. This makes checking in sets a very quick operation.

To be sure that the process is correct, each code is verified and printed to display progress while generating the code. This also allows us to inspect that everything is working as expected.

Finally, the codes are divided into the proper number of batches and each one is saved in an individual .csv file. The codes are removed one by one from codes using .pop() until batch is the proper size:

```
batch = [(codes.pop(),) for _ in range(batch_size)]
```

Note how the previous line creates a batch of the proper size of rows with a single element. Each row is still a list, as it should be for a CSV file.

Then, a file is created and, using csv.writer, the codes are stored as rows.

As a final test, the remaining codes are verified to make sure they're empty.

There's more...

In this recipe, a direct approach was used in the flow. This is in opposition to the principles presented in the *Preparing a task to run* recipe in *Chapter 2, Automating Tasks Made Easy*. Notice that, compared with the tasks presented there, this script is aimed to be run a single time to produce the codes, and that's it. It also uses defined constants, such as BATCHES, for configuration, instead of command-line parameters or config files.

Given that it is a unique task, designed to be run once, spending time structuring it into a reusable component is probably not the best use of our time.

 Over-engineering is definitively possible and choosing between a pragmatic design and a more future-facing approach may not be easy. Be realistic about maintenance costs and try to find your own balance.

In the same way, the design in this recipe on the checksum is aimed to give a minimal way to check whether a code is totally made up or looks legit. Given that codes will be checked against a system, this seems like a sensible approach, but be aware of your particular use case.

Our code space is made up of 22 characters ** 9 digits = 1,207,269,217,792 possible codes, meaning the probability of guessing one of the million generated is very small. It's also not very likely to produce the same code twice, but nevertheless, we protected our code against that with up to three retries.

These kinds of checks, as well as checking that each code has been verified and that we end up with no remaining codes, are very useful when developing this kind of script. It ensures that we are going in the right direction and things are going according to plan. Just be aware that `asserts` may not be executed in some conditions.

 As described in the Python documentation, `assert` commands are ignored if the Python code is optimized (run with the `-O` command). See the documentation here: `https://docs.python.org/3/reference/simple_stmts.html#the-assert-statement`. The usage of the `-O` argument is rare, but can be confusing if that's the case. Avoid depending heavily on `asserts`.

Learning the basics of cryptography is not as difficult as you may think. There are a small number of basic schemes that are well-known and can be easily learned. A good introduction article is `https://thebestvpn.com/cryptography/`. Python also has a good number of cryptographic functions; see the documentation at `https://docs.python.org/3/library/crypto.html`. The best approach is to find a good book and know that, while it's a difficult subject to truly master, it is definitely approachable.

See also

- The *Introducing regular expressions* recipe in *Chapter 1, Let's Begin Our Automation Journey*, to learn how to use regular expressions.
- The Reading CSV files recipe in *Chapter 4, Searching and Reading Local Files*, to learn how to work with CSV files.

Sending a notification to a customer on their preferred channel

In this chapter, we are presenting a marketing campaign divided into several tasks:

1. Detect the best moment to launch the campaign
2. Generate individual codes to be sent to potential customers
3. **Send the codes directly to users over their preferred channel, text message or email**
4. Collect the results of the campaign
5. Generate a sales report with an analysis of the results

This recipe shows *task 3* of the campaign.

Once our codes have been created for direct marketing, we need to distribute them to our customers.

For this recipe, from an input from a CSV file with the information of all customers and their preferred contact methods, we will fill the file with the codes generated previously, and then send a notification through the proper method. This will include the promotional code.

Getting ready

In this recipe, we will use several modules already presented: delorean, requests, and twilio. We need to add them to our virtual environment, if they're not already there:

```
$ echo "delorean==1.0.0" >> requirements.txt
$ echo "requests==2.23.0" >> requirements.txt
$ echo "twilio==6.37.0" >> requirements.txt
$ pip install -r requirements.txt
```

We need to define a config-channel.ini file with our credentials for the services to use, Mailgun and Twilio. A template of this file can be found on GitHub here: https://github.com/PacktPublishing/Python-Automation-Cookbook-Second-Edition/blob/master/Chapter10/config-channel.ini.

 For information on how to obtain the credentials, refer to the *Sending notifications via emails* and *Producing SMS* recipes in *Chapter 9, Dealing with Communication Channels.*

The file has the following format:

```
[MAILGUN]
KEY = <YOUR KEY>
DOMAIN = <YOUR DOMAIN>
FROM = <YOUR FROM EMAIL>
[TWILIO]
ACCOUNT_SID = <YOUR SID>
AUTH_TOKEN = <YOUR TOKEN>
FROM = <FROM TWILIO PHONE NUMBER>
```

For a description of all the contacts to target, we need to generate a CSV file, `notifications.csv`, in the following format:

Name	Contact Method	Target	Status	Code	Timestamp
John Smith	PHONE	+1-555-12345678	NOT-SENT		
Paul Smith	EMAIL	paul.smith@test.com	NOT-SENT		

Figure 10.2: Format of `notifications.csv`

Note that the `Code` column is empty and that all the statuses should be NOT-SENT or empty.

 If you are using a test account in Twilio and Mailgun, be aware of its limitations. For example, Twilio only allows you to send messages to authenticated phone numbers. You can create a small CSV file with only two or three contacts to test the script.

The coupon codes to be used should be ready in a CSV file. You can generate several batches with the `create_personalised_coupons.py` script, available on GitHub at `https://github.com/PacktPublishing/Python-Automation-Cookbook-Second-Edition/blob/master/Chapter10/create_personalised_coupons.py`.

Download the script to be used, `send_notifications.py`, from GitHub at `https://github.com/PacktPublishing/Python-Automation-Cookbook-Second-Edition/blob/master/Chapter10/send_notifications.py`.

How to do it...

1. Run `send_notifications.py` to see its options and usage:

```
$ python send_notifications.py --help
usage: send_notifications.py [-h] [-c CODES] [--config CONFIG_
FILE] notif_file


positional arguments:
  notif_file            notifications file
```

```
optional arguments:
  -h, --help            show this help message and exit
  -c CODES, --codes CODES
                        Optional file with codes. If present, the
file
                        will be populated with codes. No codes
will be
                        sent
  --config CONFIG_FILE config file (default config.ini)
```

2. Add the codes to the `notifications.csv` file:

```
$ python send_notifications.py --config config-channel.ini
notifications.csv -c codes_batch_3.csv
$ head notifications.csv
Name,Contact Method,Target,Status,Code,Timestamp
John Smith,PHONE,+1-555-12345678,NOT-SENT,CFXK-U37JN-TM,
Paul Smith,EMAIL,paul.smith@test.com,NOT-SENT,HJGX-M97WE-9Y,
...
```

3. Finally, send the notifications:

```
$ python send_notifications.py --config config-channel.ini
notifications.csv
$ head notifications.csv
Name,Contact Method,Target,Status,Code,Timestamp
John Smith,PHONE,+1-555-12345678,SENT,CFXK-U37JN-TM,2018-08-
25T13:08:15.908986+00:00
Paul Smith,EMAIL,paul.smith@test.com,SENT,HJGX-M97WE-9Y,2018-08-
25T13:08:16.980951+00:00
...
```

4. Check the emails and phones to verify the messages were received.

How it works...

Step 1 shows the use of the script. The general idea is to call it several times; the first time to fill it with codes, and the second time to send the messages. If there's an error, the script can be executed again, and only messages not previously sent will be retried.

The `notifications.csv` file gets the codes that will be injected in *step 2*. The codes are finally sent in *step 3*.

Let's analyze the code of `send_notifications.py`. Only the most relevant bits are shown here:

```
# IMPORTS

def send_phone_notification(...):
def send_email_notification(...):
def send_notification(...):

def save_file(...):
def main(...):

if __name__ == '__main__':
    # Parse arguments and prepare configuration
    ...
```

The main function goes through the file line by line and analyzes what to do in each case. If the entry is SENT, it skips it. If it has no code, it tries to fill it. If it tries to send it, it will attach the timestamp to record when it was sent or tried to be sent.

For each entry, the whole file is saved again in a file called `save_file`. Notice how the file cursor is positioned at the start of the file. The file is written and then flushed to disk:

```
def save_file(notif_file, data):
    '''
    Overwrite the file with the new information
    '''

    # Start at the start of the file
    notif_file.seek(0)

    header = data[0].keys()
    writer = csv.DictWriter(notif_file, fieldnames=header)
    writer.writeheader()
    writer.writerows(data)

    # Be sure to write to disk
    notif_file.flush()
```

This overwrites the file on each entry operation, without us having to close and open the file again.

Why write the whole file for each entry? This is an easy way to store each of the operations and allows you to retry the sending process. For example, if an entry produces an unexpected error or a timeout, or even if there's a general failure, all the progress and previous codes will be marked as SENT already and won't be sent a second time. This means the operation can be retried as needed. For a big number of entries, this is a good way of ensuring that a problem in the middle of the process doesn't make us resend messages to our customers.

For a huge number of rows, we may risk having a problem with saving the file. This can cause the file to get corrupted by an unexpected error while writing or taking too long to save. If that's the case, split the file into independent batches that can be treated independently. For very big processes, a system that guarantees the data won't get corrupted, like using a database, may be required.

For each code to be sent, the `send_notification` function decides to call either `send_phone_notification` or `send_email_notification`. It appends the current time in both cases.

Both `send` functions return an error if they can't send the message. This allows you to mark it in the resulting `notifications.csv` file and retry it later.

The `notifications.csv` file can also be changed manually. For example, imagine there's a typo in an email and that's the reason for the error. It can be changed and retried.

`send_email_notification` sends the message based on the Mailgun interface. For more information, refer to the *Sending notifications via emails* recipe in *Chapter 9, Dealing with Communication Channels*. Note that the email sent here is text only.

`send_phone_notification` sends the message based on the Twilio interface. For more information, refer to the *Producing SMS* recipe in *Chapter 9, Dealing with Communication Channels*.

There's more...

Timestamps have been deliberately written in ISO format, as it is a parsable format. This means that we can get back a proper object in an easy way, like this:

```
>>> import datetime
>>> timestamp = datetime.datetime.now(datetime.timezone.utc).isoformat()
>>> timestamp
'2018-08-25T14:13:53.772815+00:00'
>>> datetime.datetime.fromisoformat(timestamp)
datetime.datetime(2018, 9, 11, 21, 5, 41, 979567, tzinfo=datetime.timezone.utc)
```

This allows you to easily parse the timestamp back and forth.

 ISO 8601 time format is well supported in most programming languages and precisely defines the time as it includes the time zone. It is an excellent choice for recording times, if you can use it.

The strategy used in `send_notification` to route the notifications is an interesting one:

```
# Route each of the notifications
METHOD = {
    'PHONE': send_phone_notification,
    'EMAIL': send_email_notification,
}
try:
    method = METHOD[entry['Contact Method']]
    result = method(entry, config)
except KeyError:
    result = 'INVALID_METHOD'
```

The METHOD dictionary assigns each of the possible Contact Methods to a function that has the same definition, accepting both an entry and a config.

Then, based on the specific method, the function is retrieved from the dictionary and called. Note that the method variable contains the correct function to call.

This acts in a similar way to the `switch` operation that is available in other programming languages. It is also possible to achieve this through `if...else` blocks. For simple cases like this code, the dictionary method makes the code very readable.

The `invalid_method` function is used as a default. If `Contact Method` is not one of the available ones (`PHONE` or `EMAIL`), a `KeyError` will be raised and captured, and the result will be defined as `INVALID_METHOD`.

See also

- The *Sending notifications via emails* recipe in *Chapter 9, Dealing with Communication Channels*, to learn how to send emails through Mailgun.

- The *Producing SMS* recipe in *Chapter 9, Dealing with Communication Channels*, to learn how to send text messages using Twilio.

Preparing sales information

In this chapter, we are presenting a marketing campaign divided into several tasks:

- Detect the best moment to launch the campaign

- Generate individual codes to be sent to potential customers

- Send the codes directly to users over their preferred channel, text message or email

- **Collect the results of the campaign**

- Generate a sales report with an analysis of the results

This recipe shows *task 4* of the campaign.

After sending the information to users, we need to collect the sales logs from the shops to monitor how it is going and how big the campaign's impact is.

The sales logs are reported as individual files from each of the associated shops, so in this recipe, we'll see how to aggregate all the info into a spreadsheet to be able to treat the information as a whole.

Getting ready

For this recipe, we need to install the following modules:

```
$ echo "openpyxl==3.0.3" >> requirements.txt

$ echo "parse==1.15.0" >> requirements.txt

$ echo "delorean==1.0.0" >> requirements.txt

$ pip install -r requirements.txt
```

We can obtain a test structure and test logs for this recipe from GitHub at `https://github.com/PacktPublishing/Python-Automation-Cookbook-Second-Edition/tree/master/Chapter10/sales`. Please download the full `sales` directory, which contains a lot of test logs. To display the structure, we'll use the `tree` command (`http://mama.indstate.edu/users/ice/tree/`), which is installed by default in Linux and can be installed using `brew` in macOS (`https://brew.sh/`). You can use a graphical tool to inspect the directory as well.

We'll also need the `sale_log.py` module and the `parse_sales_log.py` script, available on GitHub at `https://github.com/PacktPublishing/Python-Automation-Cookbook-Second-Edition/blob/master/Chapter10/parse_sales_log.py`.

How to do it...

1. Check the structure of the `sales` directory. Each subdirectory represents a shop that has submitted its sales logs for the specified period:

```
$ tree sales
sales
├── 345
│   └── logs.txt
├── 438
│   ├── logs_1.txt
│   ├── logs_2.txt
│   ├── logs_3.txt
│   └── logs_4.txt
└── 656
    └── logs.txt
```

2. Check the log files:

```
$ head sales/438/logs_1.txt
[2018-08-27 21:05:55+00:00] - SALE - PRODUCT: 12346 - PRICE:
$02.99 - NAME: Single item - DISCOUNT: 0%
```

```
[2018-08-27 22:05:55+00:00] - SALE - PRODUCT: 12345 - PRICE:
$07.99 - NAME: Family pack - DISCOUNT: 20%

...
```

3. Call the `parse_sales_log.py` script to generate the repository:

```
$ python parse_sales_log.py sales -o report.xlsx
```

4. Check the generated Excel result, `report.xlsx`:

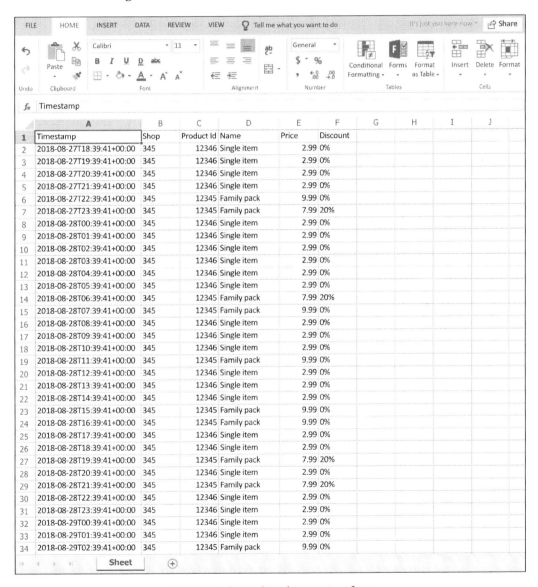

Figure 10.3: Screenshot of `report.xlsx`

How it works...

Steps 1 and *2* show how the data is structured. *Step 3* calls `parse_sales_log.py` to read all the log files and parse them, and then stores them in an Excel spreadsheet. The contents of the spreadsheet are displayed in *step 4*.

Let's see how `parse_sales_log.py` is structured:

```python
# IMPORTS
from sale_log import SaleLog

def get_logs_from_file(shop, log_filename):
    with open(log_filename) as logfile:
        logs = [SaleLog.parse(shop=shop, text_log=log)
                for log in logfile]
    return logs
def main(log_dir, output_filename):
    logs = []
    for dirpath, dirnames, filenames in os.walk(log_dir):
        for filename in filenames:
            # The shop is the last directory
            shop = os.path.basename(dirpath)
            fullpath = os.path.join(dirpath, filename)
            logs.extend(get_logs_from_file(shop, fullpath))

    # Create and save the Excel sheet
    xlsfile = openpyxl.Workbook()
    sheet = xlsfile['Sheet']
    sheet.append(SaleLog.row_header())
    for log in logs:
        sheet.append(log.row())
    xlsfile.save(output_filename)

if __name__ == '__main__':
    # PARSE COMMAND LINE ARGUMENTS AND CALL main()
```

The command-line arguments are explained in *Chapter 1, Let's Begin Our Automation Journey*. Note that the imports include `SaleLog`.

The main function walks through the whole directory and grabs all the files through `os.walk`. You can find out more about `os.walk` in *Chapter 2, Automating Tasks Made Easy*. Each file is then passed to `get_logs_from_file` to parse their logs and add them to the global `logs` list.

Note that the specific shop is stored in the last subdirectory, so it is extracted with `os.path.basename`.

Once the list of logs has been completed, a new Excel sheet is created using the `openpyxl` module. The `SaleLog` module has a `.row_header` method to add the first row, and then all the logs are converted into row format using `.row`. Finally, the file is saved.

To parse the logs, we make a module called `sale_log.py`, which abstracts parsing and dealing with rows. Most of it is straightforward and structures each of the different parameters properly, but the `parse` method requires a bit of attention:

```python
@classmethod
def parse(cls, shop, text_log):
    '''
    Parse from a text log with the format

    ...
    to a SaleLog object
    '''
    def price(string):
        return Decimal(string)

    def isodate(string):
        return delorean.parse(string)

    FORMAT = ('[{timestamp:isodate}] - SALE - PRODUCT: {product:d} '
              '- PRICE: ${price:price} - NAME: {name:D} '
              '- DISCOUNT: {discount:d}%')

    formats = {'price': price, 'isodate': isodate}
    result = parse.parse(FORMAT, text_log, formats)

    return cls(timestamp=result['timestamp'],
               product_id=result['product'],
               price=result['price'],
               name=result['name'],
               discount=result['discount'],
               shop=shop)
```

`sale_log.py` is a `classmethod`, meaning that it can be used by calling `SaleLog.parse`. It returns a new element of the class.

Classmethods are called with a first argument that stores the class, instead of the object normally stored in `self`. The convention is to use `cls` to represent it. Calling `cls(...)` at the end is equivalent to `SaleFormat(...)`, so it calls the `__init__` method.

The method uses the `parse` module to retrieve the values from the template. Note how two elements, `timestamp` and `price`, have custom parsing. The `delorean` module helps us with parsing the date, and the price is better described as a `Decimal` to keep the proper resolution. The custom filters are applied in the `formats` argument.

There's more...

The `Decimal` type is described in detail in the Python documentation here: `https://docs.python.org/3/library/decimal.html`.

The full `openpyxl` can be found here: `https:/openpyxl.readthedocs.io/en/stable/`. Also, check *Chapter 6, Fun with Spreadsheets*, for more examples on how to use the module.

The full `parse` documentation can be found here: `https://github.com/r1chardj0n3s/parse`. *Chapter 1, Let's Begin Our Automation Journey*, also describes this module in greater detail.

See also

- The *Using a third-party tool – parse* recipe in *Chapter 1, Let's Begin Our Automation Journey*, to learn more about the `parse` module.

- The *Crawling and searching directories* recipe in *Chapter 4, Searching and Reading Local Files*, to learn about how to walk and find all the files in a directory.

- The *Reading text files* recipe in *Chapter 4, Searching and Reading Local Files*, to learn how to open text files.

- The *Updating an Excel spreadsheet* recipe in *Chapter 6, Fun with Spreadsheets*, to learn how to write Excel spreadsheets using Python.

Generating a sales report

In this chapter, we are presenting a marketing campaign divided into several tasks:

1. Detect the best moment to launch the campaign
2. Generate individual codes to be sent to potential customers
3. Send the codes directly to users over their preferred channel, text message or email
4. Collect the results of the campaign
5. **Generate a sales report with an analysis of the results**

This recipe shows *task 5* of the campaign.

As the final step, all the information about each of the sales is aggregated and displayed in a sales report.

In this recipe, we'll see how to read from spreadsheets, create PDFs, and produce graphs to generate a comprehensive report automatically in order to analyze the performance of our campaign.

Getting ready

In this recipe, we'll require the following modules in our virtual environment:

```
$ echo "openpyxl==3.0.3" >> requirements.txt
$ echo "fpdf==1.7.2" >> requirements.txt
$ echo "delorean==1.0.0" >> requirements.txt
$ echo "PyPDF2==1.26.0" >> requirements.txt
$ echo "matplotlib==3.2.1" >> requirements.txt
$ pip install -r requirements.txt
```

We'll need the `sale_log.py` module, which is available on GitHub at `https://github.com/PacktPublishing/Python-Automation-Cookbook-Second-Edition/blob/master/Chapter10/sale_log.py`.

 The input spreadsheet was generated in the previous recipe, *Preparing sales information*. Refer to this recipe for more information.

You can download the script to generate the input spreadsheet, `parse_sales_log.py`, from GitHub at `https://github.com/PacktPublishing/Python-Automation-Cookbook-Second-Edition/blob/master/Chapter10/parse_sales_log.py`.

Download the raw log files from GitHub at `https://github.com/PacktPublishing/Python-Automation-Cookbook-Second-Edition/tree/master/Chapter10/sales`. Please download the full `sales` directory.

Download the `generate_sales_report.py` script from GitHub at `https://github.com/PacktPublishing/Python-Automation-Cookbook-Second-Edition/blob/master/Chapter10/generate_sales_report.py`.

How to do it...

1. Call the `parse_sales_log.py` script to generate the input file:

   ```
   $ python parse_sales_log.py sales -o report.xlsx
   ```

2. Check the input file and the use of `generate_sales_report.py`:

   ```
   $ ls report.xlsx
   report.xlsx
   $ python generate_sales_report.py --help
   usage: generate_sales_report.py [-h] input_file output_file


   positional arguments:
     input_file
     output_file


   optional arguments:
     -h, --help show this help message and exit
   ```

3. Call the `generate_sales_report.py` script with the input file and an output file:

   ```
   $ python generate_sales_report.py report.xlsx output.pdf
   ```

4. Check the `output.pdf` output file. It will contain three pages, the first a brief summary and the second and third with graphs showing the sales by day and by shop.

How it works

Step 1 shows how to use the script and *step 2* calls it on the input file. Let's take a look at the basic structure of the generate_sales_report.py script:

```
# IMPORTS
def generate_summary(logs):


def aggregate_by_day(logs):
def aggregate_by_shop(logs):


def graph(...):


def create_summary_brief(...):



def main(input_file, output_file):
    # open and read input file
    # Generate each of the pages calling the other calls
    # Group all the pdfs into a single file
    # Write the resulting PDF


if __name__ == '__main__':
    # Compile the input and output files from the command line
    # call main
```

There are two key elements—the aggregation of the logs in different ways (by shop and by day) and the generation of a summary in each case. The summary is generated with generate_summary, which, from a list of logs, generates a dictionary with its aggregated information. The aggregation of the logs is done in different styles in the aggregate_by functions.

 generate_summary produces a dictionary with the aggregated information, including start and end time, total income of all logs, total units, average discount, and a breakdown of the same data by product.

The script is better understood by starting at the end. The main functions join all the different operations. Read each of the logs and transform them into native SaleLog objects.

Then, it generates each of the pages as intermediate PDF files:

- A brief, generated by `create_summary_brief`, provides a general summary of all the data.
- The logs are `aggregate_by_day`. A summary is created, and a graph is produced.
- The logs are `aggregate_by_shop`. A summary is created, and a graph is produced.

All the intermediate PDF pages are joined, using `PyPDF2`, into a single file. Finally, the intermediate pages are deleted.

Both `aggregate_by_day` and `aggregate_by_shop` return a list with a summary of each of the elements. In `aggregate_by_day`, we detect when a day ends by using `.end_of_day` to differentiate one day from another.

The `graph` function does the following:

1. Prepares all the data that is going to be displayed. That includes the number of units per tag (day or shop) and the total income per tag.
2. Creates a top graph with the total income, split by product into stacked bars. To be able to do this, at the same time the total income is calculated, the baseline (the position where the next stack is located) is calculated.
3. It divides the bottom part of the graph into as many graphs as there are products, and displays the number of units sold on each one, per tag (day or shop).

 For a better display, the graph is defined to be the size of an A4 sheet. It also allows us, using `skip_labels`, to print one of each X label on the second graph on the X axis to avoid overlapping. This is useful when displaying the days, and it's set to show only one label per week.

The resulting graph is saved to a file.

`create_summary_brief` uses the `fpdf` module to save a text PDF page containing the total summary information.

 The template and information in `create_summary_brief` has been left deliberately simple to avoid complicating this recipe, but it can be complicated with better descriptive text and formatting. Refer to *Chapter 5, Generating Fantastic Reports*, for more details on how to use `fpdf`.

As shown previously, the `main` function groups all the PDF pages and joins them into a single document, removing the intermediate pages later:

Report generated at 2018-08-29T23:45:21.661291+00:00

Covering data from 27 Aug to 08 Oct

Summary

TOTAL INCOME: $ 14225.0

TOTAL UNIT: 3000 units

AVERAGE DISCOUNT: 2%

Figure 10.4: Sales summary

The second page shows a graph of sales by day:

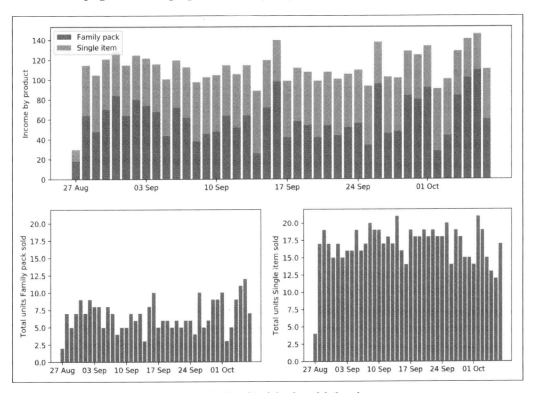

Figure 10.5: Graphical display of daily sales

The third page divides the sales by shop:

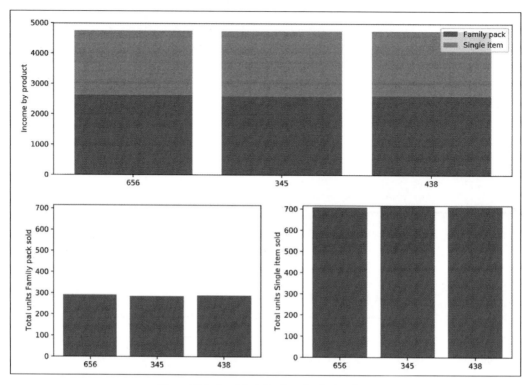

Figure 10.6: Graphical display of sales by shop

There's more...

The reports included in this recipe can be expanded. For example, the average discount could be calculated on each page and displayed as a line:

```
# Generate a data series with the average discount
discount = [summary['average_discount'] for _, summary in full_
summary]
....
# Print the legend
# Plot the discount in a second axis
plt.twinx()
plt.plot(pos, discount,'o-', color='green')
plt.ylabel('Average Discount')
```

Be careful not to put too much information in a single graph, though. It may reduce readability. In this case, another graph is probably a better way of displaying it.

Be careful to print the legend before creating the second axis, or it will display only the information on the second axis.

The size and orientation of the graphs can determine whether to use more labels or fewer so that they are clear and readable. This is demonstrated in the use of `skip_labels` to avoid clutter. Keep an eye on the resulting graphics and try to adapt to possible problems in that area by changing sizes or limiting labels in some cases.

For example, a possible limit is to have no more than three products, as printing four graphs on the second row in our graphs will probably make the text illegible. Feel free to experiment and check the limits of the code.

The complete `matplotlib` documentation can be found at `https://matplotlib.org/`. The `delorean` documentation can be found here: `https://delorean.readthedocs.io/en/latest/`.

All the documentation for `openpyxl` is available at `https://openpyxl.readthedocs.io/en/stable/`. The full documentation for the PDF manipulation modules can be found for PyPDF2 at `https://pythonhosted.org/PyPDF2/` and for `pyfdf` at `https://pyfpdf.readthedocs.io/en/latest/`.

This recipe makes use of different concepts and techniques that are available in *Chapter 5, Generating Fantastic Reports*, for PDF creation and manipulation, *Chapter 6, Fun with Spreadsheets*, for spreadsheet reading, and *Chapter 8, Developing Stunning Graphs*, for graph creation. Check them out to find out more.

See also

- The *Aggregating PDF reports* recipe in *Chapter 5, Generating Fantastic Reports,* to learn how to join multiple PDF files.

- The *Reading an Excel spreadsheet* recipe in *Chapter 6, Fun with Spreadsheets,* to learn how to get information from Excel spreadsheets.

- The *Drawing stacked bars* recipe in *Chapter 8, Developing Stunning Graphs,* to find out more about how to draw stacked bar graphs.

- The *Displaying multiple lines* recipe in *Chapter 8, Developing Stunning Graphs,* to learn how to get a single graph with multiple information lines.

- The *Adding legends and annotations* recipe in *Chapter 8, Developing Stunning Graphs,* for more information about adding legends and extra annotations to graphs.

- The *Combining graphs* recipe in *Chapter 8, Developing Stunning Graphs,* to learn how to combine different graphs into a single image.

- The *Saving charts* recipe in *Chapter 8, Developing Stunning Graphs,* to find out more about how to store graphs in different formats.

11

Machine Learning for Automation

In this chapter, we will cover the following recipes:

- Analyzing images with Google Cloud Vision AI
- Extracting text from images with Google Cloud Vision AI
- Analyzing text with Google Cloud Natural Language
- Creating your own custom machine learning model to classify text

Introduction

Machine learning is a technique that allows systems to be trained to recognize patterns without explicitly describing these patterns. The basis of machine learning is the creation and training of a model, a system that is prepared with training data and then can automatically process new data that is similar to the training data. The model learns from the training data.

For example, a traditional method to detect spam in emails is to check words or sentences that are suspicious. With machine learning techniques, instead, a list of spam and non-spam messages are provided to the model, and the system adjusts itself. It learns from the data. New emails then can be given to the model to detect whether they are spam or not.

This approach can also be used with images, so instead of trying to create a complicated shape detection algorithm to recognize a dog, a significant number of dog images can be used to train the model to detect whether there's a dog or not in an image. The same approach can be used for other areas, such as sound (speech-to-text and text-to-speech) and video.

This kind of training is called "supervised" because the training data needs to be properly labeled beforehand. This is the most mature and useful type of machine learning at the moment. There are other kinds of machine learning that work in an unsupervised way (where training data needs no labels), for example, determining from a group of pictures which ones are related to each other.

Machine learning is becoming increasingly popular. As time passes, machine learning models are becoming more capable and producing better results. This used to be a complicated field to enter, but thanks to new cloud providers, ready-to-use APIs are available to leverage the power of machine learning quickly.

Machine learning can be used in a lot of different fields. In this chapter, we will cover the following examples:

- Detecting the location in a picture
- Finding and extracting text in an image, including handwritten text
- Detecting whether the sentiment of text is positive or negative
- Translating text to other languages
- Determining what department within a store a message is addressed to, based on previous examples

In this chapter, we will use the publicly available Google resources, specifically their out-of-the-box models to detect general characteristics in images and text. Their public trained models are very powerful and allow you to detect a variety of elements. We will also cover how to create and train a custom text model that can apply our own labels to new text.

 There are three levels of machine learning application, based on their complexity. The first one is to apply an already existing ready-to-use trained model. The second is to train an existing model with your own data. The third is to create your own model from scratch. To get to the third level you need significant expertise in machine learning, so it's out of scope for this book, but the first two levels are accessible. Most of this chapter deals with the first level, but the last recipe covers the second using supervised training.

We will start our journey into machine learning by detecting already existing labels in images. To be able to do so, we will need to set up an account in Google Cloud.

Analyzing images with Google Cloud Vision AI

We will acquire basic access to Google Cloud Vision AI to detect what broad categories can be inferred from pictures automatically. These categories are called *labels* by the API. These labels identify objects (such as a box), locations (such as a landscape), animal species (such as a cat), and other things. We will use images already presented in *Chapter 4, Searching and Reading Local Files*.

In this recipe, we will set up a Google Cloud account to use its APIs. This process will work as the basis for other recipes in this chapter.

Getting ready

We first need to set up our account with Google, so go to the Google Cloud site at `https://cloud.google.com/vision`:

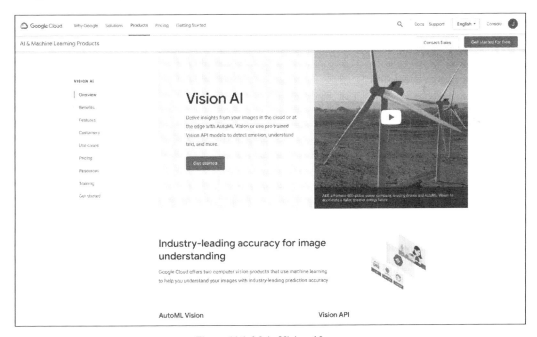

Figure 11.1: Main Vision AI page

From there, you can go to **Get started for free** and set up your account:

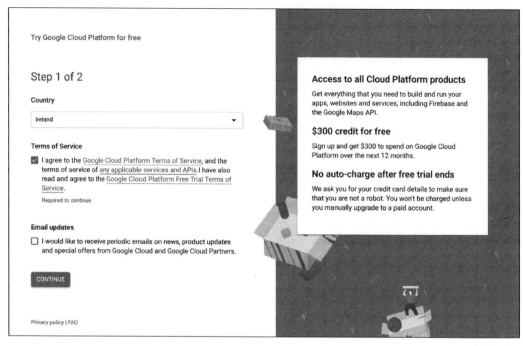

Figure 11.2: Registration page

You'll need to set up your credit card information as part of the setup. You should get some free credit to allow enough time to test, and there won't be charges, though you'll see a *Google Temporary Hold* on your credit card statement:

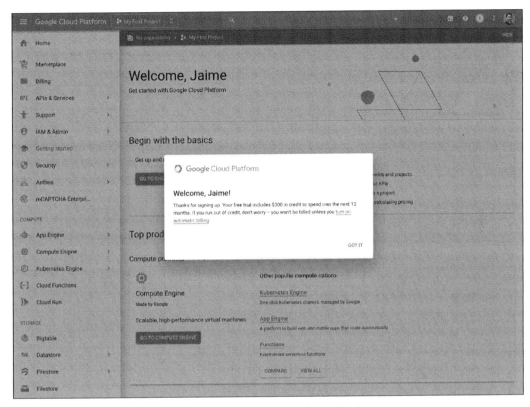

Figure 11.3: Welcome screen after registering

From there, you need to access the **APIs & Services** tab:

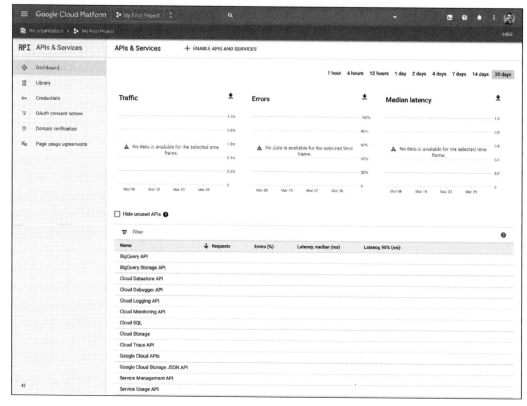

Figure 11.4: APIs & Services page

And enable the **Vision API**. You can search and filter by name, as there are lots of different APIs:

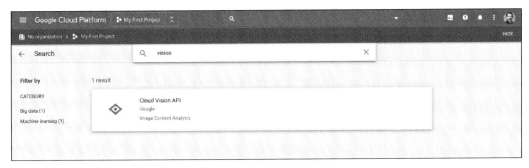

Figure 11.5: Search for Cloud Vision API

From there, enable it from the interface:

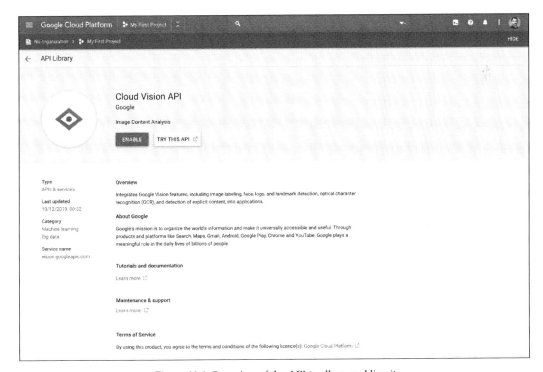

Figure 11.6: Overview of the API to allow enabling it

To access the API you'll need to create a set of credentials to authenticate. Click on **CREATE CREDENTIALS**:

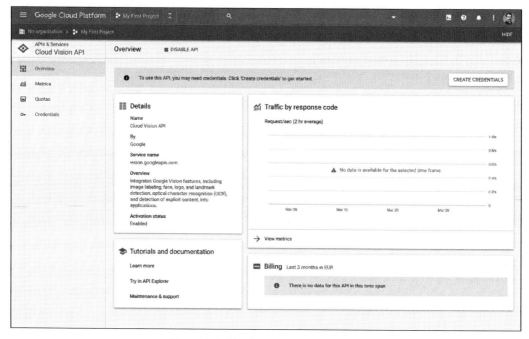

Figure 11.7: Cloud Vision API main page

You need to create a service account to use Vision API with the Python client. A service account is a set of credentials that are intended for use with an automated script or "bot," like the one we need.

Go to **credentials** to create a new one. After clicking on **CREATE CREDENTIALS**, select **Service Accounts**:

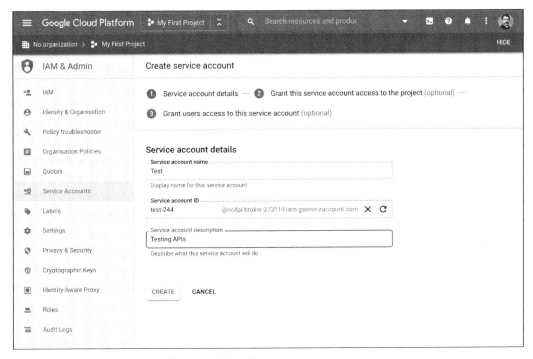

Figure 11.8: Creating a new service account

Add a descriptive name and create the service account. You don't need to fill in the other two optional steps, but they can restrict the users that can use the key or grant permissions.

Finally, create a new JSON key by hitting the **+Create Key** button and selecting it in **JSON** format:

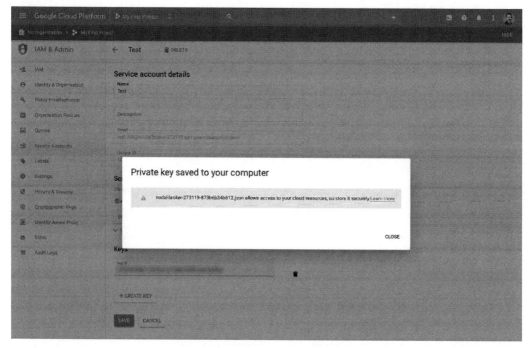

Figure 11.9: Download the JSON private key

This downloaded JSON file will contain the required credentials to access the API. We'll call it `credentials.json` throughout this chapter.

 Service account keys can be deleted. After a key is deleted, it won't work anymore. Ideally, keys should be changed regularly to avoid security problems in case they are leaked.

You also need to enable billing. Go to the **billing** section in the console, `https://console.cloud.google.com/billing`, and make sure that you have your project enabled for billing:

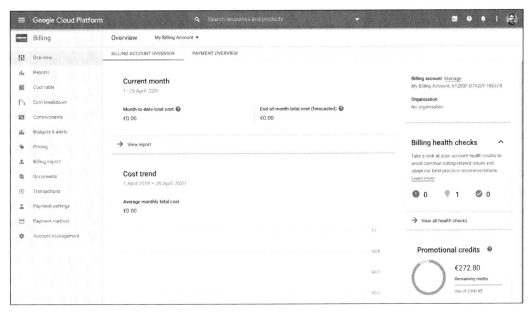

Figure 11.10: Account overview

You are now ready to access the API.

Take your time to explore the billing options in case you make use of the system for more than some tests. There are options that will allow you to limit expenses to avoid surprises.

We need to add the official Google Cloud Vision library. We should install the module, adding it to our `requirements.txt` file as follows:

```
$ echo "google-cloud-vision==1.0.0" >> requirements.txt
$ pip install -r requirements.txt
```

We will use the `image_labels.py` script and the `photo-dublin-b.png` image file, which was also used in the *Reading images* recipe in *Chapter 4, Searching and Reading Local Files*. You can download them from the GitHub repository at `https://github.com/PacktPublishing/Python-Automation-Cookbook-Second-Edition/tree/master/Chapter11`.

The images are in the `images` subdirectory.

How to do it...

1. Take a look at the `images/photo-dublin-a2.png` image:

Figure 11.11: Picture of Dublin waterfront

2. Call the `image_labels.py` script, passing the credentials and the `photo-dublin-a2.png` file:

```
$ GOOGLE_APPLICATION_CREDENTIALS=credentials.json python
image_labels.py images/photo-dublin-a2.png
Labels for the image and score:
Water 0.9388793110847473
Daytime 0.9213085770606995
River 0.9155402183532715
City 0.9150108098983765
```

```
Sky 0.9127334952354431

Waterway 0.9020747542381287

Urban area 0.8954816460609436

Human settlement 0.8528644442558289

Architecture 0.8278814554214478

Metropolitan area 0.8263764381408691
```

Notice how the labels provide a good characterization of the picture, including details such as `River` and `Daytime`.

How it works...

An important detail is the usage of the `credentials.json` credential file. Note how we set it up in the `GOOGLE_APPLICATION_CREDENTIALS` environment variable so the library can read it there. Remember to add the right path to access the file.

> Adding the variable at the start of the line makes it available for the environment on that command. This avoids having to set it up permanently in the shell environment. You can also use the `export` command to define it in an indefinite way:
>
> `export GOOGLE_APPLICATION_CREDENTIALS=credentials.json`
>
> If you're using Windows, you'll need to set up the environment variable using the equivalent command, `set`: `set GOOGLE_APPLICATION_CREDENTIALS=credentials.json`

Let's take a look at the `image_labels.py` script, used in *step 2*:

```python
import argparse
from google.cloud import vision


def landmark(client, image):
  print('Landmark detected')
    response = client.landmark_detection(image=image)
    landmarks = response.landmark_annotations
    for landmark in landmarks:
        print(f' {landmark.description}')
        for location in landmark.locations:
            coord = location.lat_lng
            print(f'  Latitude {coord.latitude}')
```

```python
                print(f'  Longitude {coord.longitude}')

    if response.error.message:
        raise Exception(
            '{}\nFor more info on error messages, check: '
            'https://cloud.google.com/apis/design/errors'.format(
                response.error.message))


def main(image_file):
    content = image_file.read()

    client = vision.ImageAnnotatorClient()

    image = vision.types.Image(content=content)

    response = client.label_detection(image=image)
    labels = response.label_annotations
    print('Labels for the image and score:')

    for label in labels:
        print(label.description, label.score)
        if(label.description == 'Landmark'):
            landmark(client, image)

    if response.error.message:
        raise Exception(
            '{}\nFor more info on error messages, check: '
            'https://cloud.google.com/apis/design/errors'.format(
                response.error.message))


if __name__ == '__main__':
    parser = argparse.ArgumentParser()
    parser.add_argument(dest='input', type=argparse.FileType('rb'),
                        help='input image')
    args = parser.parse_args()
    main(args.input)
```

The script uses `argparse` to open and pass the file as described in the call. Then, it calls `main`, which uses the Google Cloud Vision API to retrieve the labels for the image. The core of the process is this:

```
content = image_file.read()

client = vision.ImageAnnotatorClient()
image = vision.types.Image(content=content)

response = client.label_detection(image=image)
labels = response.label_annotations
print('Labels for the image and score:')

for label in labels:
    print(label.description, label.score)
```

It first extracts the content from the file. Note this is binary content as extracted by the configuration of `argparse` with `rb`.

The content is then sent to `ImageAnnotatorClient` to perform `label_detection`. The image first needs to be properly converted into `vision.types.Image`.

The response label description and score are then printed. Note how they are sorted by score. A high score means that the API considers the label a good match.

There's more...

Other than the `score` of a particular label, the interface will return the `topicality` of it. While the `score` reflects the confidence that the label is applicable to the image, the `topicality` reflects how representative the label is for the image as a whole. Typically, they are the same or very similar, but an image with a landscape can show a small house far away that has a high `score` but low `topicality` compared with the `landscape` label.

The `label_detection` interface is the most general, and will return general information about the image, but there are other interfaces available that are more specific. We added landmark detection in the `landmark` function, which is called if the `landmark` label is returned:

```
def landmark(client, image):
    print('Landmark detected')
    response = client.landmark_detection(image=image)
    landmarks = response.landmark_annotations
```

```
    for landmark in landmarks:
        print(f'  {landmark.description}')
        for location in landmark.locations:
            coord = location.lat_lng
            print(f'  Latitude {coord.latitude}')
            print(f'  Longitude {coord.longitude}')


    if response.error.message:
        raise Exception(
            '{}\nFor more info on error messages, check: '
            'https://cloud.google.com/apis/design/errors'.format(
                response.error.message))
```

If you call the script with the `photo-dublin-b.png` image, which is a picture of the General Post Office building in the center of Dublin, you'll be able to trigger it:

```
$ GOOGLE_APPLICATION_CREDENTIALS=credentials.json python3 image_labels.py
photo-dublin-b.png
Labels for the image and score:
Architecture 0.9421795010566711
Landmark 0.928507924079895
Landmark detected
  General Post Office
  Latitude 53.349369
  Longitude -6.260251
Building 0.8951834440231323
Sky 0.8857545852661133
Classical architecture 0.8762346506118774
Daytime 0.8634399771690369
Town 0.8440616726875305
City 0.82234787940979
Facade 0.8102320432662964
Street 0.75846105813980l
```

The images can be sent for analysis in binary format, like here, or also as a URL, if they are available on the web:

```
    image = vision.types.Image()
    image.source.image_uri = uri
```

This can be combined with the ideas in *Chapter 3, Building Your First Web Scraping Application*, to automatically detect some kinds of images on a web page. For example, you could detect the headshots on a corporate website, as shown by the label `Face`, or detect the pictures of red cars in a catalog of vehicles.

 There's a specific API to detect faces with `face_client.detection(image=image)`, which includes details such as the likelihood of different emotions, such as joy or sadness. It can be called in a similar fashion as `landmark_detection`.

Other available features can detect an image's dominant colors, logos in an image, explicit (adult) content, or even if an image is present somewhere on the web. Be sure to check the documentation to learn all the options.

 Be sure to check the documentation of the available types to get the returned attributes from the API. This is available at `https://googleapis.dev/python/vision/latest/gapic/v1/types.html`.

You can access the full Vision API documentation at `https://cloud.google.com/vision/docs/`. The Python client documentation is here: `https://googleapis.dev/python/vision/latest/index.html`.

See also

- The *Extracting text from images with Google Cloud Vision AI* recipe, later in this chapter, to learn about another image analyzing technique.

- The *Analyzing text with Google Cloud Natural Language* recipe, later in this chapter, to apply a similar approach to text.

- The *Creating your own custom machine learning model to classify text* recipe, later in this chapter, to learn how to train your own model. This technique is also applicable to images.

Extracting text from images with Google Cloud Vision AI

We can use the power of the Google Cloud interface to detect and extract text in images. This process is called Optical Character Recognition, or OCR.

Getting ready

We need to enable the Google Cloud Vision API and create credentials to work with it, as described in the previous recipe, *Analyzing Images with Google Cloud Vision AI*. We need to use the generated service account key in JSON format. We will call it `credentials.json` throughout the chapter.

We need to add the official Google Cloud Vision library. We should install the module, adding it to our `requirements.txt` file as follows:

```
$ echo " google-cloud-vision==1.0.0" >> requirements.txt
$ pip install -r requirements.txt
```

We will use the `image_text.py` script and the `photo-text.jpg` and `dublin-a-text.jpg` files that were also used in *Chapter 4, Searching and Reading Local Files*. You can download them from the GitHub repository at https://github.com/PacktPublishing/Python-Automation-Cookbook-Second-Edition/tree/master/Chapter11.

The images are in the `images` subdirectory.

How to do it...

1. Take a look at the `images/photo-text.jpg` image:

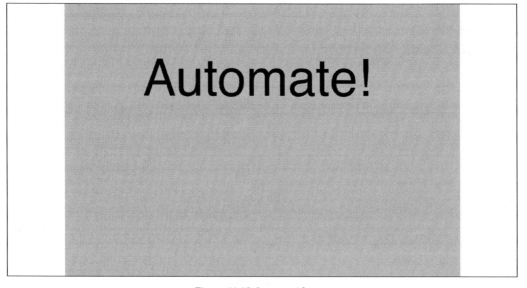

Figure 11.12: Image with text

2. Execute the `image_text.py` script passing the credentials and the `images/hoto-text.jpg` file:

```
$ GOOGLE_APPLICATION_CREDENTIALS=credentials.json   python3
image_text.py images/photo-text.jpg
Automate !
```

3. Check the `images/photo-dublin-a-text.jpg` file, which has the same text over a landscape:

Figure 11.13: Landscape with the same text as the previous picture

4. Call the `image_text.py` script passing the credentials and the `images/photo-dublin-a-text.jpg` file:

```
$ GOOGLE_APPLICATION_CREDENTIALS=credentials.json   python3
image_text.py images/photo-dublin-a-text.jpg
Automate !
```

See how it detects the text even if it's over an image.

How it works...

Let's take a look at the `image_text.py` script, used in *steps* 2 and 4:

```python
import argparse
from google.cloud import vision


def main(image_file, verbose):
    content = image_file.read()

    client = vision.ImageAnnotatorClient()
    image = vision.types.Image(content=content)
    response = client.document_text_detection(image=image)

    for page in response.full_text_annotation.pages:

        for block in page.blocks:

            if verbose:
                print('\nBlock confidence: {}\n'.format(block.
confidence))

            if block.confidence < 0.8:
                if verbose:
                    print('Skipping block due to low confidence')
                continue

            for paragraph in block.paragraphs:
                paragraph_text = []
                for word in paragraph.words:
                    word_text = ''.join([
                        symbol.text for symbol in word.symbols
                    ])
                    paragraph_text.append(word_text)
                    if verbose:
                        print(f'Word text: {word_text} '
                            f'(confidence: {word.confidence})')
                        for symbol in word.symbols:
                            print(f'\tSymbol: {symbol.text} '
                                f'(confidence: {symbol.
```

```
confidence})')

                    print(' '.join(paragraph_text))

    if response.error.message:
        raise Exception(
            '{}\nFor more info on error messages, check: '
            'https://cloud.google.com/apis/design/errors'.format(
                response.error.message))


if __name__ == '__main__':
    parser = argparse.ArgumentParser()
    parser.add_argument(dest='input', type=argparse.FileType('rb'),
                        help='input image')
    parser.add_argument('-v', dest='verbose', help='Print more
data',
                        action='store_true')
    args = parser.parse_args()
    main(args.input, args.verbose)
```

The final block configures the command-line parameters, using the `argparse` library. It configures the input file and the `verbose` parameter. We will talk about the `verbose` parameter in the *There's more* section.

The core of the code in the `main` function is as follows:

```
def main(image_file, verbose):
    content = image_file.read()

    client = vision.ImageAnnotatorClient()
    image = vision.types.Image(content=content)
    response = client.document_text_detection(image=image)

    for page in response.full_text_annotation.pages:
        ...
        for paragraph in block.paragraphs:
            paragraph_text = []
            for word in paragraph.words:
                word_text = ''.join([symbol.text for symbol in word.
symbols])

                paragraph_text.append(word_text)
```

```
print(' '.join(paragraph_text))
```

The content of the image is read and sent to the Vision API through the `document_text_detection` interface. This returns a response that's structured in blocks, then in paragraphs, words, and finally symbols.

Blocks with a low confidence are skipped. This prevents elements being printed that the API is not sure are correct.

> The confidence level has been set arbitrarily to 0.8. You can play with the value until finding one that works for you. If you're happy with any confidence level, you can directly call the text with `response.full_text_annotation.text`, though this may return spurious results if there are elements in the image that could add noise to the text, like in the `photo-dublin-a-text.jpg` image.

The symbols get aggregated as words, and then into paragraphs. Each paragraph is printed independently.

There's more...

The `verbose` flag displays more information about the margin of confidence for each symbol. For example, calling:

```
$ GOOGLE_APPLICATION_CREDENTIALS=credentials.json  python3 image_text.py
images/photo-dublin-a-text.jpg -v


Block confidence: 0.9900000095367432


Word text: Automate (confidence: 0.9900000095367432)
        Symbol: A (confidence: 0.9900000095367432)
        Symbol: u (confidence: 0.9900000095367432)
        Symbol: t (confidence: 1.0)
        Symbol: o (confidence: 1.0)
        Symbol: m (confidence: 1.0)
        Symbol: a (confidence: 1.0)
        Symbol: t (confidence: 1.0)
        Symbol: e (confidence: 0.9900000095367432)
```

```
Word text: ! (confidence: 0.949999988079071)
     Symbol: ! (confidence: 0.949999988079071)
Automate !


Block confidence: 0.3100000023841858


Skipping block for low confidence
```

This gives detailed information for each of the individual detected symbols. Notice the skipped block due to low confidence.

This interface is even capable of recognizing handwritten and non-vertical text. For example, the `images/handwrite.jpg` file, available at `https://github.com/PacktPublishing/Python-Automation-Cookbook-Second-Edition/tree/master/Chapter11` shows the following text:

Figure 11.14: Handwriting example

Running it through the script, it detects the text correctly in three blocks:

```
$ GOOGLE_APPLICATION_CREDENTIALS=credentials.json  python3 image_text.py
images/handwrite.jpg
PYTHON
AUTOMATED
COOKBOOK
```

Instead of `document_text_detection`, the `text_detection` interface can be used. This returns the text without dividing it into blocks. In this case, the position of the text is returned described as a polygon with the boundaries of the text:

```
response = client.text_detection(image=image)
for text in response.text_annotations:
    # Text
    print('"{}"'.format(text.description))
    # Bounding box
    points = ['({},{})'.format(p.x, p.y)
              for p in text.bounding_poly.vertices]
    print('box: {}'.format(','.join(points)))
```

The position information can be used to give context, such as filtering only the text in the top-right corner or similar.

 A script showing this capability called `image_text_box.py` is available on GitHub at `https://github.com/PacktPublishing/Python-Automation-Cookbook-Second-Edition/tree/master/Chapter11`. Call it with the `-v` parameter to display the position of each piece of detected text.

The position information can be used to give context, such as filtering only the text in the top-right corner or similar.

In *Chapter 4, Searching and Reading Local Files*, we introduced the `pytesseract` module as another way of extracting text from images and applying OCR. Both methods have their advantages and disadvantages. Calling the Google Cloud Vision API is likely to return a better result in worse conditions (noise, background images, handwriting), but at the same time, the access to an external API is slower and less safe. There's also a cost associated with using the Vision API, especially if it's used for bulk text extraction, while `pytesseract` is open source and free to use. The method you choose depends on the data and security requirements.

You can access the full Vision API documentation at `https://cloud.google.com/vision/docs/`. The Python client documentation is at `https://googleapis.dev/python/vision/latest/index.html`.

See also

- The *Analyzing images with Google Cloud Vision AI* recipe, earlier in this chapter, to learn how to create an account for Google Cloud interfaces.

Analyzing text with Google Cloud Natural Language

In this recipe, we will use the Google Cloud interface to evaluate text. This is similar to the earlier *Analyzing images with Google Cloud Vision AI* recipe but applied to text instead. We will be able to detect the language of a piece of text, as well as its general sentiment (how positive or negative it is). We will also translate all non-English text into English.

Getting ready

We need to enable the Google Cloud Natural Language API and create credentials to work with it. Most of the process is similar to the process described earlier in the chapter to enable the Vision API in a Google Cloud project, so we'll use the same project described in the earlier *Analyzing images with Google Cloud Vision AI* recipe.

Log into your account to go to the API dashboard at `https://console.cloud.google.com/apis`. Make sure you're using the same project as before, or the `credentials.json` file won't work:

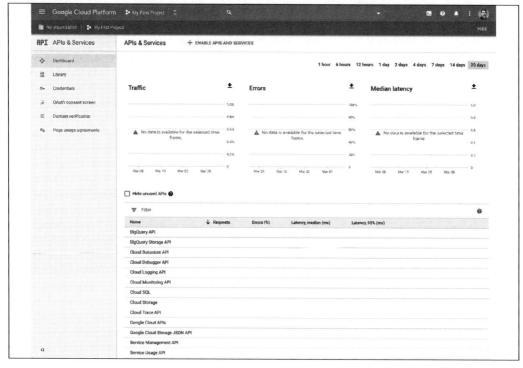

Figure 11.15: API dashboard

Click on **ENABLE APIS AND SERVICES** and search for **Natural Language** to enable it:

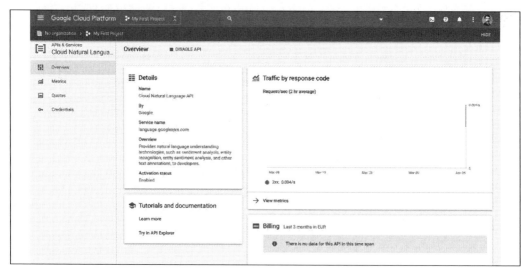

Figure 11.16: Natural Language API dashboard

Search and enable the **Cloud Translation API** as well:

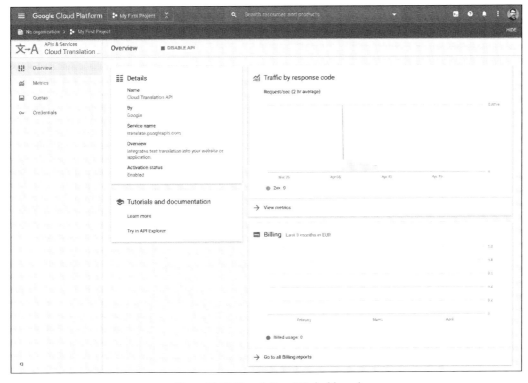

Figure 11.17: Translation API dashboard

We need to use the generated service account key in JSON format. We will call it `credentials.json` throughout the chapter.

We will use the `google-cloud-language` module. We should install the module, adding it to our `requirements.txt` file as follows:

```
$ echo "google-cloud-language==1.3.0" >> requirements.txt
$ echo "google-cloud-translate==2.0.1" >> requirements.txt
$ pip install -r requirements.txt
```

The code can be found in the GitHub repository, `https://github.com/PacktPublishing/Python-Automation-Cookbook-Second-Edition/tree/master/Chapter11`. There are some text examples in the `/texts/` subdirectory, mostly containing text from the beginning of classic novels from the 19th century in different languages.

How to do it...

1. Call the `text_analysis.py` script with the start of the novel *Pride and Prejudice* and pass the credentials:

```
$ GOOGLE_APPLICATION_CREDENTIALS=credentials.json python text_
analysis.py texts/pride_and_prejudice.txt
```

Text: It is a truth universally acknowledged, that a single man in possession of a good fortune, must be in want of a wife. However little known the feelings or views of such a man may be on his first entering a neighbourhood, this truth is so well fixed in the minds of the surrounding families, that he is considered the rightful property of some one or other of their daughters.

Language: en

Sentiment Score (how positive the sentiment is): 0.699999988079071

Sentiment Magnitude (how strong it is): 1.5

2. Call the `text_analysis.py` script with the start of the novel *La Regenta*, in Spanish, and pass the credentials:

```
$ GOOGLE_APPLICATION_CREDENTIALS=credentials.json  python text_
analysis.py texts/regenta.txt
```

Text: La heroica ciudad dormía la siesta. El viento Sur, caliente y perezoso, empujaba las nubes blanquecinas que se rasgaban al correr hacia el Norte. En las calles no había más ruido que el rumor estridente de los remolinos de polvo, trapos, pajas y papeles que iban de arroyo en arroyo, de acera en acera, de esquina en esquina revolando y persiguiéndose, como mariposas que se buscan y huyen y que el aire envuelve en sus pliegues invisibles. Cual turbas de pilluelos, aquellas migajas de la basura, aquellas sobras de todo se juntaban en un montón, parábanse como dormidas un momento y brincaban de nuevo sobresaltadas, dispersándose, trepando unas por las paredes hasta los cristales temblorosos de los faroles, otras hasta los carteles de papel mal pegado a las esquinas, y había pluma que llegaba a un tercer piso, y arenilla que se incrustaba para días, o para años, en la vidriera de un escaparate, agarrada a un plomo.

Language: es

Sentiment Score (how positive the sentiment is): 0.0

Sentiment Magnitude (how strong it is): 0.8999999761581421

IN ENGLISH

The heroic city napped. The south wind, hot and lazy, pushed the whitish clouds that ripped as they ran north. In the streets there was no more noise than the shrill noise of the swirls of dust, rags, straws and papers that went from stream to stream, from sidewalk to sidewalk, from corner to corner revoking and chasing each other, like butterflies that seek and flee and that the air envelops in its invisible folds. Like mobs of urchins, those crumbs from the garbage, those leftovers from everything gathered in a heap, they stood as if for a moment asleep and they jumped again with a start, dispersing, some climbing the walls to the trembling glass of the lanterns, others to the paper posters badly glued to the corners, and there was a pen that reached a third floor, and sand that was embedded for days, or for years, in the window of a shop window, clinging to a lead.

How it works...

Let's take a look at the `text_analysis.py` script, used in *steps 1* and *2*:

```python
import argparse
from google.cloud import language
from google.cloud import translate_v2 as translate
from google.cloud.language import enums
from google.cloud.language import types


def main(image_file):
    content = image_file.read()
    print(f'Text: {content}')
    document = types.Document(content=content,
                             type=enums.Document.Type.PLAIN_TEXT)

    client = language.LanguageServiceClient()

    response = client.analyze_sentiment(document=document)
    lang = response.language
    print(f'Language: {lang}')
    sentiment = response.document_sentiment
    score = sentiment.score
    magnitude = sentiment.magnitude
    print(f'Sentiment Score (how positive the sentiment is): {score}')
    print(f'Sentiment Magnitude (how strong it is): {magnitude}')
    if lang != 'en':
        # Translate into English
        translate_client = translate.Client()
```

```
        response = translate_client.translate(content,
    target_language='en')
        print('IN ENGLISH')
        print(response['translatedText'])



if __name__ == '__main__':
    parser = argparse.ArgumentParser()
    parser.add_argument(dest='input', type=argparse.FileType('r'),
                        help='input text')
    args = parser.parse_args()
    main(args.input)
```

The final block configures the command-line parameters using the `argparse` library. It configures the input file and opens it in text format. The `main` function performs the actions.

The first stage is to extract the text from the file. The text gets encapsulated into a `types.Document` type, defining it as plain text.

The client is created with `LanguageServiceClient` and the `analyze_sentiment` method gets called to get the results from Google servers.

This call returns both the automatically detected language, stored in `lang`, and the sentiment of the text, stored in `score` and `magnitude`.

> The sentiment is composed of both `score` and `magnitude`. `score` describes how positive the aggregated sentiment is in a text. A score of `-1.0` describes an extremely negative emotion, and `1.0` describes an extremely positive emotion. The magnitude is how clear this sentiment is in the text, with a positive number. Short sentences will be difficult to qualify correctly by the API.

If the language is different from English, then it's translated by creating a new `Client` and calling `translate`:

```
    translate_client = translate.Client()
    response = translate_client.translate(content,
                                          target_language='en')
    print('IN ENGLISH')
    print(response['translatedText'])
```

The resulting translated text gets printed.

Google Translate sometimes gets a bit of bad press in terms of getting strange translations sometimes, but it's still capable of getting pretty good results most of the time, with an impressive amount of languages covered.

An automated translation can work as an initial stage to determine what parts require a better human translation, such as idioms.

There's more...

The quality of language processing is very different for different languages. Some languages won't have the same level of support as English. Check the documentation for more details.

The Google text APIs also have other capabilities. For example, they can classify text based on predefined categories. The text_analysis_categories.py script does that, and it's available on GitHub at https://github.com/PacktPublishing/ Python-Automation-Cookbook-Second-Edition/tree/master/Chapter11. Executing it classifies the text, for example, calling it over the texts/category_ example.txt text:

```
$ GOOGLE_APPLICATION_CREDENTIALS=credentials.json  python
text_analysis_categories.py texts/category_example.txt

Text: This text talks about literature and different authors from the
XIX century. It discusses the different styles from different authors in
different languages, analysing and comparing them with their historical
context.


Categories

Category: /Books & Literature

Confidence: 0.9300000071525574
```

Let's take a look at the text_analysis_categories.py script, which is very similar to text_analysis.py:

```
import argparse
from google.cloud import language
from google.cloud.language import enums
from google.cloud.language import types


def main(image_file):
```

```
        content = image_file.read()
        print(f'Text: {content}')
        document = types.Document(content=content,
                                  type=enums.Document.Type.PLAIN_TEXT)

        client = language.LanguageServiceClient()

        print('Categories')
        response = client.classify_text(document=document)
        if not response.categories:
            print('No categories detected')

        for category in response.categories:
            print(f'Category: {category.name}')
            print(f'Confidence: {category.confidence}')


if __name__ == '__main__':
    parser = argparse.ArgumentParser()
    parser.add_argument(dest='input', type=argparse.FileType('r'),
                        help='input text')
    args = parser.parse_args()
    main(args.input)
```

To obtain the categories, it calls `classify_text`, which returns the categories along with the confidence for each detected one. The full list of categories can be obtained in the Google documentation, at `https://cloud.google.com/natural-language/docs/categories`.

 As with the sentiment, check in the documentation if the API is compatible with the specific language, since the API may not be capable of categorization certain languages. You can try to translate first into English and then perform the categorization, but the quality of the result may vary.

In all these cases, the document can also accept HTML text using the `enums.Document.Type.PLAIN_TEXT` type. That can help if you want to combine this recipe with others in this book, such as crawling the web and translating interesting articles to your native language, or categorizing blog posts from an RSS feed to filter only the relevant ones.

Go to `https://cloud.google.com/natural-language/` to see the full Natural Language API documentation. The documentation for the Python clients is available at `https://googleapis.dev/python/translation/latest/index.html` and `https://googleapis.dev/python/language/latest/index.html`.

See also

- The *Analyzing images with Google Cloud Vision AI* recipe, earlier in this chapter, to learn how to create an account to use the Google Cloud interfaces.
- The *Creating your own custom machine learning model to classify text* recipe, later this chapter, to learn how to train a model to recognize custom elements.

Creating your own custom machine learning model to classify text

Using the default interface to classify text based on sentiment or general categories is very powerful but doesn't allow us to classify different texts based on our own rules. Being able to create our own model is where the full power of machine learning lies.

Fortunately, Google offers the power to create and train our own models based on our own set of training data. This allows us to generate a collection of texts and classify them using our own labels. With this data, we will prepare our own model that can be matched against new texts.

We will see in this recipe an example of classifying emails sent to a shop that has two sections, "appliances" and "furniture." We will create a third category of "others" that should capture emails that don't fit neatly into either category.

The process is highly dependent on the quality of the data that is provided to the model. The examples presented in this recipe are simple to keep it small, but they show the potential of this technique.

Let's see how we can create and operate our own machine learning model.

Getting ready

We need to enable the Google Cloud Natural Language API and create credentials to work with it. Most of the process is similar to the process described earlier in the chapter to enable the Vision API in a Google Cloud project, so we can start with the project used in the earlier *Analyzing images with Google Cloud Vision AI* recipe.

Log into your account to go to the API dashboard at `https://console.cloud.google.com/apis`. Be sure to use the same project as before, or the `credentials.json` file won't work.

We have some text prepared for training the model. It is available on GitHub: `https://github.com/PacktPublishing/Python-Automation-Cookbook-Second-Edition/tree/master/Chapter11`.

In the `shop_training` subdirectory, there are three subdirectories (`appliances`, `furniture`, and `others`), each containing ten text files with email content. Each of the subdirectories corresponds to a label, so all the emails in each subdirectory should be qualified on that label.

The data is zipped in a file called `shop.zip`. This contains the same information, but Google requires it to be uploaded in zip format.

 Each email text is simulating a request to the shop for either two departments or other stuff. You can take a look at them.

We need to create a new model. Go to `https://console.cloud.google.com/natural-language` and select **AutoML text and document classification**:

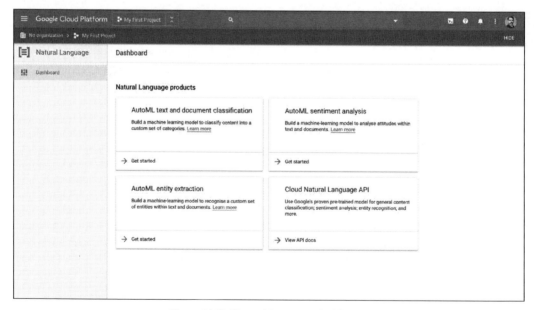

Figure 11.18: Natural Language dashboard

Now we need to add a new data set with our example:

Figure 11.19: Data set list

Select that our data set is for **Single-label classification** (each text will have a single label):

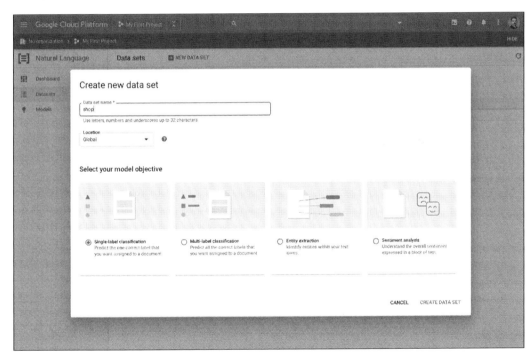

Figure 11.20: Creating a new data set

To upload the files, select a ZIP file. You'll need to create a new bucket to store the data. Keep in mind that the bucket name needs to be globally unique, so you'll need to specify your own.

Follow the instructions to create one. Add the ZIP file:

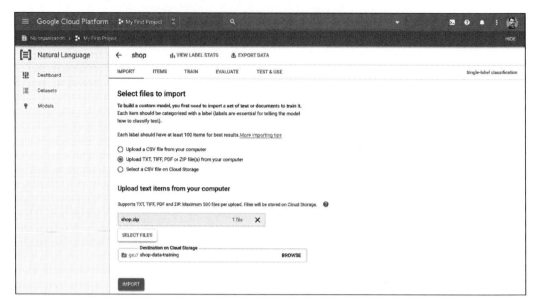

Figure 11.21: Import the training set

Importing the data will take a few minutes. Once it is imported, you'll see all the data available as different items:

Figure 11.22: The imported data

With this data, we can now train the model. Click on the **TRAIN** tab and then **START TRAINING**, which can take *several hours*, so be patient. You'll get an email when it's done:

11.23: Start the training

As you can see, to properly label data, each label should have 100 examples or more. Our data is not that ambitious. The more examples, the better the model will work, though it will take longer to train. Keep in mind that training the model requires computing power that will be charged to your account. With the free account, the credit should be enough to make some tests, but keep in mind potential charges when using the platform.

After the training is done, you can see the evaluation of the model. The system will leave some elements of your training data as tests to evaluate how good your model is:

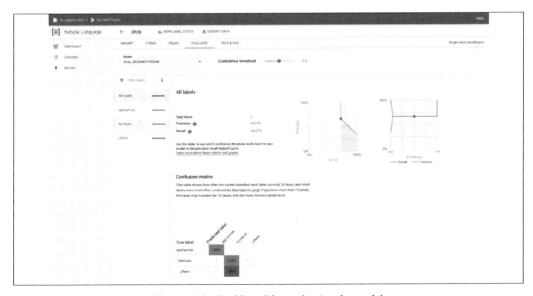

Figure 11.24: Dashboard for evaluating the model

The two most important parameters here are `precision` and `recall`.

> `precision` is the ability of the model to predict the correct label, while `recall` is the ability to not assign an incorrect label. A model with low precision will have more false positives – results with labels attached that are not correct. For example, it will detect a smile when there isn't one. A model with low recall will produce false negatives – results that should have a label attached will not have one. For example, it won't detect a smile when there is one.

The confusion matrix displays the detection patterns based on the training data. A perfect matrix will show a 100% diagonal, which will mean that the data is properly categorized and there are no mistaken elements. You can see that's not the case here.

> Our precision and recall parameters of 66.67% are not fantastic. This is in part due to the small number of samples generated. In real life, aim to have around 90% or higher.

The next tab, **TEST & USE**, has all the information that we require to use it, but to be able to call the API, we need to add the proper permissions to our service account.

> Copy the model reference at the end of the **TEST & USE** tab for Python. This will look similar to `projects/<PROJECT ID>/ locations/us-central1/models/<ID>`. We will use it later as `REFERENCE`.

Remember that the service account is linked to the credentials. To add them, go to `https://console.cloud.google.com/iam-admin/`:

Figure 11.25: Dashboard with the defined users

We need to add the service account as a user and grant it the **AutoML Editor** role. Go to the **Service accounts** page to get the name of our created service account:

 Check out the first recipe in this chapter, *Analyzing images with Google Cloud Vision AI*, to see the process of creating the service account.

Figure 11.26: Service account list

Copy the name of the service account and go back to the **IAM** tab to create a new user with that name. Use the **ADD** button at the top. Put the service account name and add the extra role of **AutoML Editor**:

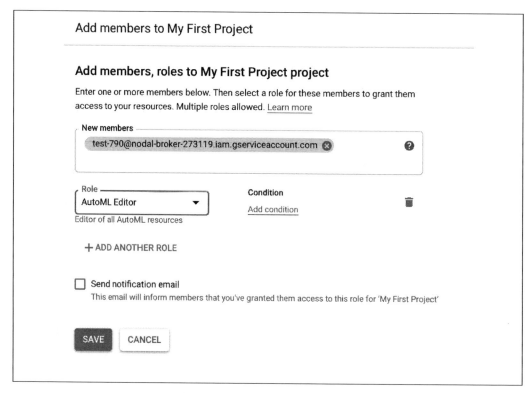

Figure 11.27: Add a role to the member

Once saved, the model is ready to use authentication with the `credentials.json` file. Remember to annotate the REFERENCE for the model, as it will be used later.

We will use the `google-cloud-automl` module. We should install the module, adding it to our `requirements.txt` file as follows:

```
$ echo " google-cloud-automl==0.10.0" >> requirements.txt
$ pip install -r requirements.txt
```

The code can be found in the GitHub repository: `https://github.com/PacktPublishing/Python-Automation-Cookbook-Second-Edition/tree/master/Chapter11`. There are some text examples with the name `example_shopX.txt`. The script we will use is `text_predict.py`. Remember the training data is in the `shop_training` subdirectory and compressed as `shop.zip`.

`precision` and `recall` oppose each other and can be tweaked to a certain extent.

How to do it...

1. Check the message from `example_shop1.txt` and categorize it using `text_predict.py`, `credentials.json`, and REFERENCE for the model:

   ```
   $ cat example_shop1.txt
   ```

   Hello:

      Are there any offers in fridges? I'm searching to replace mine. I live in a fifth floor and the lift is broken, would that be a problem? I'll be fine with paying an extra.

      Thanks a lot,

        Carrie

   ```
   $ GOOGLE_APPLICATION_CREDENTIALS=credentials.json python text_predict.py -m projects/<project_id>/locations/us-central1/models/<id> example_shop1.txt
   ```

   ```
   Label: appliances : 0.99986
   ```

   ```
   Label: furniture : 0.00014
   ```

   ```
   Label: others : 0.00000
   ```

   Check the result is correctly labelled as `appliances`.

2. Look at the message from `example_shop2.txt` and categorize it using `text_predict.py`, `credentials.json`, and REFERENCE for the model:

   ```
   $ cat example_shop2.txt
   ```

   Hello:

      Are there any offers in fridges? I'm looking to replace mine that is old. I live in a fifth floor and the lift is broken, would that be a problem? I'll be fine with paying an extra.

      I think you also have a furniture department, right? What are the prices for mattresses?

      Thanks a lot,

        Carrie

   ```
   $ GOOGLE_APPLICATION_CREDENTIALS=credentials.json python text_predict.py -m projects/<project_id>/locations/us-central1/models/<id> example_shop2.txt
   ```

   ```
   Label: furniture : 0.99995
   ```

   ```
   Label: appliances : 0.00005
   ```

   ```
   Label: others : 0.00000
   ```

Check the result is correctly labeled as `furniture`.

3. Look at the message from `example_shop3.txt` and categorize it using `text_predict.py`, `credentials.json`, and REFERENCE for the model:

```
$ cat example_shop3.txt
Hello:


    I need your full details including your address and phone for an
    invoice. Can you please send them to me?


    Thanks a lot,
        Carrie
$ GOOGLE_APPLICATION_CREDENTIALS=credentials.json python text_
predict.py -m projects/<project_id>/locations/us-central1/
models/<id> example_shop3.txt
Label: others : 1.00000
Label: furniture : 0.00000
Label: appliances : 0.00000
```

Check the result is correctly labelled as `others`.

How it works...

Let's take a look at the `text_predict.py` script, used in all steps:

```python
import argparse

from google.api_core.client_options import ClientOptions
from google.cloud import automl_v1

def main(content, model_name):
    content = args.input.read()
    options = ClientOptions(api_endpoint='automl.googleapis.com')
    prediction_client = automl_v1.PredictionServiceClient(
        client_options=options
    )
    payload = {'text_snippet': {
'content': content,
'mime_type': 'text/plain'}
    }
    params = {}
```

```
request = prediction_client.predict(model_name, payload, params)
for result in request.payload:
    label = result.display_name
    match = result.classification.score
    print(f'Label: {label} : {match:.5f}')


if __name__ == '__main__':
    parser = argparse.ArgumentParser()
    parser.add_argument(dest='input', type=argparse.FileType('r'),
                        help='input text')
    parser.add_argument('-m', dest='model', type=str, help='model
ref')
    args = parser.parse_args()

    main(content, args.model)
```

The final part of the script file deals with the parsing of arguments, which was described in detail in *Chapter 2, Automating Tasks Made Easy*. It accepts a file and the details for the model.

The main function reads the input text and calls the Google API for AutoML. The data needs to be sent in a standard structure including the `mime_type`. The result of `prediction_client.predict` is printed. Note it's sorted so the most relevant label is located at the start:

```
for result in request.payload:
    label = result.display_name
    match = result.classification.score
    print(f'Label: {label} : {match:.5f}')
```

The score match is displayed up to 5 decimal places with `{match:.5f}`.

You can create your own messages and test to see if they are properly labeled.

There's more...

The classification of text into different categories can help to direct emails towards the correct department, to assign them with different priorities, to generate statistics against a database of messages, or to divide them into different groups.

In our example, we used a simple single-label detection model, but the API allows more complex processes, such as recognizing multiple labels instead of a single one per text or recognizing custom sentiments or entities. Be sure to check out the full documentation at `https://cloud.google.com/natural-language/automl/docs`.

> Try to use the simplest model possible. As with every tool, there's a return on investment in terms of configuration and tweaking. In our example, the simple division of an email by department could be better than trying to set up multiple labels. Use a sensible approach, and start small before generating complex models. A complex model will also take longer to tweak.

The most important step of the process is selecting an adequate set of data to train the model. It's recommended that a minimum of 100 samples should be used for each label. The selection of the set is also important as it has to be representative of the things you want to detect; both to check things that should be labeled, and things that should not.

> A machine learning model is so dependent on the training set, so it is easy to fall into the trap of reinforcing biases in the training set. Machine learning is, at its core, something that uses bias to get results. Creating a set of diverse data is very important. This is easy to explain with pictures. If you only use pictures of cats sitting to train a model to recognize cats, it will probably not recognize a jumping or running cat as a cat.
>
> Minimizing hidden bias can be difficult. Include ample examples in your training data of rare cases of your match, so the common case won't overload them completely.

We talked about precision and recall earlier. Though they are not completely dependent on one another, they are definitively related and can be adjusted dependently. The model allows a bit of tweaking in the form of the **confidence threshold**. You can change it on the **EVALUATE** tab of the model:

Figure 11.28: The confidence threshold can be tweaked from the EVALUATE panel

You can also use this page to see the different tags and how they relate.

 Tweaking the training set and adjusting the model is an essential part of the process if you want to get good results. Spend enough time testing and adjusting the model that you want to use in a real operation.

Following the same parameters, you can also use the AutoML Vision product, which works in the same way but with images. You train the model to identify and categorize different labels with a set of pictures and then analyze new pictures with that.

You can use it to train the detection of custom elements in pictures. For example, it could be trained to count different subspecies of bears in a national park or specific car models. You can use AutoML Vision to identify specific expressions, such as smiles, or more complex ones such as winking the left eye or raising eyebrows. This, combined with a camera capturing multiple photos per second, can enable fast interfaces to communicate actions in environments where the hands cannot be used and sound is not an option, such as industrial environments. The possibilities are only being discovered now.

You can learn more in the full documentation for AutoML Vision at `https://cloud.google.com/vision/overview/docs#automl-vision`.

See also

- The *Analyzing images with Google Cloud Vision AI* recipe, earlier in this chapter, to learn how to create an account to use the Google Cloud interfaces.

- The *Analyzing text with Google Cloud Natural Language* recipe, from the previous section, to learn about other possibilities of text analysis using pre-trained models.

12

Automatic Testing Routines

In this chapter, we will cover the following recipes:

- Writing and executing test cases
- Testing external code
- Testing using dependency mocking
- Testing using HTTP call mocking
- Preparing testing scenarios
- Running tests selectively

Introduction

When the code and the complexity of your software grows, generating tests to ensure your program does what it is supposed to do is the best tool to provide you with a firm footing over rocky terrain.

Tests are, in essence, double-checking the code is valid and doing what it is supposed to do. This is a deceptively simple statement, but in practice, it can be very difficult.

 Mastering the ability to test is a difficult task and is worth a book or two. The tasks introduced in this chapter move from business-oriented tasks to software engineering tasks, which is a different approach. The objective of this chapter is to present some practical aspects of testing to introduce the subject.

The most important thing about a test is that it tries to check the code that is being tested independently. This involves a mindset of looking at the code and the inputs and outputs and approaching the task with a fresh look, and to not be influenced by the internal implementation. In some cases, the people testing the software may be different from the people writing the code in the first place, to ensure that there's a good understanding of what the code should and should not do. Try to design your tests with this approach and create well-defined interfaces to work with.

In summary, testing checks the code does what it is supposed to do, and doesn't do what it is not supposed to do.

The first part of the sentence is easier, but the second part is very difficult or even impossible. Writing tests has a cost, both in time and in maintenance. Only in highly critical software is code tested extensively to ensure that nothing unexpected happens. Try to find your balance in how many tests are adequate for your needs.

Tests are typically classified depending on how many different parts of the software they test. A test that only covers a small part of the code, like a function, is normally called a unit test, while a test that covers the whole system is called a system test. A test that covers the integration of different software elements is called an integration test. This is a very fluid definition, as not everyone agrees on what the system is, or how big a unit test can be before it becomes an integration test, or whether there's a significant difference between integration and system tests. But it helps to understand that different tests cover different areas of software – some are bigger, some are smaller – and have different requirements.

To have a team of developers working on the same software, ensuring it is of high quality, and the discipline of adding and running tests continuously is crucial. That's why there are lots of types of tests to help with that task. Continuous integration, or CI, includes the practice of running tests for each change to the software and before merging them with changes by other developers. CI tools allow you to run tests in the background automatically and notify developers of any problem, ensuring that there are no unexpected failures.

In this chapter, we will cover the usage of `pytest` as a tool to run various tests. This is one of the most complete Python test frameworks. `pytest` enables the easy setup of tests and provides a lot of useful options to run subsets of tests, run tests quickly, and detect problems when tests fail.

It has also an extensive ecosystem of plugins that allows you to integrate with other systems, like databases and web services, and to extend `pytest` with additional features, such as code coverage, running tests in parallel, and performance benchmarking. Let's start writing and running some simple tests.

Writing and executing test cases

In this recipe, we will learn how to define and run tests using the `pytest` library.

Getting ready

We will use the `pytest` module. We should install the module, adding it to our `requirements.txt` file as follows:

```
$ echo "pytest==5.4.1" >> requirements.txt
$ pip install -r requirements.txt
```

We will use the file test_case.py. You can download it from the GitHub repository at https://github.com/PacktPublishing/Python-Automation-Cookbook-Second-Edition/tree/master/Chapter12/tests.

How to do it...

1. Check the file `tests/test_case.py`, which contains the definition of four tests:

```
LIST = [1, 2, 3]


def test_one():
    # Nothing happens
    pass


def test_two():
    assert 2 == 1 + 1


def test_three():
    assert 3 in LIST
```

```
     def test_fail():
          assert 4 in LIST
```

2. Run pytest to run the test file:

```
$ pytest tests/test_case.py

===================. test session starts =====================
platform darwin -- Python 3.8.2, pytest-5.4.1, py-1.8.1,
pluggy-0.13.1
rootdir: /Python-Automation-Cookbook/Chapter12
collected 4 items


tests/test_case.py ...F
[100%]


============================== FAILURES ============================
_____ test_fail _____
     def test_fail():
>         assert 4 in LIST
E         assert 4 in [1, 2, 3]


tests/test_case.py:16: AssertionError
==================== short test summary info ====================
FAILED tests/test_case.py::test_fail - assert 4 in [1, 2, 3]
==================== 1 failed, 3 passed in 0.03s =================
```

Congratulations, you've run your first suite of tests. Notice
how one of the tests has failed.

How it works...

`pytest` allows you to define tests simply as functions.

 Not every function will be interpreted as a test. By default, only functions starting with `"test"` will be treated as such. This is a very handy default configuration, but it can be changed if needed. The documentation can be found at `https://docs.pytest.org/en/latest/goodpractices.html#test-discovery`.

Each function in `tests/test_case.py` defines a test, as we see in *step 1*.

The four tests defined in the file `tests/test_case.py` define the basis of a `pytest` test: code that executes and contains one or more assertions verifying the code is correct. Note that these first tests are very simple. We will see more complicated tests later in the chapter:

- `test_one` doesn't have any assertions, so it can only pass.
- `test_two` checks that the addition is correct with an `==` operator.
- `test_three` uses the `in` operator to check whether a value is contained in a list.
- `test_fails` uses the `in` operator to check whether a value is contained in a list. It is not, so this test will fail, as seen in *step 2*.

In *step 2*, `pytest` collects all the tests at the start and then runs them:

```
collected 4 items


tests/test_case.py ...F
[100%]
```

Each passing test is represented by a dot, while each failed test shows an F.

 If color is available in the terminal, the failures will be marked in red and passes marked in green.

For failed tests, the details on the exact line where an assertion failed are shown:

```
                                    test_fail
    def test_fail():
>          assert 4 in LIST
E          assert 4 in [1, 2, 3]


tests/test_case.py:16: AssertionError
========================= short test summary info =========================
FAILED tests/test_case.py::test_fail - assert 4 in [1, 2, 3]
```

A brief summary of failed tests, total tests, and time taken is displayed later. This information is very useful to be able to act and fix the code to make the tests pass.

There's more...

The displayed information shows almost nothing on passing tests by default. This allows you to focus on the failing tests. If you want to display every single test, you can call `pytest` with the verbose flag (`-v` or `–verbose`) activated:

```
$ pytest -v tests/test_case.py
========================= test session starts =========================
platform darwin -- Python 3.8.2, pytest-5.4.1, py-1.8.1, pluggy-0.13.1 --
/usr/local/opt/python@3.8/bin/python3.8
cachedir: .pytest_cache
rootdir: Python-Automation-Cookbook/Chapter12
collected 4 items

tests/test_case.py::test_one PASSED                             [ 25%]
tests/test_case.py::test_two PASSED                             [ 50%]
tests/test_case.py::test_three PASSED                           [ 75%]
tests/test_case.py::test_fail FAILED                            [100%]


============================== FAILURES ==============================
                                    test_fail
    def test_fail():
>          assert 4 in LIST
E          assert 4 in [1, 2, 3]


tests/test_case.py:18: AssertionError
===================== short test summary info =====================
FAILED tests/test_case.py::test_fail - assert 4 in [1, 2, 3]
==================== 1 failed, 3 passed in 0.03s ====================
```

The usage of the `assert` keyword in Python is very flexible and easy to understand. The test needs to be defined in a way that it `asserts` that something evaluates as `True`.

`pytest` will not only show the line that's failing but also give some context, as shown in our example, making it easy to see the problem.

 Try to fix the error to make all the tests pass.

You can access the full `pytest` documentation at the following link: `https://docs.pytest.org/`.

See also

- The *Running tests selectively* recipe, later in this chapter, to learn how to run only a subsection of the tests.
- The *Testing external code* recipe, next up in this chapter, to learn how to test code in other modules.

Testing external code

The main objective of testing is to be able to check code that's out of the boundaries of the test files. We can import code easily in the tests, and then verify whether it is working as expected. Let's see how to do it.

Getting ready

We will use the `pytest` module. We should install the module, adding it to our `requirements.txt` file as follows:

```
$ echo "pytest==5.4.1" >> requirements.txt
$ pip install -r requirements.txt
```

We will use the test files `tests/test_external.py` and `code/external.py`. You can download them from the GitHub repository at `https://github.com/PacktPublishing/Python-Automation-Cookbook-Second-Edition/tree/master/Chapter12`, under the subdirectories `tests` and `code`.

The tree should look like this:

```
├── code
│    ├── __init__.py
│    └── external.py
├── conftest.py
└── tests
     └── test_external.py
```

How to do it...

1. The `__init__.py` file and `conftest.py` are empty, but define the structure of the modules.

2. Check the file `code/external.py`, which contains the definition of a division function:

    ```python
    def division(a, b):
        return a / b
    ```

3. The test file `tests/test_external.py` contains some tests about the `division` function:

    ```python
    import pytest
    from code.external import division


    def test_int_division():
        assert 4 == division(8, 2)


    def test_float_division():
        assert 3.5 == division(7, 2)


    def test_division_by_zero():
        with pytest.raises(ZeroDivisionError):
            division(1, 0)
    ```

4. Run `pytest` on `tests/test_external.py` to see all the tests pass:

```
$ pytest tests/test_external.py
======================== test session starts =======================
platform darwin -- Python 3.8.2, pytest-5.4.1, py-1.8.1,
pluggy-0.13.1
rootdir: Python-Automation-Cookbook/Chapter12
collected 3 items


tests/test_external.py ...                                  [100%]



======================== 3 passed in 0.01s =======================
```

How it works...

The tree structure allows `pytest` to detect the different modules in the structure:

- The `__init__.py` file defines that the subdirectory `code` contains a Python module. This is a standard Python definition.
- The file `conftest.py` contains specific information for `pytest`. Even if it's empty, it defines the root directory for the tests.
- The files starting with `test` are detected as containing tests. Inside these files, the functions prefixed with `test` are detected and run.

The `code` module content is defined in *step 1*. The file `external.py` contains the function `division`.

In *step 3*, the test file is defined. Note the import:

```
from code.external import division
```

That allows you to use external code defined outside of the boundaries of the test file. The function is then verified in three situations:

- `test_int_division` checks that `division` divides two integers and returns the correct integer result.
- `test_float_division` verifies that dividing two integers can produce a float result.
- `test_division_by_zero` checks that the correct exception is raised if trying to divide by zero.

The first two tests contain a simple assertion checking the result of the function call, but `test_division_by_zero` requires that you verify that the code raises an exception. This is done through a `with` block using `pytest.raises`:

```
def test_division_by_zero():
    with pytest.raises(ZeroDivisionError):
        division(1, 0)
```

This block will generate an assertion error if the call doesn't generate the exception, allowing you to check the behavior. Note that the specific exception needs to be passed as an argument.

Step 4 runs the tests, checking that all tests are correct and the code does what it is supposed to do.

There's more...

To be able to define the exceptions to be captured, you'll need to import the exception definitions from the module code or the relevant library.

Raising an exception in any part inside of the `with` block will capture it. Try to include the smallest possible call that is expected to raise the exception, to avoid capturing spurious exceptions. For the same reason, the most precise exception should be declared.

When running `pytest` without specifying a file, it will try to detect possible test files and capture all the tests in the subdirectory. Be sure that the modules are properly defined as defined by `__init__.py` and `conftest.py`.

 We will see more of `conftest.py` later in this chapter.

See also

- The *Writing and executing test cases* recipe, in the previous section, to learn the basics of how to define tests.

- The *Testing using HTTP call mocking* recipe, later in this chapter, to learn how to use testing modules that mock specific libraries.

Testing using dependency mocking

One of the biggest advantages of using Python is having a rich library of resources at our disposal. That includes modules in the standard library, like the `csv` module to read and write CSV files or the `re` library to use regexes.

Others can be external, like `Beautiful Soup` to parse HTML or `matplotlib` to generate graphs. We can also create our own libraries or structure our code in different files and encapsulate the functionality in a way that's reusable and improves readability.

When creating tests, sometimes using external elements and library calls to the core of the test is not advisable. For example, to test that a report is correctly processed, it may be necessary to read a CSV file that contains the report. But preparing the test by preparing a file, in this case, becomes cumbersome and can lose focus on the actual objective of the test.

In these cases, it can be convenient to simulate those dependencies to simplify the tests or to avoid external calls such as calls to network access or other kinds of hardware. This kind of simulation, which replaces the external dependencies during testing, is known as a *mock*.

 Mocks are closely related to unit tests, in that they are small focused tests that cover a single unit of code, like a function, a class, or even a small module. This allows you to test such units of code in isolation from external elements, or, more precisely, fully controlling the external elements the code accesses. Keep in mind that exactly how big a unit test can get before it is no longer a unit test is up for debate.

This can be done through the library `mock` in the Python standard library, which allows you to replace the behavior of external dependencies.

Getting ready

We will use the `pytest` module. We should install the module, adding it to our `requirements.txt` file as follows:

```
$ echo "pytest==5.4.1" >> requirements.txt
$ pip install -r requirements.txt
```

We will use the test files `tests/ test_dependencies.py` and `code/dependencies.py`. You can download them from the GitHub repository at `https://github.com/PacktPublishing/Python-Automation-Cookbook-Second-Edition/tree/master/Chapter12`, under the subdirectories `tests` and `code`.

The tree should look like this:

```
├── code
│   ├── __init__.py
│   └── dependencies.py
├── conftest.py
└── tests
    └── test_dependencies.py
```

How to do it...

1. The __init__.py file and conftest.py are empty, but define the structure of the modules.

2. Check the file code/dependencies.py, which contains the definition of calculating areas for certain shapes:

```python
PI = 3.14159


def rectangle(sideA, sideB):
    return sideA * sideB


def circle(radius):
    return 2 * PI * radius


def calculate_area(shape, sizeA, sizeB=0):
    if sizeA <= 0:
        raise ValueError('sizeA needs to be positive')

    if sizeB < 0:
        raise ValueError('sizeB needs to be positive')

    if shape == 'SQUARE':
        return rectangle(sizeA, sizeA)

    if shape == 'RECTANGLE':
        return rectangle(sizeA, sizeB)

    if shape == 'CIRCLE':
        return circle(sizeA)

    raise Exception(f'Shape {shape} not defined')
```

3. Check the tests in the file tests/test_dependencies.py, validating the calculations of calculate_area:

```python
from unittest import mock
```

```
from code.dependencies import calculate_area


def test_square():
    result = calculate_area('SQUARE', 2)

    assert result == 4


def test_rectangle():
    result = calculate_area('RECTANGLE', 2, 3)

    assert result == 6


def test_circle_with_proper_pi():
    result = calculate_area('CIRCLE', 2)

    assert result == 12.56636


@mock.patch('code.dependencies.PI', 3)
def test_circle_with_mocked_pi():
    result = calculate_area('CIRCLE', 2)

    assert result == 12


@mock.patch('code.dependencies.rectangle')
def test_circle_with_mocked_rectangle(mocked_rectangle):
    mocked_rectangle.return_value = 12

    result = calculate_area('SQUARE', 2)

    assert result == 12
    mocked_rectangle.assert_called()
```

4. Run `pytest` to run the test file:

```
$ pytest tests/test_dependencies.py
======================== test session starts ========================
platform darwin -- Python 3.8.2, pytest-5.4.1, py-1.8.1,
pluggy-0.13.1
rootdir: Python-Automation-Cookbook/Chapter12
collected 5 items


tests/test_dependencies.py .....
[100%]


======================== 5 passed in 0.10s ========================
```

How it works...

The `code` module content is defined in *step 1*. The file `dependencies.py` contains the following elements:

- The definition of the variable `PI`.

- Two internal functions that calculate the areas of rectangles (based on two sides) and circles (based on the radius).

- The `calculate_area` function, which accepts several kinds of shapes and channels the request to the correct internal one. It understands that a square is a kind of rectangle with four equal sides, for example.

In *step 3*, the test file is defined. Note the imports, both of the `mock` module and the function to test:

```
from unittest import mock
from code.dependencies import calculate_area
```

The first three tests (`test_square`, `test_rectangle`, and `test_circle_with_proper_pi`) are straightforward.

The test `test_circle_with_mocked_pi` uses a `mock.path` decorator to replace the `PI` variable with 3 in the `code.dependencies` module:

```
@mock.patch('code.dependencies.PI', 3)
def test_circle_with_mocked_pi():
    result = calculate_area('CIRCLE', 2)

    assert result == 12
```

This changes the `PI` constant while the test is running, affecting the result. Once the test is done, the mock is disabled and the variable is again the previously defined value.

The test `test_circle_with_mocked_rectangle` mocks the `rectangle` function. As a replacement is not defined in the decorator, it is passed as a parameter to the function `mocked_rectangle`:

```
@mock.patch('code.dependencies.rectangle')
def test_circle_with_mocked_rectangle(mocked_rectangle):
    mocked_rectangle.return_value = 12

    result = calculate_area('SQUARE', 2)

    assert result == 12
    mocked_rectangle.assert_called()
```

The function, during the test, is replaced with a `MagicMock` object. To specify the value returned when this object is called as a function, use the attribute `.return_value`. As we see in the result, it replaces the area calculation. The mock can also be checked to see whether it has been called with `.assert_called()`.

In *step 4*, the tests are called to see that all tests are working as expected.

There's more...

Mocks are very flexible and there are different ways of checking whether they have been called and how. A few possibilities are listed here:

- `.assert_called_once()`: Raises an error if not called or called more than once.
- `.assert_called_with(args)`: Raises an error if not called or called with different arguments. The arguments will be checked against the last call of the mock.
- `.call_count`: Counts the number of times i has been called.

A `Mock` object will create another mock automatically if any attribute is accessed or called. For example:

```
>>> from unittest.mock import Mock
>>> mock = Mock()
>>> mock.attribute
<Mock name='mock.attribute' id='4337292000'>
>>> mock.other_attribute
<Mock name='mock.other_attribute' id='4337292144'>
>>> mock.other_attribute()
<Mock name='mock.other_attribute()' id='4337353728'>
```

This means mocks have a flexible API that adapts easily to most calls of a module.

In our example, we mocked a function and a constant in our code, but you can also mock any library, either in the Python standard library or any other installed package.

Keep in mind that you need to mock in the correct path. You need to mock the object where it's imported to, not where it's originally defined. For example, if you're importing `from extpck import extfunction` into your package `code.module`, you need to mock it as follows:

`@mock.patch('code.module.extfunction')`

It's an easy mistake to make, even for seasoned mocking users. Remember that you need to mock *where it's used, not where it's defined.*

If you need to raise an exception when a mock is called, you can do so using the `.side_effect` attribute. This is very useful for testing error conditions in external libraries and making sure your code can correctly handle them:

```
>>> from unittest.mock import Mock
>>> mock = Mock()
>>> mock.side_effect = Exception('Custom error')
>>> mock()
Traceback (most recent call last):
  File "<stdin>", line 1, in <module>
  File "/usr/local/Cellar/python@3.8/3.8.2/Frameworks/Python.framework/
Versions/3.8/lib/python3.8/unittest/mock.py", line 1081, in __call__
```

```
    return self._mock_call(*args, **kwargs)
  File "/usr/local/Cellar/python@3.8/3.8.2/Frameworks/Python.framework/
Versions/3.8/lib/python3.8/unittest/mock.py", line 1085, in _mock_call
    return self._execute_mock_call(*args, **kwargs)
  File "/usr/local/Cellar/python@3.8/3.8.2/Frameworks/Python.framework/
Versions/3.8/lib/python3.8/unittest/mock.py", line 1140, in _execute_
mock_call
    raise effect
Exception: Custom error
```

The same `.side_effect` attribute, assigning an iterator, can be used if the mock needs to return different results for multiple calls:

```
>>> from unittest.mock import Mock
>>> mock = Mock()
>>> mock.side_effect = (1, 2, 3)
>>> mock()
1
>>> mock()
2
>>> mock()
3
```

We mentioned that `mock.patch` can be used as a decorator. This is a Python concept that, in essence, modifies the function it is decorating, usually by adding extra functionality before and/or after the function process.

Decorators are a very useful concept and, in essence, they replace the function with a modified version. You can gain a deeper understanding of how decorators work from this article: `https://medium.com/hasgeek/python-decorators-demystified-5ab4081fd0fe`.

`patch` can also be used as a `with` block. If that's the case, the module is mocked while inside the block:

```
>>> from unittest.mock import patch
>>> from code.dependencies import circle
>>> with patch('code.dependencies.PI', 2):
...     print(circle(2))
...
8
>>> circle(2)
12.56636
```

You can read the full documentation for mocks at `https://docs.python.org/3/library/unittest.mock.html`.

See also

- The *Testing external code* recipe, earlier in this chapter, to learn how to test code in other modules.

- The *Testing using HTTP call mocking* recipe, up next, to learn how to use testing modules that mock specific libraries.

Testing using HTTP call mocking

Working with mocks is a common operation when testing. Some dependencies are typically mocked in most tests.

One common dependency to be mocked is external HTTP calls. Performing these calls while running tests is costly, slow, and can produce unreliable results if the network connection fails.

Though external calls can be mocked through the library `mock` in the Python standard library, as shown in the previous recipe, *Testing using dependency mocking*, there are specific testing modules that allow you to simulate HTTP calls and responses. Also, there are specific libraries that mock other specific libraries. This produces easier and better mocks, as they are adapted to the behavior of the mock.

We have previously used the fantastic `requests` library (introduced in the *Installing third-party packages* recipe from *Chapter 1, Let's Begin Our Automation Journey*, but also used throughout the book). We will look at how to mock this library specifically. We will use the testing library `responses`, which allows us to generate expected requests and their responses.

> Note that this testing library doesn't mock general HTTP access, but specifically the `requests` module.

Getting ready

We will use the `pytest` module, along with the `requests` and `responses` libraries. We should install the modules, adding them to our `requirements.txt` file as follows:

```
$ echo "pytest==5.4.1" >> requirements.txt
```

```
$ echo "requests==2.23.0" >> requirements.txt
$ echo "responses==0.10.12" >> requirements.txt
$ pip install -r requirements.txt
```

We will use the test files `tests/test_requests.py` and `code/code_requests.py`. You can download them from the GitHub repository at `https://github.com/PacktPublishing/Python-Automation-Cookbook-Second-Edition/tree/master/Chapter12/tests`, under the subdirectories `tests` and `code`.

The tree should look like this:

```
├── code
│   ├── __init__.py
│   └── code_requests.py
├── conftest.py
└── tests
    └── test_requests.py
```

How to do it...

1. The `__init__.py` file and `conftest.py` are empty, but define the structure of the modules.

2. Check the file `code/code_requests.py`, which contains a call to an external form in `https://httpbin.org/post` to order a pizza:

   ```python
   import requests
   from datetime import datetime, timedelta


   RECIPES = {
       'DEFAULT': {
           'size': 'small',
           'topping': ['bacon', 'onion'],
       },
       'SPECIAL': {
           'size': 'large',
           'topping': ['bacon', 'mushroom', 'onion'],
       }
   }
   ```

```
def order_pizza(recipe='DEFAULT'):

    delivery_time = datetime.now() + timedelta(hours=1)
    delivery = delivery_time.strftime('%H:%M')

    data = {
        'custname': "Sean O'Connell",
        'custtel': '123-456-789',
        'custemail': 'sean@oconnell.ie',
        # Indicate the time
        'delivery': delivery,
        'comments': ''
    }

    extra_info = RECIPES[recipe]
    data.update(extra_info)
    resp = requests.post('https://httpbin.org/post', data)
    return resp.json()['form']
```

3. Check the tests in the file tests/test_requests.py, checking that the code behaves correctly:

```
import pytest
import requests
import responses
import urllib.parse
from code.code_requests import order_pizza


@responses.activate
def test_order_pizza():
    body = {
        'form': {
            'size': 'small',
            'topping': ['bacon', 'onion']
        }
    }
    responses.add(responses.POST, 'https://httpbin.org/post',
                  json=body, status=200)
```

```
result = order_pizza()
assert result['size'] == 'small'
# Decode the sent data
encoded_body = responses.calls[0].request.body
sent_data = urllib.parse.parse_qs(encoded_body)
assert sent_data['size'] == ['small']


@responses.activate
def test_order_pizza_timeout():
    responses.add(responses.POST, 'https://httpbin.org/post',
                  body=requests.exceptions.Timeout())

    with pytest.raises(requests.exceptions.Timeout):
        order_pizza()
```

4. Run `pytest` to run the test file:

```
$ pytest tests/test_requests.py
===================== test session starts =====================
platform darwin -- Python 3.8.2, pytest-5.4.1, py-1.8.1,
pluggy-0.13.1
rootdir: Python-Automation-Cookbook-Second-Edition/Chapter12
collected 2 items

tests/test_requests.py ..                            [100%]


===================== 2 passed in 0.12s =====================
```

How it works...

The `code` module content is defined in *step 1*. The file `code_requests.py` contains the following elements:

- A section of imports.
- The definition of two kinds of pizzas in the RECIPES constant.
- The `order_pizza` function selects the pizza, composes the form data, and then POSTs it to `https://httpbin.org/post`.

The form rendered in `https://httpbin.org/forms/post` and it's POSTing url `https://httpbin.org/post` were introduced in the *Interacting with forms* recipe from *Chapter 3, Building Your First Web Scraping Application*. It presents a form to order a pizza and returns the same information that is posted in the form in JSON format.

Let's take a closer look at the `order_pizza` function.

The code uses the current time to calculate the delivery time, adding an hour. The time is described in the format HH:MM using `delivery_time.strftime('%H:%M')`. The function `strftime` formats the time and the string `'%H:%M'` prints only the hours and minutes of the time:

```
delivery_time = datetime.now() + timedelta(hours=1)
delivery = delivery_time.strftime('%H:%M')
```

The full data is composed of both a predefined `data` dictionary and the recipe information. The recipe information gets selected from the `RECIPE` dictionary and is then added to the `data` dictionary using `.update()`:

```
data = {
    'custname': "Sean O'Connell",
    'custtel': '123-456-789',
    'custemail': 'sean@oconnell.ie',
    # Indicate the time
    'delivery': delivery,
    'comments': ''
}
extra_info = RECIPES[recipe]
data.update(extra_info)
```

Finally, the information is sent to the URL using `requests.post`. The response data, once decoded from JSON, is returned by the function:

```
resp = requests.post('https://httpbin.org/post', data)
return resp.json()['form']
```

In *step 3*, the test file is defined. Note the import of the `responses` module. The first test, `test_order_pizza`, starts by activating the `responses` module with the decorator `@responses.activate`:

```
@responses.activate
def test_order_pizza():
```

```
body = {
    'form': {
        'size': 'small',
        'topping': ['bacon', 'onion']
    }
}
responses.add(responses.POST, 'https://httpbin.org/post',
              json=body, status=200)


result = order_pizza()
assert result['size'] == 'small'
# Decode the sent data
encoded_body = responses.calls[0].request.body
sent_data = urllib.parse.parse_qs(encoded_body)
assert sent_data['size'] == ['small']
```

The first thing it does is define the expected HTTP request as `https://httpbin.org/post` and the response that should be returned:

```
body = {
    'form': {
        'size': 'small',
        'topping': ['bacon', 'onion']
    }
}
responses.add(responses.POST, 'https://httpbin.org/post',
              json=body, status=200)
```

The call to `responses.add` specifies the method (POST), the URL, the response in JSON format, and the status code. When our code makes a request to the given URL, it will receive this information, instead of making an external call to the network.

The next block is the call to `order_pizza()` and the assertion of the result, which is straightforward.

After that, the following block checks the data sent and captured by `responses`:

```
# Decode the sent data
encoded_body = responses.calls[0].request.body
sent_data = urllib.parse.parse_qs(encoded_body)
assert sent_data['size'] == ['small']
```

The `responses` library keeps track of all the captured requests. We retrieve the body of the first request and store it in the `encoded_body` variable. This data has been encoded and sent as part of the POST into `application/x-www-form-urlencoded` format, which is the default for POST requests. We decode it using the default library, `urllib`, and `parse_qs()` to transform it into a dictionary.

> The full documentation for `urllib.parse` can be found in the Python official documentation: `https://docs.python.org/3/library/urllib.parse.html`.

The second test, `test_order_pizza_timeout`, shows how to raise an exception when requesting a particular URL:

```
@responses.activate
def test_order_pizza_timeout():
    responses.add(responses.POST, 'https://httpbin.org/post',
                body=requests.exceptions.Timeout())

    with pytest.raises(requests.exceptions.Timeout):
        order_pizza()
```

The `responses.add` call, in this case, specifies an `Exception` in the body that will be raised when the URL is requested with the defined method.

> Because the exception is raised instantly when the request is done, this speeds up the generation of a `Timeout` exception, which normally would require seconds or minutes to be generated.

Step 4 runs the tests to check that the code works as expected.

There's more...

The `responses` library is very useful for generating error conditions and preparing your code for them. The STATUS argument can be used to generate error codes in external systems, such as `"403 Forbidden,"` `"404 Not Found,"` `"500 Internal Server error,"` and `"503 Service Unavailable."` Properly handling the different situations that can be produced and reacting to them will improve the reliability of your code.

Notice that some of these errors can happen without any changes at your end, like 503. In some cases, a wait-and-retry strategy can be adequate, and in others, the proper notification of "external service unavailable" can be better. Don't assume that external services will always behave perfectly, as they can (and will) have problems.

Once you enable `responses.activate` to capture all the HTTP requests, any request to an unexpected URL will raise an error:

```
E           requests.exceptions.ConnectionError: Connection refused by
Responses - the call doesn't match any registered mock.
E
E           Request:
E           - POST https://httpbin.org/otherurl
E
E           Available matches:
E           - POST https://httpbin.org/post
```

This makes every test that uses `responses` self-contained and means they won't leak any external calls due to mistakes or changes.

The `pytest` plugin `pytest-responses` allows the activation of responses for all tests automatically. You can read its documentation here: `https://github.com/getsentry/pytest-responses`.

The full documentation of the `responses` library can be found here: `https://github.com/getsentry/responses`.

`responses` is not the only example of a library created to mock some specific aspects when testing. Another example is `freezegun`, which allows you to set the time. Take this test, for example:

```
import responses
import urllib.parse
from freezegun import freeze_time
from code.code_requests import order_pizza


@responses.activate
@freeze_time("2020-03-17T19:34")
def test_order_time():
    body = {
```

```
        'form': {
            'size': 'small',
            'topping': ['bacon', 'onion']
        }
    }
    responses.add(responses.POST, 'https://httpbin.org/post',
                  json=body, status=200)

    order_pizza()
    # Decode the sent data
    encoded_body = responses.calls[0].request.body
    sent_data = urllib.parse.parse_qs(encoded_body)
    assert sent_data['delivery'] == ['20:34']
```

This test uses the `freeze_time` decorator to set the time to 19:34, no matter when the test is run. Note that it also sets the date.

> The test is available on GitHub as `tests/test_requests_time.py`. Remember to install the package `freezegun` using `pip`.

The full documentation of `freezegun` can be accessed here: `https://github.com/spulec/freezegun`.

See also

- The *Testing external code* recipe, earlier in this chapter, to learn how to test code in other modules.

- The *Testing using dependency mocking* recipe, from the previous section, to learn how to mock any kind of package or function.

Preparing testing scenarios

Tests are typically prepared in batches. Similar tests require a similar setup and cleanup, and they only differ on small details. Repeating the same preparation over and over generates boilerplate code and it's less readable.

The term *boilerplate* comes from 19th century local newspapers printing already-prepared news stamped onto metal plates by distribution companies. This meant the same news, in the same format, was repeated all across different newspapers. Boilerplate code is reused code that presents little or no variation, and, in most cases, mainly adds clutter. When creating tests, it is easy to fall into this pattern, which makes the code cumbersome.

In this recipe, we will see how to prepare setup scenarios to run tests using `pytest` fixtures.

Getting ready

We will use the `pytest` module. We should install the modules, adding them to our `requirements.txt` file as follows:

```
$ echo "pytest==5.4.1" >> requirements.txt
$ pip install -r requirements.txt
```

We will use the test files `tests/test_fixtures.py` and `code/code_fixtures.py`. You can download them from the GitHub repository at `https://github.com/PacktPublishing/Python-Automation-Cookbook-Second-Edition/tree/master/Chapter12/`, under the subdirectories `tests` and `code`:

The tree should look like this:

```
├── code
│   ├── __init__.py
│   └── code_fixtures.py
├── conftest.py
└── tests
    └── test_fixtures.py
```

How to do it...

1. The `__init__.py` file and `conftest.py` are empty, but define the structure of the modules.

2. Check the file `code/code_fixtures.py`, which contains the code to store data in a zip file and retrieve it:

    ```
    from zipfile import ZipFile
    ```

```
INTERNAL_FILE = 'internal.txt'


def write_zipfile(filename, content):
    with ZipFile(filename, 'w') as zipfile:
        zipfile.writestr(INTERNAL_FILE, content)


def read_zipfile(filename):
    with ZipFile(filename, 'r') as zipfile:
        with zipfile.open(INTERNAL_FILE) as intfile:
            content = intfile.read()

    return content.decode('utf8')
```

3. Check the tests in the file `tests/test_fixtures.py`, checking that the code behaves correctly:

```
import os
import random
import string
from pytest import fixture
from zipfile import ZipFile
from code.code_fixtures import write_zipfile, read_zipfile


@fixture
def fzipfile():
    content_length = 50
    content = ''.join(random.choices(string.ascii_lowercase,
k=content_length))
    fnumber = ''.join(random.choices(string.digits, k=3))

    filename = f'file{fnumber}.zip'

    write_zipfile(filename, content)
    yield filename, content

    os.remove(filename)
```

```python
def test_writeread_zipfile():
    TESTFILE = 'test.zip'
    TESTCONTENT = 'This is a test'
    write_zipfile(TESTFILE, TESTCONTENT)
    content = read_zipfile(TESTFILE)

    assert TESTCONTENT == content


def test_readwrite_zipfile(fzipfile):
    filename, expected_content = fzipfile
    content = read_zipfile(filename)

    assert content == expected_content


def test_internal_zipfile(fzipfile):
    filename, expected_content = fzipfile
    EXPECTED_LIST = ['internal.txt']

    # Verify only a single file exist in the zipfile
    with ZipFile(filename, 'r') as zipfile:
        assert zipfile.namelist() == EXPECTED_LIST
```

4. Run `pytest` to run the test file:

```
$ pytest tests/test_fixtures.py
======================== test session starts =====================
platform darwin -- Python 3.8.2, pytest-5.4.1, py-1.8.1,
pluggy-0.13.1
rootdir: /Users/jaime/Dropbox/code/Packt/Python-Automation-
Cookbook/Chapter12New
collected 3 items


tests/test_fixtures.py ...
[100%]


======================== 3 passed in 0.01s =====================
```

5. Check that a new file called `test.zip` has been created in the directory:

```
$ ls test.zip
test.zip
```

How it works...

The `code` module content is defined in *step 1*.

As described in *step 2*, the file `code_fixtures.py` contains two functions to store and save information in a zip file. This uses the standard Python `zipfile` module to deal with zip files:

`write_zipfile` creates a zip file with an internal compressed file, `internal.txt`, which contains the data passed as an argument. This is written using the method `.writestr()`:

```python
def write_zipfile(filename, content):

    with ZipFile(filename, 'w') as zipfile:
        zipfile.writestr(INTERNAL_FILE, content)
```

`read_zipfile` reads the file and extracts the content from the internal file:

```python
def read_zipfile(filename):
    with ZipFile(filename, 'r') as zipfile:
        with zipfile.open(INTERNAL_FILE) as intfile:
            content = intfile.read()

    return content.decode('utf8')
```

`read_zipfile` follows the same pattern as the write. It searches for the defined internal file inside the zip file and reads its content. The content needs to be decoded as it's encoded in UTF-8.

Zip files are a collection of files that are compressed. We need to define at least one file to store information inside a zip file. You can learn more about the `zipfile` module here: https://docs.python.org/3/library/zipfile.html.

The tests are defined in *step 3*. The test `test_writeread_zipfile` first generates a file and then reads it, testing the whole lifecycle and ensuring that a file can be written, then read:

```python
def test_writeread_zipfile():
    TESTFILE = 'test.zip'
    TESTCONTENT = 'This is a test'
    write_zipfile(TESTFILE, TESTCONTENT)
    content = read_zipfile(TESTFILE)

    assert TESTCONTENT == content
```

This test works correctly but doesn't perform any cleanup, which leaves the file `test.zip` in the working directory.

For the other two tests, use the declared fixture `fzipfile`. Note the `@fixture` decorator. Let's take a look at it:

```python
import os
import random
import string
from pytest import fixture

@fixture
def fzipfile():
    content_length = 50
    content = ''.join(random.choices(string.ascii_lowercase,
k=content_length))
    fnumber = ''.join(random.choices(string.digits, k=3))

    filename = f'file{fnumber}.zip'

    write_zipfile(filename, content)
    yield filename, content

    os.remove(filename)
```

The fixture generates some random content in the shape of a string of 50 lowercase characters. It also generates a random filename. It then writes this file and `yields` both the generated filename and the content. Finally, it removes the file with a call to `os.remove`.

The `yield` keyword in Python allows us to pause the execution of code, return a value, and then resume the code. In a fixture, everything that goes before `yield` will be executed before the start of a test, and everything after `yield` will be executed at the end of the test.

 yield is typically used within generator functions that act as iterators, but each time a new value is requested, the code keeps executing until another `yield` is found; for example:

```
>>> def generator():
...     yield 1
...     yield 2
...     for _ in range(3):
...         yield 3
...
>>> list(generator())
[1, 2, 3, 3, 3]
```

You can learn more about generators at https://realpython.com/introduction-to-python-generators/.

The fixture then performs some setup (creates a zip file), returns the values (randomly generated name and content) to work with, and finally cleans up (deletes the file).

The other two tests use this fixture to set up the test. `test_readwrite_zipfile` is very straightforward; it reads the file created by the fixture:

```
def test_readwrite_zipfile(fzipfile):
    filename, expected_content = fzipfile
    content = read_zipfile(filename)

    assert content == expected_content
```

Note that the value returned by the fixture `fzipfile` is a tuple with two elements, the filename and the content.

`test_internal_zipfile` uses the fixture to then check that there's only one file inside the zip file and that it has the correct name. It opens the zip file and uses `.namelist()` to get a list of the files inside to verify them:

```
def test_internal_zipfile(fzipfile):
    filename, expected_content = fzipfile
    EXPECTED_LIST = ['internal.txt']
```

```
# Verify only a single file exist in the zipfile
with ZipFile(filename, 'r') as zipfile:
    assert zipfile.namelist() == EXPECTED_LIST
```

There's more...

Fixtures can be shared across multiple test files. You don't need to import them. Add them instead to the `conftest.py` file. You can generate local `conftest.py` files in the subdirectory for fixtures that are local to that directory only.

 To use a fixture, the name of the parameter in the test needs to have the name of the fixture. Be careful not to overwrite these names unintentionally.

`pytest` provides some built-in fixtures available for common operations. For example, the fixture `caplog` captures the logs emitted while running tests, and `tmp_path` creates a temporary subdirectory that's unique to each test. Go to the fixture documentation for more details.

There are a lot of `pytest` plugins that include fixtures to deal with a lot of common scenarios or tools; for example, connecting to databases, web frameworks, external APIs, and so on. It's worth running a search on `pypi.org` before creating a fixture, or checking the non-exhaustive list of `pytest` plugins at `http://plugincompat.herokuapp.com/`.

`pytest` also adds context for the specific data on fixtures when there's a failing test. This helps with understanding behavior and debugging problems, either on the fixture or in the code that's being tested:

```
$ pytest tests/test_fixtures.py
========================= test session starts =========================
platform darwin -- Python 3.8.2, pytest-5.4.1, py-1.8.1, pluggy-0.13.1
rootdir: /Users/jaime/Dropbox/code/Packt/Python-Automation-Cookbook
Second-Edition/Chapter12
collected 3 items


tests/test_fixtures.py ..F                                      [100%]


============================== FAILURES ===============================
```

```
_____ test_internal_zipfile _____
```

```
fzipfile = ('file989.zip',
'ldrnfqwqodcwmkxkehfcaaxzaocxasbduixouchvrzqyfgaaxv')
```

FAILURE

Remember to perform a cleanup stage in your fixtures. As we've seen in the example of `test_writeread_zipfile`, not cleaning up can lead to spurious data being stored on the hard drive or any other place where the fixture created spurious data. Putting code in the fixture after the `yield` keyword will definitely be called even if there's an exception or some other kind of error.

The full `pytest` fixture documentation is available here: `https://docs.pytest.org/en/latest/fixture.html`.

See also

- The *Writing and executing test cases* recipe, earlier in this chapter, to learn the basics of how to define tests.
- The *Testing external code* recipe, earlier in this chapter, to learn how to test code in other modules.

Running tests selectively

Detecting and running all the defined tests in a project is good to verify that everything is working. But most of the development work done while dealing with tests benefits from executing only a subset of all tests.

When adding new code or new tests, it is crucial to iterate quickly through a specific part of the tests and code to narrow your focus.

In this recipe, we will see how to run a subset of available tests with `pytest` and what parameters to use in different scenarios.

Getting ready

We will use the `pytest` module among others. We should install the modules by adding them to our `requirements.txt` file as follows:

```
$ echo "pytest==5.4.1" >> requirements.txt
$ echo "requests==2.23.0" >> requirements.txt
```

```
$ echo "responses==0.10.12" >> requirements.txt
$ echo "freezegun==0.3.15" >> requirements.txt
$ pip install -r requirements.txt
```

We will use the test files introduced in the previous recipes of the chapter. You can download them from the GitHub repository at https://github.com/ PacktPublishing/Python-Automation-Cookbook-Second-Edition/tree/ master/Chapter12, under the subdirectories tests and code:

```
├── code
│   ├── __init__.py
│   ├── code_fixtures.py
│   ├── code_requests.py
│   ├── dependencies.py
│   └── external.py
├── conftest.py
└── tests
    ├── test_case.py
    ├── test_dependencies.py
    ├── test_external.py
    ├── test_fixtures.py
    ├── test_requests.py
    └── test_requests_time.py
```

How to do it...

1. Run all the tests with pytest:

    ```
    $ pytest
    ======================= test session starts =====================
    platform darwin -- Python 3.8.2, pytest-5.4.1, py-1.8.1,
    pluggy-0.13.1
    rootdir: /Python-Automation-Cookbook-second-Edition/Chapter12
    collected 18 items

    tests/test_case.py ...F
    [ 22%]
    tests/test_dependencies.py .....
    [ 50%]
    tests/test_external.py ...
    ```

```
[ 66%]

tests/test_fixtures.py ...
[ 83%]

tests/test_requests.py ..
[ 94%]

tests/test_requests_time.py .
[100%]


============================ FAILURES ============================
_____ test_fail _____


>    ???
E    assert 4 in [1, 2, 3]


/Python-Automation-Cookbook-Second-Edition/Chapter12/tests/test_
case.py:18: AssertionError
========================= short test summary info ================
FAILED tests/test_case.py::test_fail - assert 4 in [1, 2, 3]
==================== 1 failed, 17 passed in 0.28s ==================
```

Note that `test_fail` is failing.

2. Run `pytest --collect-only`:

```
$ pytest --collect-only
========================= test session starts =====================
platform darwin -- Python 3.8.2, pytest-5.4.1, py-1.8.1,
pluggy-0.13.1
rootdir: /Python-Automation-Cookbook-Second-Edition/Chapter12
collected 18 items
<Module tests/test_case.py>
  <Function test_one>
  <Function test_two>
  <Function test_three>
  <Function test_fail>
<Module tests/test_dependencies.py>
  <Function test_square>
  <Function test_rectangle>
  <Function test_circle_with_proper_pi>
  <Function test_circle_with_mocked_pi>
```

```
      <Function test_circle_with_mocked_rectangle>
   <Module tests/test_external.py>
      <Function test_int_division>
      <Function test_float_division>
      <Function test_division_by_zero>
   <Module tests/test_fixtures.py>
      <Function test_writeread_zipfile>
      <Function test_readwrite_zipfile>
      <Function test_internal_zipfile>
   <Module tests/test_requests.py>
      <Function test_order_pizza>
      <Function test_order_pizza_timeout>
   <Module tests/test_requests_time.py>
      <Function test_order_time>


===================== no tests ran in 0.23s =====================
```

3. Run `pytest -v -k time`:

```
$ pytest -v -k time

======================= test session starts =======================
platform darwin -- Python 3.8.2, pytest-5.4.1, py-1.8.1,
pluggy-0.13.1 -- /usr/local/opt/python@3.8/bin/python3.8
cachedir: .pytest_cache
rootdir: / Python-Automation-Cookbook-Second-Edition/Chapter12
collected 18 items / 16 deselected / 2 selected


tests/test_requests.py::test_order_pizza_timeout PASSED
[ 50%]
tests/test_requests_time.py::test_order_time PASSED
[100%]


================== 2 passed, 16 deselected in 0.22s ===============
```

4. Run `pytest -v -k time tests/test_requests.py`:

```
$ pytest -v -k time tests/test_requests.py

======================= test session starts ===================
platform darwin -- Python 3.8.2, pytest-5.4.1, py-1.8.1,
pluggy-0.13.1 -- /usr/local/opt/python@3.8/bin/python3.8
```

```
cachedir: .pytest_cache
rootdir: / Python-Automation-Cookbook-Second-Edition/Chapter12
collected 2 items / 1 deselected / 1 selected


tests/test_requests.py::test_order_pizza_timeout PASSED
[100%]


================= 1 passed, 1 deselected in 0.10s =============
```

5. Run `pytest -v tests/test_requests_time.py::test_order_time`:

```
$ pytest -v tests/test_requests_time.py::test_order_time
======================= test session starts ==================
platform darwin -- Python 3.8.2, pytest-5.4.1, py-1.8.1,
pluggy-0.13.1 -- /usr/local/opt/python@3.8/bin/python3.8
cachedir: .pytest_cache
rootdir: /Python-Automation-Cookbook-Second-Edition/Chapter12
collected 1 item


tests/test_requests_time.py::test_order_time PASSED
[100%]


========================= 1 passed in 0.38s ==================
```

6. Run `pytest -v --lf`:

```
$ pytest -v --lf
======================= test session starts ==================
platform darwin -- Python 3.8.2, pytest-5.4.1, py-1.8.1,
pluggy-0.13.1 -- /usr/local/opt/python@3.8/bin/python3.8
cachedir: .pytest_cache
rootdir: /Python-Automation-Cookbook-Second-Edition/Chapter12
collected 11 items / 10 deselected / 1 selected
run-last-failure: rerun previous 1 failure (skipped 3 files)


tests/test_case.py::test_fail FAILED
[100%]


============================= FAILURES ========================
_____ test_fail _____
```

```
    def test_fail():
>       assert 4 in LIST
E       assert 4 in [1, 2, 3]

tests/test_case.py:18: AssertionError
===================== short test summary info =================
FAILED tests/test_case.py::test_fail - assert 4 in [1, 2, 3]
================= 1 failed, 10 deselected in 0.30s ============
```

How it works...

In *step 1*, the call to `pytest` is done with no arguments. This runs all the tests defined under the subdirectory.

Note that it displays how many tests it collects:

`collected 18 items`

Step 2 shows how to get the list of tests collected, but without running them. This is done through the `--collect-only` parameter. It presents them all but doesn't run them.

To run only certain tests, *step 3* shows how to generate a matching string that will limit the tests to run. Using `-k` allows matching by string, so all the tests that match the string `time` will be executed.

 The option `-v` makes the output verbose and displays a line per test, instead of a line per test file.

Note how the total number of tests is still present. `pytest` collects them all, but then only runs the ones that match the `-k` parameter:

`collected 18 items / 16 deselected / 2 selected`

To limit the number of collected tests, a file path can be specified, as done in *step 4*, where the path of a specific file is added to the command. In this case, the number of collected tests is only the ones located in the file path:

```
$ pytest -v -k time tests/test_requests.py
...
collected 2 items / 1 deselected / 1 selected
```

Step 5 shows how to specify a single test, using the full file path and descriptor. This is easy to copy from the output when using the -v argument:

```
$ pytest -v tests/test_requests_time.py::test_order_time
...
collected 1 item
```

Finally, in *step 6*, a different argument is used, --lf. This runs only the last failed tests:

```
$ pytest -v --lf
...
collected 11 items / 10 deselected / 1 selected
run-last-failure: rerun previous 1 failure (skipped 3 files)
```

If no test has failed in the last run, --lf will run all the tests.

There's more...

Keep in mind that all these parameters can be combined. For example, --collect-only can be used with -k to check whether the selected tests are correct.

In the same way, multiple file paths and tests can be added. For example:

```
$ pytest -v tests/test_external.py::test_int_division tests/test_requests.py
=========================== test session starts ===========================
platform darwin -- Python 3.8.2, pytest-5.4.1, py-1.8.1, pluggy-0.13.1 --
/usr/local/opt/python@3.8/bin/python3.8
cachedir: .pytest_cache
rootdir: / Python-Automation-Cookbook-Second-Edition/Chapter12
collected 3 items


tests/test_external.py::test_int_division PASSED                   [ 33%]
tests/test_requests.py::test_order_pizza PASSED                    [ 66%]
tests/test_requests.py::test_order_pizza_timeout PASSED            [100%]


=========================== 3 passed in 0.11s ===========================
```

Collecting tests, when the number of tests grows, can take a significant amount of time. When the number of tests is in the hundreds or thousands, collecting and filtering using -k can take so much time as to delay the execution of tests (by half a minute or more). This makes it important to know how to reduce the number of collected tests by specifying the files to collect tests from.

To stop the execution of tests when a failure is detected, use the parameter -x:

```
$ pytest -v -x
=========================== test session starts ===========================
platform darwin -- Python 3.8.2, pytest-5.4.1, py-1.8.1, pluggy-0.13.1 --
/usr/local/opt/python@3.8/bin/python3.8
cachedir: .pytest_cache
rootdir: /Python-Automation-Cookbook-Second-Edition/Chapter12
collected 18 items

tests/test_case.py::test_one PASSED                                   [  5%]
tests/test_case.py::test_two PASSED                                   [ 11%]
tests/test_case.py::test_three PASSED                                 [ 16%]
tests/test_case.py::test_fail FAILED                                  [ 22%]


============================== FAILURES ==============================
_____ test_fail _____


    def test_fail():
>       assert 4 in LIST
E       assert 4 in [1, 2, 3]


tests/test_case.py:18: AssertionError
======================== short test summary info ========================
FAILED tests/test_case.py::test_fail - assert 4 in [1, 2, 3]
!!!!!!!!!!!!!!!!!!!!!!!!!! stopping after 1 failures
!!!!!!!!!!!!!!!!!!!!!!!!!
===================== 1 failed, 3 passed in 0.38s =====================
```

When developing, it's common to iterate through a test or a small number of tests to fix them. In these situations, `--lf` can greatly help to run the whole test suite at once, and then repeat with only the failing tests. As the code is fixed, tests that pass will be removed from the execution group, until finally the last test passes. Then, `--lf` will run all the tests again.

With small numbers of tests in a test suite, most of this advice won't be necessary, as tests will be very quick. As the number of tests increases, using these parameters becomes more important so as to not waste time executing tests that are not directly related to the specific part of the code being developed. Just remember to run the whole suite once at the end to ensure that your changes didn't have a disruptive effect on an unexpected part of the code. This is actually something that happens more times than developers would like!

See also

- The *Writing and executing test cases*, earlier in this chapter, to learn the basics of how to define tests.

- The *Testing external code*, earlier in this chapter, to learn how to test code in other modules.

13
Debugging Techniques

In this chapter, we will cover the following recipes:

- Learning Python interpreter basics
- Debugging through logging
- Debugging with breakpoints
- Improving your debugging skills

Introduction

Writing code is not easy. Actually, it is very hard. Even the best programmer in the world can't foresee every possible alternative and flow of the code.

This means that executing our code will always produce surprises and unexpected behaviors. Some will be very evident, while others will be very subtle, but the ability to identify and remove these defects in the code is critical to building solid software.

These defects in software are known as **bugs**, and therefore removing them is called **debugging**.

Inspecting the code just by reading it and reasoning about its execution image will never be enough to cover all the possible outcomes on non-trivial code. There are always surprises, and complex code is difficult to follow. That's why the ability to debug by stopping execution and taking a look at the current state of things is important.

Everyone, and I mean EVERYONE, introduces bugs in the code, only to be surprised by them later. Some people have described debugging as *being the detective in a crime movie where you are also the murderer.*

Any debugging process roughly follows this path:

1. You realize there's a problem.
2. You understand what the correct behavior should be.
3. You discover why the current code produces the bug.
4. You change the code to produce the proper result.

95% of the time, everything but *step 3* is straightforward. *Step 3* is the bulk of the debugging process.

Realizing the *why* of a bug, at its core, follows a scientific methodology:

1. Measure and observe what the code is doing.
2. Produce a hypothesis on why that is.
3. Validate or disprove the hypothesis, through either a specifically designed experiment (for example, a test) or the examination of the execution of a test (which can be considered a natural experiment).
4. Use the resulting information to fix the bug or to iterate the process.

Debugging is a skill, and as such, it will improve over time. Practice plays an important role in developing intuition on what paths look promising to identify an error, but there are some general ideas that may help you:

*   **Divide and conquer**: Isolate small parts of the code so that it is possible to understand the code. Simplify the problem as much as possible.

There's a format of this method called the **Wolf fence algorithm**, described by Eduard Gauss:

"There's one wolf in Alaska; how do you find it? First, build a fence down the middle of the state, wait for the wolf to howl, and determine which side of the fence it is on. Repeat this process on that side only, until you get to the point where you can see the wolf."

*   **Move backward from the error**: If there's a clear error at a specific point, the bug is likely located in the surroundings. Move progressively backward from the error, following the track until the source of the error is found.

- **You can assume anything you want, as long as you prove your assumption is true**: Code is very complex to keep in your head all at once. You need to validate small assumptions that, when combined, will provide solid ground to move forward with detecting and fixing the problem. Make small experiments that allow you to rule out parts of the code that work and focus on untested ones.

Or, in the words of Sherlock Holmes:

"Once you eliminate the impossible, whatever remains, no matter how improbable, must be the truth."

Remember to prove any assumption you make. Avoid unproven assumptions, as they'll distract you from the location of the bug. It's very easy to think that the error happens in one part of the code and look at another.

This may sound a bit scary, but most bugs are pretty evident. Maybe a typo, or a piece of code not ready for a particular value. Try to keep things simple. Simple code is easier to analyze and debug.

Check out *Chapter 12, Automatic Testing Routines*, to learn how to work with tests. Tests are excellent tools to help you debug, find problems, and add validation points. Debugging the code in a defined test allows you to create a small environment where you can focus on the expected inputs and outputs and search for bugs.

In this chapter, we will look at several tools and techniques for debugging and apply them specifically to Python scripts. The scripts will contain some bugs that we will fix as part of the recipe.

Learning Python interpreter basics

In this recipe, we'll cover some of Python's built-in capabilities to examine code, investigate what's going on, and detect when things are not behaving properly.

We can also verify when things are working as expected. Remember that being able to rule out part of the code as the source of a bug is incredibly important.

While debugging, we typically need to analyze unknown elements and objects that come from an external module or service. Code in Python is highly discoverable at any point in its execution. This ability to examine the types and properties of the code while it is being executed is called *introspection*.

Everything in this recipe is included by default in Python's interpreter.

How to do it...

1. Import `pprint`:

   ```
   >>> from pprint import pprint
   ```

2. Create a new dictionary called `dictionary`:

   ```
   >>> dictionary = {'example': 1}
   ```

3. Display `globals` in this environment:

   ```
   >>> globals()
   {...'pprint': <function pprint at 0x100995048>,
   ...'dictionary': {'example': 1}}
   ```

4. Print the `globals` dictionary in a readable format with `pprint`:

   ```
   >>> pprint(globals())
   {'__annotations__': {},
    ...
    'dictionary': {'example': 1},
    'pprint': <function pprint at 0x100995048>}
   ```

5. Display all of the attributes of `dictionary`:

   ```
   >>> dir(dictionary)
   ['__class__', '__contains__', '__delattr__', '__delitem__',
   '__dir__', '__doc__', '__eq__', '__format__', '__ge__', '__
   getattribute__', '__getitem__', '__gt__', '__hash__', '__init__',
   '__init_subclass__', '__iter__', '__le__', '__len__', '__lt__',
   '__ne__', '__new__', '__reduce__', '__reduce_ex__', '__repr__',
   '__reversed__', '__setattr__', '__setitem__', '__sizeof__', '__
   str__', '__subclasshook__', 'clear', 'copy', 'fromkeys', 'get',
   'items', 'keys', 'pop', 'popitem', 'setdefault', 'update',
   'values']
   ```

6. Show the help for the `dictionary` object:

   ```
   >>> help(dictionary)
   ```

```
Help on dict object:

class dict(object)
 |  dict() -> new empty dictionary
 |  dict(mapping) -> new dictionary initialized from a mapping
object's
 |  (key, value) pairs
...
```

How it works...

After importing `pprint` (pretty print) in *step 1*, we create a new dictionary to work in, as shown in *step 2*.

Step 3 shows how the global namespace contains, among other things, the defined dictionary and the module. `globals()` displays all imported modules and other global variables.

 There's an equivalent `locals()` for local namespaces.

`Pprint` helps display the `globals` in a more readable format in *step 4*, adding more space and separating the elements by line.

Step 5 shows how to use `dir()` to obtain all the names of the attributes of a Python object. Note that this includes all the double underscore values, such as `__len__`.

The use of the built-in `help()` function will display relevant information for objects.

There's more...

`dir()`, in particular, is extremely useful for inspecting unknown objects, modules, or classes. If you need to filter out the default attributes and clarify the output, you can filter the output using a list comprehension:

```
>>> [att for att in dir(dictionary) if not att.startswith('__')]
['clear', 'copy', 'fromkeys', 'get', 'items', 'keys', 'pop', 'popitem',
'setdefault', 'update', 'values']
```

In the same way, you can do this if you're searching for a particular method (such as something that starts with `set`).

`help()` will display the `docstring` of a function or class. `docstring` is the string defined just after the definition to document the function or class:

```
>>> def something():
...     '''
...     This is help for something
...     '''
...     pass
...
>>> help(something)
Help on function something in module __main__:

something()
    This is help for something
```

Notice how the `"This is help for something"` string is displayed just after the definition of the function.

> `docstring` is normally enclosed in triple quotes to allow writing string with multiple lines. Python will treat everything inside triple quotes as a big string, even if there are newlines. You can use either `"or"` characters, as long as you use three of them. You can find more information about `docstrings` at https://www.python.org/dev/peps/pep-0257/.

The documentation for the built-in functions can be found at https://docs.python.org/3/library/functions.html#built-in-functions, while the full documentation for `pprint` can be found at https://docs.python.org/3/library/pprint.html.

See also

- The *Improving your debugging skills* recipe, later in this chapter, to pick up more debugging tools.
- The *Debugging through logging* recipe, next in this chapter, to learn how to debug elements by setting traces.

Debugging through logging

Debugging is, after all, detecting what's going on inside our program and finding out what unexpected or incorrect effects may be happening. A simple, yet very effective, approach is to output variables and other information at strategic parts of your code to allow the programmer to follow the flow of the program.

The simplest form of this approach is called **print debugging**. This technique consists of inserting print statements at certain points to print the value of variables or points while debugging.

But taking this technique a little further and combining it with the logging techniques presented in *Chapter 2, Automating Tasks Made Easy*, allows us to create a trace of the execution of the program. This tracing information can be really useful when detecting issues in a running program. Logs are also typically displayed when running tests using a test framework.

> pytest, introduced in *Chapter 12, Automatic Testing Routines*, automatically shows logs of failed tests. Other test frameworks may need to be configured. Logging is presented in this book in *Chapter 2, Automating Tasks Made Easy*.

Getting ready

Download the debug_logging.py file from GitHub: https://github.com/PacktPublishing/Python-Automation-Cookbook-Second-Edition/blob/master/Chapter13/debug_logging.py.

This contains an implementation of the bubble sort algorithm (https://www.studytonight.com/data-structures/bubble-sort), which is one of the simplest ways to sort a list of elements. It iterates several times over the list, and within each iteration, two adjacent values are checked and interchanged, so the bigger one comes after the smaller. This makes the bigger values ascend like bubbles in the list.

> Bubble sort is a simple but naive way of implementing a sort, and there are better alternatives. Unless you have an extremely good reason not to, rely on the standard .sort method in lists.

When run, it checks the following list to verify that it is correct:

```
assert [1, 2, 3, 4, 7, 10] == bubble_sort([3, 7, 10, 2, 4, 1])
```

We have a bug in this implementation, so we can fix it as part of the recipe!

How to do it...

1. Run the `debug_logging.py` script and check whether it fails:

    ```
    $ python debug_logging.py
    INFO:Sorting the list: [3, 7, 10, 2, 4, 1]
    INFO:Sorted list:      [2, 3, 4, 7, 10, 1]
    Traceback (most recent call last):
      File "debug_logging.py", line 17, in <module>
        assert [1, 2, 3, 4, 7, 10] == bubble_sort([3, 7, 10, 2, 4, 1])
    AssertionError
    ```

2. Enable debug logging by changing the second line of the `debug_logging.py` script:

    ```
    logging.basicConfig(format='%(levelname)s:%(message)s',
    level=logging.INFO)
    ```

    Change the preceding line to the following one:

    ```
    logging.basicConfig(format='%(levelname)s:%(message)s',
    level=logging.DEBUG)
    ```

    Note the different `level`.

3. Run the script again, with more information inside:

    ```
    $ python debug_logging.py
    INFO:Sorting the list: [3, 7, 10, 2, 4, 1]
    DEBUG:alist: [3, 7, 10, 2, 4, 1]
    DEBUG:alist: [3, 7, 10, 2, 4, 1]
    DEBUG:alist: [3, 7, 2, 10, 4, 1]
    DEBUG:alist: [3, 7, 2, 4, 10, 1]
    DEBUG:alist: [3, 7, 2, 4, 10, 1]
    DEBUG:alist: [3, 2, 7, 4, 10, 1]
    DEBUG:alist: [3, 2, 4, 7, 10, 1]
    DEBUG:alist: [2, 3, 4, 7, 10, 1]
    DEBUG:alist: [2, 3, 4, 7, 10, 1]
    DEBUG:alist: [2, 3, 4, 7, 10, 1]
    INFO:Sorted list : [2, 3, 4, 7, 10, 1]
    Traceback (most recent call last):
    ```

```
File "debug_logging.py", line 17, in <module>
    assert [1, 2, 3, 4, 7, 10] == bubble_sort([3, 7, 10, 2, 4, 1])
AssertionError
```

4. After analyzing the output, we realize that the last element of the list is not sorted. We analyze the code and discover an off-by-one error in line 7. Do you see it? Let's fix it by changing the following line:

    ```
    for passnum in reversed(range(len(alist) - 1)):
    ```

    Change the preceding line to the following one:

    ```
    for passnum in reversed(range(len(alist))):
    ```

    Notice the removal of the `-1` operation.

5. Run it again and you will see that it works as expected. The debug logs are not displayed here:

    ```
    $ python debug_logging.py
    INFO:Sorting the list: [3, 7, 10, 2, 4, 1]
    ...
    INFO:Sorted list    : [1, 2, 3, 4, 7, 10]
    ```

How it works...

Step 1 presents the script and shows that the code is faulty, as it's not sorting the list properly.

The script already has some logs to show the start and end result, as well as some debug logs that show each intermediate step. In *step 2*, we activate the display of the DEBUG logs, as in *step 1*, only the INFO ones were shown.

> Note that the logs are displayed by default in the standard error output. This is displayed by default in the terminal. If you need to direct the logs somewhere else, such as a file, you can configure a different handler. See the logging configuration in Python for more details: https://docs.python.org/3/howto/logging.html.

Step 3 runs the script again, this time displaying extra information, showing that the last element in the list is not sorted.

The bug is an off-by-one error, a very common kind of error, as it should iterate to the whole size of the list. This is fixed in *step 4*.

Check the code to understand why there's an error. The whole list should be compared, but we made the mistake of reducing the size by one.

Step 5 shows that the fixed script runs correctly.

There's more...

In this recipe, we have strategically located the debug logs beforehand, but that may not be the case in a real-life debugging exercise. You may need to add more or change the location as part of the bug investigation.

The biggest advantage of this technique is that we're able to see the flow of the program, being able to inspect the output of one block of the code execution to the next and make sense of the flow. The disadvantage is that we can end up with a wall of text that doesn't provide specific information about our problem. You need to find a balance between too much and too little information.

Be verbose if you have to, but to reduce clutter, try to avoid long and confusing logs. Keep the text as short and as descriptive as possible. Keep each log concise, as you can always create more logs if you have to.

Remember to turn down the logging level after fixing the bug. You may need to delete some logs afterward as they won't be useful in the long term.

The quick and dirty version of this technique is to add print statements instead of debug logs. While some people are resistant to this, it is a valuable technique to use for debugging purposes. But remember to clean them up when you're done.

All the introspection tools are available while generating logs, so you can create logs that display, for example, all the results of a call to a dir(object) object:

```python
logging.debug(f'object {dir(object)}')
```

Anything that can be displayed as a string can be presented in a log.

See also

- The *Learning Python interpreter basics* recipe, earlier in this chapter, to learn the basics of Python introspection tools.

- The *Improving your debugging skills* recipe, later in this chapter, to see a whole example of debugging covering different problems.

Debugging with breakpoints

Python has a built-in debugger called pdb. Stopping the execution of the code at any point is possible by setting a breakpoint. A breakpoint will jump into command-line mode. From the command line, the current status can be analyzed. Given that Python is interpreted, any new code can be executed from this stage. This is very flexible and allows you to create flexible breakpoints and change the current state to analyze the behavior of the program.

Let's see how to do it.

Getting ready

Download the debug_algorithm.py script, available from GitHub: https://github.com/PacktPublishing/Python-Automation-Cookbook-Second-Edition/blob/master/Chapter13/debug_algorithm.py.

In the next section, we will analyze the execution of the code in detail. The code checks whether numbers fulfil certain criteria:

```python
def valid(candidate):
    if candidate <= 1:
        return False

    lower = candidate - 1
    while lower > 1:
        if candidate / lower == candidate // lower:
            return False
        lower -= 1
    return True


assert not valid(1)
assert valid(3)
assert not valid(15)
assert not valid(18)
assert not valid(50)
assert valid(53)
```

It is possible that you recognize what the code is doing, but bear with me so that we can analyze it interactively.

How to do it...

1. Run the code to see that all the assertions are valid:

    ```
    $ python debug_algorithm.py
    ```

2. Add `breakpoint()`, after the `while` statement, just before line 7, resulting in the following:

    ```
    while lower > 1:
        breakpoint()
        if candidate / lower == candidate // lower:
    ```

3. Execute the code again, and see that it stops at the breakpoint, entering into the interactive `Pdb` mode:

    ```
    $ python debug_algorithm.py
    > .../debug_algorithm.py(8)valid()
    -> if candidate / lower == candidate // lower:
    (Pdb)
    ```

4. Check the value of the candidate and the two operations. This line is checking whether dividing `candidate` by `lower` is an integer (float and integer division is the same):

    ```
    (Pdb) candidate
    3
    (Pdb) candidate / lower
    1.5
    (Pdb) candidate // lower
    1
    ```

5. Continue to the next instruction with n. Check that it ends the `while` loop and returns `True`:

    ```
    (Pdb) n
    > ...debug_algorithm.py(10)valid()
    -> lower -= 1
    (Pdb) n
    > ...debug_algorithm.py(6)valid()
    -> while lower > 1:
    (Pdb) n
    ```

```
> ...debug_algorithm.py(12)valid()
-> return True
(Pdb) n
--Return—
> ...debug_algorithm.py(12)valid()->True
-> return True
```

6. Continue the execution until another breakpoint is found with c. Note that this is the next call to `valid()`, which has `15` as an input:

```
(Pdb) c
> ...debug_algorithm.py(8)valid()
-> if candidate / lower == candidate // lower:
(Pdb) candidate
15
(Pdb) lower
14
```

7. Continue running and inspecting the numbers until what the `valid` function is doing makes sense. Are you able to find out what the code does? (If you can't, don't worry and check the next section.) When you're done, exit with `q`. This stops the execution:

```
(Pdb) q
...
bdb.BdbQuit
```

How it works...

The code is, as you probably know already, checking whether a number is a prime number. It tries to divide the number by all integers lower than it. If, at any point, the number is exactly divisible by any of them, it returns `False`, because it's not a prime number.

 This is actually a very inefficient way of checking for a prime number, as it will take a very long time to deal with big numbers. It is fast enough for our teaching purposes, though. If you're interested in finding primes, you can take a look at math packages such as SymPy (https://docs.sympy.org/latest/modules/ntheory.html?highlight=prime#sympy.ntheory.primetest.isprime).

After checking the general execution in *step 1*, in *step 2*, we introduced a `breakpoint` in the code.

When you execute the code in *step 3*, it will stop at the `breakpoint` position, entering an interactive mode.

In the interactive mode, we can inspect the values of any variable, as well as perform any kind of operation. As demonstrated in *step 4*, sometimes, a line of code can be better analyzed by reproducing its parts.

The code can be inspected and regular operations can be executed in the command line. The next line of code can be executed by calling `n (next)`, as implemented in *step 5* several times, to see the flow of the code.

Step 6 shows how to resume the execution with the `(continue)` command, in order to stop in the next breakpoint. All these operations can be iterated to see the flow and values, and to understand what the code is doing at any point.

The execution can be stopped with `q (quit)`, as demonstrated in *step 7*.

There's more...

To see all the available operations, you can call `h (help)` at any point.

You can check the surrounding code at any point using the `l (list)` command. For example, in *step 4*:

```
(Pdb) l
  3     return False
  4
  5     lower = candidate - 1
  6     while lower > 1:
  7        breakpoint()
  8 ->    if candidate / lower == candidate // lower:
  9           return False
 10        lower -= 1
 11
 12    return True
```

The other two main debugger commands are `s (step)`, which will execute the next step, including entering a new call (as in *stepping into*), and `(return)`, which will continue the execution of the current function until it executes a `return` statement, and then stops. Note that at the end of any Python function, there's an implicit `return None`.

You can set up (and disable) more breakpoints using the pdb command (break). You need to specify the file and line for the breakpoint, but it's actually more straightforward and less error-prone to just change the code and run it again.

You can overwrite variables as well as read them. Or create new variables. Or make extra calls. Or anything else you can imagine. The full power of the Python interpreter is at your service! Use it to check how something works or verify whether something is happening.

 Avoid creating variables with names that are reserved for the debugger, such as calling a list l. It will make things confusing and interfere with pdb commands, sometimes in non-obvious ways.

The breakpoint() function was introduced in Python 3.7 and is highly recommended if you're using a compatible version. In previous versions, you need to replace it with the following:

```
import pdb;
pdb.set_trace()
```

They work in exactly the same way. Note the two statements in the same line, which is not recommended in Python in general, but it's a great way of keeping the breakpoint in a single line.

 Remember to remove any breakpoints once debugging is done! Especially when committing to a version control system such as Git.

You can read more about the new breakpoint call in the official PEP at https://www.python.org/dev/peps/pep-0553/.

The full pdb documentation can be found here: https://docs.python.org/3.7/library/pdb.html#module-pdb. It includes all the debug commands.

See also

- The *Learning Python interpreter basics* recipe, earlier in this chapter, to learn the basics of Python introspection tools.
- The *Improving your debugging skills* recipe, next in this chapter, to see an example of debugging covering different problems.

Improving your debugging skills

In this recipe, we will analyze and fix some bugs using a small script that replicates a call to an external service. We will show different techniques to improve your debugging skills.

The script will send some personal names to an internet server (httpbin.org, a test site) to get them back, simulating its retrieval from an external server. It will then split them into first and last names and prepare them to be sorted by surname. Finally, it will sort them.

We used this test site previously in the Interacting with forms recipe, *Chapter 3, Building Your First Web Scraping Application*. Note that the URL https://httpbin.org/forms/post renders the form, but internally calls the URL https://httpbin.org/post to send the information. We only need to use the second URL for this recipe..

The script contains several bugs that we will detect and fix.

Getting ready

For this recipe, we will use the requests and parse modules and include them in our virtual environment:

```
$ echo "requests==2.18.3" >> requirements.txt
$ echo "parse==1.8.2" >> requirements.txt
$ pip install -r requirements.txt
```

The debug_skills.py script is available from GitHub: https://github.com/PacktPublishing/Python-Automation-Cookbook-Second-Edition/blob/master/Chapter13/debug_skills.py. Note that it contains bugs that we will fix as part of this recipe.

How to do it...

1. Run the script, which will generate an error:

    ```
    $ python debug_skills.py
    Traceback (most recent call last):
      File "debug_skills.py", line 26, in <module>
      raise Exception(f'Error accessing server: {result}')
    Exception: Error accessing server: <Response [405]>
    ```

2. Analyze the status code. We get **405**, which means that the method we sent is not allowed. We inspect the code and realize that for the request on line 24, we used GET when we should have used POST (as described in the URL). Replace the code with the following:

```
# ERROR Step 2. Using .get when it should be .post
# (old) result = requests.get('http://httpbin.org/post',
json=data)
result = requests.post('http://httpbin.org/post', json=data)
```

We keep the old buggy code commented with (old) for clarity of changes that we made.

3. Run the code again, which will produce a different error:

```
$ python debug_skills.py
Traceback (most recent call last):
  File "debug_skills_solved.py", line 34, in <module>
    first_name, last_name = full_name.split()
ValueError: too many values to unpack (expected 2)
```

4. Insert a breakpoint in line 33, one preceding the error. Run it again and enter debugging mode:

```
$ python debug_skills_solved.py
..debug_skills.py(35)<module>()
-> first_name, last_name = full_name.split()
(Pdb) n
> ...debug_skills.py(36)<module>()
-> ready_name = f'{last_name}, {first_name}'
(Pdb) c
> ...debug_skills.py(34)<module>()
-> breakpoint()
```

Running n does not produce an error, meaning that it's not the first value. After a few runs on c, we realize that this is not the correct approach, as we don't know what input is the one generating the error.

5. Instead, wrap the line with a try...except block and produce a breakpoint at that point:

```
    try:
        first_name, last_name = full_name.split()
    except:
        breakpoint()
```

6. We run the code again. This time, the code stops at the moment the data produced an error:

```
$ python debug_skills.py
> ...debug_skills.py(38)<module>()
-> ready_name = f'{last_name}, {first_name}'
(Pdb) full_name
'John Paul Smith'
```

7. The cause is now clear; line 35 only allows us to split two words, but raises an error if a middle name is added. After some testing, we settle into this line to fix it:

```
# ERROR Step 6 split only two words. Some names has middle
names
# (old) first_name, last_name = full_name.split()
first_name, last_name = full_name.rsplit(maxsplit=1)
```

8. We run the script again. Be sure to remove `breakpoint` and the `try..
except` block. This time, it generates a list of names! And they are sorted alphabetically by surname. However, a few of the names look incorrect:

```
$ python debug_skills_solved.py

['Berg, Keagan', 'Cordova, Mai', 'Craig, Michael', 'Garc\\u00eda,
Roc\\u00edo', 'Mccabe, Fathima', "O'Carroll, S\\u00e9amus", 'Pate,
Poppy-Mae', 'Rennie, Vivienne', 'Smith, John Paul', 'Smyth, John',
'Sullivan, Roman']
```

Who's called `O'Carroll, S\\u00e9amus`?

9. To analyze this particular case but skip the rest, we must create an `if` condition to break only for that name in line 33. Notice the `in` to avoid having to be totally correct:

```
        full_name = parse.search('"custname": "{name}"', raw_
result)['name']
        if "O'Carroll" in full_name:
            breakpoint()
```

10. Run the script once more. The breakpoint stops at the proper moment:

```
$ python debug_skills.py
> debug_skills.py(38)<module>()
-> first_name, last_name = full_name.rsplit(maxsplit=1)
(Pdb) full_name
"S\\u00e9amus O'Carroll"
```

11. Move upward in the code and check the different variables:

```
(Pdb) full_name
"S\\u00e9amus O'Carroll"
(Pdb) raw_result
'{"custname": "S\\u00e9amus O\'Carroll"}'
(Pdb) result.json()
{'args': {}, 'data': '{"custname": "S\\u00e9amus O\'Carroll"}',
'files': {}, 'form': {}, 'headers': {'Accept': '*/*', 'Accept-
```

```
Encoding': 'gzip, deflate', 'Connection': 'close', 'Content-
Length': '37', 'Content-Type': 'application/json', 'Host':
'httpbin.org', 'User-Agent': 'python-requests/2.18.3'}, 'json':
{'custname': "Séamus O'Carroll"}, 'origin': '89.100.17.159',
'url': 'http://httpbin.org/post'}
```

12. In the `result.json()` dictionary, there's actually a different field that seems to be rendering the name properly, which is called `'json'`. Let's look at it in detail; we can see that it's a dictionary:

```
(Pdb) result.json()['json']
{'custname': "Séamus O'Carroll"}
(Pdb) type(result.json()['json'])
<class 'dict'>
```

13. Now, we need to change the code. Instead of parsing the raw value in `'data'`, use the `'json'` field directly from the result. This simplifies the code, which is great!

```
# ERROR Step 11. Obtain the value from a raw value. Use
# the decoded JSON instead
# raw_result = result.json()['data']
# Extract the name from the result
# full_name = parse.search('"custname": "{name}"', raw_result)
['name']
raw_result = result.json()['json']
full_name = raw_result['custname']
```

14. Run the code again. Remember to remove the `breakpoint`:

```
$ python debug_skills.py
['Berg, Keagan', 'Cordova, Mai', 'Craig, Michael', 'García,
Rocío', 'Mccabe, Fathima', "O'Carroll, Séamus", 'Pate, Poppy-Mae',
'Rennie, Vivienne', 'Smith, John Paul', 'Smyth, John', 'Sullivan,
Roman']
```

This time, it's all correct! You have successfully debugged the program!

How it works...

The structure of this recipe is divided into three different problems. Let's analyze it in small blocks:

1. **First error—Wrong call to the external service**:

   After showing the first error in *step 1*, we read the resulting error with care, saying that the server is returning a `405 status code`.

This corresponds to a `method not allowed` error, indicating that our calling method is not correct.

Inspect the following line:

```
result = requests.get('http://httpbin.org/post', json=data)
```

This gives us the indication that we are sending a GET request to one URL that accepts only POST requests, so we make the change in *step 2*.

> Notice that no specific debug steps have been required to detect this error, only a careful reading of the error message and the code. Remember to pay attention to error messages and logs. Often, this is enough to discover the issue or at least a very important piece of the puzzle.

We run the code in *step 3* to find the next problem.

2. **Second error — Wrong handling of middle names**:

In *step 3*, we get an error of too many values to unpack. We can create a `breakpoint` to analyze the data in *step 4* at this point but discover that not all the data produces this error. The analysis done in *step 4* shows that it may be very confusing to stop the execution when an error is not produced, thus having to continue until it does. We know that the error is produced at this point, but only for specific data.

As we know that the error is being produced at some point, we capture it in a `try..except` block in *step 5*. When the exception is produced, we trigger the `breakpoint`.

This causes the *step 6* execution of the script to stop when `full_name` is `'John Paul Smith'`. This produces an error as the `split` expects two elements, not three.

This is fixed in *step 7*, allowing everything except the last word to be part of the first name, grouping any middle name(s) into the first element. This fits our purpose for this program, to sort by last name.

> Names are actually quite complex to handle. Check out this article if you want to be delighted by the vast numbers of incorrect assumptions one can make regarding names: `https://www.kalzumeus.com/2010/06/17/falsehoods-programmers-believe-about-names/`.

The following line does that with `rsplit`:

```
first_name, last_name = full_name.rsplit(maxsplit=1)
```

It divides the text by words, starting from the right and making a maximum of one split, guaranteeing that only two elements, at most, will be returned.

> This may produce an error if a name with no surname is defined, for example. We may need to amend the code if the input data changes.

When the code is changed, *step 8* runs the code again to discover the next error.

3. **Third error—Using an incorrect returned value by the external service**:

   Running the code in *step 8* displays the list and does not produce any errors. But, by examining the results, we can see that some names are incorrectly processed.

   We pick one example in *step 9* and create a conditional breakpoint. We only activate the `breakpoint` if the data fulfils the `if` condition.

> The `if` condition, in this case, stops at any time the `"O'Carroll"` string appears, not having to make it stricter with an equal statement. Be pragmatic about this code, as you'll need to remove it after the bug is fixed anyway.

The code is run again in *step 10*. Once we've validated the data is as expected, we work backward to find the root of the problem. *Step 11* analyzes previous values and the code up to that point, trying to find out what led to the incorrect value.

We then discover that we used the wrong field of the server response. The value in the `json` field is better for this task and it's already parsed for us. *Step 12* checks the value and sees how it should be used.

In *step 13*, we change the code to properly decode the JSON content using the `existing .json()` method. Notice that the `parse` module is no longer needed and that the code is cleaner using the `json` method.

> This outcome, using already existing tools, is more common than it looks, especially when dealing with external interfaces. We may use it in a way that works, but maybe it's not the best. Take a little bit of time to read the documentation to keep an eye on improvements and learn how to better use the tools.

Once this is fixed, the code is run again in *step 14*. Finally, the code is doing what's expected, sorting the names alphabetically by surname. Notice that the other name that contained strange characters is fixed as well.

There's more...

The fixed script is available from GitHub: `https://github.com/PacktPublishing/Python-Automation-Cookbook-Second-Edition/blob/master/Chapter13/debug_skills_fixed.py`. You can download it and see the differences.

There are other ways of creating conditional breakpoints. There's actually support from the debugger to create breakpoints that stop, but only if some conditions are met. When possible, I find it easier to work directly with code, as it is persistent between runs and easier to remember and operate. You can check how to create it in the Python `pdb` documentation: `https://docs.python.org/3/library/pdb.html#pdbcommand-break`.

The kind of breakpoint that catches an exception, as shown in the first error, is a demonstration of how making conditions in code is straightforward. Just be careful to remove them afterward!

There are other debuggers available that have an increased set of features; for example:

- `ipdb` (`https://github.com/gotcha/ipdb`): Adds tab completion and syntax highlights.
- `pudb` (`https://documen.tician.de/pudb/`): Displays an old-style, semi-graphical, text-based interface, in the style of early 90s tools that displays the local scope variables automatically.
- `web-pdb` (`https://pypi.org/project/web-pdb/`): Opens a web server to access a graphic interface with the debugger.

Read the preceding debuggers' documentation to learn how to install and run them.

 There are more debuggers available. A search on the Internet will give you more options, including Python IDEs. In any case, be aware of adding dependencies. It is always good to be able to use the default debugger.

The new breakpoint commands allow us to change easily between debuggers using the `PYTHONBREAKPOINT` environment variable; for example:

```
$ PYTHONBREAKPOINT=ipdb.set_trace python my_script.py
```

This starts `ipdb` on any breakpoint in the code. You can learn more about this in the `breakpoint()` documentation, which can be found here: `https://www.python.org/dev/peps/pep-0553/#environment-variable`.

An important effect on this is to disable all breakpoints by setting `PYTHONBREAKPOINT=0`, which is a great tool to ensure that code in production is never interrupted by a `breakpoint()` left by mistake.

The Python `pdb` documentation can be found here: `https://docs.python.org/3/library/pdb.html`. The entire documentation regarding the `parse` module can be found at `https://github.com/r1chardj0n3s/parse,` while the whole `requests` documentation can be found at `https://requests.readthedocs.io/en/master/`.

See also

- The *Learning Python interpreter basics* recipe, earlier in this chapter, to learn the basics of code introspection in Python.

- The *Debugging with breakpoints* recipe, from the previous section, to learn the basics of setting up breakpoints.

Other Books You May Enjoy

If you enjoyed this book, you may be interested in these other books by Packt:

Python Machine Learning - Third Edition

Sebastian Raschka, Vahid Mirjalili

ISBN: 978-1-78995-575-0

- Master the frameworks, models, and techniques that enable machines to 'learn' from data
- Use scikit-learn for machine learning and TensorFlow for deep learning
- Apply machine learning to image classification, sentiment analysis, intelligent web applications, and more

- Build and train neural networks, GANs, and other models
- Discover best practices for evaluating and tuning models
- Predict continuous target outcomes using regression analysis
- Dig deeper into textual and social media data using sentiment analysis

Pandas 1.x Cookbook - Second Edition

Matt Harrison, Theodore Petrou

ISBN: 978-1-83921-310-6

- Master data exploration in pandas through dozens of practice problems
- Group, aggregate, transform, reshape, and filter data
- Merge data from different sources through pandas SQL-like operations
- Create visualizations via pandas hooks to matplotlib and seaborn
- Use pandas, time series functionality to perform powerful analyzes
- Import, clean, and prepare real-world datasets for machine learning
- Create workflows for processing big data that doesn't fit in memory

Leave a review - let other readers know what you think

Please share your thoughts on this book with others by leaving a review on the site that you bought it from. If you purchased the book from Amazon, please leave us an honest review on this book's Amazon page. This is vital so that other potential readers can see and use your unbiased opinion to make purchasing decisions, we can understand what our customers think about our products, and our authors can see your feedback on the title that they have worked with Packt to create. It will only take a few minutes of your time, but is valuable to other potential customers, our authors, and Packt. Thank you!

Index

D

data
  extracting, from structured strings 19-21
data center (DC) 326
DataFrame 262
debugging
  about 475
  through logging 481-483
  with breakpoints 485-488
debugging, skills
  improving 490-495
Decimal, Degrees (DD) 137
Decimal type, Python
  reference link 378
declarative 265
default text editor, setting in Linux
  reference link 57
Degrees, Decimal, Minutes (DDM) 137
Degrees, Minutes, Seconds (DMS) 137
Delorean module documentation
  reference link 245, 385
dependency mocking
  used, for performing tests 443-447
dialects 126
Dillinger
  URL 161
directories
  crawling 114-116
  searching 114-116
documents
  scanning, for keyword 147-149

E

email
  notifications, sending via 329-333
  reading 321-323
email newsletter
  subscribers, adding 325-328
email notifications
  sending 65-68
Email Regex
  URL 31
email templates
  working with 312-315
encodings
  dealing with 120-122

  reference link 122
errors
  capturing 59-63
escaping 14
Excel spreadsheet
  cell formats, working with 216-219
  charts, creating 213-215
  new sheets, creating 209-211
  reading 203, 204
  updating 206-208
Exchangeable Image File (EXIF) 133
ExchangeRate-API
  URL 239
exif metadata
  reference link 133
external code
  testing 439-441

F

feedparser module documentation
  URL 88
feeds
  subscribing 86-88
file metadata
  reading 130, 131
Fiona documentation
  reference link 296
formatted values
  used, for creating strings 11-14
formatter_class argument
  reference link 58
forms
  interacting with 93-98
FPDF documentation
  reference link 182
freezegun documentation
  reference link 458

G

get current axes (gca) 295
Google Cloud Natural Language
  used, for analyzing text 411-417
Google Cloud Vision
  used, for analyzing images 389-401
  used, for extracting text from
      images 403-408

R

regex101
URL 32
regex denial-of-service attack 33
regexes 28
regexes, usage
input data, validating 28
scrapping 28
string, parsing 28
words replacement 28
regular expression operations
reference link 38
regular expressions
about 28-34
working 30-36
reports
creating, in plain text 152, 153
templates, using for 155-157
requests-futures
reference link 110
responses library 456
RESTful 89
RFC3339
URL 250
RGB colors
reference link 271
RSS feeds
reference links 357

S

sales graph
plotting 268-270
sales information
preparing 373-378
sales report
generating 379-384
scatter plot
drawing 286-288
Selenium
using, for interactions 99-101
working 102
shop.zip file 420
Simple Mail Transfer Protocol (SMTP) 316
SMS
receiving 339-345

SMS messages
producing 334-338
smtplib documentation
reference link 321
somesite
URL 79
stacked bars
drawing 272-274
stack trace 64
standard output (stdout) 58
strings
creating, with formatted values 11-14
manipulating 14-17
reference link 17
structure
generating, in Word documents 169-174
structured strings
data, extracting from 19-21
subscribers
adding, to email newsletter 325-328
supervised training 388
system test 434

T

tasks
preparing 46-50
Telegram bot
creating 347-351
reference link 353
telepot module documentation
reference link 353
templates
using, for reports 155-157
test cases
executing, with pytest library 435-437
writing, with pytest library 435-437
testing scenarios
preparing 458-464
tests
performing, with dependency
mocking 442-447
performing, with HTTP call mocking 450-456
running, selectively 466-472
text
analyzing, with Google Cloud Natural
Language 411-417
formatting, in Markdown 159, 160

Printed in Great Britain
by Amazon